A NEW CONSTITUTION FOR AUSTRALIA

A NEW CONSTITUTION FOR AUSTRALIA

Bede Harris
BA (Mod) (Dublin), LLB (Rhodes), DPhil (Waikato)
Senior Lecturer, School of Law
University of Canberra

Routledge
Taylor & Francis Group
LONDON AND NEW YORK

First published 2002 by Cavendish Publishing Limited

This edition published 2013 by Routledge
2 Park Square, Milton Park, Abingdon, Oxon OX14 4RN
711 Third Avenue, New York, NY 10017

Routledge is an imprint of the Taylor & Francis Group, an informa business

Harris, Bede

A new constitution for Australia

1 Australia. Constitution 2 Constitutional law – Australia

I Title

342.9402

ISBN 1 876905 06 9

[Cover picture: Ian Waldron, *Hey Bros*, 1998, acrylic on canvas, 122x176 cm.]

To my wife, Veronica, and my daughter, Elizabeth

PREFACE

This book is the product of my peripatetic life as a teacher of constitutional law in South Africa, New Zealand and Australia. Exposure to a variety of constitutional issues in these three jurisdictions was the inspiration for a project which would draw upon the constitutional law of these and other countries in order to draft the best possible Constitution for Australia.

When I began teaching constitutional law in South Africa in 1987, that country was still in the throes of its struggle towards freedom. Debate over what type of Constitution the country should have was the stuff of everyday news. The Interim Constitution of 1993 and the Final Constitution of 1996 marked a departure from the positivist theories upon which South African constitutional law had previously operated, to one based on subordination of positive law to human rights.

The constitutional environment which I encountered in New Zealand was equally challenging, but in a different way. The former government of Sir Geoffrey Palmer had enacted significant constitutional reforms, and New Zealand was, and indeed still is, in the process of determining the constitutional implications of the Treaty of Waitangi. The introduction of the Mixed Member proportional representation system changed the political environment in which the system of parliamentary government operates.

By contrast, in Australia, constitutional development appears stultified. Indeed, with the possible exception of the change to proportional representation for elections to the Senate in 1949, there has been no significant institutional change since the Commonwealth came into existence in 1901. The comprehensive and well thought out recommendations contained in the report of the 1988 Constitutional Commission were never implemented. Such constitutional debate as there has been has focussed on the issue of a republic, and, while this is an important issue, there are many areas of our Constitution that are in far more urgent need of reform. The 1999 referendum on the republic was, however, significant in that it exposed the lack of awareness on the part of many people in relation to how the Constitution works. Clearly there is a need to devote more resources to civics education, both in schools and among the public generally. Only an engaged citizenry can participate meaningfully in constitutional debate.

Each chapter in the book addresses a specific area of constitutional law, and suggests what a new Australian Constitution should provide in relation thereto. The book concludes with a draft new Constitution, which I have optimistically entitled 'the Constitution of the Commonwealth of Australia Act 2002', and which reflects the recommendations made in the preceding chapters.

There is a strong comparative element in this book. I have drawn heavily on the Constitutions of South Africa, Germany, Ireland, Canada, the United States and New Zealand in suggesting changes to our Constitution. The often traumatic experiences of those countries over the past century have forced them to confront difficult constitutional issues, and their experiences, and the solutions they have arrived at, provide us with useful lessons in reforming the Australian Constitution.

Finally, a word about the cover art, which I chose for this book at my wife's suggestion: I first saw Ian Waldron's *Hey Bros* at the Museum and Art Gallery of the Northern Territory in 1998. My initial impression was that the National Gallery in London had generously lent Constable's *The Hay-Wain* to its counterpart in the Northern Territory. As Constable's painting has long been a favourite of my mother's, I stepped forward for a closer inspection. I then realised that I was viewing something very different from Constable's bucolic work. Who can guess what the insouciant figure in the bottom right hand corner of *Hey Bros* plans to do? Perhaps he proposes to claim Somerset or Derbyshire as *terra nullius*. He is certainly likely to disrupt the established order. I hope that this book does the same.

Bede Harris
University of Canberra
July 2002

ACKNOWLEDGMENTS

There are many people to whom I owe a debt of gratitude for their assistance and support in writing this book. The staff of the Library at the University of Canberra, and, in particular, Hugh Malcolm, were ever eager to render me assistance. Thanks are also due to the staff of the Library at the Australian University and of the National Library of Australia. I was privileged to participate in a Fulbright American Studies Institute in 2001, and the knowledge gained through that programme contributed significantly to this book. I would like to extend my gratitude to Mark Darby, of the Australian-American Fulbright Commission in Canberra, for his assistance in Australia, and to Professor John Kincaid, Director of the Robert B and Helen S Meyner Centre for the study of State and Local Government at Lafayette College, for the superb programme he constructed. My gratitude also extends to many others who participated in the running of the programme, either as teachers or as administrators, including the inimitable Donald Lutz, Barbara Allen, Ellis Katz, Joseph Marbach, Morey Myers, Stephen Schechter, Conrad Weiler, Jerome Heavey, Wes Leckrone and Terry Cooper. I received valuable assistance from my friend and former colleague, Jonathan Burchell, Professor of Law at the University of Cape Town, who responded generously to emailed requests for references from South African sources. My colleagues at the University of Canberra also deserve acknowledgment – Keturah Whitford, who, as Head of School, unfailingly supported my research, and accommodated my visit to the United States on the Fulbright scholarship, as well as all my other colleagues who, perhaps unbeknown to them, contributed to this book through vigorous discussions in the staff room. Special thanks are due to Ian Waldron, who gave permission for the use of the artwork on the cover. Above all, however, my thanks go to my wife Veronica, and my daughter, Elizabeth, for it is their unfailing support, and their understanding of the demands made on family life by the authorship of a book, that made this project possible. It is to them that this book is fittingly dedicated.

CONTENTS

TABLE OF CASES

TABLE OF LEGISLATION

AUSTRALIA

Australian Capital Territory

Commonwealth

New South Wales

Northern Territory

Queensland

South Australia

Victoria

Western Australia

AUSTRIA

BAHAMAS

BARBADOS

CANADA

COMOROS

DOMINICA

FIJI

GERMANY

GRENADA

INDIA

SOUTH AFRICA

SPAIN

UNITED KINGDOM

UNITED STATES OF AMERICA

ZIMBABWE

INTERNATIONAL DOCUMENTS

TABLE OF ABBREVIATIONS

AC	Appeal Cases
AD	Appellate Division reports
AJLR	Australian Law Journal Reports
All ER	All England Reports
ALR	Australian Law Reports
ALRC	Australian Law Reform Commission
ATSIC	Aboriginal and Torres Strait Islander Commission
BAC	Bantu Appeal Cases
BCLR	Butterworths Constitutional Law Reports
CCLT	Canadian Cases on the Law of Torts
ChD	Chancery Division Reports
CLR	Commonwealth Law Reports
CRR	Canadian Rights Reporter
DLR	Dominion Law Reports
ER	English Reports
F	Federal reports
FCR	Federal Court Reports
FLR	Federal Law Reports
ICJ Rep	International Court of Justice Reports
KB	King's Bench reports
LRC	Law Reform Commission
NAC	Native Appeal Cases
NSWLR	New South Wales Law Reports
NTLR	Northern Territory Law Reports
NTR	Northern Territory Reports
NYS	New York State reports
NZLR	New Zealand Law Reports
Qd R	Queensland Reports
SA	South African Law Reports
SASR	South Australian State Reports

SCR (NSW)	Supreme Court Reports (New South Wales)
SR (NSW)	State Reports (New South Wales)
US	United States Reports
VR	Victorian Reports

CONSTITUTIONAL REFORM

1.1 THE NEED FOR CONSTITUTIONAL DEBATE

It could well be said that anyone writing a book as a result of which he or she hopes to effect constitutional reform in Australia must either be optimistic to the point of foolhardiness or be expecting to live beyond the normal human lifespan. The fate of proposed constitutional amendments in Australia is well known: of 44 referenda conducted since the coming into force of the Constitution, only eight have cleared both hurdles set by s 128 of the Constitution by securing majority support of votes cast nationwide and majority support in a majority of States (in other words, in four of the six States). Most recently, the referendum held in 1999 on whether Australia should become a Republic suffered a crushing defeat, with 5,273,000 votes cast in favour of the Republic, 6,410,000 cast against, and without securing a majority in any State or Territory, bar the Australian Capital Territory (ACT).

While of symbolic importance, the issue of the Republic is of relatively little importance from a functional point of view. As we shall see in Chapter 10, most countries in the international Commonwealth have adopted a republican form of government, with a president performing the same functions as the former Governor-General, with a minimum of fuss. I should at this stage declare my preference for Australia becoming a republic, simply because I believe we should have an Australian as our Head of State. However, in my view the issue of whether we should become a republic is of relatively minor importance in comparison with the many far more pressing constitutional issues we face. Similarly, the actual result of the 1999 referendum pales into insignificance when compared with the appalling, although perhaps understandable, lack of public knowledge on the basic functioning of the Constitution which became evident during the referendum campaign. This lack of knowledge is understandable because the offering of subjects covering government and law is a relatively recent development in High School curricula, and, for the most part, Australians who left school before such programmes were introduced are rarely exposed to formal education as to the purpose and function of the federal or State Constitutions. This work is thus to some extent inspired by the referendum of 1999, and I hope that its publication will create awareness and understanding of the problems underlying current constitutional arrangements in a way that the referendum process failed to do even in relation to the specific issue of the republic.

1.2 DO WE NEED A NEW CONSTITUTION?

Does Australia need a new Constitution? Our system of government works, and the stability and freedom it provides are factors which make it a highly attractive destination for migrants. Although marred by some obvious flaws – principal among which are the incompatibility of the Senate's blocking power of financial legislation with the doctrine of parliamentary government, and the mutual ability of the Prime Minister and the Governor-General to dismiss each other – the Commonwealth Constitution is functional. Is constitutional reform something that should concern us? The answer to this is, in my view, a resounding 'yes'. The 'If it ain't broke, don't fix it' philosophy, in which complacency about the Constitution finds its roots, is really an argument for mediocrity. The best response that can be given to that argument takes the form of another adage: 'The good is enemy of the best'. Surely Australia should have a Constitution which is the best we can devise, rather than one which is merely serviceable? Can it really be true that the experiences gained by operating the Constitution during the past century have yielded no lessons as to how that document could be improved? Given that necessary reforms have been implemented in every other area of law during the same period – in some cases on several occasions – surely it would be beneficial for the Constitution to be reviewed? Yet the only occasion upon which a thoroughgoing review of the Constitution was undertaken – when the then government established the 1988 Constitutional Commission, which recommended a set of useful, but by no means radical, constitutional reforms – was not followed up with political action, with the result that the enormous body of work contained in the Commission's report was left unexploited. Surely we should draw upon our experiences, and those of other countries, to revise our Constitution, so that it reflects the best of contemporary thought, both local and international?

This introduces another prominent theme of this book – the usefulness of looking at the experience of other jurisdictions in deciding how we would like to reform Australia's Constitution. Constitution-making should not be affected by misplaced national pride which denies that there are any useful ideas that can be adopted from overseas. On the other hand, the fact that something is done overseas is also not in itself a reason to adopt the practice here. But, that having been said, where another country has an institution or rule that operates well, we should avail ourselves of that experience as a source of ideas for reform of our own Constitution. For that reason, this book draws substantially on the constitutional law of other jurisdictions. The 20th century was unparalleled in the extent and speed of developments which had a bearing on constitutional thought: democratisation, decolonisation and the terrible experience of tyrannies, such as Communism and Nazism, which led to the wholesale slaughter of populations on the basis of class or race. All of these developments provide useful lessons from a variety of jurisdictions on what should and should not be done when reforming a Constitution.

Finally, one should recognise that tradition is to some extent an impediment to constitutional reform. Of course a country's Constitution reflects its history, and in examining the Constitution one cannot avoid acknowledging that history and the sentimental attachment that people have to their constitutional institutions – an attachment which is, indeed, a major defence available to the Constitution, should it ever be threatened by unconstitutional action. However, we should not be held prisoner by history, and so provisions of the Constitution should not be retained merely because they reflect an historical need, if that need is no longer important. The difficulty that has attended attempts to amend Australia's Constitution is undoubtedly due in part to the suspicion with which voters view proposals for reform, there being a presumption in the mind of the voters that proposals for change to the federal Constitution – particularly any proposal emanating from the mouth of a politician – is motivated by a desire to increase governmental power.[1]

A constitutional provision may exist simply because it has existed for a long time, because experience shows that it works, or because it is just. I would argue that the first is the weakest reason for retaining a provision. Ideally, we should have a Constitution which serves both the second and the third. One would hope that, in time, a new Constitution would itself become part of our traditions, and would draw strength from that fact. That having been said, there is no merit in constitutional change for its own sake. Current institutions which accord with constitutional principle, and which work effectively, should be retained. It is only where a constitutional rule or institution is defective, or could be improved by alteration, that change is warranted.

Finally, even setting aside changes required to the substance of the Constitution, I would argue that we need a new Constitution because the current one is written in language which is archaic, uninspiring and difficult to understand. Such a circumstance is obviously incompatible with the Constitution being a document which the people hold dear. As is stated by Lutz:[2]

> ... the whole point of a written constitution is to make available to the average citizen a description of the institutions and rules whereby a people govern themselves. Any constitution that cannot be understood by its citizens is, in effect, *not* a constitution. [Original emphasis.]

1.3 CONSTITUTIONAL VALUES

What is a 'good' constitution? To answer this we should perhaps first enquire as to what is the purpose of a constitution. Most constitutional scholars writing in the context of free societies say that the purpose of a constitution (and indeed of constitutional law generally) is to define and limit the powers of the state. Under this theory (usually referred to as the doctrine of constitutionalism), constitutional law serves to bring the State down to the level of the individual by subjecting the state to law in the same way as the individual is. So constitutional law has an important levelling function. Once this is understood, one realises that what constitution-making is essentially concerned with is striking an appropriate balance between the citizen and the organs of the state – defining in what circumstances the state may validly limit the freedom of the individual, and how the different organs of the state interact among themselves. This analysis is useful, because it illuminates an important principle which is not adequately appreciated in the Australian constitutional tradition, namely that good constitution-making requires a *focus on the citizen*. It is from the perspective of the citizen that a constitution should be evaluated, and from this it follows that in drafting the rules contained in a Constitution, one should have the question of what impact will this have on the citizen in the forefront of one's mind.

1 Hughes, 1994, 164.
2 Lutz, 1990, 266.

This was certainly not the perspective adopted by the framers of Australia's Constitution. As they saw it, their task was to draft not a charter regulating the relationship between the citizen and the various governments in Australia, but rather what was really a compact[3] or treaty between the separate Australian colonies, delineating the terms upon which they would agree to federate. Our Constitution thus bears more of the features of an inter-governmental agreement than a set of principles regulating the relationship between the individual and the State. Although it is true that the Constitution does contain some sections which confer rights on citizens, it is arguable that, with the exception of the s 80 right to trial by jury for indictable offences against the Commonwealth, these were included largely in order to serve some federal purpose, rather than to protect the individual against the organs of government. Thus, the prohibition against restrictions on inter-State trade, commerce and intercourse (s 92) was designed to ensure free trade within the Commonwealth; the prohibition against establishment of religion (s 116) was inserted partly in order to prevent the Commonwealth from becoming involved in the politically sensitive issue of State policies towards churches, or from enacting legislation that favoured any of the contending churches;[4] the requirement of equality of treatment as between residents of different States (s 117) sought to ensure that neither the Commonwealth nor other States would impose restrictions on residents of a State when they were in other States;[5] and it is arguable that the s 51(xxxi) requirement of just terms compensation was inserted in order to address the States' fears that the Commonwealth might use its enumerated powers as a means of expropriating their property.

Delegates to the Conventions rejected the idea that the Constitution contain a Bill of Rights, preferring instead to rely on common law rights, and a belief that the Commonwealth and State legislatures could be trusted not to exercise their power to override such rights.[6] This reveals another feature of 19th century Australian constitutionalism which is still prevalent today: an acceptance of the right of Parliaments to subject the citizen to law. The fact that Parliaments are the product of the general will is seen as sufficient justification for the subjection of the citizen to the will of Parliament. There was, and is, little credit given to the idea that the individual should have a sphere of rights which are immune from override by the majority acting through the agency of Parliament. This again illustrates a failure to focus on the primacy of the citizen, and stands in contrast to the attitude which governed constitution-making in South Africa in the 1990s, for example, where the starting point was that the dignity of the citizen as a human being entitled him or her to a core set of freedoms to which the legislature was subordinate. In Australia, the attitude seems rather to be 'If Parliament, representing the majority, has chosen to enact legislation restricting freedom, what ground is there for complaint?', which implies a default position that Parliament has power over the citizen, and that the citizen should be satisfied with whatever residual sphere of liberty

3 The term 'compact' has a specific meaning in the context of constitutional law, and is discussed at 5.2.1, below.

4 See Ely, 1976.

5 La Nauze, 1972, 229–31.

6 *Ibid*, 227, 231.

Parliament chooses to leave to him or her. A citizen-focused approach to constitutionalism is the reverse – the rights of the citizen should be affirmatively stated and protected against invasion by government, which can then operate in the residuum left to it.

A further consequence of what almost might be called the contractual nature of the Constitution was that, like all contracts, it was the product of a compromise, and that in order to achieve that compromise, the delegates sacrificed positions which, if the process had been driven by principle and logic, would have been maintained. Chief among these was undoubtedly what came to be known as the 'Compromise of 1891', that each State should have equality of representation in the Senate irrespective of population, and that the Senate should have a power of veto over the House of Representatives, including over financial legislation.[7] This compromise was objectionable for two reasons: it offended against the principle of equality of representation, in that it made the weight of a person's vote depend upon which State they lived in, and it was incompatible with the doctrine of responsible government, in that it made the government which by definition had a majority in the House of Representatives dependant for supply (and thus tenure of office) upon the Senate, in which it might well not have a majority. This fundamental incompatibility between a powerful Senate and responsible government would be starkly revealed during the constitutional crisis of 1975.

It will be apparent from the above that this book adopts a stance to constitutional development which is very different to that which has been accepted in Australia over the last century, and, consistent with what has been said above, I would suggest that for purposes of this book we should define a 'good' Constitution as one which satisfies two essential requirements – one of principle, namely that it must accord with fundamental principles of justice, the other of practicality, namely that it must allow the machinery of government to work efficiently.

The question of what fundamental principles of justice should underlie that Constitution is very broad, but I would suggest that the following are important:

- human dignity – served by a recognition that each person is entitled to a basic core set of rights, which are protected from unreasonable impairment by the rest of society, and thus by government as the repository of legal authority in society; and
- equality – served by a recognition that each person should enjoy (at the very minimum) equality in the formal sense of equality of opportunity, the same rights of participation in the political process, and the same degree of influence over the political process as every other person, and that when power is applied to a person, it should be done in a non-discriminatory manner.

Reference will frequently be made to these values when analysing current institutions and suggesting how best they should be reformed.

It is in the light of these principles that I address such issues as whether Australia should have a Bill of Rights, and, if so, what its content should be (Chapter 2); how we should select our judges (Chapter 3); what rules should govern the liability of the executive under statute and common law (Chapter 4); what the appropriate balance between the States and the Commonwealth should be in the Australian federation

7 Galligan, 1995, 75.

(Chapter 5); what constitutional arrangements need to be made in order to protect the rights of Australia's indigenous population (Chapter 6); what the direct legislative role of the citizen should be (Chapter 7); how to ensure that each citizen's vote is of equal weight (Chapter 8); what the balance of power should be between the two Houses of Parliament (Chapter 9); and how our Head of State should be chosen (Chapter 10). This is a broad outline of the major issues addressed by the book, but there are a multitude of other specific matters that would need to be taken into account in drafting a new Constitution, and attention is, of course, paid to these as well.

1.4 THE PRACTICALITIES OF REFORM

An issue which I will not address until Chapter 11, the very last chapter in this book, is the practicality of constitutional reform. The hurdle presented by s 128 has, I would argue, had a deadening effect on constitutional debate in Australia, and breeds a degree of pusillanimity among those who write on the topic. Those arguing for reform propose modest options which they feel have the best chance of success, rather than presenting more radical proposals which are best on the merits. Others give up on constitutional reform altogether, with the result that much academic writing on constitutional matters takes the form of dry statutory interpretation. The approach I have adopted is different. Let us assume, for the purposes of this book, that we have a blank sheet, and can reform the Australian Constitution *de novo*. Would we end up drafting the same document that we have now? I think not. If that is the case, then surely it means that we should begin by examining what the best Constitution for Australia would be, and then address the practical question of how to achieve reform? Let us, at least, prepare an alternative which is worthwhile presenting to the Australian people, before worrying about how reform is to be achieved. Such an alternative is presented for consideration in the Appendix, which contains the text of a new Constitution, drafted in accordance with the recommendations found in the rest of the book.

A BILL OF RIGHTS

2.1 WHY WE NEED A BILL OF RIGHTS

It is assumed that most Australians would recoil from the proposition that a law, even one enacted by a democratically elected Parliament, should be valid irrespective of its substantive content. Yet there is no doubt that, except for a narrow range of rights expressly and impliedly protected by the Commonwealth Constitution, this proposition is correct. This was vividly illustrated by the interchange between Kirby J and Mr G Griffith QC, counsel for the Commonwealth, during the hearing of *Kartinyeri v Commonwealth* (*Hindmarsh Bridge* case):[1]

> **KIRBY J**: How would you apply that distinction to the case of Nuremberg-type laws which, after all, were race laws or to land area laws such as were enacted in South Africa? Would they be permissible under [the race] power?
>
> **MR GRIFFITH**: Your Honour, they may well be. The races power is an inherently discriminatory law ... One might say one stands back and adopts a different approach as to power as from the issue of whether or not it is objectionable *per se* that a law under the races power which to be valid must discriminate on the basis of race may validly discriminate in a way which operates adversely rather than generally beneficially with respect to its subject matter.

As Williams notes, in his book on human rights in Australia,[2] one could also point to the following part of the transcript from later in the case:

> **KIRBY J**: Can I just get clear in my mind, is the Commonwealth's submission that it is entirely and exclusively for the Parliament to determine the matter upon which special laws are deemed necessary or whatever the words say or is there a point at which there is a justiciable question for the Court? I mean, it seems unthinkable that a law such as the Nazi race laws could be enacted under the race power and that this Court could do nothing about it.
>
> **MR GRIFFITH**: Your Honour, if there was a reason why the Court could do something about it, a Nazi law, it would, in our submission, be for a reason external to the races power.

Kirby J was putting to counsel for the Commonwealth the extreme proposition that Parliament is free to legislate as unjustly as it pleases (so long as it stays within the heads of power conferred by the Constitution), thereby illustrating the morally unacceptable implication of the argument that nothing in the Constitution impeded Parliament from enacting racist laws. In so doing he may have been hoping to secure from counsel a withdrawal of the argument. Yet no withdrawal was forthcoming, and for good reason, because, as the law stands, counsel for the Commonwealth was correct in arguing as he

1 (1998) 195 CLR 337.
2 Williams, 2000, 8.

did. Furthermore, there is nothing anywhere else in the Constitution which would invalidate such a law. Although one might find that result abhorrent, the case does at least focus our attention on the reason why we should have a Bill of Rights.

2.2 HUMAN RIGHTS IN AUSTRALIA

To what extent are rights protected in Australia? There are a number of legal rules which protect rights, but none of them gives the complete protection that would be afforded by a comprehensive Bill of Rights.

The Commonwealth Constitution expressly protects a few rights from legislative over-ride – the right to jury trial for indictable offences under Commonwealth law (s 80), freedom of religion (s 116), the right to equal treatment as between residents of different States (s 117), and the requirement of just terms compensation when the Commonwealth acquires property (s 51(xxxi)). As well as being limited to the specific matters they cover, the four express freedoms are also limited in the scope of coverage they provide: because the s 80 right to jury trial applies only to crimes prosecuted on indictment, and it is up to Parliament to determine which crimes are to be so prosecuted, the right is obviously vulnerable to erosion. Furthermore, except for s 117, the express rights limit the law-making capacity only of the Commonwealth Parliament, not the Parliaments of the States.

In addition to the express freedoms, the High Court has found that the Constitution contains an implied freedom of political communication, first recognised in *Australian Capital Television v Commonwealth (No 2)*.[3] Although a minority of justices in *Leeth v Commonwealth*[4] found that the Constitution also impliedly protected the right to equality (a conclusion which has not yet found support among a majority in any subsequent case), and in *Durham Holdings v New South Wales*[5] two justices left open the question as to whether additional freedoms might be implicit in the Constitution,[6] it is doubtful whether that avenue has more to offer beyond the implied freedom of political communication already recognised. At most, the Constitution protects such freedoms as are necessary for the conduct of representative government, not freedoms protecting personal autonomy. Furthermore, the ambit of the former category is not that broad – it is to be noted that in the *Australian Capital Television* case, the High Court was careful to use the term 'implied freedom of political communication' rather than 'implied freedom of expression', while in *McGinty v Western Australia*,[7] High Court held that the doctrine of representative government did not imply a right to 'one vote, one value'.

3 (1992) 177 CLR 106.
4 (1992) 174 CLR 455.
5 (2001) 177 ALR 436.
6 *Ibid*, Kirby J, 457 and Callinan J, 458.
7 (1996) 136 CLR 140.

Although the Commonwealth,[8] and the States and Territories,[9] have enacted anti-discrimination laws, such laws essentially protect only one right – that to equality – and can be overridden by an inconsistent enactment of the relevant legislature. Although s 10 of the Racial Discrimination Act 1975 (Cth) overrides all legislation (both Commonwealth and State) which is inconsistent with its terms, the Commonwealth Parliament could exempt legislation from the scope of s 10, or, indeed, repeal s 10 in its entirety, by means of an ordinary enactment.

There are common law doctrines which protect rights, but their very status as rules of the common law makes them vulnerable to legislative override. It is trite law that Parliament can enact legislation overriding the common law whenever it chooses. It seems that this was not always the case. In 1610, in *Dr Bonham's* case,[10] England's great Chief Justice Coke enunciated the principle that:

> [I]t appears in our books, that in many cases, the common law will controul (*sic*) Acts of Parliament, and sometimes adjudge them to be utterly void for when an Act of Parliament is against common right and reason, or repugnant, or impossible to be performed, the common law will controul (*sic*) it, and adjudge such Act to be void.

That view waned in the face of the gradual ascendancy of Parliament in the 17th and 18th centuries until, in the case of *Edinburgh and Dalkeith Rwy Co v Wauchope*,[11] one finds the court declaring that it could not invalidate Acts of Parliament on substantive grounds. However, some support continues to be expressed for the view that there may be a situation where a court, faced with a law that infringed fundamental freedoms, should declare that the common law forbids Parliament from passing such an enactment. In New Zealand, in *Fraser v State Services Commission*,[12] Cooke J (as he then was) asked whether 'some common law rights may go so deep that even Parliament cannot be accepted by the courts to have destroyed them'. Subsequently, in *Taylor v New Zealand Poultry Board*,[13] he stated that:

> I do not think that literal compulsion, by torture for instance, would be within the lawful power of Parliament. Some common law powers presumably lie so deep that even Parliament could not override them.

Finally, speaking extra-judicially, he categorised the operation of independent courts as a 'lawfully unalterable' principle,[14] echoing earlier *obiter* statements questioning whether Parliament could enact legislation to remove from the courts the jurisdiction to determine whether ouster clauses were valid,[15] or to remove the right of access to the courts.[16]

8 See the Racial Discrimination Act 1975 (Cth), the Sex Discrimination Act 1984 (Cth); and the Disability Discrimination Act 1992 (Cth).

9 All States, with the exception of Tasmania, have enacted such laws: see the Anti-Discrimination Act 1991 (Qld); the Anti-Discrimination Act 1977 (NSW); the Equal Opportunity Act 1995 (Vic); Equal Opportunity Act 1984 (SA); Equal Opportunity Act 1984 (WA); the Discrimination Act 1991 (ACT); and the Anti-Discrimination Act 1992 (NT).

10 (1610) 8 Co Rep 113; 77 ER 647.

11 (1842)8 Cl & F 710; 8 ER 279.

12 [1984] 1 NZLR 116, 121.

13 [1984] 1 NZLR 394.

14 Cooke, 1988.

15 *L v M* [1979] 2 NZLR 519, 527.

16 *New Zealand Drivers' Association v New Zealand Road Carriers* [1982] 1 NZLR 374, 390.

In Australia, Murphy J not only found a number of rights implicit in the text of the Commonwealth Constitution[17] (thereby anticipating the High Court's finding in *Australian Capital Television v Commonwealth (No 2)*[18]), but also stated, in *McGraw-Hinds (Australia) Pty Ltd v Smith*,[19] that some implied rights arose 'from the nature of the society which operates the Constitution'. This idea of common law rights was noted by the High Court in *Union Steamship Co of Australia Pty Ltd v King*,[20] which declined to either accept or reject the principle.

However, in *Durham Holdings Pty Ltd v New South Wales*,[21] the High Court rejected the argument that the right to full compensation for compulsorily acquired property was a common law right which 'lay so deep' in the legal system as to have the effect of curbing the legislative competence of a State Parliament. Gaudron, McHugh, Gummow and Hayne JJ appeared to leave open the *Union Steamship dictum* as an avenue leading towards the development of common law rights superior to the legislative will, by confining their decision to the particular right at hand (that of adequate compensation), stating that:

> ... whatever may be the scope of the inhibitions on legislative power involved in the question identified but not explored in *Union Steamship*, the requirement of compensation which answers the description 'just' or 'properly adequate' falls outside that field of discourse.

Callinan J, too, reserved his position on the *Union Steamship* issue.[22] By contrast, after reviewing the history of the common law rights argument, Kirby J concluded that turning the clock back to the position as stated in *Dr Bonham's case* would amount to a judicial revolution, inverting the relationship between courts and Parliament and, as such, was a course upon which, from a political perspective, it would be inappropriate for the courts to embark. Regrettably, one must agree with this analysis. The opprobrium directed against the High Court from some quarters when it took the far less radical step of recognising the implied right to political communication, a right which the court has re-emphasised exists only because it is implicit in the text of the Constitution rather than being derived from broader social values,[23] would pale into insignificance in comparison with what would happen if the courts recognised rights standing outside the text of the Constitution. Practically speaking, then, a Bill of Rights is likely to come into existence only if included in the text of the Constitution, or if found implicit in the text of the Constitution as it currently stands, although it may be doubted whether the latter option has more to offer beyond the already discovered implied freedom of expression.

Furthermore, on a philosophical level, given that the common law reflects the prevailing norms of society (albeit as enunciated by the courts), the theory that a Bill of Rights could, or should, be founded upon the common law offers insufficient protection

17 For a collection of the cases in which Murphy J recognised implied rights, see Winterton, 1986, 228, n 42.

18 (1992) 177 CLR 106.

19 (1979) 144 CLR 633, 668.

20 (1988) 166 CLR 1.

21 (2001) 177 ALR 436.

22 *Ibid*, 458.

23 *Lange v Australian Broadcasting Corporation* (1997) 189 CLR 520, 567.

for rights, as it suggests that ultimately rights are dependant upon such norms, whereas an essential feature of a Bill of Rights is surely that it protects the right to engage in conduct and hold opinions which are *contrary to* prevailing norms. Finally, on a more practical level, the piecemeal nature of litigation means that a judge-made Bill of Rights would come into existence in an *ad hoc* manner, rather than as an integrated document, and, as was explained in the English case of *Malone v Metropolitan Police Commissioner*[24] (where the court refused to create a new common law right to privacy), leaving to the courts the task of defining a Bill of Rights would impose upon them a burden which they would find it difficult, and perhaps impossible, to discharge.

2.3 ARGUMENTS AGAINST A BILL OF RIGHTS

Assuming then that the law as it currently stands does not provide adequate protection to human rights, it would seem that the case for a Bill of Rights is incontrovertible, and that the Bill of Rights should protect freedoms from infringement not only by the Commonwealth government but also by the governments of the States and Territories. Yet, the issue of whether Australia should have a Bill of Rights has engendered a significant body of debate.[25] The main argument in favour of a Bill of Rights is that procedural regularity is, in itself, not sufficient to ensure the validity of law, and that validity also requires that the substance of the law should conform to an external code of values. Those opposing this argument do so on a number of grounds.

2.3.1 Legal positivism

The first argument against a Bill of Rights directly challenges the natural rights theory upon which Bills of Rights are based, and asserts that values are relative to societies rather than being absolute, and that attempts to draft such a set of values are vain. According to this view, the validity of laws is to be tested in accordance with the theory of legal positivism, the central planks of which are that laws are valid if they are made in accordance with prescribed procedures and if they are effective.

Addressing, firstly, the point about relativism and rights, an argument for the existence of a basic principle can be founded on the ideas of Kant, and the linkage he made between dignity and equality. Kant based a rationalist (that is, non-theistic) theory of rights upon human dignity,[26] emphasising the obligation to consider the human being as an end not as a means – in other words, that the inherent dignity of each person makes it impermissible for one to be subordinated to another, or to be prevented by that other from exercising free will.[27] Thus, as Rotenstreich noted in his analysis of Kant:[28]

24 [1979] Ch 344.

25 For an account of the history of attempts to introduce a Bill of Rights in Australia, see Galligan, 1995, 142–58. See also Goldsworthy, 1992, 160–76.

26 Kant, 1969, 53–54.

27 *Ibid*, 47.

28 Rotenstreich, 1983, 154. See also *ibid*, 161–62.

> Kant himself associates mankind with dignity and asserts that this is so because one human being cannot take advantage of another human being; not only can he not do so but he cannot regard even himself merely as a means since he has always been regarded as an end. His dignity lies precisely in that position which elevates him above the position of those entities which are mere things. What actually happens is that every human being recognises on the level of practice the dignity of mankind in each human individual, and along with that recognition comes the duty to express respect and reverence for every human being.

Kant identified equality as a crucial link in the chain from the 'is' (the individual has a quality – dignity – which derives from his uniqueness as an autonomous being endowed with free will), to the 'ought' (the individual should be guaranteed rights to prevent interference with that autonomy). He did this by arguing that once one asserts that one's own inherent dignity as a human being entitles one to freedom of action, one is logically bound to recognise that freedom in all other human beings as well. Thus, from the 'is' of asserting one's own dignity proceeds the 'ought' of respecting the dignity of others.[29] It follows that the only ground upon which one can deny the dignity and autonomy of one's fellow human beings is by saying that they are *not* equal to ones-self, notwithstanding the obvious common humanity one shares with them. But then, one faces the burden of showing *why* they are not equal which, since the argument for inequality is not based on any rational principle, is a burden that can ultimately be discharged only by basing the claim on will coupled with power – in other words, one says that the others are not equal simply because one wishes it to be so, and has the means to enforce that view. Thus, Kant's position is that since dignity is an inherent aspect of being human, all human beings must be entitled to it, and thus each human being has the right to have his or her dignity – and thus rights – respected by all other human beings.[30] As Rotenstreich points out,[31] Kant held that although man has unique dignity *qua* man, no individual is 'more unique' than any other, and hence each human being's dignity must be accorded equal respect.[32]

The above argument confronts positivists with a difficult problem: in the absence of a set of ethical values external to the law, the only theory left to explain the validity of law is power. Ideally, the power will be wielded democratically, but even if it is, all that that does is ensure that power is wielded in accordance with the will of the majority, and it is worth remembering at this juncture that, on a strictly black-letter view of the law in Germany, as it then stood, Hitler took power legitimately in 1933, and with the subsequent benefit of democratic approval voiced in a plebiscite held in 1934. If, on the other hand, power is not exercised democratically, positivism's lack of values means that it offers no argument as to why it *should* be democratic – after all, in the absence of values, all one can do is evaluate governments pragmatically, and pragmatic notions of social cohesion, tranquillity and efficiency may conceivably lead to the conclusion that undemocratic governments are more efficient than democratic ones. Once one understands that positivism elevates power to the position of supreme constitutional

29 Kant, 1965, 44. See also Mulholland, 1990, 184 and 215. For a discussion of Kant's contribution to theories of autonomy, see Feinberg, 1986, 36–37.

30 The same rationale of shared humanity formed the basis of Locke's theory of rights – see Macpherson, 1967, 7–8. For a general overview of rationalist and natural law theories of rights, see Shestack, 2000.

31 Rotenstreich, 1983, 149.

32 Rawls, 1980, 515–19.

principle, it is easy to see why the positivist road ultimately ends in the Gulags or at Auschwitz.

2.3.2 A Bill of Rights would make our society litigious

Probably the weakest, and yet the most frequently voiced, argument against a Bill of Rights is that if Australia were to have a Bill of Rights we would become an increasingly litigious society, the United States often being held up as a spectre in this regard, although it may be noted that the overwhelming majority of suits filed in the United States are civil damages claims, not actions brought under the Constitution. This argument has attracted support from across the political spectrum, which is perhaps indicative of the fact that, irrespective of their political hue, governments would prefer not to be subject to the limitations imposed by a Bill of Rights. Thus, in response to a call by former Prime Minister Malcolm Fraser for a Bill of Rights, John Howard said:[33]

> If you have a Bill of Rights, you open up a whole new opportunity for court cases because people say their rights have been infringed [and] they go to court to get redress.

The flaw in this argument is that, taken to its logical conclusion, it invites one to deny the very existence of the rule of law. After all, if it is a bad thing for people to go to court to assert their rights, why have any rules limiting the government at all? Why subject the government to law, and why not move back to the pre-Magna Carta era, where the word of the monarch was law with no right of redress in the courts? One has only to voice this argument to realise that at best it is facile, and at worst could be used to justify the abrogation of the constitutional order.

A variant on the 'litigious society' argument is that the increase in litigation would put additional strain on an already overstretched legal system.[34] Here, too, the response should be that society is not improved by the abolition of law, but rather by the government allocating adequate resources to the courts so that justice is done speedily and efficiently.

2.3.3 A Bill of rights would be ineffective

This argument is to the effect that, since a Bill of Rights will not prevent a government that is determined to breach fundamental rights from acting unconstitutionally, it is pointless to have a Bill of Rights. This argument, too, begs the question of why have constitutional law at all, because surely the entire Constitution, and not just a Bill of Rights, is vulnerable to overthrow? If that is the case, is it not futile even to have a Constitution? Why bother to have the Commonwealth Constitution if it could be overthrown by a determined coup leader? At the end of the day, the constitutional order of *any* country depends upon the willingness of its citizens to resist unconstitutional

33 Ross Peake, 'PM rejects Fraser's call for Rights Bill' (2000) *Canberra Times*, 26 August, 3.

34 This argument was made by New South Wales Premier, Bob Carr, in his submission to the New South Wales parliamentary inquiry into whether the State should have a Bill of Rights – see Standing Committee on Law and Justice, 2001, 6.50–52.

action. A good example of this was provided when, in 1991, the people of Moscow massed outside the Russian Parliament to defend the Russian government of Boris Yeltsin from the coup leaders who had overthrown the Soviet government of Mikhail Gorbachev. Thankfully, we have never had to call upon the population to defend the Constitution in Australia. Furthermore, given our tradition of democratic government which accepts subjection to the rule of law, it is unlikely that we will ever need to. But this, surely, means that Australia is an environment where, compared to most other countries, a Bill if Rights (and the rest of the Constitution) is *least* likely to be overthrown, which, in turn, reveals the implausibility of the argument based on ineffectiveness. Furthermore, if Australia was ever subject to the threat of tyranny, surely it is likely that a Constitution in which the people's rights were declared would be even more likely to be defended by the people than one which did not?

2.3.4 We do not need the protection of a Bill of Rights

An argument based on naive optimism about the trustworthiness of governments is to the effect that we do not need a Bill of Rights because ours is a free society in which governments do not infringe human rights. While no-one would deny that, compared with most countries, Australia enjoys a large measure of freedom, the fact remains that Australian legislatures do sometimes seek unreasonably to limit fundamental freedoms. A few examples serve to illustrate this fact: in 2002 the Minister of Foreign Affairs, exercising powers under the Diplomatic Privileges and Immunities Act 1967 (Cth), prohibited demonstrators protesting against the denial of religious freedom to Falun Gong adherents in China from using banners across the street from the Chinese embassy.[35] This order undoubtedly infringed the protesters' right to freedom of expression. Furthermore, there is little doubt that such an order would be found to constitute an unreasonable limitation on the freedom, as the protesters were acting peacefully. This incident also highlights an important feature of human rights litigation: even if a statute limiting a freedom is valid on the face of it, the courts may rule that a specific application of a discretion conferred by the statute is unlawful under a Bill of Rights. Such 'as applied' challenges are a common feature of human rights litigation in other jurisdictions.

As an example of State legislation breaching rights, one can point to the famous case of the Builders' Labourers' Federation, whose registration as a union was cancelled by an exercise of executive discretion by the Minister for Industrial Relations of the New South Wales government, and whose right to judicial review of that decision was then retrospectively extinguished by the Building Industry Act 1985 (NSW). The Supreme Court of New South Wales upheld the validity of this scheme in *Building Construction Employees and Builders' Labourers' Federation of New South Wales v Minister for Industrial Relations*.[36] This saga involved a breach both of the right of the members of the Federation to freedom of association, and of the Federation's right to review of administrative action. As a final example, one can cite the fact that in 2001 the validity of the Coal Acquisition

35 Craig Skehan, 'Downer shackles Falun Gong for visiting Minister' (2002) *Sydney Morning Herald*, 19 March, 4.

36 (1986) 7 NSWLR 372.

(Amendment) Act 1990 (NSW), which limited to far below market value the amount of compensation payable to owners of coal mines expropriate by the State, was upheld by the High Court.[37] The outcome of this case was inevitable, given that there is no rule of the common law which entitles people to just terms compensation for expropriation of their property by a State, and that to find a right to compensation would not only have required the court to create such a rule, but also to find that such a common law rule overrode statute law, something which the court correctly stated would have amounted to a judicial revolution.

2.3.5 A Bill of Rights would disrupt the federal balance

Since the idea of having a Bill of Rights derives from the principle that human rights deserve protection from infringements by any level of government, it would follow that in order to be effective, a Bill of Rights contained in a new Australian Constitution should be expressly stated to bind not only the Commonwealth government, but State and Territory governments as well. (I also argue later in this chapter that a Bill of Rights should also bind private actors). Some might argue that extending the each of a Bill of Rights to the States would disrupt the federal balance by further restricting the powers of State governments. While it is undoubtedly true that the scope of action of State governments would be constrained by a Bill of Rights in a way that it is not at the moment, this would not mean that the federal government's power *vis-à-vis* the States would be enhanced: the federal government itself would be constrained by the Bill of Rights to the same extent as State governments, and so their powers relative to each other would not be affected. The key issue in determining the balance of power in a federation is the way in which legislative competence and financial resources are distributed between the federal and State governments. This topic is addressed in Chapter 5.

2.3.6 Specifying rights in a Bill of Rights will eliminate common law rights

Some have argued against a Bill of Rights on the ground that by defining rights in a Bill of Rights, we would, by implication, be saying that no other rights exist, and that we would, therefore, lose the common law rights we have. In response to this, it is firstly necessary to realise that to say that we have common law 'rights', in the sense of entitlements that cannot be removed, is wrong. All rules of the common law are at the mercy of a simple majority of Parliament. Declaring what rights we have in a Bill of Rights can, therefore, only strengthen rights, as it would put them out of reach of Parliament. Secondly, any fear that the *expressio unius est exclusio alterius* principle could lead to a finding that common law freedoms not mentioned in a Bill of Rights were done away with, could be assuaged simply through the inclusion of a section in the Bill of Rights to the effect that the declaration of rights therein was not to be taken to have removed any other rights existing under law.

37 *Durham Holdings Pty Ltd v New South Wales* (2001) 177 ALR 436.

2.3.7 A Bill of Rights would place the courts over the Commonwealth and State Parliaments

There is no doubt that putting a Bill of Rights to which the legislature was subject, and in relation to which the judiciary had a testing right, would increase the power of the judiciary relative to Parliament, and would thus be incompatible with unrestrained majority rule. However, this appears to be more of a concern for politicians than for voters: Galligan notes that the most recent survey on this issue, conducted in the early 1990s, found that while 72% of voters favoured the entrenchment of a Bill of Rights in the Constitution, the opposite was true of elected State and Commonwealth representatives, 76% of whom believed that it should be the legislature rather than the courts that was the final arbiter of human rights.[38]

The argument that having a Bill of Rights is anti-democratic must be treated with caution. Much depends on how one defines 'democracy'. If one defines it as 'a society in which the will of the majority prevails', then having a Bill of Rights is, indeed, 'anti-democratic'. However, I would imagine that if posed the question 'should a 51% majority of society, acting through their representatives in Parliament, be able to legislate to permit the acquisition of evidence from suspects by torture?', most of us would vehemently disagree with the proposition, despite its formal compatibility with democratic principles. In other words, in modern times at least, 'democracy' has come to mean more than commitment to a specific process by which laws are made, but also to imply a certain minimum standard relating to the content of the law. So I would argue that, nowadays, when most people use the word 'democracy', they are referring not just to a society in which the will of most people prevails but to 'a State in which the will of the majority prevails, subject to fundamental rights'. Once one accepts this, the concept of the courts applying a Bill of Rights to restrain tyrannical majorities becomes not only palatable but desirable. In short, if one accepts that there is a core of rights to which our human dignity entitles us as individuals, it follows that that core must be put beyond the reach of mere majorities, and the only way to do that is to give the courts the power to give effect to those rights.

2.3.8 A Bill of Rights would involve the courts in policy decisions

A variation on the argument that the courts should not be given the power to test legislation for consistency with a Bill of Rights, put by Brennan[39] and others,[40] is that the courts are not equipped to make the types of decision which a Bill of Rights would require them to make. This argument is to the effect that in deciding contentious issues (such as whether the right to life would mean that abortion or euthanasia should be permitted, or whether freedom of expression would mean that sexually explicit material, or material which denigrated particular racial groups, could be published), the courts would be engaging in policy-making rather than the application of law. Policy-making is, it is argued, the function of the legislature and executive rather than of the judiciary. This

38 Galligan, 1995, 134.

39 Brennan, 1998.

40 See the submissions discussed in Standing Committee on Law and Justice, 2001, 6.10–12.

argument thus appears to relate to the type of decision-making process, rather than to the question of whether a Bill of Rights skews the balance of power between the courts and Parliament (the issue addressed in the preceding paragraph). But what type of decision do courts make when they apply a Bill of Rights? Essentially this depends on how one drafts one's Bill of Rights. The more specific the rights are, the less room for interpretation there is by the courts – so if, for example, instead of stating that suspects were entitled to 'due process' while in police custody, the Bill of Rights specified what 'due process' meant (for example, being informed of why one was being arrested and of one's right to legal counsel, *et cetera*), the courts would not be put in the position of having to give meaning to the term 'due process'. Decisions of that type do not involve policy, rather they require the courts to determine whether conduct accords with a procedure mandated by law, an inquiry which lies at the heart of trial work handled by courts every day. Determining whether legislation is consistent with constitutional requirements is also a type of inquiry which the courts are well used to – as, for example, when determining questions of inconsistency between Commonwealth and State legislation under s 109 of the Constitution.

The second point to note is that, apart from the degree of specificity with which a Constitution defines rights, how it provides for the *limitation* of rights is also an important factor which determines the scope of decision-making left to the courts. In no jurisdiction where there is a Bill of Rights does the law adopt an absolutist approach to the application of such a document. Clearly, it would lead to absurd consequences if it did, because, to take an obvious example, the right to freedom of expression would be *prima facie* incompatible with a law which forbade conspiracy or incitement to crime. The source of many of the problems highlighted by Brennan in his survey of decisions of the United States Supreme Court on that country's Bill of Rights[41] is that nowhere in the United States Constitution is there a textual criterion which the courts are to use to determine whether legislation or conduct amounts to a breach of rights of sufficient gravity to fail judicial review. This has meant that the courts have had to devise their own standards of review. To this end, they have developed three levels of judicial review:[42] In cases involving infringements of rights which are considered to be fundamental (the right to vote, freedom of movement and freedom of expression), or where a law operates unequally in relation to so-called 'suspect classes' (for example, those involving categorisations of race, alienage or national origin), the courts apply 'strict scrutiny', and the law will be justified only where the infringement of rights serves a 'compelling' governmental interest. The number of 'suspect categories' recognised by the courts increased during the 1960s, but it appears that no new categories of discrimination will be subject to strict scrutiny, as none have been added since then.[43] An intermediate level of review applies where the law discriminates on the ground of gender. In such cases, 'heightened scrutiny' applies, and the law will be valid if it serves an important, but not necessarily compelling, government interest.[44] The third, and least exacting, level of judicial review, which applies in all other cases, requires the application of a 'rational

41 What is commonly referred to as the Bill of Rights is contained in the first 10 amendments to the United States Constitution.

42 For a summary of the levels of review, see Vile, 2001, 96.

43 Rich, 1995, 12–13.

44 See, eg, *Frontero v Richardson* 411 US 677 (1973).

basis' test, under which limitations of freedoms will be upheld if the government is able to demonstrate that the law was passed in pursuit of a legitimate governmental interest and is reasonably related to that interest.[45] These judicially-created tests for judicial review are unsatisfactory for three principal reasons: the existence of different standards of review suggests that some rights are more deserving of protection than others; the vagueness of the tests creates a penumbra of uncertainty in relation to the fundamental constitutional question of how far the legislature and executive can go in limiting rights; and, finally, as products of judicial invention, the tests are vulnerable to modification, and even whole-scale elimination, by the courts which created them. It would surely be far preferable if the Constitution were itself to contain a test which the courts were required to apply in determining whether legislative or executive action should be struck down.

This situation can be contrasted with that in Canada, where the Canadian Charter of Rights and Freedoms itself contains the test to be used in determining whether infringements of rights are valid or not. Section 1 of the Charter provides that rights may be subject to such 'reasonable limits prescribed by law as can be demonstrably justified in a free and democratic society'. This was interpreted by the Canadian Supreme Court, in the leading case of *R v Oakes*,[46] as requiring that the party seeking a remedy under the Charter prove (on a balance of probabilities) that a right had been infringed, whereupon the onus rested on the other party to show (again on a balance of probabilities) that the infringement of the right:

- was prescribed by law (in other words, proceeded from common or statute law);
- served a sufficiently important objective to justify a limitation of fundamental freedoms (in the words of the court, that the social interest which limitation of the right sought to further related to concerns that are 'pressing and substantial in a free and democratic society'); and
- was 'reasonable and demonstrably justified' which, the court said, meant that the infringement must be shown to have satisfied a proportionality test which required that:

    the limitation of rights must, in fact, serve (in the words of the court, must be 'rationally connected' to) the important objective;

    the limitation must impair the freedom no more than is necessary to serve the objective; and

    the extent to which the right is limited must be proportionate to the interest served (in other words, a drastic limitation of a right could not be justified by an objective of only modest importance).

The above clearly provides a far more detailed guideline to the courts than does the test developed by the United States Supreme Court. Furthermore, an examination of decisions by the Canadian courts shows that the 'sufficiently important objective' criterion leaves the legislature a wide scope of operation, because the courts have generally interpreted that limb of the limitations test in a manner which is deferential to the legislature, and have been very slow to find that legislation does not relate to a

45 For examples of the application of the 'rational basis' test, see *Allegheny Pittsburgh Coal v Webster County* 488 US 336 (1989); and *Chapman v United States* 500 US 453 (1991).

46 (1986) 26 DLR (4th) 200.

sufficiently important social objective.[47] To put it differently, the courts are far less willing to substitute their opinion for that of Parliament as to the latter's determination of whether a topic is of sufficient importance to warrant legislative action limiting fundamental freedoms, than they are to find that legislation fails the proportionality test in that it limits freedom to a greater extent than is reasonable in a free and democratic society.

But even where the courts are guided by an explicit test, as in Canada, does their determination of the question of whether a law disproportionately limits freedom involve them in policy decisions? The process involved in answering such a question certainly requires the courts to balance competing social interests. For example, in considering whether a law which makes racist speech illegal breaches the right to freedom of expression, the courts would have to balance the interest of members of ethnic groups not to be subject to emotional harm caused by insult (and, some would also argue, from the deterrent effect that such speech has upon their participation in public life and thus their right to equality), against the interest of having all political points of view aired in a democracy. But, in balancing such rights, the courts are not doing anything out of the ordinary. Even in the absence of a Bill of Rights, the courts are constantly charged with the task of balancing interests. To take a simple example, under the law of torts, courts determine liability by inquiring whether the plaintiff owed the defendant a duty of care and did not take such steps as a reasonable person would have in discharging that duty. Such questions surely involve matters of 'policy' in so far as they involve the courts firstly determining under what circumstances society would say one has a duty of care to the plaintiff, and then in determining what steps society would say are reasonable in the circumstances. Furthermore, just as the law of torts commonly involves the balancing of the rights of different groups (for example, drivers versus pedestrians, doctors versus patients), a similar decision-making process is used in many other branches of law, as, for example, in the development of the common law of evidence, where the courts balance the rights of the accused against those of the prosecution. Furthermore, the outcome of cases in all branches of the law has implications for the rights and duties not only of the immediate parties but also those of others, such as insurers, law enforcement personnel, the health system, *et cetera*. If we are willing to allow the courts to take such apparently 'policy'-laden factors into account when deciding cases on torts and evidence, why should we think them any less capable of weighing interests in cases involving human rights? In short, the courts are already daily making decisions which affect the rights of the individual *vis-à-vis* the rest of society. Having a Bill of Rights will not cast the courts in a new role, nor require them to adopt new methods of reasoning. Assuming one accepts the underlying philosophical principle that human beings are entitled to certain fundamental freedoms even in the face of the will of Parliament, and that those freedoms should be curtailed only in ways that are reasonable, there can be no difficulty in concluding that the courts are entirely capable of determining that balance, within the framework of the phraseology of the Bill of Rights and the limitations clause it contains.

It should be apparent from the above that the limitations clause in a Bill of Rights is as important as those provisions which protect substantive rights. The limitations clause provides a counterweight on the side of legislation and executive action to balance the

---

47 See Beaudoin and Mendes, 1996, § 3.12–20; Hogg, 1992, 870; and Hiebert, 1996, 74–75.

power of judicial review conferred on the courts, and provides the courts with a criterion which they are bound to apply in determining the validity of legislation and executive action. The rest of this Chapter, and, in particular, the discussion in 2.5, below, of what specific rights should be protected in a Bill of Rights, proceeds on the assumption that all rights would be subject to a clause permitting their limitation in accordance with the same formula that appears in the Canadian Charter – namely, whether the limitation is one which is reasonable in a free and democratic society.

2.3.9 A counter-argument based on the South African experience

Perhaps the most powerful argument that can be made in support of a judicially-enforced Bill of Rights comes from an examination of the history of South Africa, which reveals both the potential for abuse of power in the absence of any restraint upon the legislative branch in relation to the substantive justice of laws it enacts, and how people who have been subject to oppression view judicial review by the courts, rather than unrestrained democracy, as providing the ultimate security for fundamental rights. The history of apartheid reveals the consequences for fundamental rights when the legislature is not subject to substantive restraints. Commencing with legislation which removed coloured and black voters from the voters' roll,[48] the South African Parliament progressively constructed a legislative edifice consisting of a wide range of racially discriminatory laws governing virtually all aspects of life, buttressed by an equally wide range of enactments restricting civil liberties.[49] These laws were designed to stifle opposition to the government and imposed censorship of news and political discussion, provided for detention without trial, denied detainees access to legal counsel, and ousted the jurisdiction of the courts to hear applications for release from detention. The application of such laws placed the judiciary in a moral dilemma, as they were required by their judicial oath to enforce the will of Parliament (there, of course, being no Bill of Rights which overrode the will of Parliament), a course of conduct which, some argued, meant that judges were complicit in the oppression being inflicted by the state and ought, therefore, to resign. On the other hand, most judges argued that a society with bad law is better than one with no law at all, and that resignation would have achieved nothing to ameliorate the condition of the population. To their credit, what many judges did was use canons of statutory interpretation to fight a rearguard action against Parliament, which led to a cat-and-mouse game between Parliament and the courts as the former closed loopholes found in legislation by the latter. When both the 1993 Interim Constitution and the 1996 Final Constitution were being drafted,[50] all major parties were agreed on the

48 Under ss 35 and 152 of the then South African Constitution (the Union of South Africa Act 1910), franchise rights as they existed in the Cape and Natal prior to the formation of the Union were entrenched in the Constitution. The non-racial (albeit otherwise qualified) franchise in these two provinces meant that in a number of electorates the votes of black, coloured (mixed race) and Indian voters could have an important effect on elections. Black voters were moved onto a separate roll, electing separate Members of Parliament in 1936. In 1951 the government enacted the Separate Representation of Voters Act 1951 to do the same thing to coloured voters.

49 For a general discussion of laws restricting civil liberties, see Mathews, 1986.

50 The 1993 interim Constitution was the product of a political agreement negotiated at the Multi-Party Negotiating Process (MPNP). The 1996 final Constitution was enacted by Parliament sitting as a Constitutional Assembly. The history of the Constitution-making process is outlined in van Wyk, 1994, 137–43; and in Gloppen, 1997, 200–10.

necessity of including a Bill of Rights in the Constitution. Why this is remarkable is because despite the fact that they would enjoy a legislative majority, representatives of black political organisations recognised the moral imperative (born of their own bitter experiences when they were subject to untrammelled legislative power), of restricting the competence of Parliament by means of a Bill of Rights which gave a testing power to the courts. The commitment of these parties to a Bill of Rights, even though such a document would restrict the exercise of legislative power they had struggled so hard to win, is indicative of a rare commitment to purity of principle, which, indeed, was the touchstone of the Constitution-making process in that country.[51] What is equally remarkable is that, despite having a legislative majority, those parties preferred to repose ultimate faith in protection of rights in the judiciary, rather than in politicians in the legislature. Clearly, the judiciary (acting through the new Constitutional Court) were seen as providing a neutral forum for the determination of questions involving the balancing of rights – questions which were likely to arise frequently as the majority began enacting its legislative programme in a highly politically-charged atmosphere. Thus, far from the enactment of a Bill of Rights being seen as something which would 'politicise the judiciary', leaving it to the courts to be the ultimate arbiters of whether the Bill of Rights or the popular will should prevail was, in fact, seen as de-politicising those questions, because they would be determined by impartial, politically neutral judges, rather than by self-interested politicians.

To summarise, the South African experience illustrates a number of important points: how vulnerable rights are to legislative abrogation in the absence of a Bill of Rights, the necessity for majorities to put principle above expediency when engaged in Constitution-making, and the fact that people who have had the misfortune of experiencing oppression, and who are thus best placed to determine which institution is most worthy of trust in defending them against future oppression, chose to allocate that role to the courts rather than to politicians. The value of the South African experience is that it provides results from Constitution-making in one of the harshest social laboratories in the world. Surely if people to whom constitutional rights have literally been a matter of life and death have reached the conclusion that an entrenched Bill of Rights, enforced by the courts, provides the best defence for freedom, we should pay heed to that result? And if their example is not persuasive enough, then perhaps the following consideration might be: given the high level of mistrust Australians evince for politicians, surely it is anomalous that we are willing to entrust a bare majority of self-interested politicians with the defence of our most basic freedoms?

51 The South African Bill of Rights was certainly not a charter of 'white rights' put in place in order to protect white privilege, as is asserted by Brennan, 1998, 177. The Bill of Rights confers strong protection on the right to equality (s 9), and while it protects the rights of different groups to maintain their own culture, this right is expressly stated in s 31(2) as being subject to a prohibition against the exercise of the right in a manner inconsistent with the rest of the Bill of Rights, obviously, and perhaps most importantly, including s 9.

2.4 WHAT IS THE SOURCE OF HUMAN RIGHTS?

Earlier in this chapter I criticised the positivist school for its rejection of anything other than a purely formal test for the validity of law, and argued instead that the principles of equality and human dignity in combination provide a philosophical foundation for the principle that governmental power should be subject to protection of human rights. However, the question remains who defines what human rights mean? Is there an objective content to human rights? The rejection of positivism earlier in this chapter proceeded on the basis that such an objective set of rules does exist, because by rejecting positivism one is saying that there is something external and superior to the values of a particular society, at a particular time, as expressed through that society's law-making mechanism. But whence does one derive this code? What is the authority for it? Can one really treat such rules as being objective in the same way as one treats the laws of gravity as being objective? Surely the value system of one society is as valid as that of the next? Who is to say that the concept of rights developed by the liberal societies of the (mostly) ethnically European western world are objectively valid?

2.4.1 Ancient jurisprudence and the classification of law

A useful lens through which to examine these questions is provided by the *Institutes* of Justinian, one of the works commissioned as part of his great codification of Roman law. This exposition of Roman law began with a discussion of the nature of law. The authors of the *Institutes* distinguished between *ius naturale* – natural law, which was divine in origin and superior to human law; *ius gentium* – the law of peoples, which was positive in the sense that it was devised by human beings, but which was supra-national in that it represented a consensus among nations; and *ius civile* – the civil law of Rome which comprised the laws of the Roman people as they stood from time to time.[52] It was acknowledged that some practices which were accepted under *ius gentium* and *ius civile* were prohibited by *ius naturale* – slavery being a prime example.[53] In other words, the Romans recognised a set of principles beyond human law, and conceded that human law was imperfect when measured against those principles.

The reason why the Romans' basic taxonomy of law is useful to us is that its threefold division between *ius naturale*, *ius gentium* and *ius civile* is reflected in modern jurisprudence. We, too, speak of natural law as a value code external to the positive law of any given society, although, as is shown in the next paragraph, modern concepts of natural law are based upon rationalist philosophies rather than on the theistic foundation upon which it rested in ancient and medieval times. *Ius gentium* has its modern analogue in customary international law, which is also discussed below. Finally, the modern-day analogue of *ius civile* is positive law – in other words, a given society's common and statute law, the content of which depends upon the outcomes of the political process within that society and which, to a greater or lesser extent, reflects the prevailing value system of that society.

---

52 *Inst* 1.2.pr–1.2.2, and 1.2.11. Citations are from Thomas, JAC (trans), *The Institutes of Justinian*, 1995, North Holland, Amsterdam.

53 *Inst* 1.2.2.

2.4.2 Natural rights

The most significant development in natural law theory occurred during the Enlightenment when, having been shorn of its religious underpinnings, natural law came to be conceived of as a set of principles which could be rationally deduced from the nature of humankind. I have already mentioned how Kant did this by linking equality and freedom, using an argument which obliges a person denying the obligation to respect natural rights to admit that by so doing, they accept that they themselves cannot claim any rights, and that ultimately, in a valueless system, there is no principle that they can have recourse to to deny the primacy of force, including force employed against themselves. Other contemporary philosophers also provide a rationalist justification for fundamental rights. Rawls, who posed the question of what fundamental values would be agreed upon if a group of people were to construct a legal order behind a 'veil of ignorance', unaware of what position they would hold in the society once it was created, said that such a group would produce a set of rules which (i) would confer upon everyone the maximum degree of individual liberty compatible with the enjoyment of liberty by others, and (ii) which would address social and economic inequalities by creating a system which would confer greatest benefit on the least advantaged.[54] Obviously there is some tension between principle (i) relating to liberty and principle (ii) relating to equality. The point is, however, that this methodology indicates that a human society designed according to rational principles would produce a set of rules in which the exercise of individual freedoms was maximized, subject only to intervention by rules designed to ensure that no-one could exercise their rights in such a way as to interfere with the exercise of rights by others, and to ensure that economic well-being was maintained above a certain minimum.

I would argue that rationalist natural rights theories provide the most principled basis upon which to found the obligation to protect human rights. But a significant difficulty that needs to be addressed is how to reconcile the universalist claims of natural rights theory with the observable fact that the body of rights, which are accepted by the proponents of that theory as being included within it, change over time. A good example mentioned by Piotrowicz and Kaye is that of slavery, which was accepted as an institution even by 18th century natural rights supporters such as Thomas Jefferson.[55] But if, as proponents of the natural rights theory would now assert, slavery violates a fundamental human right, and has always done so, how could it have been accepted by proponents of that same theory two hundred years ago? Are not natural rights supposed to be universal both with respect to time and place? The answer to this problem lies in the rationalist nature of contemporary human rights theory, as compared to the theistic character of the theory in ancient and medieval times. Whereas proponents of theistic natural law claimed to be in possession of 'the truth' as revealed by a moral order that ultimately drew its authority from revelation, Enlightenment and post-Enlightenment philosophers saw natural rights as scientific truth, understandable by human reason, but subject to changes in human understanding thereof, in common with other scientific truths. Thus, just as one can say that the laws of Newtonian physics appear to be objectively true but may yet

54 Rawls, 1971, 302; and Rawls, 1993, 5–7.

55 Piotrowicz and Kaye, 2000, 8–9.

conceivably be replaced by a new objective truth which always existed but was not comprehended, so, too, the changing definition of what constitutes natural rights simply reflects the evolutionary nature of human understanding of that concept, which may thus lead to institutions (such as slavery), which are accepted during one era, being found to be incompatible with fundamental rights in another.

On a practical level, this means that, paradoxical as it may seem given the universalist claims of natural rights theory, no single view as to the content of natural rights can be claimed to be definitively true. But this is by no means fatal to the natural rights project – commitment to the Kantian principle that there are fundamental values (even though their content is open to debate) is as important as discovering the content of those principles. Kant does at least force one to choose between a world with values (even though their content may be disputed), and a world where brute force is the final arbiter in human affairs. Assuming one accepts the first alternative (and, as I have already shown in my discussion of the obstacle Kant's ideas put in the path of positivists, anyone who accepts the second implicitly accepts that they themselves have no rights), one thereby acknowledges that there are rights, and that their content should be discovered through the application of reason. The major strength of the natural rights theory is that it provides a very strong argument supporting the assertion that rights exist (even though it cannot definitively say what those rights are), and that it prescribes commitment to a particular process by which questions about rights are to be resolved – that is, through rational debate. That process also requires tolerance for the views of others which may differ from one's own. The important division among legal philosophers is between those who assert that rights exist (who are bolstered by the strong theory put forward by Kant), and those who do not (who must perforce rely on the weak and ultimately self-defeating arguments proposed by legal positivists). In comparison with that divide, differences between proponents human rights over the substantive content of human rights are of reduced significance.

2.4.3 Customary international law

Even if one does not accept the rationalist arguments of theorists such as Kant and Rawls, this does not mean that one must therefore surrender to moral relativism, and to the propositions that every moral order is of equal value, that every society's value system is of equal worth, and that the mandates of a Nazi government would be as valid as those of one which respected fundamental rights. This is because the concept of customary international law provides a source from which one can infer both an obligation to respect fundamental rights, as well as the content of those rights. While there are numerous international treaties imposing obligations to respect human rights, they are regarded at international law as being binding only on their signatories, and hence cannot be regarded as imposing obligation on other, non-signatory, States. The argument based on customary international law counters this weakness by saying that there are some rules of international law (including some rules regarding human rights), which are so generally accepted as to have been elevated to the status of being binding, even in the absence of treaties imposing specific obligations. It was for infringements of these rules of customary international law that the defendants at Nuremberg were tried, an event which was significant because the Nuremberg war crimes court held that not only states, but also individuals, could be tried for breaches of these rules. Customary international law is defined as that body of law which is recognised as binding by a sufficient number of states (this recognition being referred to in international law as the *opinio juris* element) and which is generally obeyed by them as a matter of practice.[56] It is a body of rules agreed by states in a condition of dispassion. It is, by definition, a construct arrived at in the absence of contention, reflecting the principles which states are prepared to adopt while they are in agreement with each other. Although it might occur that states breach these rules when they are subject to internal or external strife, the fact remains that, once such rules have been generally accepted by the international community, States feel bound by them, their own positive law notwithstanding. A sub-set of this body of law are rules which are considered to be peremptory norms of international law (often referred to as *ius cogens*). These are rules which are so fundamental as not to be able to be overridden under any circumstances.[57] Examples of *ius cogens* referred to by international lawyers are the prohibitions of slavery, genocide and torture,[58] and there are cases in which domestic courts, applying customary international law as part of their own law, have held aliens liable for breaches of *ius cogens* which occurred outside their boundaries.[59]

A weakness of customary international law theory is the difficulty of identifying precisely which rules of law have been elevated to the status of international customary law, and also of determining how many states must accept and abide by a rule as *opinio juris* before it can be said that that rule has won general acceptance. Further problems are presented by the question of what happens if states express acceptance of a rule in theory while breaching it in practice – does that mean that if a sufficient number of states (and how many is a sufficient number?) breach the rule, even while continuing to do it lip service, that rule no longer forms part of customary international law?[60] The content of customary international law is thus, to some extent, indeterminate.

Using the norms of customary international law as the foundation of a general theory of human rights also exposes one to the criticism that the mere fact that a majority of nations, or even most of them, happen to agree on a set of rules does not vest those rules with any greater authority than the rules that might be developed by an individual society. Who is to say which of these sets of rules is superior to the other? Are they not both just positivist codes, one generated by the community of nations, the other by a community within a single state? It is true that basing the argument in favour of universal human rights on customary international law makes it less easy to defend in principle than is the argument based on natural rights. This is because customary international law is still positivist and subjective, representing, as it does, human agreement on what the law is, rather than a set of values derived from natural law, which is objective and external to the law or the views of human society at a particular time. Nevertheless, I

56 Davidson, 1993, 56–57.

57 *Ibid*, 58–59. This definition of *ius cogens* is to be found in Art 53 of the Vienna Convention on the Law of Treaties 1969, 155 UNTS 331.

58 Schachter, 1991, 338. See also the decision of the International Court of Justice in the *Barcelona Traction* case [1970] ICJ Rep 33–34, in which the court stated that the 'basic rights of the human person' at international law included the prohibition of slavery, racial discrimination, genocide and aggression.

59 See, eg, *Filartiga v Pena-Irala* (1980) 630 F2d 876, in which a United States court held that torture committed in Paraguay amounted to a breach of 'the law of nations' which United States courts could enforce by virtue of the Alien Tort Statute 28 USC § 1350.

60 For an analysis of these questions, see Higgins, 1994, 19.

would argue that customary international law offers a greater chance of according with natural law than does reference merely to the laws of a particular society. Support for this emerges from the writings of Grotius, who was both a natural lawyer and the first international law theorist. According to Grotius, questions of what was just (that is, what was in accordance with natural law) would be determined by reference to what was generally agreed upon as being correct, that is, *ius gentium*,[61] and to 'the testimony of those who are skilled' in law.[62] Although, given that natural law is immutable and general sentiment might be erroneous, *ius gentium* would not automatically coincide with natural law, in Grotius' opinion it could be said that it was at least likely that *ius gentium* would come close to natural law, simply because it reflected the accumulated wisdom of nations – in other words, the greater the accumulation of authority, the greater the likelihood that *ius gentium* would approach the objective truth of natural law, unattainable as the latter might be given the fallacy of human wisdom.[63] In other words, *ius gentium* provided the best available evidence as to the content of *ius naturale*.

Before leaving this discussion of customary international law, it is necessary to address the argument posed by cultural relativists who question the authority of human rights norms, both as derived from natural rights theory and from customary international law. In essence, their argument is that natural rights have no objective reality as a source of rules which vests them with universal authority, and that the authority of customary international law rests simply upon majoritarian sentiment among the nations of the world, and that this too is insufficient to vest its dictates with moral authority.[64] A couple of points can be made in response: first, the foundation of the cultural relativists own argument is to the effect that the imposition of human rights standards on states by the international community is wrong because it undermines these states' cultural rights. This argument has been used both by Third World countries when arguing that the imposition of human rights obligations threatens their own cultural values, and by other regimes which argue against the universality of human rights on the ground that they are seeking to preserve their sovereignty. Both variants of the relativist argument are frequently couched in terms that the world should be tolerant of cultural and political diversity, and that the universalist character of human rights ignores that entitlement. The problem with these arguments (and it is, indeed, the same problem I identified earlier in this chapter when discussing positivist opponents of Kant's theories), is that by claiming an entitlement to cultural autonomy and tolerance, the relativists are themselves claiming a right which presumably they would see as belonging to all societies – in other words, something that is universal.[65] The second point that can be made is that even proponents of cultural relativism do not deny the inherent dignity of the human being, rather they argue that respect for dignity does not necessarily require adherence to international human rights concepts. However, surely once one has accepted the principle of human dignity, this implies at least some limits as to what human beings may be subjected to – in other words, acceptance of a basic core of rights?[66] This being the case, it may be that

61 Grotius, 1925, 1.1.12.2. See also Scott's introduction at xxxiv.

62 *Ibid*, Grotius, 1.1.14.2.

63 Grotius, 1899, 1.2.12.

64 For a discussion summarising the relativist position see Steiner and Alson, 2000, 366–68.

65 For a critique of the relativist position exposing its self-contradictory nature, see Treson, 1985, 133–42.

66 For a discussion of this argument, see Schachter, 1983, 848.

even the cultural relativists disagreement is not so much with the concept of rights as with their content, upon which, as has been noted, even proponents of natural rights theories also disagree.

2.4.4 Constitutional implications

I would submit that the arguments presented above, based both on natural law and on customary international law, present a compelling case for the inclusion of a justiciable Bill of Rights in a new Australian Constitution. Such a document should be drafted in accordance with the principle that maximum protection should be given to human dignity and autonomy – in other words, the Bill of Rights should be comprehensive, and should protect as wide range of legal interests as is necessary to reflect the totality of human activity, subject only to the overarching principle that rights may be limited by law to the extent that is reasonable in a free and democratic society.

Finally, it is worthwhile noting that it may well be that the argument that Australia should have a Bill of Rights has often been cast in terms which have failed to win popular support: by focusing on the failure of the legal system to comply with human rights norms as embodied in international documents, proponents of a Bill of Rights may have given the impression that by enacting such a document, Australia would be submitting to the dictates of an external authority and, to that extent, would be compromising its sovereignty at least in a political, even if not in a legal, sense. While not denying the ethical force of the international documents, it is vital to present the argument in terms that it is the entitlement *of the Australian people* to have their own rights protected, and that what is being proposed is a Bill of Rights, drafted by Australians in order to protect the human dignity of Australians. This is not to contradict the argument made earlier in this chapter regarding the universality of human rights. However, from a tactical perspective, it will probably be more rewarding for proponents of a Bill of Rights in Australia to emphasise that the obligation resting upon the legal system to respect human rights derives from a value which one assumes is shared by broad Australian society, namely respect for the inherent dignity and equality of the individual.

2.5 WHAT RIGHTS SHOULD BE PROTECTED?

What rights should an Australian Bill of Rights protect? This part of the chapter examines a number of rights commonly found in Bills of Rights in various jurisdictions, and discusses the interests they serve – in other words, why they merit protection – and the challenges involved in delineating their scope. This discussion does not pretend to be comprehensive. A full discussion of what should be included in a Bill of Rights would require a book of its own, in which a discussion of each of these rights could take a separate chapter. The purpose of the rest of this chapter is simply to give a general overview of the sorts of rights that an Australian Bill of Rights might contain.

2.5.1 Life

As the most fundamental right, in the sense that it is the one upon which all others are dependant, it would seem that, as a bare minimum, a Bill of Rights should protect the right to life. Nevertheless, the inclusion of such an obvious right has the capacity to give rise to the most heated controversies. In other jurisdictions, issues such as the death penalty, euthanasia and abortion have all given rise to debate, in some cases accompanied by violence. Controversy over these issues is unavoidable: it will either confront the drafters of a Bill of Rights if they attempt to define in the document whether capital punishment, abortion and euthanasia, *et cetera* are permitted as exceptions to the right, or it will confront the courts if the drafters simply include an unqualified right to life in the Bill of Rights, leaving it to the judicial branch to determine the scope of the right using the Bill of Rights' limitations clause. According to Brennan, because it is unlikely that drafters of a Bill of Rights would reach agreement on these issues, and because of what he sees as the demonstrable inability of the courts in the United States to frame principled rules on these matters, an entrenched Bill of Rights should not be used for protecting these (or, indeed, other) rights.[67] In his view, these questions should be left to the workings of the common law, as modified by statutory intervention by legislatures responding to public opinion. This argument has already been countered above, but it is useful to re-emphasise a number of points.

First and foremost, the very concept of human rights is rendered meaningless if the scope of rights is determined by self-interested politicians and prejudiced majorities. That point has already been made on several occasions in this chapter. Secondly, as has also been noted, the United States is not a particularly good example to choose in determining the utility or otherwise of a Bill of Rights to determine these questions, because the United States Bill of Rights lacks a limitations clause, and this has meant that the courts have had to determine the scope of rights unaided by any general test. Nevertheless, the case law that has developed in the United States under the rubric of the right to privacy (discussed below under the heading of the right to personal autonomy), provides useful lessons in relation to the right to life, by no means all of them negative. Thirdly, although the questions related to the right to life may engender heated debate, they are conceptually no different to questions raised by other rights, or, indeed, to questions addressed by the courts in their development of the common law, under which the right to life is weighed against the right to self-defence every time an appeal court determines the circumstances in which that defence operates. Recently, the courts in the United Kingdom were called upon to determine whether it was lawful to end the life of the weaker of a pair of conjoined twins in order that the stronger might live, a case which involved the balancing of the rights of the infants, their parents, medical practitioners and the public interest.[68] So, too, in the case of a constitutionally-protected right to life in an Australian Bill of Rights, the courts would adopt the same techniques of judicial reasoning to weigh a woman's right to privacy and physical integrity against the foetus' right to life in the case of abortion. In other words, these questions may be difficult, but they are not unique. There is, therefore, no reason to omit protection of this most

67 Brennan, 1998, 91–94.

68 *Re A (Children)* [2001] 2 WLR 480 (CA).

fundamental right from an Australian Bill of Rights. It, like all other rights, would be able to be interpreted by the courts within the parameters of the reasonable limitations clause, assisted by the precedent that has been built up in other jurisdictions.

2.5.2 Liberty of the person and due process rights

The coercive power of the State over individual liberty has long been recognised as being open to abuse, and consequently the need to limit that power has long been acknowledged. In English law, protection of personal liberty and the requirement of due process for the deprivation thereof were recognised in Chapters 39 and 40 of Magna Carta,[69] which state as follows:

> 39 No freemen shall be taken or imprisoned or disseised or exiled or in any way destroyed, nor will we go upon him nor send upon him, except by the lawful judgment of his peers or by the law of the land.
>
> 40 To no one will we sell, to no one will we refuse or delay, right or justice.

In Australia, the circumstances in which an individual may be deprived of personal liberty are nowadays regulated primarily by statute law,[70] although residual protection is also provided by basic common law principles of the law of torts, under which an unlawful arrest is false imprisonment[71] and an unlawful search a trespass.[72]In addition, in *Chu Kheng Lim v Minister for Immigration, Local Government and Ethnic Affairs*,[73] the High Court held that the power to detain citizens was punitive in character, and thus one which, under the doctrine of separation of powers found in Chapter III of the Constitution, could lawfully occur only as a result of a judgment by a court.[74] For this reason, it was held that the Commonwealth did not have the power to enact legislation authorising detention of a citizen,[75] other than in certain limited circumstances where detention was to be considered non-punitive, namely arrest and detention in order to bring an accused before the courts, detention in cases of mental illness or contagious disease and detention in times of war (although this was raised only as a possibility and was expressly left open by the court).[76] A survey of criminal procedural law of every jurisdiction in Australia is obviously beyond the scope of this work.[77] It is true to say that, in general, Commonwealth and State statutory regimes carefully circumscribe powers of arrest and search, and provide significant protection for the accused while in custody and in order to ensure fair trial procedures. However, the fact that this area of the law is ultimately subject to the will of the legislature obviously makes liberty of the person

69 Magna Carta 1215.

70 For a general overview of this area, see Tronc, Crawford and Smith, 1996.

71 *R v Macquarie* (1875) 13 SCR (NSW) 264; *Greenwood v Ryan* (1846) 1 Legge 275; *Squires v Mahon* [1922] SASR 447.

72 *Entick v Carrington* (1765) 95 ER 807; 19 St Tr 1029.

73 (1992) 176 CLR 1.

74 Note, however, that in *Lim* the issue involved the detention of non-citizen asylum seekers. Their detention was upheld on the ground that it was non-punitive detention authorised by the s 51(xix) naturalisation and aliens power.

75 *Ibid*, 27.

76 *Ibid*, 28.

77 A concise overview of this area of the law is provided by Leaver, 1997.

potentially vulnerable to unreasonable limitation. As Joseph and Castan point out in their analysis[78] of *Kable v Director of Public Prosecutions (NSW)*,[79] although the High Court was able to use the doctrine of separation of powers to invalidate a State law which conferred on a body exercising the judicial power of the Commonwealth (in casu the Supreme Court of New South Wales), there would have been no constitutional doctrine that would have invalidated a law enacted under the State's plenary legislative power which authorised a member of the executive to detain people. Furthermore, the fact that there is no single national code governing liberty of the person in Australia means that the extent to which this right is protected varies from jurisdiction to jurisdiction. I would, therefore, argue that given the importance of the right to personal liberty, an Australian Bill of Rights should set a minimum floor of rights in relation to matters such as arrest, search, interrogation and criminal trial procedure.

Most Bills of Rights formulate the right to personal liberty as a primary prohibition of arbitrary interference with personal liberty – in other words, they provide that interferences with personal liberty not authorised by law are invalid.[80] However, even where deprivation of liberty is authorised by law, it may, nevertheless, infringe fundamental rights because the deprivation is unreasonable. The simplest way of capturing both the need for deprivations of liberty to be authorised by law and to be reasonable is to put into the Bill of Rights a blanket provision to the effect that no person may be deprived of their liberty, and then to leave it to the limitations clause, (which would permit limitations of rights which were performed under law and which were reasonable in a free and democratic society), to determine which deprivations of liberty are permissible. Note that it would be important to frame the right as relating to deprivations of liberty, rather than to a narrower term such as 'arrest'. The protection of the right to personal liberty would obviously lose much of its substance if the Bill of Rights did not offer protection of individual liberty in circumstances where no formal arrest had taken place. Indeed, the absence of such protection would invite legislatures to evade the provisions of the Bill of Rights by legislating for administrative detention as a category of deprivation of liberty distinct from arrest.

Assuming a deprivation of liberty under a constitutionally valid law, what procedural protections should a Bill of Rights provide to persons who have been deprived of their liberty? At a minimum, the Bill of Rights should include the requirement that a person who has been deprived of their liberty be informed without delay of the reason for the deprivation, of the fact that that they have a right to contact a legal adviser without delay, of the fact that they have a right of silence and of the consequences of their waiving the right to silence. Such information must be given to the person in a language they understand or via a translator. Following upon that, the person should be afforded the right to contact a legal adviser. The Bill of Rights should also specify that a person must be formally arrested and charged, or be released, within a specified time, and that a

78 Joseph and Castan, 2001, 146.

79 (1996) 189 CLR 51.

80 The New Zealand Bill of Rights Act 1990, s 22 states that 'Everyone has the right not to be arbitrarily arrested or detained'; the Constitution of the Republic of South Africa 1996, s 12(1) states that everyone has the right 'not to be deprived of freedom arbitrarily or without just cause' and 'not to be detained without trial'; while the Canadian Charter of Rights and Freedoms 1982, s 9 states that 'Everyone has the right not to be arbitrarily detained or imprisoned'.

person who has been deprived of their liberty has a right to appear before court within a specified time after deprivation of their personal liberty, in order to have the validity of their detention or arrest determined.

Those who have been charged with an offence must be accorded the right to a public trial by an impartial court[81] within a reasonable time, and must not be denied bail without cause. Where the language of the court is not understood by the accused, a translator must be provided. Accused persons must have the right to be presumed innocent until proven guilty, and must not be compelled to give evidence against themselves. A person who has been tried and acquitted should not be able to be tried for the offence again, and if found guilty of the offence should not be able to be tried or punished for it again.

Allied to rights relating to personal liberty are those relating to search and seizure of property. Bills of Rights commonly require that search and seizure not be arbitrary, and be subject to a test of reasonableness[82] or probable cause.[83] Just as in relation to the right to personal liberty, framing the right as a prohibition against 'unreasonable' search and seizure is unnecessary if the Constitution contains a general limitations provision, as it will follow from such a provision that restrictions on the right taking the form of reasonable search and seizure will be constitutional. Effective protection of the interest served by the right not to be subject to search and seizure requires that the right be formulated in such a way as to include the right not to be subject to surveillance by the state, or to have private communications interfered with. In some jurisdictions, protection has been extended to that right by means of judicial interpretations of the concept of search and seizure,[84] while in others it is recognised as a dimension of a right to privacy.[85]

The above rights are fundamental to any fair system of justice, and are unlikely to prove controversial in Australia. However, there are some aspects of criminal procedural rights which are more open to debate.

Should a Bill of Rights protect a right to legal counsel, in the sense that the state is obliged to provide an accused with a lawyer if the accused is unable to afford one? Bills of Rights evince different answers to this question in different jurisdictions: in the United States, judicial interpretation of the right to have the 'assistance of counsel' found in the Sixth Amendment, coupled with the 'due process' clause of the Fourteenth Amendment, is to the effect that a fair trial requires the provision of state-funded representation where the accused may be subjected to imprisonment.[86] In South Africa, the Bill of Rights

81 Subject to an exception (see, eg, the Canadian Charter of Rights and Freedoms, s 11(f)) that members of the defence force who are being tried for offences against military law may be tried by a military tribunal. However, in all other aspects the rights of persons appearing before such tribunals should be the same as those enjoyed by accused appearing before ordinary courts.

82 See, eg, the Canadian Charter of Rights and Freedoms 1982, s 8; and the Constitution of the Republic of South Africa 1996, ss 14 and 36.

83 Constitution of the United States of America 1787, Amendment IV.

84 Eg, in the United States the Amendment IV protection of freedom from search and seizure has been interpreted as including the right not to be subject to electronic surveillance – see *Katz v United States* 389 US 342 (1967).

85 Eg, the Constitution of the Republic of South Africa 1996, s 14(d) protects the right to privacy of communications.

86 See *Gideon v Wainwright* 372 US 335 (1963); and *Scott v Illinois* 440 US 367 (1979).

provides that the right to a fair trial includes the right 'to have a legal practitioner assigned to the accused person by the State and at State expense if substantial injustice would otherwise result'.[87] In this context, the courts have interpreted 'substantial injustice' as existing if an unrepresented accused might face imprisonment if convicted.[88] In Australia, while expressly rejecting the argument that under the common law an accused is entitled to publicly-funded defence counsel, the High Court in *Dietrich v R*[89] held that a trial would be unfair where an accused faced a serious charge when unable to afford representation. What is meant by a 'serious offence' was not elaborated upon by the court, save to say that in the case before it, the fact that the accused faced narcotics charges, which carried substantial penalties of imprisonment, met the test. The Commonwealth and all the States and Territories have statutory legal aid schemes which vest the Attorney-General (Commonwealth) or a Legal Aid Commission (State or Territory) with the power to grant legal aid on application by a party seeking it.[90] Applications are subject to a means test in all jurisdictions, most of which apply a common National Means Test model.[91] The operation of the legal aid schemes is assisted by those private practitioners who provide voluntary assistance to the Legal Aid Commissions, and who charge less than market rates when representing those who have been granted legal aid, a practice which enables Commission funds go further than they otherwise would.[92] Representation is also provided to those unable to afford it by virtue of *pro bono* work undertaken by practitioners.[93] Given that the right to counsel has been put in the Constitution in South Africa, even though the resources available to the government are extremely limited, I would argue that a comparatively wealthy society such as ours should accept the same obligation, at least in respect of accused persons facing imprisonment. Including such a right in the Constitution would formalise the current situation where representation relies upon the voluntary acceptance by governments of an obligation to fund statutory legal aid schemes, and the goodwill of the legal profession. Legal aid schemes might well continue to provide assistance in cases other than those where the accused faces imprisonment, but the Constitution would at least provide a floor entitlement in relation to that category.

Another possibly controversial right is that to trial by jury. Currently, s 80 of the Commonwealth Constitution provides for a right to jury trial for offences against Commonwealth law triable on indictment. However, given that, as was held in *R v Archdall*,[94] the Commonwealth Parliament can freely determine which offences are prosecuted by indictment and which by summons, the scope of the right is obviously limited. While jury trials are used by all States and Territories in Australia, there is significant variation between them with regard to which offences are triable summarily and which on indictment, and, in relation to the latter category, which indictable offences

87 Constitution of the Republic of South Africa 1996, s 35(3)(g).

88 *S v Mfene* 1998 (9) BCLR 1157 (N).

89 (1992) 177 CLR 292.

90 For an overview of the Commonwealth, State and Territory schemes, see Fleming, 1994.

91 *Ibid*, 34–44.

92 *Ibid*, 81.

93 Weisbrot, 2001, 216–22.

94 (1928) 41 CLR 128. The interpretation of s 80 in *Archdall* was upheld by the High Court in *Kingswall v R* (1985) 159 CLR 264; and in *Cheng v The Queen* (2000) 203 CLR 248.

may, as opposed to *must*, be tried by jury.[95] Furthermore, while some continue to assert the importance of the jury in ensuring fairness in the criminal justice process,[96] others point to the lack of expertise of juries, the secretiveness of the jury process, the susceptibility of juries to emotional manipulation and the pressurised environment in which jury members make decisions, as a recipe for bad decision-making, and thus as strong arguments for the abandonment of trial by jury.[97] For present purposes, it suffices to say that trial by jury cannot be said to be fundamental to the fairness of a criminal trial in the way that other procedural rights discussed in preceding paragraphs. A criminal justice system can operate with fairness and integrity without the use of juries. On balance, there thus seems to be no good reason to include a blanket right to trial by jury in a Bill of Rights. The preferable course would, therefore, be to leave the current position undisturbed, with the question of whether an offence is triable on indictment (and thus by jury) or summarily (and thus by judge alone) being addressed by the relevant legislature.

Finally, in respect of procedural rights, the issue of laws creating retrospective criminal offences must be considered. This matter was considered by the High Court in *Polyukhovich v The Queen*.[98] The court rejected the argument that, by imposing guilt in respect of conduct which was not an offence under Australian law when committed, Parliament had usurped the judicial function. By contrast, the United States Constitution prohibits both federal and State legislatures from enacting such legislation,[99] as does the Canadian Charter[100] and South Africa's Bill of Rights.[101] The argument put to the court in *Polyukhovich* was founded only on the separation of powers doctrine. Indeed, there is no other principle of Australian constitutional law which could have been relied upon as an argument to invalidate a retrospective statute, despite the obvious affront such laws present to notions of criminal responsibility. I would, therefore, argue that such legislation ought to be expressly proscribed in a Bill of Rights.

2.5.3 The right not to be subject to slavery, torture and cruel or inhuman treatment

Many Bills of Rights extend the protection of the person to include prohibitions against slavery, torture and cruel or inhumane imprisonment or treatment.

The obligation to prevent slavery has already been accepted by Australia in international law through its ratification of the International Convention to Suppress the Slave Trade and Slavery.[102] No-one would deny that protection from slavery should be

95 Chesterman, 2000, 130–31.

96 See, eg, the statements by Deane J in *Kingswall v R* (1985) 159 CLR 264, 300–01.

97 Kerr, 1987. See also Crispin Hull, 'Time has now come to put the jury system to the test' (2000) *Canberra Times*, 20 May, 1; and Crispin Hull, 'Questions arise in trial by jury' (2000) *Canberra Times*, 17 August, 9.

98 (1991) 172 CLR 501.

99 Constitution of the United States of America 1787, Art 1, ss 9 and 10.

100 Canadian Charter of Rights and Freedoms 1982, s 11(g).

101 Constitution of the Republic of South Africa 1996, s 35(3)(l).

102 League of Nations Treaty, Geneva, 25 September 1926.

included in a Bill of Rights. More controversial, however, is the question of whether a Bill of Rights should include a broader prohibition against forced labour. Forced labour is prohibited under the International Labour Organisation's Convention concerning Forced or Compulsory Labour.[103] Article 2 of that Convention defines forced labour as 'all work or service which is exacted from any person under the menace of any penalty and for which the said person has not offered himself voluntarily', but excludes compulsory military or civic service, service required as part of a sentence following conviction for an offence, or service required in emergency situations. It is something of an irony, given the hard fought struggle against conscription during the First World War, and the social division caused by the anti-conscription movement during the war in Vietnam, that while the s 51(xxiiiA) welfare power prohibits civil conscription for the purpose of providing medical or dental services, nothing in the Constitution prohibits military conscription. The prohibition against civil conscription was included in the Constitution as a consequence of a political compromise designed to placate fears of the medical profession that the welfare power might be used to nationalise the provision of medical services in Australia.[104] It would seem anomalous to extend the protection against compulsory service to civil conscription while denying it in relation to military conscription, in relation to which there are far more pressing ethical reasons justifying a constitutional prohibition. I would, therefore, argue that the Bill of Rights should include a prohibition on forced labour, expressly mentioning military and civil conscription as specific aspects of the general prohibition.

Australia has also ratified international conventions prohibiting torture and inhuman treatment, such as the International Covenant on Civil and Political Rights,[105] and the Convention Against Torture and Other Inhuman or Degrading Treatment or Punishment.[106] It is important to note that most modern Bills of Rights usually refer to treatment which is 'cruel or inhuman' rather than to that which is 'cruel or unusual'. The 'cruel or inhuman' formulation imports a more objective test, in that it requires a court interpreting the provision to assess conduct against a general standard of humaneness (in other words, a standard that focuses on the effect of the conduct on the person who is subject to it), rather than against a standard which focuses primarily on prevailing usual practice, which may or may not be objectively humane. The deficiencies of the 'cruel and unusual' formula become evident when one considers case law that has arisen under the 'cruel and unusual punishment' clause of the Eighth Amendment to the United States Constitution, which has been interpreted as *not* prohibiting the death penalty, on the basis that the punishment, far from being unusual, is widely imposed.[107] By contrast, in one of its first decisions under the 1993 Interim Constitution, the South African Constitutional Court held the death penalty to be inconsistent with the right conferred under the

103 Convention Concerning Forced or Compulsory Labour (ILO No 29), 1 May 1932.

104 Hanks, 1996, 452–53.

105 GA Res 2200 A (XXI), 16 December 1966. Article 7 of the Covenant provides that no-one may be subject to 'torture, cruel, inhuman or degrading treatment or punishment'.

106 GA Res 39/46, 10 December 1984. Article 1 of the Convention prohibits torture, while Art 2 requires signatories to take appropriate legislative measures to prevent torture within their jurisdictions and Art 4 requires parties to make torture an offence under their criminal law. In addition, Art 16 obliges signatories to prevent 'acts of cruel, inhuman or degrading treatment or punishment which does not amount to torture' taking place within their jurisdiction.

107 See *Gregg v Georgia* 428 US 153 (1976).

Constitution not to be treated or punished in a 'cruel, inhuman or degrading way'.[108] Members of the court stated that the death penalty was objectively inhumane, gave primacy to retribution over all other factors in sentencing (thereby discounting the possibility if rehabilitation), was unnecessary in that there was no evidence that life imprisonment would not equally serve to deter the criminal and protect society, and stripped the individual of dignity by reducing him to the status of an object to be disposed of by the State. Although the death penalty was last used in Australia in 1967 and was abolished in all jurisdictions by 1985,[109] there is no legal barrier to its reintroduction. An Australian Bill of Rights ought, therefore, to expressly prohibit it, as well as protecting the broader right not to be subject to cruel and inhuman treatment.

2.5.4 Expression

As we have already seen, the importance of freedom of expression in a democracy has been given some recognition in Australian law through the reading into the Constitution of an implied right to political communication. Of particular importance is the deliberately narrow terminology used by the High Court – what has been recognised is not a general right to freedom of expression, but a highly specific freedom to engage in communication about political matters. The right thus does not extend to freedom of artistic expression or to communication in relation to anything other than the political – and these are undeniably important dimensions of expressive conduct. Restricting the freedom only to such expression as is necessary to sustain democracy is to adopt an instrumentalist view of freedom of expression in particular, and of human rights in general, and is to ignore the fact that freedoms warrant protection not only for utilitarian reasons, but also for the broader reason that, by respecting them, one respects the individual's right to self-fulfilment.[110] One would, therefore, hope that an Australian Bill of Rights would specify a non-exclusive set of categories of expressive conduct which were protected. Such an approach would confer certainty of coverage in respect of the nominated categories, while leaving it to the courts extend coverage to other dimensions of expressive conduct.

The issue of what limits should be placed on freedom of expression has provoked spirited debate among academics, and has produced a substantial volume of case law. Perhaps this is because the need to express oneself is a core aspect of individual autonomy, generating passionate defence from those who see any attempt to limit expression as suppressing their very identity. By contrast, those arguing in favour of limits on freedom of expression point to the fact that it is the very power of expression that creates the potential for harm caused to feelings and to reputation by negative speech. Here is not the place to canvass the nuances of the debate on the likely

108 *S v Makwanyane* 1995 (6) BCLR 665 (CC).

109 The last jurisdiction to abolish the death penalty was New South Wales, by the enactment of the Crimes (Death Penalty Abolition) Amendment Act 1985 (NSW). At the federal level, the death penalty was abolished by the Death Penalty Abolition Act 1973 (Cth).

110 For an enunciation of this view, see Emmerson, 1963, 879; and Smolla, 1993, 9–10 and 119.

constitutional validity of restrictions on hate speech[111] and on sexually explicit material[112] – issues which have proved highly controversial in other jurisdictions. However, one point that needs to be emphasised is that the most dangerous type of restriction on freedom of expression is that which attempts to limit the range of ideas open for discussion and evaluation and, perhaps even more insidiously, which seeks to establish an official orthodoxy as to what attitudes it is permissible to hold. Perhaps the most powerful argument in the armoury of those who favour a broad interpretation of freedom of expression (and a correspondingly strict construction of restrictions on the freedom) is that prohibitions on the expression of ideas amount to a declaration by the legal system that it has discovered 'the truth' about a particular matter – in other words, to a declaration of official infallibility – something which is surely incompatible with a rational society. The legitimate focus of restrictions on freedom of expression must be the prohibition of expression which urges unlawful conduct, not expression which amounts to the propagation of ideas which it is sought by lawful persuasion to seek society to adopt. Once the expression of a certain idea has been restricted, the law has, in fact, passed beyond merely restricting expression and on to the regulation of attitudes.[113] Freedom of expression thus serves to protect not only the enunciation of ideas, but also the even more intimate freedom to hold particular ideas within one's head.

In some jurisdictions, freedom of expression is supplemented by an express protection of the right of peaceful assembly and to engage in public protest.[114] Arguably, such freedoms are implicit in freedom of expression, as they essentially amount to forms of expressive conduct. In Australia, the High Court has recognised that the implied freedom of political communication extends to symbolic speech taking the form of conduct.[115] Nevertheless, it would eliminate any uncertainty in relation to these aspects of expressive conduct if they were expressly mentioned in the Bill of Rights.

2.5.5 Franchise and political participation

Given that exercising a vote represents the most fundamental act of political participation in a democracy – and, indeed, for the vast majority of people, the only type of political participation they are likely to engage in – it would seem obvious that a Bill of Rights ought to protect the right to vote. It would also seem fundamental in a democracy to include a right to stand for public office.

111 'Hate speech' is not a legal term but, rather, one describing a range of conduct extending from expression which incites others to commit criminal acts against members of a certain race, that which defames members of a race, that which insults members of a race and, finally, that which does not fall into any of the preceding categories but which simply contains ideas which members of a racial group find offensive – see Harris, 1999, 261–68. There is an enormous amount of literature on this topic. The views for and against restriction of hate speech are particularly well put by Lawrence, 1990; and Browne, 1991.

112 For a clear articulation of views for and against the censorship of sexually explicit material, see Dworkin and MacKinnon, 1988, and Strossen, 1993.

113 For an early critique of attitudinal regulation, see Mill, 1991, 96. For recent writing, see Dority, 1991; and Smolla, 1993, 10–11.

114 See, eg, the Constitution of the Republic of South Africa 1996, s 17.

115 *Levy v Victoria* (1997) 189 CLR 579.

2.5.5.1 The right to vote

Currently, the text of the Constitution affords little protection to franchise rights. Section 41 provides that a person who has acquired the right to vote in elections for the more numerous house of a State Parliament must be permitted to vote in elections for the Commonwealth Parliament. However, in *R v Pearson ex parte Sipka*[116] the High Court interpreted s 41 as having only transitory effect, spanning the time federation was formed and the time the Commonwealth first used its power under s 30 of the Constitution to legislate on voting rights in Commonwealth elections.[117] The High Court reasoned that if an ambulatory meaning was given to s 41, it would mean that the States could have set differing franchise qualifications for Commonwealth elections, thus subverting the uniform franchise scheme put in place by the Commonwealth Parliament.

Since the decision in *Sipka*, the High Court has read into the Constitution a right to freedom of communication, implied from the system of representative government established principally by ss 7 and 24 of the Constitution which require that members of the Senate and House of Representatives be 'directly chosen by the people'.[118] The implied freedom of political communication was discussed earlier in this chapter. The High Court has never been called upon to determine whether the system of representative government means that there is also an implied right to the franchise in the Constitution – the question being moot so long as universal adult suffrage is conferred by the Commonwealth Electoral Act 1918 (Cth). Of course, given the emphasis placed on representative government in the implied freedom of political communication cases, it would seem highly likely that, if ever presented with the question, the High Court would affirm such an implied right. Indeed, in *McGinty v Western Australia*[119] there are *dicta* to the effect that universal adult franchise is a *sine qua non* of representative democracy, and that it is implicit in the Constitution.[120] Nevertheless, the right to vote is obviously a freedom meriting express constitutional protection. A Bill of Rights ought, therefore, to state that every citizen who has attained the age of 18 years has the right to vote. The same qualifications ought to entitle a person to stand for public office – the precise rules which should govern eligibility to be a member of Parliament are discussed later in this section.

An interesting issue that might arise in the context of Australian electoral law is the interaction between compulsory voting (a somewhat misleading term, in that what is required by s 245(1) of the Commonwealth Electoral Act 1918 (Cth) is attendance at the polls and the placing of a ballot paper in the box), and freedom of expression. In *Langer v Commonwealth*,[121] a voter challenged the validity of s 240 of the Commonwealth Electoral Act 1918 (Cth) (which required that voters must vote preferences sequentially), and s 329A, which made it an offence to encourage voters to mark their ballot papers in any way other than that required by s 240. The High Court rejected Langer's argument that, because ss 7 and 24 of the Constitution required that members of Parliament be 'chosen'

116 (1983) 152 CLR 254.

117 By enacting the Commonwealth Franchise Act 1902 (Cth).

118 The implied freedom was first recognised in *ACTV Pty Ltd v Commonwealth* (1992) 177 CLR 106.

119 (1996) 186 CLR 140.

120 *Ibid*, 201, 221–22 and 287.

121 (1996) 186 CLR 302.

by the people, s 240 was inconsistent with these sections of the Constitution in that it mandated how that choice was to be expressed. In other words, the concept of choice as embodied in the Constitution did not, according to the High Court, protect the right to make a choice taking the form of an informal vote. This was despite the fact that s 270 of the Commonwealth Electoral Act 1918 (Cth) specifically addressed the question of how informal ballots (that is, ballots marked other than in accordance with the requirements of s 240) were to be counted. The court also came to the conclusion that the prohibition in s 329A was not inconsistent with the implied freedom of political communication, even though it effectively punished a person who advised fellow voters on how to vote informally – a course of conduct specifically addressed by s 270! Unfortunately, Langer did not directly challenge the constitutional validity of s 245(1) of the Act, which compels voters to attend the polls and put a ballot in the box. Nonetheless, it is clear that the challenges to ss 240 and 329A were motivated by a desire to attack the institution of compulsory voting, and argument for Langer proceeded on the basis that, in a democracy, the political and expressive rights of a citizen must at least include the right to manifest his or her opinion of the political system by voting other than in the way mandated by the system.[122] Certainly there are strong arguments which support the proposition that political rights include the right not to participate in the political process, and that abstention can itself constitute potent political expression in relation to the system.[123] Yet the High Court's conception of democratic rights and freedom of political communication (both of which, one might think, exist to protect the individual's right to political autonomy), led it to the bizarre conclusion that the state can compel the citizen to engage in political participation, and can criminalise the conduct of the citizen who advises others to cast their ballots in an informal manner for which provision is made in the electoral law. The High Court reached the same decision when faced with a challenge to almost identical provisions in State law in *Muldowney v South Australia*.[124] What the fate of compulsory voting would be in the event that Australia had a Bill of Rights which gave express protection both to the franchise and freedom of expression, is a matter for conjecture.

Another area in which the High Court's treatment of franchise rights has been unsatisfactory relates to its rejection of the argument that the concept of representative government implies that each citizen has the right not just to a vote but to an equal vote. The principle that the vote of every citizen should be of equal weight appears so fundamental as not to require defence, yet in cases decided both before[125] and after[126] the High Court found that rights were implied by representative government, the court rejected the argument that representative government required an electoral system conforming to the principle of 'one vote one value'. This issue is explored in Chapter 8, in which I address the concept of fair representation. Here, it is only necessary to note that, in light of the arguments presented in that chapter, the protection afforded to the franchise in the Bill of Rights must be worded in such a way as to make it explicit that

122 For a discussion of arguments both for and against compulsory voting, see Hill, 2001.

123 For a discussion of compulsory voting from a United States perspective, see Hasen, 1996.

124 (1996) 186 CLR 352.

125 *Attorney-General (Cth); ex rel McKinlay v Commonwealth* (1975) 135 CLR 1.

126 *McGinty v Western Australia* (1996) 186 CLR 140.

every adult citizen has the right to a vote which is of equal weight to that exercised by every other citizen, at least in the House of Representatives. Franchise rights in relation to the Senate and how they are affected by the powers of that chamber, are examined in Chapter 9.

2.5.5.2 The right to stand for election and to sit as a member of Parliament

Attention must also be given to the issue of the qualifications required to stand for election as a member of Parliament. Assuming that the Constitution stated that every citizen who had attained the age of 18 years had a right to stand for election to public office, what restrictions, if any, should the Constitution place on that right and on the entitlement of elected candidates to sit in Parliament? Currently these issues are governed by ss 16, 34 and 43–47 of the Constitution

Section 16 provides that the qualification for being a senator shall be the same as those for being a member of the House of Representatives, which in s 34 are stated as being that a person must be 21 years of age, must be entitled to vote for the House of Representatives, must have resided in the Commonwealth for three years and must be a 'subject of the Queen'. Sections 43–47 provide as follows:

> 43 A member of either House of the Parliament shall be incapable of being chosen or of sitting as a member of the other House.
>
> 44 (1) Any person who–
>
> (i) Is under any acknowledgment of allegiance, obedience, or adherence to a foreign power, or is a subject or a citizen or entitled to the rights or privileges of a subject or a citizen of a foreign power; or
>
> (ii) Is attained of treason, or has been convicted and is under sentence, or subject to be sentenced, for any offence punishable under the law of the Commonwealth or of a State by imprisonment for one year or longer; or
>
> (iii) Is an undischarged bankrupt or insolvent; or
>
> (iv) Holds any office of profit under the Crown, or any pension payable during the pleasure of the Crown out of any of the revenues of the Commonwealth; or
>
> (v) Has any direct or indirect pecuniary interest in any agreement with the Public Service of the Commonwealth otherwise than as a member and in common with the other members of an incorporated company consisting of more than 25 persons,
>
> shall be incapable of being chosen or of sitting as a senator or a member of the House of Representatives.
>
> (2) But Sub-section (iv) does not apply to the office of any of the Queen's Ministers of State for the Commonwealth, or of any of the Queen's Ministers for a State, or to the receipt of pay, half pay, or a pension, by any person as an officer or member of the Queen's navy or army, or to the receipt of pay as an officer or member of the naval or military forces of the Commonwealth by any person whose services are not wholly employed by the Commonwealth.
>
> 45 If a senator or member of the House of Representatives–
>
> (i) Becomes subject to any of the disabilities mentioned in the last preceding section; or

(ii) Takes the benefit, whether by assignment, composition, or otherwise, of any law relating to bankrupt or insolvent debtors; or

(iii) Directly or indirectly takes or agrees to take any fee or honorarium for services rendered to the Commonwealth, or for services rendered in the Parliament to any person or State,

his place shall thereupon become vacant.

46 Until the Parliament otherwise provides, any person declared by this Constitution to be incapable of sitting as a senator or as a member of the House of Representatives shall, for every day on which he so sits, be liable to pay the sum of one hundred pound to any person who sues for it in any court of competent jurisdiction.

47 Until the Parliament otherwise provides, any question respecting the qualification of a senator or of a member of the House of Representatives or respecting a vacancy in either House of the Parliament, and any question of a disputed election to either House, shall be determined by the House in which the question arises.

These provisions are antiquated and in need of reform. Given that the individual's right to stand for, and serve in, public office is fundamental to the democratic system, the right should be restricted to the minimum extent necessary. The basic entitlement both to vote and to stand for office should be that a person is an Australian citizen who has attained the age of 18 years.

The s 43 prohibition on dual membership of the House of Representatives and the Senate is an obvious consequence of the federal system and should therefore be retained. So far as s 44 is concerned, I would argue that many of the recommendations of the 1988 Constitutional Commission are worthy of adoption. Thus the restrictions on foreign citizens being able to stand for election should be removed.[127] This would mean that a candidate would have to be an Australian citizen, but would not be ineligible to stand simply because they held dual citizenship. The prohibition relating to conviction for offences should be restricted to those who have been convicted of treason or who are currently serving a sentence of imprisonment.[128] The prohibition on bankrupts and insolvents, which reflects the values of an age when those situations were thought to indicate moral turpitude, should also be removed,[129] along with the related provision in s 45(ii). So far as the provisions of s 44(iv) relating to office-holding are concerned, the Constitutional Commission recommended that these provisions be replaced with a set of categories of office-holding which reflected the need to maintain separation of powers between the judiciary and the other branches of government, which reflected the federal structure of Australia (by prohibiting a person from sitting in the Commonwealth Parliament and that of a State simultaneously), and which better reflected the purpose of the rule against office-holders being members of Parliament. Thus the Commission recommended that a person who became the holder of judicial office, a member of the federal, State or Territory public service, a member of the Defence Force, a member of any other Australian legislature and a member, officer or employee of a public authority, be

127 *Constitutional Commission*, 1988, 4.797.

128 *Ibid*, 4.800 – the Commission actually recommended that conviction for treason be an automatic disqualification and that Parliament should have the power to disqualify a person while serving a sentence of imprisonment.

129 *Ibid*, 4.819.

disqualified from being a member of the Commonwealth Parliament if they were one already,[130] but that a person who fell into one of the disqualified categories be permitted to stand for election, and be deemed to have ceased to hold the disqualifying position they day before they were elected to Parliament if their candidacy was successful.[131] This would obviate the necessity for people who were in disqualifying positions resigning before even being able to stand as a candidate, which is the current unsatisfactory position under s 44. The Commission's recommendations would also remove the necessity for a specific exemption in the Constitution relating to Ministers, Assistant Ministers and Parliamentary Secretaries, as they would not be captured by the prohibition relating to the public service. The Commission recommended the retention of the conflict of interest provision in s 44(v), but with the additional entitlement of Parliament to legislate to disqualify members who have other interests which might create the risk of conflict of interest, or who have committed offences relating to corrupt practices or improper influence. The Commission did, however, recommend that the s 45(iii) prohibition against members of Parliament receiving fees or honoraria be removed from the Constitution. A new ground for disqualification, which the Constitutional Commission recommended be added to the Constitution, is that of being of unsound mind.[132] Including that as a ground of disqualification would enable voters represented by the parliamentarian concerned to obtain new representation.

The enforcement provisions of this part of the law also require reform. The penalty provision in s 46 is obviously antiquated. The conferral upon Parliament of jurisdiction under s 47 to determine cases over the qualifications of members and over disputed returns, while in accordance with notions of Parliamentary privilege, carries the risk that such matters might be politicised. Although current practice is for Parliament to use the provisions of s 376 of the Commonwealth Electoral Act 1918 (Cth), and to refer disputes relating to the qualifications of members of either house of Parliament, or relating to vacancies in either house, to the High Court, there is much to be said for the matter of the validity of elections, and of the eligibility of members of Parliament to sit in either house, to be de-politicised by having them fall within the jurisdiction of the courts as a matter of course. Thus, at 3.5.2.4, below, I argue that jurisdiction in relation to electoral matters should be removed from the Commonwealth Electoral Act 1918 (Cth) and be put into the Constitution as part of the High Court's entrenched original jurisdiction.

2.5.6 Association

Allied to traditional political rights of voting, and of standing for office, is the broader right of freedom of association. By protecting that right, a Bill of Rights acknowledges that much human activity takes place through individuals forming groups in order to enhance the effectiveness of their political, industrial, entrepreneurial and social activity. Indeed, freedom to associate and to organise is fundamental to the operation of what is known as 'civil society' – the aggregate of non-governmental groups formed by people in the exercise of their role as citizens.

130 *Ibid*, 4.837.
131 *Ibid*, 4.838.
132 *Ibid*, 4.827.

One aspect of freedom of association which has proved controversial is the question of whether freedom of association includes the right of the individual *not* to associate. Logically, the case for reading freedom of association as including the right not to associate is compelling: if the underlying rationale for the recognition of the freedom is to enable individuals to pool their strength in order to facilitate an underlying shared objective, it would be inconsistent for the law to allow individuals to be coerced into lending their names, funds or efforts to an association which was striving towards an objective which they did not share. The issue of whether the freedom includes the right not to associate has been of particular relevance in relation to contracts of employment in unionised industries, which sometimes impose a 'closed shop' (workers must be union members in order to be employed), 'union shop' (workers must join the union after obtaining employment) or 'agency shop' (workers must pay dues to a union but do not have to become members).[133] Unions argue that non-union workers who derive benefits from industry wages set through the collective bargaining power of union members are 'freeloaders' on the system,[134] and ought at the very least to contribute financially to the union. However, compulsory union membership raises the problem that individuals who object to union membership on religious grounds, or because they disagree with political postures adopted by the union, face the choice of losing their jobs or abandoning their principles. Furthermore, it could be argued that, at base, the 'freeloader' argument rests on the same ethically flawed foundation as does that used to justify military conscription, which is that the person who objects on conscientious or other grounds to military service is taking advantage of the benefits conferred by the state without being willing to contribute to them. At the very least, it is clear that there are important individual interests which require protecting through explicit recognition of a right not to associate, and that such a right should be afforded explicit protection in a Bill of Rights, along with the right to freedom of association. The precise boundary between the two rights would be determined by the courts on a case by case basis. In the United States the Supreme Court has ruled that 'agency shop' contracts infringe First Amendment rights if workers are required to contribute financially to political and other activities of unions that are not strictly related to worker representation.[135] By contrast, the Supreme Court of Canada has recognised that freedom not to associate is a dimension of freedom of association, but has nevertheless upheld 'agency shop' arrangements,[136] and has held that freedom not to associate is not infringed by the requirement that workers obtain bare membership of one of a wide range of unions.[137] Australian courts would no doubt find such precedents useful when interpreting an Australian Bill of Rights.

133 This analysis is taken from Hogg, 1992, 994–95, which also contains a discussion of freedom of association and union membership under the Canadian Charter.

134 For a general discussion of freedom of association in the context of industrial relations, see Leader, 1992; and Orr, 2001.

135 *Communications Workers of America v Beck* 487 US 735 (1988).

136 *Lavigne v OPSEU* (1991) 81 DLR (4th) 545.

137 *R v Advance Cutting and Coring Ltd* (2002) 205 DLR (4th) 385.

2.5.7 Religion

As already mentioned, freedom of religion is already protected by s 116 of the Constitution. Given that the interpretation of this provision is governed by precedent which is both long-standing and clear (a fact which, it might be observed, gives the lie to the argument that Australian courts would find themselves in uncharted waters when interpreting a Bill of Rights), there would seem to be every reason to incorporate it in a new Constitution with its essential terms unaltered. The High Court has avoided interpreting the anti-establishment clause in s 116 as erecting a rigid 'wall of division separation between church and State'[138] in the way the Supreme Court in the United States has done.[139] Thus, in contrast to the United States Supreme Court's prohibition of financial aid to religious schools in *Lemon v Kurtzman*,[140] the High Court in *Attorney-General (Vic); ex rel Black v Commonwealth* (*DOGS* case)[141] held that the anti-establishment clause was not infringed when the government subsidised religious schools. In that case, the High Court held that what is required by s 116 is that the State not give preference to one religion over another, and that the channelling of Commonwealth grants money to the States on condition that they use it for the specified purpose of funding religious schools was not inconsistent with s 116, provided that funding was provided to religious schools of all denominations on an equal basis. Section 116 would thus be infringed if the government discriminated between private schools run by different religious denominations and, it is probably also true to say, between religious and non-religious private schools, in its allocation of financial assistance.

The fact that the Commonwealth government has had a longstanding policy of supporting private schools established by religious and ethnic groups means that the *entitlement* of such groups to the benefits of such a policy has not been an issue, at least in recent times. Yet it can be argued that not only is it permissible under s 116 for the government to make such arrangements, but also that modern human rights law recognises that the state is required to protect the cultural rights of cultural groups, and that provision of education in culturally-based schools is an important dimension of that right. This brings us to the next right to be discussed – the right to culture.

2.5.8 Culture

The right to practice and preserve culture was not conceived of in the individualistic intellectual milieu of the Enlightenment. Rather, it is the product of 20th century concerns with the rights of minorities which first came to prominence in the aftermath of the First World War. In particular, the dissolution of the Austro-Hungarian Empire created numerous problems involving ethnic minority groups within the often artificial States created at Versailles – problems which bedevilled the Balkans throughout the 1990s.[142] The League of Nations sought to address the problem of how to define and protect the

138 *Reynolds v United States* 98 US 145 (1879), 164.

139 For a discussion of the differences between the anti-establishment clause of the First Amendment in the United States and s 116 in Australia, see Rich, 1995, 21–22.

140 403 US 602 (1971).

141 (1981) 146 CLR 559.

142 For a general overview of the rights of ethnic minorities, see Lerner, 1991; and Hannum, 1990.

rights of minorities living in states which, although conforming to the norms of democratic government, put ethnic groups at a disadvantage because of their inability to control government.

It is certainly true that many dimensions of the 'right to culture' can be adequately protected through the mechanism of other rights – for example, the right to free exercise of religion can protect minority religions from being suppressed, while the right to freedom of expression arguably includes the right of members of minority groups to express themselves in their own language. However, there are other minority group interests which are not adequately accommodated by the purely negative rights prohibiting interference with freedom of religion or of religious exercise: in the circumstance where a minority group lives in a country dominated by a powerful majority, or, equally, in the situation where the population consists of numerous minorities without a single dominant majority group, survival of a particular minority culture will often depend on questions of resource allocation, and it is the positive right to receive a fair share of resources that is often involved in questions of minority rights. To take the most obvious example, members of a minority group who contribute to the financing of the public education system through their taxes may feel justifiably aggrieved if public education is provided only through the medium of the majority group's language. While it is true that such a minority group could establish their own private schools to provide native-tongue education, that would obviously place an added financial burden on the community. The important feature of this theory of minority rights is that it casts a positive obligation on the state to provide an equitable share of resources to minority groups, in relation to public services which have a cultural dimension. Although education is the most obvious of these, it could be argued that the provision of health services, too, could be seen as having a cultural aspect. Having acknowledged that such rights should, in principle, be protected, it is, however, necessary to note that factors such as population distribution and numbers will determine the economic feasibility of providing separate educational and other services to cultural groups. Such aspects of the right to culture ought, therefore, to be subject to the qualification that the state is obliged to provide such facilities to the extent that resources make it reasonably practical to do so.

Cultural rights were given formal recognition with the establishment of the United Nations and the promulgation of the Universal Declaration on Human Rights.[143] Article 27 of the Declaration reads as follows:

> In those States in which ethnic, religious or linguistic minorities exist, persons belonging to such minorities shall not be denied the right, in community with the other members of their group, to enjoy their own culture, to profess and practise their own religion, or to use their own language.

The proposal to include minority rights in the Universal Declaration attracted controversy, and this impacted upon the way the right was framed. This is because the concept of 'minority rights' is very broad. Furthermore, because the vulnerability of minority groups essentially derives from the fact that, in a democracy, decisions are taken by majorities, it is unsurprising that some minority groups have gone further than simply

143 GA Res 217 A (III), 10 December 1948.

to claim a *pro rata* share of resources and the provision of separate educational and health services, and have also read into the right to culture more fundamental entitlements, such as the right to sharing political power through such mechanisms as regional autonomy (where the ethnic group live in distinct geographic areas), communal autonomy (where the group is intermingled in the general population), weighted voting systems, constitutionally-mandated coalitions or a combination of these.[144] Many states were suspicious that the inclusion of cultural rights in the Universal Declaration would serve as a springboard for secession by ethnic minorities, and have thus always insisted that the right be limited to an obligation to preserve minority cultures within existing boundaries. The political autonomy dimension of minority rights is discussed in the context of the position of indigenous Australians in Chapter 6.

2.5.9 Privacy

The concept of privacy as a legal interest is not known to Anglo-Australian common law.[145] However, in other jurisdictions, and in the United States in particular, protection is given to two separate legal interests (albeit ones which share a common root),[146] both of which are referred to as the 'right to privacy': the first of these refers to the recognition by the courts from the late 19th century of a right to privacy as an aspect of the common law of torts. Actions in tort are available for four types of invasion of privacy: intrusion (for example, the act of eavesdropping on the plaintiff); publication of private facts (for example, through media reports of intimate facts about the plaintiff's personal life); appropriation (where the plaintiff's image is used without permission for commercial gain) and false light depiction (a tort which is similar to defamation in that it involves a false statement about the plaintiff, but which lacks the element of diminution of reputation).[147]

'Privacy' in this sense raises constitutional issues in two respects: first, it is necessary to protect privacy in so far as it relates to the need to protect the individual from unreasonable surveillance by the state, an issue which has already been discussed at 2.5.2, above, in the context of the right not to be subject to search and seizure. There, it will be recalled, I argued that the interest the individual has in being secure from physical search and seizure will not be fully protected unless express protection is also given to freedom from surveillance and interception of private communications.

The second privacy interest requiring constitutional protection is that of informational privacy – in other words, the right of individuals to have such information about themselves as has been collected not disclosed to parties who have no lawful interest in

144 The range of specific rights which fall into the broad category of ethnic rights are listed in Lerner, 1991, 34–37.

145 *Victoria Park Racing and Recreation Grounds Co Ltd v Taylor* (1937) 58 CLR 479. In *Australian Broadcasting Corporation v Lenah Game Meats Pty Ltd* (2001) 185 ALR 1 the High Court declined to create a common law action to remedy invasions of privacy, but left open the possibility that such an action might be recognised in suitable cases in the future.

146 The common source of privacy both in the torts sense and the constitutional sense is the article by Warren and Brandeis, 1890.

147 For an overview of this aspect of the law of torts, see Christie, Meeks, Prior and Sanders, 1997, 1192–257; and Dobbs, Keeton and Owen, 1984, 851–54.

receiving it. Progress has already been made in Australia, in that the Privacy Act 1988 (Cth) requires government bodies and corporations to comply with a statutory regime which restricts the purpose for which personal information may be collected, and the ways in which it may be used and transmitted to others, and which provides remedies enabling individuals to obtain access to and, if necessary, to correct, information held about them. These interests could be protected by a provision in a Bill of Rights which stated that individuals had a right of privacy in relation to the collection, dissemination, verification and correction of personal information relating to them. Including such a provision in the Bill of Rights would have the effect of casting the onus on those who were in possession of personal information about others to show that their handling of that information was reasonable, and that it therefore fell within the scope of the reasonable limitations clause of the Bill of Rights.

2.5.10 Autonomy

The other, very different, meaning of the 'right to privacy' developed in the United States is privacy used in the sense of what is really a right to personal autonomy. In the United States, the origins of this right can be traced to the dissenting opinion of Brandeis J in *Olmstead v United States*,[148] in which he argued for recognition of 'the most comprehensive of rights and the right most valued by civilised men ... the right to be let alone'.[149] Later, in *Meyer v Nebraska*,[150] McReynolds J held[151] that where the due process clause of the Fourteenth Amendment protects 'liberty' this:

> ... denotes not merely freedom from bodily restraint but also the right of the individual to contract, to engage in any of the common occupations of life, to acquire useful knowledge, to marry, establish a home and bring up children, to worship God according to the dictates of his own conscience, and generally enjoy those privileges long recognised at common law as essential to the orderly pursuit of happiness by free men.

Probably the most influential case in the area of privacy was that of *Griswold v Connecticut*,[152] in which the court struck down legislation criminalising the supply of contraceptives, holding that marital privacy was one of the rights guaranteed by the Constitution. Although justification for this position was found primarily in the Ninth Amendment (which states that all the enumeration of specified rights in the Constitution should not be construed as to deny the existence of other rights), the court also held that the Fifth Amendment protected a 'zone of privacy' secure from intrusion by the State. Thus, Goldberg J held that:

> ... the Ninth Amendment lends strong support to the view that the 'liberty' protected by the Fifth and Fourteenth Amendments from infringement by the Federal Government or the States is not restricted to rights specifically mentioned in the first eight amendments.

148 277 US 438 (1928).

149 The conceptual link between the common law tort and the constitutional right was expressly noted by Murphy J in his dissenting judgment in *Goldman v United States* 316 US 129 (1942), 136–37, and by Bloustein, 1964, 994–95.

150 162 US 390 (1923).

151 *Ibid*, 399.

152 381 US 479 (1965).

Similarly, in their concurring judgments in *Griswold*, Justices Harlan and White stated that the legislation was unconstitutional on the ground that it infringed the Fourteenth Amendment which, according to the earlier decision in *Palko v Connecticut*,[153] included within its protective ambit 'basic values implicit in the concept of ordered liberty'. In other words, the decision in *Griswold* laid a firm foundation for the development of a general right to what the court called 'privacy', but which was, in reality, 'autonomy' – a zone of essentially private decision-making in which the state is not permitted to interfere, unless it can meet the 'strict' standard of constitutional scrutiny, which is that the state must show that the limitation is both necessary and narrowly tailored to serve a compelling governmental interest.[154] The right to a 'zone of privacy' was subsequently used by the court in cases such as *Loving v Virginia*[155] to strike down a State law prohibiting inter-racial marriage, and *Eisenstadt v Baird*[156] to uphold the right of unmarried persons to have access to contraceptives. This was soon followed by the landmark decision of *Roe v Wade*,[157] in which the court stated that the right to privacy found in the Fourteenth Amendment[158] made unconstitutional prohibitions on abortion within the first trimester of pregnancy, a finding that has since been upheld in a line of abortion cases to reach the court.[159]

The difficulty of setting limits to a broad right to personal autonomy in the absence of a test in the text of the Constitution was revealed when the court came to consider the issue of homosexual conduct. In *Bowers v Hardwick*,[160] the Court upheld the validity of a Georgia statute prohibiting consensual homosexual acts, and rejected the argument that homosexual conduct was protected by the Fifth, Fourteenth and Ninth Amendments, stating that the privacy precedents discussed above related to 'family, marriage [and] procreation'[161] which, in the opinion of the court, homosexual activity did not. The court further cited precedent[162] to the effect that such freedoms as might be implied by these Amendments were restricted to those that were 'implicit in the concept of ordered liberty' in the sense that 'neither liberty or justice would exist if they were sacrificed', and to abolish them would be to violate a 'principle of justice so rooted in the traditions and conscience of our people as to be ranked as fundamental' (*Palko v Connecticut*,[163] reaffirmed in *Paris Adult Theatre I v Slaton*[164]), or were 'deeply rooted in this Nation's

153 302 US 319 (1932).

154 *Griswold v Connecticut* 381 US 479 (1965), 496–98; citing *Bates v Little Rock* 361 US 516 (1960), 524. For a concise discussion of the development of the right to privacy, see Feinberg, 1986, 87–94.

155 338 US 1 (1967).

156 405 US 438 (1972).

157 410 US 113 (1973).

158 Interestingly, the court held that the alternative foundation of the Ninth Amendment would also support this aspect of the right to privacy.

159 The *Roe* decision that choice in the matter of abortion is an aspect of the right to privacy was upheld in several cases, including *Akron v Akron Center for Reproductive Health Inc* 462 US 416 (1983); *Thornburgh v American College of Obstetricians and Gynaecologists* 476 US 747 (1986); and *Planned Parenthood of Southeastern Pennsylvania v Casey* 505 US 833 (1992).

160 478 US 186 (1986).

161 *Bowers v Hardwick* 478 US 186 (1986) 190.

162 *Ibid*, 191–92.

163 302 US 319 (1937), 325.

164 413 US 49 (1973), 65.

history and traditions' (*Moore v East Cleveland*[165]), and that, far from being an indispensable aspect of liberty, homosexual conduct had traditionally been widely proscribed. Leaving aside, for the moment, the broader issue of the methodology used in discovering what rights are implicit in the Constitution (which is dealt with in the paragraphs below), the court's reading of the precedents was surely wrong – restrictions on intimate activity had been struck down in these earlier cases not because there was anything special about these activities *per se*, but because they were simply aspects of a fundamental right of privacy, in the sense of autonomy, which was (successfully) argued for in all of them. The reasoning in *Hardwick* was, nevertheless, adopted in *Barnes v Glen Theatre, Inc*,[166] where, in his concurring judgment, Scalia J rejected the idea that the Constitution embodied a general protection for all conduct that was not harmful or which was engaged in consensually. Consequently, he also rejected the idea that a prohibition on conduct was unconstitutional simply because the prohibition was based on morality, citing sadomasochism, bestiality, suicide, drug use and prostitution as examples of activities that were proscribed on the basis that they offended public morality, rather than that they caused harm to a victim.[167]

By contrast, a more liberal approach was adopted in *Planned Parenthood of Southeastern Pennsylvania v Casey*,[168] in which the court explicitly reiterated that the Fourteenth Amendment right not to be deprived of liberty without due process embraced more than just the rights protected in the other Amendments, and stated that 'it is a promise of the Constitution that there is a realm of personal liberty which the government may not enter'.[169] Later, the court held[170] that its previous refusals to countenance governmental intervention in areas such as marriage, procreation, contraception, *et cetera* were based upon the principle that these were matters:

> ... involving the most intimate and personal choices a person may make in a lifetime, choices central to personal dignity and autonomy, [which are] essential to the liberty protected by the Fourteenth Amendment.

Similarly, in upholding the view that the Constitution protected a degree of freedom of choice as regards abortion, Stevens J linked autonomy and dignity, holding that:[171]

> The authority to make such traumatic and yet empowering decisions is an element of basic human dignity,

and that:[172]

> Part of the constitutional liberty to choose is the equal dignity to which each of us is entitled.

Casey thus represents a swing back towards a more generous understanding of autonomy, in keeping with cases like *Griswold v Connecticut* and *Roe v Wade*, an outcome which, it is

165 431 US 494 (1977), 503.
166 501 US 560 (1991).
167 *Ibid*, 575.
168 505 US 833 (1992).
169 *Ibid*, 847.
170 *Ibid*, 851.
171 *Ibid*, 916.
172 *Ibid*, 920.

submitted, relates to the difference in methodology used in this decision, as compared with that used in *Bowers*, to determine the extent of the right to 'autonomy': In *Bowers v Hardwick*, and subsequently in *Michael H v Gerald D*,[173] the court adopted an approach based squarely on 'tradition', essentially holding that new rights would be found to be implicit in the Constitution only if the traditions of American society indicated that they were worthy of protection. The incompatibility of this approach with the concept of individual liberty is obvious. As Justice Brennan pointed out in his dissenting opinion in *Michael H v Gerald D*, the adoption of that approach in many of the early cases on privacy would probably have led to different results, in that the rights claimed in those cases (for example, the right of access to contraceptives vindicated in *Griswold v Connecticut*), were certainly not traditionally protected by society at the time the cases were heard by the court. Further he stated that:[174]

> In construing the Fourteenth Amendment to offer shelter only to those interests specifically protected by historical practice, moreover, the plurality ignores the kind of society in which our Constitution exists. We are not an assimilative, homogenous society, but a facilitative, pluralistic one, in which we must be willing to abide someone else's unfamiliar or even repellent practice because the same tolerant impulse [p]rotects our own idiosyncrasies ... In a community such as ours, 'liberty' must include the freedom not to conform.

In contrast to the majority approach in *Michael H*, the court in *Casey* stated firstly that in determining the scope of liberty conferred by the due process clause the court was called to 'exercise that same capacity which by tradition courts have always exercised: reasoned judgment'.[175] Furthermore, the court held that in making its decisions it had to:[176]

> ... speak and act in ways that allow people to accept its decisions on the terms the Court claims for them, as grounded in principle, *not as compromises with social and political pressures* having, as such, no bearing on the principled choices the Court is obliged to make. (Emphasis added).

In other words, the court in *Casey* adopted an approach through which the ambit of individual autonomy would be determined objectively and, therefore, I would argue, in a manner more in keeping with the natural rights doctrine upon Bill of Rights are based, which sees objective values as existing independently of, and yet being discoverable by, human will, rather than as the product of societal pressures.[177] This is not to say, however, that social values and expectations are irrelevant to the understanding of human rights[178]– to use the analogy from Roman law referred to earlier in this chapter, *ius gentium* is often good evidence of *ius naturale* – but, clearly, the idea of human rights as providing protection for individuals is stripped of much of its usefulness once the ambit of rights is limited by what is acceptable to society, because it is, of course, in protecting what is *unacceptable* to society that the concept of human rights frequently comes into its own.

173 491 US 110 (1989), 122–29.

174 *Ibid*, 141.

175 *Planned Parenthood of Southeastern Pennsylvania v Casey* 505 US 833 (1992).

176 *Ibid*, 997.

177 See, eg, Paust, 1984, 220–22, where he argues that since the United States Constitution was drafted in order to give expression to unwritten natural rights, it is appropriate to adopt an objective approach in interpreting that document, and in particular the Ninth Amendment's reservation of rights to the people.

178 *Ibid*, 204–10.

The contrast between the approach based on tradition, and that based on an objective weighing of interests, has been illustrated with particular clarity in a number of cases dealing with what is, perhaps, the most difficult aspect of individual autonomy – that relating to the right of patients to refuse medical treatment and, more controversially, the right to voluntary euthanasia. Central to this position is the argument that patients should, at a stage when they still have the capacity to reason, be allowed to use that reason to exercise a measure of control over the timing and manner of their death, rather than to be the object of decisions by the medical profession. Active suicide clearly raises profound issues regarding the limits of autonomy. In *Cruzan v Director, Missouri Department of Health*,[179] the Supreme Court upheld the validity of a statute which made withdrawal of life support conditional upon relatives of a patient in a vegetative state being able to adduce sufficient proof that that would have been her wish, holding that such a requirement did not violate the patient's right to liberty inherent in the Fourteenth Amendment. However, the court noted that it was willing to accept for the purposes of the case that the Constitution would grant to a competent patient (which, of course, the patient in this case was not) the right to refuse medical treatment, even if this hastened death.

More difficult to decide, however, was the question of active euthanasia (as opposed to mere refusal of treatment): in *Washington v Glucksberg*,[180] the Supreme Court upheld the validity of a State statute which prohibited physician-assisted suicide. Rehnquist CJ (speaking for the court) held that because the history of American law revealed an almost universal[181] acceptance that physician-assisted suicide was a criminal act, it could not be said that physician-assisted suicide was a fundamental liberty interest upheld by the right to privacy/personal autonomy. The decision in this case thus appears, at first sight, to have been decided upon the basis of the legal tradition criterion. However, Rhenquist CJ also stated that a number of factors – the State's interest in preserving life, the need to preserve the integrity of the medical profession, the need to protect the vulnerable from being pressured into accepting supposedly voluntary euthanasia and the risk that euthanasia might come to be used in cases other than those of the terminally ill – which provided reasons why the statutory prohibition should be upheld. Thus there were a number of *objective* factors which the court could have balanced against the right to physician-assisted suicide, allowing it to reach the same conclusion without reference to the argument based on historical tradition.

What implications would this useful United States case law have for Australia, if we enacted a Bill of Rights? Should an Australian Bill of Rights include a right to autonomy? If it did, how broad a scope should the Bill of Rights give to that right? In light of the United States' case law, there would seem to be a strong argument for the recognition by a Bill of Rights of a zone of individual autonomy. The philosophy underlying the very concept of a Bill of Rights, which sees the human being as a dignified, autonomous entity,

179 497 US 261 (1990).

180 521 US 702 (1997). A similar finding (upholding a New York statute prohibiting assisted suicide) was reached by the Supreme Court in *Vacco v Quill* 521 US 793 (1997).

181 Although it should be noted that Oregon's Death With Dignity Act 1994 (ORS 127.800–97) permits physician-assisted suicide. A patient may request a medical practitioner to provide him or her with medication that will end his or her life, which the patient then administers to him or herself.

rather than as one who is subject to the power of others, suggests that such a right ought to be protected.

The idea of protecting a right to autonomy raises an interesting question: should the Bill of Rights give protection to autonomy *in general* – to 'freedom to be free', as it were? Indeed, are not the specific freedoms usually mentioned in Bills of Rights really just dimensions of an overarching right of the individual not to be subject to unreasonable restriction? Is not the question 'Why protect freedom of expression?', for example, simply part of the larger question 'Why protect freedom to engage in activity in general?' Seen in this context, expression, equality, assembly and movement, *et cetera* are simply aspects of a general right to individual autonomy, and the classification of rights and freedoms under headings such as 'freedom of expression', 'freedom of religion', 'freedom of movement' is useful only to the extent that it indicates the range of activities which that autonomy implies. At first sight, this would suggest that a Bill of Rights should simply state that everyone enjoys a right to autonomy without qualification. However, two problems arise here: first, the inclusion of such a broadly-phrased provision would expose the entire range of governmental and private activity to review by the courts. The courts would be required to review all rules of statute and common law, not because the applicant could point to a specific right which was limited, but simply because the law limited human conduct. Of course, it may well be that, in applying the limitations clause[182] contained in the Bill of Rights, most challenges would fail, but, notwithstanding this, the inclusion of such a broad, non-specific right would unnecessarily constitutionalise every case which came before the courts. The second argument against the inclusion of such a right is that in many cases the courts would be required to evaluate legislation and conduct which could not be measured against the standard of what is 'reasonable' in a free and democratic society (assuming that that was the test used in the Bill of Rights' limitation clause). How, for example, would a court determine whether the rates imposed in an income tax Act were 'reasonable'? This is clearly not a question which involves legal values, but rather one which involves matters of financial policy dictated by economic conditions, the government's fiscal position and spending priorities, *et cetera*. Budget and taxation legislation is but one example of a class of rules (and thus restrictions on human behaviour) which are of such a nature as to make them not amenable to judicial review. Hence, it would be impractical to include a right to autonomy in the sense of a broad 'right to be free' in a Bill of Rights.

The situation would be very different if the Bill of Rights included a right to autonomy which was narrowly tailored to cover only those activities which lie closest to the individual's personality – in other words, to matters touching upon intimate choices relating to one's body and relationships with others, as is the position under case law as it has been developed in the United States. Such a right could perhaps be formulated as a 'right to autonomy with regard to choices relating to bodily integrity and intimate relationships'. Australian courts would be well able to determine which types of activity and relationship were covered by the right, and to what extent it was reasonable for the State to regulate such relationships.

---

182 In 2.3.8 of this chapter, above, I suggested that a limitations clause (such as those found in the Bills of Rights of Canada and South Africa) which permitted the limitation of rights to an extent that was reasonable in a free and democratic society would be most suitable for an Australian Bill of Rights.

2.5.11 Equality

As has already been noted, the right to equality is already given some protection by Commonwealth and State legislation which, although subject to override like any other legislation, does, nevertheless, outlaw discrimination on a number of grounds. We therefore have ready-made models for the type of provision that could be used to protect this right in the Constitution. Such legislation commonly prohibits discrimination on a wide range of grounds. For example, the Anti-Discrimination Act 1991 (Qld), which is typical of State anti-discrimination Acts, prohibits discrimination on grounds of sex, marital status, pregnancy, parental status, breastfeeding, age, race, impairment, religion, political belief or activity, trade union activity, lawful sexual activity and association with a person identified on the basis of any of these attributes.[183] Examples of other grounds of discrimination prohibited in Australian jurisdictions include sexuality,[184] being of transgender,[185] physical features[186] and status as a carer.[187] Section 117 of the Commonwealth Constitution 1901 prohibits discrimination on grounds of residence in a particular State, and thus residence in a particular part of Australia should be listed as a prohibited ground of discrimination in order to include this right in a new Constitution.

In the case of all Australian anti-discrimination statutes, provision is also made for specific exemptions in relation to particular grounds – to mention some obvious examples, religious discrimination is permitted in respect of employment by religious institutions,[188] discrimination on political grounds is permitted in respect of employment by political parties,[189] racial discrimination is permitted where required for purposes of authenticity in theatrical productions,[190] and discrimination is permitted in relation to the provision of accommodation (for example where accommodation is leased) where the provider lives in the same accommodation him or herself.[191] The multitude of situations in which exemptions might apply would make it impossible to include them in a Bill of Rights. However, such a course would, in any event, be unnecessary, given the reasonable limitations clause which the Bill of Rights would contain. The Bill of Rights could simply list prohibited grounds of discrimination, and such exemptions as were permitted by Commonwealth and State law would remain in effect, unless found not to be reasonable in a free and democratic society. Given the comprehensiveness of the Commonwealth and State codes, and the careful way in which their exemptions provisions have been drafted, it is unlikely that many of them would be found wanting if subjected to constitutional review.

An important and controversial issue which arises in relation to the right to equality is that of affirmative action, sometimes referred to as positive or reverse discrimination. An example of affirmative action is provided by s 8(1) of the Racial Discrimination Act 1975

183 Anti Discrimination Act 1991 (Qld), s 7(1).
184 Equal Opportunity Act 1984 (SA), s 29(1)(b).
185 Anti-Discrimination Act 1977 (NSW), s 38A.
186 Equal Opportunity Act 1995 (Vic), s 6(f).
187 *Ibid*, s 6(l).
188 *Ibid*, s 76.
189 *Ibid*, s 12.
190 Equal Opportunity Act 1984 (WA), s 50.
191 Equal Opportunity Act 1995 (Vic), s 54.

(Cth), which exempts from the concept of discrimination measures covered by Art 1.4 of the Convention on the Elimination of All Forms of Racial Discrimination,[192] which refers to 'special measures taken for the sole purpose of securing adequate advancement of certain racial or ethnic groups or individuals requiring such protection as may be necessary in order to ensure such groups or individuals equal enjoyment or exercise of human rights and fundamental freedoms'. Section 8(1) was applied by the High Court in *Gerhardy v Brown*,[193] in which it was held that, although s 19 of the Pitjantjatjara Land Rights Act 1981 (SA), which prohibited non-Aborigines from entering certain areas, was discriminatory, it was saved by s 8(1) because it was a measure designed to protect the tribal lands of Aborigines. The *Gerhardy* case shows how, in some circumstances, a law or policy which, on the face of it, amounts to discrimination and thus breaches the right to equality, is held to be justified on the ground that it is necessary to confer an advantage on a group with a particular characteristic, in order to remedy some disadvantage experienced by that group in the past. In the case of the Pitjantjatjara Land Rights Act, the advantage conferred on indigenous people was exclusive access to a particular area, and the corollary was the disadvantage experienced by non-indigenous people of denial of access to those areas. One could rationalise the discrimination in that case on the basis that the preservation of indigenous culture which (whether intentionally or not) had suffered as a result of the process of colonisation, required that access to tribal lands be restricted to indigenous people. Other examples of affirmative action could be given – Commonwealth programmes such as ABSTUDY can be seen as forms of affirmative action, in that benefits are directed towards groups that are perceived as having experienced, or as still experiencing, disadvantage. More controversial would be the situation where, for example, legislation required that employers achieve certain targets in relation to females, indigenous people or people with disabilities in their workforce. In such situations, the disadvantage caused by the affirmative action would be more personalised than in the case of affirmative action programmes such as ABSTUDY which, practically speaking, diffuses the disadvantage throughout the taxpaying community. In the case of affirmative action in the employment context, however, there would be specific identifiable individuals (in the example posited, males, non-indigenous people and non-disabled people) who, but for the affirmative action legislation, would have obtained employment. For this reason, affirmative action programmes are often perceived, however inaccurately, as exacting retribution from advantaged groups, the individual members of which understandably feel that they ought not to be penalised for the past experiences of members of disadvantaged groups. How, then, should these competing considerations be reconciled? The answer to this would lie in the fact that the tension between the right to equality, on the one hand, and affirmative action policies on the other would be able to be resolved by applying the general limitations test contained in the Bill of Rights. That being the case, it would not even be necessary for a Bill of Rights to mention affirmative action as an exception to the right to equality, because affirmative action programmes which passed the test of reasonableness would survive constitutional review, simply because they fell within the scope of the limitations clause of the Bill of Rights.

192 GA Res 2106 (XX), 21 December 1965.
193 (1985) 159 CLR 70.

2.5.12 Freedom of movement and of commercial activity

It is a truism to say that a federal system involves a balancing of State autonomy, on the one hand, and national uniformity on the other. To a large extent that balance is achieved through the distribution of legislative powers. However, from its inception, the Commonwealth Constitution has recognised the need to balance the legislative authority of the States against the freedom of people to move from State to State and to engage in inter-State trade. These rights are currently protected by s 92 of the Constitution, which binds both the Commonwealth and the States, and which provides that:

> On the imposition of uniform duties of customs, trade, commerce and intercourse among the States, whether by means of internal carriage or ocean navigation, shall be absolutely free.

As a preliminary, one should note that the section is grammatically inelegant: it is not apparent on first reading that the first part of the section ending with the word 'customs' is an adverbial phrase after which there is a definite pause – it would have been better had the section read:

> Trade, commerce and intercourse among the States, whether by means of internal carriage or ocean navigation, shall be absolutely free on the imposition of uniform duties of customs.

The section provided the High Court with one of its most difficult interpretative challenges, but stability was achieved with the decision in *Cole v Whitfield*,[194] in which the High Court held that the purpose of the section was to prohibit laws which, either on their face or in their effect, imposed 'discriminatory burdens of a protectionist kind'. In other words, to fall foul of s 92, a law would have to target (discriminate against) inter-State trade, and would have to have the effect of protecting a State from inter-State competition. The *Cole v Whitfield* test was amplified in an important way in the decision in *Castlemaine Tooheys Ltd v South Australia*.[195] In that case, the court held that legislation which had a protectionist effect might, nevertheless, not be invalid under s 92 if it satisfied a proportionality test, which required that it serve a legitimate non-protectionist objective and that the degree of protectionism caused be no greater than that which was needed to achieve the objective. *Cole v Whitfield* and *Castlemaine Tooheys Ltd v South Australia* dealt only with the inter-State trade aspect of s 92, but s 92 also covers inter-State 'intercourse', and here, too, the proportionality test was applied by the High Court in cases such as *Nationwide News Pty Ltd v Wills*[196] and *AMS v AIF*.[197] The proportionality test formalises what has long been recognised: that the rights conferred by s 92 are not absolute[198] and can be limited in order to achieve objectives such as preventing the spread of disease,[199] or the enforcement of public morality.[200]

194 (1988) 165 CLR 360.
195 (1990) 169 CLR 436.
196 (1992) 177 CLR 1.
197 (1999) 199 CLR 160.
198 *Duncan v Queensland* (1916) 22 CLR 556.
199 *Ex parte Nelson* (1928) 42 CLR 209; *Hughes & Vale Pty Ltd v New South Wales (No 1)* (1954) 93 CLR 1.
200 *Mansell v Beck* (1956) 95 CLR 550.

The same freedoms as lie within the scope of s 92 would be protected by a provision in a Bill of Rights acknowledging freedom of movement and freedom of commercial activity, in combination with one which protected freedom of expression. Indeed, provisions drafted in those terms would cover not only inter-State movement and commercial activity but also movement and activity which takes place within States. The proportionality test used in interpreting s 92 is very similar to the type of reasonable limitations test which I have suggested that an Australian Bill of Rights should contain. It could, therefore, be expected that the courts would continue to draw upon case law generated by s 92 in interpreting analogous freedoms in a Bill of Rights.

2.5.13 Socio-economic rights

A particularly difficult issue in relation to the content of Bills of Rights is whether such a document should protect so-called 'socio-economic rights' – in other words, declare that citizens have a right to housing, education, welfare, *et cetera*. Although this issue has received little attention in developed countries, it has assumed significance in countries where acute divisions of wealth lead to claims by the disadvantaged that the Bill of Rights should enshrine some degree of equality of outcome rather than only equality of opportunity. The argument is that the usual range of civil and political rights (sometimes referred to as 'first generation' rights) are of little value to the impoverished, whose capacity to enjoy such rights is undermined by their need to concentrate on food, shelter and the necessities of basic survival. To them, rights to a basic minimum standard of living ('second generation' rights) are as important.

The standard argument adopted against including socio-economic rights in a Bill of Rights is that, whereas civil and political rights are negative, essentially requiring that others refrain from interfering in the holder's freedom of expression, personal liberty, freedom of religion, *et cetera,* second generation rights cast a positive obligation on the state to provide food, shelter, education, *et cetera,* which it may not have the resources to do. Practically speaking, can one impose upon the state an obligation to appropriate money for specific purposes? Surely the issue of resource-allocation involves quintessentially political, rather than legal, decisions, properly taken by the government rather than by the courts?

In the first place, the supposed dichotomy between 'resource-neutral first generation' and 'resource-dependant second generation' rights is false. Civil and political rights can quite conceivably require the allocation of resources by the state to ensure their protection – the right not to be subject to inhuman punishment may involve the state providing minimum standards for prisoners, while criminal procedural rights would, at a minimum, require that adequate police resources be provided to ensure that detainees are informed of their rights. Conceivably, the rights of an accused person might encompass access to publicly funded legal representation – even in the absence of a Bill of Rights the High Court held in *Dietrich v R*[201] that it amounts to a miscarriage of justice to proceed with a prosecution of someone for a serious criminal offence if they are unable to afford legal representation.

201 (1992) 177 CLR 292.

Secondly, the difficulty of applying socio-economic rights in concrete cases has been overstated. Much depends on how the entitlement is drafted in the Bill of Rights. South Africa's Bill of Rights confers a range of socio-economic rights to housing (s 26), health care, food, water and social security (s 27), the social rights of children (s 28) and education (s 29). In each case, however (with the notable exception of emergency medical treatment which cannot be denied),[202] the obligation cast on the State is 'to take *reasonable* legislative and other measures, within its *available resources*, to achieve the *progressive realisation*' of the right (emphasis added). Precisely what this means in practice was determined by the constitutional Court in *Government of the Republic of South Africa v Grootboom*.[203] In that case, the respondent,[204] who lived under plastic sheeting in an open field, alleged breach of her s 26 rights and the s 28 rights of her children, in that the national, provincial and municipal governments had failed to provide her family with adequate shelter. In defining the obligation of the various levels of government under the Constitution, Yacoob J, speaking for a unanimous court, held that the constitutional requirement to take 'reasonable steps' gave the government a degree of leeway: there might be a wide range of possible steps that could be taken; it was not for the court to say which of these might be the best, and so long as the steps that had been taken were reasonable, the Constitution had been fulfilled. The fact that the government had begun implementing a coherent national plan to cater for the housing needs of people amounted to such reasonable steps. However, the evidence also showed that the plan did not adequately cater for the short term needs of those most desperately in need of assistance, in that it did not provide adequate budgetary support for municipal authorities confronted by people who had no shelter at all. For this reason, the court found that the respondent's s 26 rights had been breached, and thus ordered that the state devise, fund, implement and supervise, a programme to provide measures to assist those in desperate need. It should be noted that the court did not make an order that the particular respondents be provided with immediate relief, rather it ordered that the state implement a general plan for the benefit of all similarly situated people, which plan would, of course, be assessable against the criterion of reasonableness in the light of available resources. In other words, the *Grootboom* case shows that there is little reason to fear that the recognition of socio-economic rights will lead to judicial micro-management of government spending – so long as a government can show that it is acting within the bounds of reasonableness in light of the resource constraints and competing demands it faces, its spending decisions will not be able to be challenged, nor will particular individuals be able to claim immediate provision of public services from the state if an overall plan is being implemented – indeed, the satisfaction of such a claim might itself cause socio-economic injustice if there are other claimants whose needs are even more pressing, and to whom the state ought, therefore, give preference to in the orderly implementation of its plan.

202 Republic of South Africa Constitution Act 1996, s 27(3).

203 2000 (11) BCLR 1169 (CC). For another decision of the Constitutional Court on socio-economic rights, see *Soobramoney v Minister of Health, Kwa-Zulu Natal* 1997 (12) BCLR 1696 (CC).

204 The case was brought on appeal by the government against a decision favourable to the respondent in a lower court.

The recognition of socio-economic rights is to be expected in a country such as South Africa, which came into existence as a result of political struggles which had economic redistribution among their principal objectives. More surprising, however, is the fact that several State Constitutions in the United States protect socio-economic rights. Thus, to name but a few examples,[205] the Constitution of New York provides that 'The aid, care and support of the needy are public concerns and shall be provided by the State',[206] that of Alabama provides that 'It shall be the duty of the legislature to require the several counties of this State to make adequate provision for maintenance of the poor',[207] and that of Connecticut provides that 'There shall always be free public elementary and secondary schools in the State. The general assembly shall implement this principle by appropriate legislation'.[208]

Australian human rights tribunals and courts are used to balancing the competing claims between the requirements of human rights statutes, on the one hand, and resource constraints on the other. Furthermore, anti-discrimination statutes enacted by the Commonwealth and State legislatures all recognise that, in the case of some rights – disability rights being an example – compliance may require the expenditure of resources, which the party against whom the claim has been brought may not have. To take one such example, s 35(1) of the Anti-Discrimination Act 1991 (Qld) states that discrimination on grounds of disability is not unlawful where the person discriminated against would require special services, and it would impose 'unjustifiable hardship' on the party which has allegedly engaged in discrimination to provide such services. Section 5 of the Act states that whether 'unjustifiable hardship' exists will be determined by having reference to factors including the costs of supplying the services and the number of people who would benefit or be disadvantaged, the financial position of the discriminating party, the disruption the supply of services would cause and, in general, 'the nature of any benefit or detriment to all people concerned'.[209] There is, therefore, no reason why an Australian Bill of Rights should not extend protection to basic socio-economic rights, such as food, shelter, medical care and education, subject to the caveat that the government's obligations are limited to taking such steps as are reasonable in the light of competing claims on its resources.

2.5.14 Judicial review of administrative decisions

The availability to the citizen of a remedy when governmental power has been abused is central to the doctrine of constitutionalism. In 2.8, below, I argue that an Australian Bill of Rights ought to contain a remedies clause empowering the courts to make such orders as are necessary to enforce the Bill of Rights. However, a more specific provision which

205 For an overview of socio-economic rights in State Constitutions, see Stark, 1992; Rava, 1998 and Rotunno, 1996.

206 New York State Constitution 1938, Art XVII, s 1. The New York Supreme Court enforced this right in the case of *Tucker v Toia* (1977) 390 NYS 2d 794, striking down a State statute which made the provision of social benefits to the needy contingent on recipients' taking legal action to obtain assistance from any relatives who owed them a duty of support.

207 Constitution of Alabama 1901, Art IV, s 88.

208 Constitution of Connecticut 1965, Art VIII, s 1.

209 Anti-Discrimination Act 1991 (Qld), s 5(e).

ought also to be included in the Constitution, and which can be seen both as a right and as a remedy, is the right to judicial review of administrative action. This right is, indeed, already protected by the 1901 Constitution, at least in so far as the actions of Commonwealth officers are concerned, because s 75(v) includes, as part of the constitutionally-entrenched jurisdiction of the High Court, actions in which 'a writ of Mandamus or prohibition or an injunction is sought against an officer of the Commonwealth'. As I argue in Chapter 3, this jurisdiction should be transferred to the Federal Court of Australia, which should be given constitutional recognition, rather than remaining a creature of statute, as at present. However, a section such as s 75(v) offers no guarantee of judicial review of the administrative acts of State and Territory governments. Such a guarantee would thus need to be included in the Bill of Rights which would apply to all branches of government at all levels, Commonwealth, State and Territory.

2.5.15 Compensation following expropriation of property

The right to own property is protected by Bills of Rights in many jurisdictions. However, it is also often necessary for the State to expropriate property in the public interest. In Australia, these contending interests are balanced by s 51(xxxi) of the Constitution, which states that the Commonwealth has legislative power with respect to:

> The acquisition of property on just terms from any State or person for any purpose in respect of which the Parliament has power to make laws.

This phraseology echoes the provisions of the Fifth Amendment to the United States Constitution, which prohibits the taking of private property for public use without just compensation, and Australian courts have interpreted the section as imposing upon the Commonwealth the obligation to pay full market compensation when it acquires property.[210]

Early cases on s 51(xxxi) established that the concept of 'property' includes not only obvious interests such as the right to own property, but also interests, such as leaseholder's right to income from property,[211] the right to control property one owns,[212] and rights to intangible property, such as vested choses in action against the Commonwealth or its instrumentalities, extinguishment or limitation of which was held to amount to the taking of a benefit by the Commonwealth.[213]

The right to just terms compensation is, however, subject to limitation. The courts have held that the right does not apply where mere regulation rather than actual acquisition has occurred.[214] The distinction between acquisition and regulation is one of degree: very many exercises of legislative power have an effect on property right, either directly or indirectly, and that alone should not suffice to have such exercises classified as acquisitions under s 51(xxxi). On the other hand, the precedent of *Bank of New South Wales*

210 *Georgiadis v Australian & Overseas Telecommunications Corporation* (1994) 179 CLR 297.

211 *Minister of State for the Army v Dalziel* (1944) 68 CLR 261.

212 *Bank of New South Wales v Commonwealth* (1948) 76 CLR 1.

213 See *Georgiadis v Australian and Overseas Telecommunications Corporation* (1994) 179 CLR 297; *Commonwealth v Mewett* (1997) 191 CLR 471; and *Smith v ANL Ltd* (2000) 204 CLR 297.

214 *Trade Practices Commission v Tooth & Co Ltd* (1979) 142 CLR 397.

v Commonwealth,[215] in which assumption of control over an enterprise without actually expropriating it was held to amount to an acquisition for purposes of s 51(xxxi), shows that, in some circumstances, purported regulation will have to be characterised as acquisition if s 51(xxxi) is to retain its integrity. Another aspect of s 51(xxxi) which limits the scope of protection it affords is the fact that it mentions only 'acquisition' of property, rather than deprivation, as giving rise to the obligation to pay just terms compensation. Thus in *Commonwealth v Tasmania* (*Tasmanian Dams* case),[216] the court held that compensation would not be payable if property rights were extinguished by the Commonwealth without there being any acquisition by it. As Joseph and Castan point out, this would mean that where, for example, diseased cattle were destroyed by the Commonwealth, no right to compensation would be imposed by s 51(xxxi).[217]

The above cases are relatively uncomplicated. What has, however, proved problematic is the interaction between s 51(xxxi) and the rest of s 51. In a line of cases decided since 1994, the High Court has held that where the Commonwealth acquires property incidentally to the exercise of some power in s 51 other than s 51(xxxi), the obligation to pay just terms compensation does not arise. Clearly, there is a need for some exception to the rule that an acquisition requires compensation: as was stated by the court in *Mutual Pools and Staff Ltd v Commonwealth*,[218] many enumerated powers inevitably involve acquisition of property by the Commonwealth – for example, taxation (s 51(ii)), seizure of enemy property during war (s 51(vi)) and forfeiture of illegally imported goods (s 51(i)). It would be absurd if acquisition of property through use of the taxation power, for example, was said to give rise to a right to compensation. Thus the court in *Mutual Pools* held that when the acquisition of property is merely incidental to the use of one of these other powers, s 51(xxxi) is not engaged, because the law is properly characterised as being with respect to something other than the acquisition of property. In similar vein, the court in *Re DPP ex parte Lawler*[219] upheld the validity of a Commonwealth law which authorised the confiscation of a vessel used by a person found guilty of illegal fishing (under s 51(x)), even in circumstances where the owner of the vessel had not been the one using it for that purpose; while in *Nintendo v Centronic*[220] it was held that a law enacted under the s 51(xxviii) copyright power, which effected a change in intellectual property law in Australia, and diminished the property rights of an electronic circuitry company, was not an acquisition under s 51(xxxi). Yet another example of this reasoning was provided by *Health Insurance Commission v Peverill*,[221] in which the court held that retrospective amendments to welfare laws reducing the amount claimable by medical practitioners for services they had already provided, had been validly made under s 51(xxiiiA), and did not amount to an acquisition under s 51(xxxi). It was also held that s 51(xxxi) could not be used to prevent the government from varying statutory rights, as these are inherently susceptible to variation, being dependent upon changing

215 (1948) 76 CLR 1.
216 (1983) 158 CLR 1.
217 Joseph and Castan, 2001, 289.
218 (1994) 19 CLR 155.
219 (1994) 179 CLR 270.
220 (1994) 181 CLR 134.
221 (1994) 179 CLR 226.

government policies and its resource allocation priorities – in other words, where the government confers a statutory right to property (which would not exist had the government not created it), it will not be compelled to pay compensation if, for policy reasons, it later finds that it must extinguish the right. Finally, in *Airservices Australia v Canadian Airlines International Ltd*,[222] a challenge was launched to provisions of the Civil Aviation Act 1988 (Cth), which entitled the Civil Aviation Authority (a Commonwealth agency) to take liens over aircraft in respect of unpaid fees for services provided by the Authority. In the case before the court, the liens had been incurred by companies which had leased the aircraft from overseas owners. The owners argued that subjecting their property to liens in respect of conduct which they had had nothing to do with, amounted to acquisition by the Commonwealth. A majority of the High Court held that s 51(xxxi) did not apply – the imposition of the liens was merely incidental to the Commonwealth's exercise of its s 51(i) inter-State and overseas trade and commerce power.

One can appreciate the rationale behind these decisions: many of the s 51 powers (the s 51(ii) taxation power being an obvious example) would be rendered inoperative if subject to s 51(xxxi). On the other hand, this line of cases has the potential severely to undermine the protection afforded by s 51(xxxi), as it suggests that, so long as a law can be characterised as falling within an enumerated power other than s 51(xxxi), and as having acquisition of property as merely its secondary rather than primary characteristic, the obligation to pay just terms compensation can be evaded. But the problem is even more fundamental than that, because the s 51(xxxi) power to acquire property is not a free-standing power, but is, rather, one which, according to the wording of the Constitution, entitles the Commonwealth to acquire property *for any purpose in respect of which Parliament has the power to make laws* – which purposes are of course found in the other enumerated powers. Logically, then, if the s 51(xxxi) acquisition power is to be used only in support of the other enumerated powers and is not a free-standing power in and of itself, it would appear that if the reasoning in the cases discussed above was pushed to its logical conclusion, compensation might never be payable, because all acquisitions must surely be incidental to the exercise of another enumerated power. Of course, it is unlikely that the courts would reason in that fashion, but if one starts from the point (as, indeed, the text of the Constitution compels one to) that all acquisitions occur as a result of exercising some other s 51(xxxi) power, one has to enunciate a theory of interpretation which enables one to distinguish between acquisitions which give rise to a right to compensation and those which do not. The rationale advanced by Justices of the High Court who formed majorities in the line of cases following *Mutual Pools* is, with respect, unsatisfactory, in that it relies on a test of whether the acquisition was a direct acquisition, presumably effected under s 51(xxxi) itself, or merely an incidental acquisition effected under another enumerated power. But if, in fact, s 51(xxxi) is not a free standing power, and all acquisitions are effected under another enumerated power, this argument does not hold water. A solution to these interpretative problems has, however, been presented by Evans, who, instead of using the High Court's device of characterisation as the tool for determining whether acquisition has occurred, suggests that the problem should be approached by applying a test of proportionality.[223] Under this test, the question to be

222 (1999) 202 CLR 133.
223 Evans, 2000, 201–04.

asked is whether an acquisition effected by Parliament's use of a s 51 power was an appropriate and adapted, or proportionate, use of that power. As Joseph and Castan point out,[224] this really amounts to the courts applying a balancing test or a test of reasonableness. If the acquisition was a reasonable means of exercising the 'other' s 51 power, then no compensation will be payable. If, however, the acquisition was not reasonably justified by the use of the power, compensation will be payable. The problem at the moment is that the courts are reluctant to apply a test of reasonableness openly, as this may lead to charges that they are determining limits to legislative power with reference to a criterion not contained within the Constitution.[225] Nevertheless, the decisions in *Mutual Pools*, and the cases thereafter, are perfectly consistent with such a test, which has, after all, been applied in other contexts such as cases on the implied right of freedom of political communication,[226] s 92,[227] the 'nationhood' power[228] and s 51(xxix).[229]

How should a new Constitution address this complex area? First, both the Commonwealth's power and the person's right to compensation should be phrased in terms which refer to deprivation of property rather than to acquisition, as at present, so as to fill the gap in the current formulation identified in the *Tasmanian Dams* case, discussed above. This would make the right to compensation available whenever a person was deprived of their property by the Commonwealth, irrespective of whether the Commonwealth acquired anything. Secondly, the difficulties arising from the interaction between s 51(xxxi) and the other enumerated powers could be avoided if the power to deprive of property was separated from the right to just terms compensation. The part of the Constitution defining the powers of the federal Parliament ought, therefore, simply to state that Parliament may deprive persons of property for any purpose in respect of which it has the power to make laws. A section in the Bill of Rights should state that persons have a right to compensation where property is subject to deprivation. So far as the exceptions to the right to compensation are concerned, it should be remembered that the right to compensation would, along with all other rights in the Bill of Rights, be subject to the overall exception that rights could be limited to an extent that was reasonable in a free and democratic society. This would give Parliament and avenue via which it could acquire property without having to pay compensation, because under the test of reasonableness, the courts would validate laws raising revenue, laws imposing penalties for breaches of the law, laws authorising seizure of enemy property, *et cetera*, on the ground that they were reasonable exercises of enumerated powers. Much the same result as has been achieved under existing s 51(xxxi) case law would be achieved under the new regime, but on a basis that was intellectually far more satisfying.

---

224 Joseph and Castan, 2001, 299–300.

225 Evans, 2000, 203–04.

226 See *Australian Capital Television Pty Ltd v Commonwealth (No 2)* (1992) 177 CLR 106 and the cases in which it was followed.

227 *Castlemaine Tooheys v South Australia* (1990) 169 CLR 436.

228 *Davis v Commonwealth* (1988) 166 CLR 79.

229 *Commonwealth v Tasmania* (*Tasmanian Dams* case) (1983) 158 CLR 1.

2.6 TO WHOM SHOULD THE BILL OF RIGHTS APPLY?

An important issue to be addressed in drafting a Bill of Rights would be to decide to whom it should apply. I have already argued that to be effective, a Bill of Rights should bind all levels of government, Commonwealth, State and Territory. But should the Bill of Rights regulate only relationships between individuals and the state, or should it be applicable in relations between individuals as well? This is a question to which the law has given different answers in different jurisdictions. The question is made more complex by the fact that it tends to be confused with the different but related question of whether a Bill of Rights is applicable to statute law only, or to both statute and common law.

2.6.1 The United States

In the United States, the starting point is that the Bill of Rights is engaged only by 'state action', in other words, that which is to the effect that constitutional guarantees bind only the state in its dealings with citizens and not relations between private individuals.[230] In theory, one might expect that this would mean that the Bill of Rights would be applicable only where a challenge was made to the constitutionality of a statute, or to governmental acts undertaken by virtue of statutory and common law powers. However, in practice a degree of relaxation has occurred in the application of the doctrine over the past 50 years or so.[231] A good example of this is the case of *Shelley v Kraemer*,[232] in which the court declared a private contract embodying a restrictive covenant based on race to be invalid, holding that the 'state action' requirement was satisfied because, like any contract, the covenant would have to be enforced by the courts. This decision provided an avenue whereby the equal protection clause could be used to prevent racial and other types of discrimination by actors who, on the face of it, were not engaged in state action.

In a similar way, beginning with *New York Times v Sullivan*,[233] the law of defamation was 'constitutionalised' through the Supreme Court's holding that private defamation actions were subject to First Amendment rights, where the defamed party was a public official or public figure. Although the defamation action in *New York Times v Sullivan* was brought under a statute, subsequent Supreme Court decisions were to the effect that the First Amendment applied to defamation actions brought by public officials and public figures even under the common law.[234] Whereas one might be able to argue that a defamation action brought by a public official satisfied the state action doctrine indirectly – in that such litigation could be used by the government as a vehicle for suppressing speech which was critical of it – the same cannot be said of defamation actions brought by public figures. In other words, the defamation cases reveal no principled finding as to why the state action requirement was ignored. Furthermore, in other areas of law, the First Amendment is not relevant where private conduct is involved and so, for example,

230 The basic principle was enunciated by Bradley J in *The Civil Rights* cases 109 US 3 (1883).

231 In *Shelley v Kraemer* 334 US 1 (1948), eg, it was held that court enforcement of a racially discriminatory restrictive covenant constituted 'state action'.

232 334 US 1 (1948).

233 376 US 254 (1964).

234 See the discussion by Tribe, 1988, 1711–20.

First Amendment guarantees of freedom of expression are not applicable were a private employer to impose restrictions on what employees could say at their place of work.[235]

Of course, if applied generally, the rule in *Shelley v Kraemer* would erase the distinction between private and public law, because all law must ultimately be enforced by the courts. This has not happened. Instead, as the examples relating to the First Amendment show, exceptions to the state action doctrine have developed haphazardly, with the result that, as most commentators agree, the exceptions cannot be explained by any general theory.[236]

2.6.2 Canada

In Canada, the courts have refused to apply the Charter to private, as distinct from governmental, action. Thus in *RWDSU v Dolphin Delivery*[237] the Supreme Court held that the Charter applied only to state action, and could not be availed of by private parties in the absence of their reliance on statute or on governmental action. Applying this rule, the court held that a union which had been made subject to an interlocutory injunction prohibiting secondary picketing could not rely on the Charter guarantee of freedom of expression. The court came to this conclusion on the ground that s 32 of the Charter makes the Charter applicable 'to the Parliament and government of Canada ... and ... to the legislature and government of each province'. The court interpreted 'government' as meaning the executive and not the judiciary, and thus rejected the notion that the courts were subject to the Charter when applying the common law to private litigants.[238] Note, however, that the court held that since the executive was subject to the Charter, that branch would be bound by the Charter whether exercising statutory or common law powers.[239]

2.6.3 South Africa

In South Africa, the question of whether the Bill of Rights applied only 'vertically' (that is, only to actions between private persons and organs of the state) or both 'vertically' and 'horizontally' (that is, in litigation between private persons as well as in cases between private persons and the state), was a live issue in the first few years after democratisation. Following the demise of apartheid, the South African Parliament enacted the Republic of South Africa Constitution Act 1993 (the Interim Constitution),[240] which contained a Bill of Rights which would apply until Parliament, sitting as a constituent assembly, had drafted a Final Constitution, a process eventually completed with the enactment of the Constitution of the Republic of South Africa Act 1996.[241] Although the Bills of Rights

235 The issue of the speech rights (or, rather, the lack thereof) of private employees is discussed by Browne, 1991, 511–15.

236 Tribe, 1988, 1688–91.

237 (1987) 33 DLR (4th) 174. See also *Pangilinan v Chaves* (1988) 47 CRR 371 (Man CA); and *Coates v The Citizen* (1988) 44 CCLT 286 (NSSC).

238 (1987) 33 DLR (4th) 174, 194–95.

239 *Ibid*.

240 Act 200 of 1993.

241 Act 108 of 1996.

contained in the 1993 and 1996 Constitutions were substantially the same in so far as the rights they protected were concerned, they differed significantly in relation to their scope of application.

Section 7(1) of the Interim Constitution 1993 stated that the Bill of Rights bound 'all legislative and executive organs of State at all levels of government'. In *Du Plessis v De Klerk*,[242] the Constitutional Court interpreted this as meaning that the Bill of Rights was not of horizontal application, on the ground that the omission of any reference to the judicial branch in s 7(1) reflected a conscious decision on the part of the drafters of the Interim Constitution to leave to the courts the development of the common law as between private persons (albeit having 'due regard to' the spirit of the Constitution as mandated by s 35(3)).

The Final Constitution was enacted after the decision in *Du Plessis v De Klerk*. In light of the changes made in the formulation in the 1996 Constitution, as compared with that of 1993, it is difficult to resist the inference that the later document was drafted in order to eliminate doubt as to the supremacy of the Constitution over all branches of government, including the courts, in their application of the common law. Section 8(1) of the Final Constitution 1996 provides as follows:

> **Section 8 Application**
>
> (1) The Bill of Rights applies to all law, and binds the legislature, the executive, the judiciary and all organs of State.
>
> (2) A provision of the Bill of Rights binds a natural or a juristic person if, and to the extent that, it is applicable, taking into account the nature of the right and the nature of any duty imposed by the right.
>
> (3) When applying a provision of the Bill of Rights to a natural or juristic person in terms of subsection (2), a court–
>
> (a) in order to give effect to a right in the Bill, must apply, or if necessary develop the common law to the extent that legislation does not give effect to that right; and
>
> (b) may develop rules of the common law to limit the right, provided that the limitation is in accordance with section 36(1).[243]

The significance of the revision of his section of the Constitution in the wake of *Du Plessis v De Klerk* was highlighted by Heher J in *Protea Technology Ltd v Wainer*,[244] who stated that the re-drafting was indicative of a radical legislative change of intention to ensure that the judiciary was bound by the Bill of Rights when applying the common law, noting that:[245]

> (i) the Bill of Rights now applies to 'all law' (which includes the common law) and it binds the judiciary (section 8(1)); (ii) a provision of the Bill of Rights binds a natural person or a juristic person if, and to the extent that, it is applicable, taking into account the nature of the right and the nature of any duty imposed by the right (section 8(2)); (iii) the obligation to promote the spirit, purport and objects of the Bill of Rights 'in the

242 1996 (3) SA 850 (CC).

243 Section 36 is the limitations section of the Bill of Rights. Under it, rights can be limited only to the extent that limitations can be shown to be 'reasonable and justifiable in an open and democratic society based on human dignity, equality and freedom'.

244 1997 (9) BCLR 1225 (W).

245 *Ibid*, 1238.

> application and development of the common law' in section 35(3) of the Interim Constitution has become 'when developing the common law' in section 39(2) of the 1996 Constitution ...

2.6.4 The 'quasi state action' doctrine in Australia

Not having a Bill of Rights has meant that Australian courts have not directly confronted the issue of horizontal versus vertical applications of rights. However, the issue was addressed tangentially in *Lange v Australian Broadcasting Corporation*,[246] in which the High Court considered the scope of the implied constitutional freedom of political communication. In that case, the court held that the freedom of political communication, which is implicit in the Constitution, was not available as a defence to a defamation action between individuals, because constitutional rights (or immunities from unconstitutional legislation as the court preferred to characterise them) are, it held, applicable only in cases where legislation or governmental action are challenged. The rationale advanced for this finding was both brief and unsatisfactory: the court dismissed the constitutionalisation of defamation law in the United States in two pages,[247] on the ground that, whereas the common law in the United States was 'fragmented' (in the sense that there is no single court of appeal for the common law), the High Court in Australia provides a unifying forum for the declaration of the common law, and that, because one cannot talk of separate systems of State common law in Australia, there is no need to use the law of the Constitution to set limits to rights of action in the law of torts. With respect, this is a non-sequitur: whether the judicial system provides for a nation-wide court of common law appeals is not determinative of whether the source of the rules of law balancing freedom of communication with reputational rights should be the Constitution or the common law. Certainly it is true that, not having any jurisdiction to entertain appeals on rules of State common law, the United States Supreme Court had perforce to look to the Constitution to find a rule of law to set limits on the law of defamation. But that does not mean that, because the High Court in Australia has a national common law jurisdiction, it must use that law to determine questions of that kind. Rather, the High Court can choose to find rules either in the Constitution or in the common law. Why the High Court chose the latter route, departing from prior cases in which the constitutional right had been found applicable to defamation actions,[248] is not articulated in *Lange* – all that appears from the judgment is the rejection of the American approach. The High Court created what might be called a 'quasi state action' doctrine by limiting the application of constitutional rights to governmental parties.

2.6.5 Separating the questions

Part of the reason why state action questions are difficult to resolve is that courts tend to conflate what are two separate issues: the application of constitutional rights to rules of the common law and the application of constitutional rights to non-governmental parties.

---

246 (1997) 189 CLR 520.

247 *Lange v Australian Broadcasting Corporation* (1997) 189 CLR 520, 563–64.

248 See *Theophanous v Herald & Weekly Times* (1994) 182 CLR 104; and *Stephens v West Australian Newspapers* (1994) 182 CLR 211.

There is no doubt that, even in jurisdictions whose law contains a state action doctrine, Bills of Rights apply not only to statute law and to governmental action taken under statutory powers, but also to governmental action taken by virtue of common law (or prerogative) powers. Thus, in Canada the Supreme Court held that the Canadian Charter of Rights and Freedoms applies to the executive both in its exercise of statutory and common law powers,[249] and when the application of the Bill of Rights in South Africa was restricted to the legislative and executive branches of government under the 1993 Constitution, it was accepted that the Bill of Rights would apply to the executive in its exercise of common law powers.[250] Constitutional review of prerogative powers of the executive was also asserted by the Zimbabwean Supreme Court.[251] This makes it even more puzzling why the Australian High Court, in reaching its decision in *Lange* that constitutional rights were inapplicable to defamation law, based its decision on the fact that that area of the law is in general governed by the common law. The High Court did accept that the Constitution would apply to statutes dealing with defamation law. Why should it not apply to rules of defamation derived from the common law?

If the source of the law is not a rational criterion to use when determining the circumstances in which the Bill of Rights should apply, should the status of the actor determine this question? Certainly that is the case in the United States, Canada and New Zealand. As we have seen, the restrictiveness of the rule that the state must be an actor before the Bill of Rights will be engaged in the United States has led to attempts to stretch the state action doctrine to breaking point, and to categorise as state actors a variety of *ad hoc* categories of private individuals who really have nothing to do with the state at all other than that, for example, they rely on state enforcement of a racially restrictive covenant.[252] As we have also seen, once the effect of excluding the judiciary from the ambit of the Bill of Rights became apparent in South Africa after the *Du Plessis v De Klerk* decision taken under the 1993 Constitution, the 1996 Constitution expressly made the Bill of Rights applicable to that branch of government. Under the 1993 Constitution the courts had, of course, had to apply the Bill of Rights to state actors whether they were employing statutory or common law powers, and to private persons relying on statutes, as the Bill of Rights bound the legislature and executive without qualification. After 1996 the courts had also to apply the Bill of Rights to private individuals using the common law, because by bringing the judiciary within the ambit of the Bill of Rights, the 1996 Constitution required that they comply with its terms when applying the common law even to private actors.

If Australia had a Bill of Rights there would seem to be no reason why, in addition to applying to Parliament in its enactment of legislation, to the executive in exercising statutory or common law powers and to private persons relying on statutes, the Bill of Rights should not also apply to private individuals using the common law and to the judiciary in applying it. Indeed, there would, to a certain extent, be little that was novel about that situation: for example, all Commonwealth, State and Territory anti-

249 See *Operation Dismantle v The Queen* (1985) 18 DLR (4th) 481; and *Idziak v Canada (Minister of Justice)* (1993) 97 DLR (4th) 577.

250 *President of the Republic of South Africa v Hugo* 1997 (4) SA 1 (CC).

251 *Patriotic Front ZAPU v Minister of Justice Legal and Parliamentary Affairs* 1986 (1) SA 532 (ZSC).

252 *Shelley v Kraemer* 344 US 1 (1948).

discrimination Acts already prohibit not only governments, but also private parties from discriminating when using the common law – as when employing someone under a contract of employment or leasing premises under a rental contract. The application of a Bill of Rights to the common law will no doubt require the courts to confront interesting questions regarding the extent to which the law will allow a party to a contract to submit himself or herself to conditions which restrict freedoms – an employer imposing conditions relating to employees' freedom of expression being a good example. Yet these questions are not insurmountable. The courts are used to determining the very similar question of which contracts are unenforceable on the ground that they offend public policy or are *contra bonos mores*. In Bill of Rights cases, the courts will simply balance competing interests using the test the Bill of Rights contains permitting the limitation of rights. In the example of employer-imposed restrictions on freedom of expression, one might expect that the courts would come to a different conclusion in relation to a person employed by a political party than it would in the case of a person employed as an accounts manager of a department store. In the latter case, the restriction is irrelevant to the job and thus unreasonable, whereas in the former, the nature of the job is such that some direction by the employer in relation to what employees might say would not be unexpected.

2.7 PROTECTING A BILL OF RIGHTS THROUGH ENTRENCHMENT

A crucial issue in assessing the usefulness of any Bill of Rights is the extent to which it is protected from legislative override. Although many jurisdictions have a 'Bill of Rights', documents sharing this generic title may have very different legal effects. This section focuses on the extent to which Bills of Rights provide an effective restraint on the legislature. Not all Bills of Rights do so, as the following examples show.

The New Zealand Bill of Rights Act 1990 affirms the existence of certain rights, many of which are similar to those found in the Canadian Charter of Rights and Freedoms. However, the Act has the status of ordinary legislation, and can therefore be overridden by Parliament. The Act does attempt to impose a political cost on a government seeking to legislate contrary to its provisions, in that s 7 of the Act obliges the Attorney-General to inform Parliament when proposed bills are inconsistent with the rights protected by the Act. However, compliance with this provision does not form part of the legislative process, and so non-compliance does not invalidate offending legislation.[253]

The Canadian Charter of Rights and Freedoms offers more security for rights than does the New Zealand document, but it is, nevertheless, deficient. The advantage that the Charter has over the New Zealand Bill of rights is that under s 1 of the Charter, freedoms protected by the Charter may be subject only to such limitations as are reasonable in a free and democratic society. In the event that a right is subject to an unreasonable limitation, the courts may provide a remedy. Nevertheless, the Canadian Charter suffers from the weakness that s 33(1) expressly permits a Parliament (federal or provincial) to exempt legislation from the operation of the Charter, simply by including an express

253 *Mangawaro Enterprises Ltd v Attorney-General* [1994] 2 NZLR 451.

provision to that effect in legislation. The exemption lapses after five years under s 33(3), but can be renewed. When the Charter came into force in 1982, the Quebec legislature enacted a blanket override provision covering all existing legislation,[254] and also inserted an override clause into all subsequent enactments.[255] Override clauses were no longer inserted into new legislation after a change of government in 1982, and the blanket override provision was allowed to lapse in 1987. However, the Quebec Parliament did insert an override clause in highly controversial circumstances in 1988, when it shielded from challenge under the Charter a statute which forbade the display of English language shop signs in the province.[256] The existence of s 33(1) provides governments with too great a temptation during times of crisis or in relation to highly controversial issues, which is precisely when a Bill of Rights ought to be secure from override. This is, indeed, well illustrated by the language signs case itself: given the contentious nature of language rights in Canada, the Charter should have served as a bulwark for minority language rights and freedom of expression. A Bill of Rights is not needed in the easy cases which everyone agrees on. Its true worth becomes manifest precisely on those occasions when fundamental issues are involved, and when the urge towards a decision based on political power, rather than on principle, is at its strongest.

An even more vivid example of what can happen if a Bill of Rights is exposed to legislative override is provided by the case of Zimbabwe, where, under the Constitution[257] negotiated for Zimbabwe in late 1979 between the British government and the various participants in the civil war which had taken place in Rhodesia since 1972, it was agreed that Chapter III of the Constitution would contain a Bill of Rights providing comprehensive protection for a range of freedoms. Unfortunately, s 25 of the Constitution provides that if the President declares a state of emergency which is approved by a simple resolution of Parliament under s 31J, then a range of rights listed in Schedule 2 of the Constitution can be suspended, including fundamental rights such as the right to personal liberty. These provisions rendered nugatory most of the rights theoretically protected by the Constitution, and enabled the governing party to use its parliamentary majority to perpetuate a state of emergency for a decade after independence, during which time political opponents of the government were detained without trial. In stark contrast to Zimbabwe, the South African Constitution, although providing for the derogation of some rights in a state of emergency declared by Parliament,[258] gives to the courts the power to determine whether the state of emergency was validly declared (in other words, whether the circumstances justifying the

254 An Act Respecting the Constitution Act, SQ 1982, c 21.

255 For a discussion of s 33, see Hogg, 1992, 892–93.

256 An Act to Amend the Charter of the French Language, SQ 1988, c 54.

257 The Constitution of Zimbabwe 1980 is a Schedule to the Zimbabwe Order 1979 (SI 1979/1600 of the United Kingdom).

258 Republic of South Africa Constitution Act 1993, s 37(1) provides as follows:

> A state of emergency may be declared only in terms of an Act of Parliament, and only when–
>
> (a) the life of the nation is threatened by war, invasion, general insurrection, disorder, natural disaster or other public emergency; and
>
> (b) the declaration is necessary to restore peace and order.

declaration objectively exist)[259] and, perhaps most importantly, provides that certain core rights are absolutely non-derogable, even in a state of emergency.[260]

Bills of Rights in most countries are included in the Constitution, and are, therefore, protected in that whatever special procedures must be used to amend the Constitution have to be complied with to amend the Bill of Rights. In South Africa, for example, constitutional amendment requires a two-thirds majority in the National Assembly, and the assent of six provinces in the House of Provinces.[261] The United States Constitution (including the Bill of Rights) can be amended only by a two-thirds majority in each House of Congress along with the approval of the legislatures of three-quarters of the States.[262] Approval by the legislature followed by a referendum is a common requirement for amendment in other jurisdictions.[263] The Namibian Constitution goes further, and states that the chapter in the Constitution forming the Bill of Rights is *absolutely* entrenched – in other words, the Constitution may never be amended in such a way as to reduce the degree of protection afforded by the Bill of Rights.[264] The same applies to amendment provisions[265] in the German Constitution protecting the right to human dignity[266] and the right to resist unconstitutional action.[267] In the discussion on the sources of human rights at 2.4.2, above, it was noted that modern natural rights theories, being based on reason, avoid claims to infallibility. Declaring provisions of a Bill of Rights, or any other constitutional document, unamendable is incompatible with that theory, and so I do not recommend that any part of an Australian Constitution or Bill of Rights be absolutely entrenched. Nevertheless, the German example serves to illustrate how a society whose history reveals the awful potential for denial of human rights has come to recognise the importance of protecting the Constitution from interference by the legislature.

In Australia, some have argued for a Bill of Rights which is subject to Parliamentary override.[268] But, as the examples from other jurisdictions show, such a document would offer scant protection for rights, particularly in relation to controversial issues where the temptation of legislative override is at its strongest, and where the need for the Bill of Rights is thus greatest. Australians deserve better protection of their rights than is offered by second best options. The Bill of Rights, as part of the Constitution, ought, therefore, to be subject to the same protection as is given to the rest of the document by the provision governing constitutional amendment. The precise formulation of those provisions is discussed at 5.8, below.

---

259 *Ibid*, s 37(3).

260 *Ibid*, s 37(5).

261 *Ibid*, s 74(2).

262 Constitution of the United States 1787, Art V.

263 There are a multitude of Constitutions which contain this feature. See, eg, the Constitution of the Republic of Ireland 1938, Art 47; the Constitution of Austria 1929, Art 44; and the Constitution of Spain 1978, Art 168(3).

264 Constitution of Namibia 1990, Arts 131 and 132(5).

265 Constitution of Germany 1949, Art 79(3).

266 *Ibid*, Art 1.

267 *Ibid*, Art 20.

268 See, eg, Williams, 1999, 262–64; and Goldsworthy, 1992, 173–76.

2.8 JUSTICIABILITY, REMEDIES AND STANDING

A Bill of Rights is of little use unless, in addition to being secure from legislative override, it provides remedies when it is infringed. In other words, a Bill of Rights should be justiciable. The necessity for this is starkly illustrated by the following example from Southern Africa: under its policy of apartheid, the South African government carved out small, underdeveloped, rural areas to which it purported to give independence. This device was designed to deprive black South Africans of their South African citizenship, and to replace it with the citizenship of supposedly independent tribal 'homelands' where, it was argued, they could exercise the franchise and other rights of self-government. Quite apart from the obvious injustice of the policy, it was wholly impractical from an economic and social point of view, given that most black South Africans had moved from rural areas to find employment in large cities, and many had had no connection with their supposed 'homeland' for more than a generation. One of these 'homelands', Ciskei, was given independence under a Constitution[269] which, on the face of it, met all the criteria of what a progressive Constitution should contain, including a Bill of Rights. However, the Constitution expressly denied the courts the power to invalidate legislation which contravened the Bill of Rights.[270] The government of Ciskei engaged in widespread oppression, to which the Bill of Rights provided no impediment. Indeed, it was arguably worse to include the unenforceable Bill of Rights than it would have been to omit it altogether, cruelly holding out as it did the illusory promise of fundamental freedoms while not protecting them in reality.

2.8.1 Justiciability and remedies

It is, therefore, crucial that a Bill of Rights should be justiciable – in other words, that it should be enforceable by the courts, and that a range of remedies should be available to address particular infringements complained of. As in the case of immunity to legislative override, Bills of Rights in different jurisdictions comply with the principle of justiciability in varying degrees.

The operational sections of the New Zealand Bill of Rights Act 1990 expressly exclude the power of the courts to review legislation against the Act. Sections 4–6 of the Act provide as follows:

> **4 Other enactments not affected**
>
> No court shall, in relation to any enactment (whether passed or made before or after the commencement of this Bill of Rights),
>
> (a) Hold any provision of the enactment to be impliedly repealed or revoked, or to be in any way invalid or ineffective; or
>
> (b) Decline to apply any provision of the enactment–
>
> by reason only that the provision is inconsistent with any provision of this Bill of Rights.

269 Ciskei Constitution Act 1981.

270 *Ibid*, s 19(3).

5 Justified limitations

Subject to section 4 of this Bill of Rights, the rights and freedoms contained in this Bill of Rights may be subject only to such reasonable limits prescribed by law as can be demonstrably justified in a free and democratic society.

6 Interpretation consistent with Bill of Rights to be preferred

Wherever an enactment can be given a meaning that is consistent with the rights and freedoms contained in this Bill of Rights, that meaning shall be preferred to any other meaning.

The effect of these is to reduce the status of the Bill of Rights Act to an interpretative aid. The courts must interpret legislation in conformity with the Bill of Rights Act, but if the legislation is incompatible with the Bill of Rights Act, the legislation must be given effect to. Within these parameters the most the courts can do is to 'read down' ambiguous legislation in cases of ambiguity, and to adopt that interpretation which is consistent with the Bill of Rights.[271]

The New Zealand situation, where the Bill of Rights expressly excludes the power of the courts to review legislation is obviously the least satisfactory from the perspective of effective protection of human rights. Somewhat less unsatisfactory would be the situation where the Constitution or Bill of Rights was silent as to the issue of justiciability. Silence may be taken by the judiciary as meaning that it was the intention of the legislature that no remedy be available. Sometimes, however, judicial boldness may lead to the creation of a remedy where none is expressly made available. Such was the case in the United States, where the courts took the initiative of reading a remedy into the Bill of Rights on the basis of the *ubi ius, ibi remedium* principle. In *Marbury v Madison*,[272] the Supreme Court declared that implicit in the Constitution was the power to review and invalidate legislation which infringed the Constitution, on the ground that if such an implication did not exist, the Constitution would become a dead letter.

Having the courts fashion a remedy for breaches of rights is obviously better than having no remedy at all, but clearly the best course is for the Constitution explicitly to confer upon the courts the ability to grant remedies for breaches of its provisions, including the Bill of Rights. As an example of such a provision, one might point to s 24 of the Canadian Charter of Rights and Freedoms, which provides as follows:

Enforcement of guaranteed rights and freedoms

24 (1) Anyone whose rights and freedoms, as guaranteed by this Charter have been infringed or denied may apply to a court of competent jurisdiction to obtain such remedy as the court considers appropriate and just in the circumstances.

Similarly, in South Africa ss 2 and 38 of the Constitution state as follows:

Supremacy of the Constitution

2 This Constitution is the supreme law of the Republic; law or conduct inconsistent with it is invalid, and the obligations imposed by it must be fulfilled.

271 *Ministry of Transport v Noort* [1992] 3 NZLR 260. For a discussion of the interaction between ss 4, 5 and 6 of the New Zealand Bill of Rights Act, see Joseph, 1993, 856–61; and Rishworth, 1995, 94–107.

272 (1803) 1 Cranch 137; 5 US 137.

Enforcement of rights

> 38 Anyone ... has the right to approach a competent court, alleging that a right in the Bill of Rights has been infringed or threatened, and the court may grant appropriate relief ...

A Bill of Rights without an effective remedy provides the illusion of protection of fundamental freedoms. An Australian Bill of Rights ought, therefore, to include a remedies clause drafted in sufficiently broad terms as to enable the courts to grant such remedy as they see fit. Although the most important of these remedies would undoubtedly be the power to declare invalid legislation or executive action which was inconsistent with the Bill of Rights, the courts would also find it useful to develop additional remedies which would be applicable in cases where a declaration of that type would not address the harm caused. For example, breaches of provisions of the due process provisions of a Bill of Rights might be remedied by orders excluding evidence obtained as a result of such breaches, while one could imagine many situations in which breaches would be remedied by mandatory or prohibitory orders. Some jurisdictions, for example the United States,[273] have recognised the existence of the so-called 'constitutional tort' – in other words, that a breach of the constitution causing harm gives rise to a right to claim damages. Ironically, despite the express denial by the New Zealand Bill of Rights Act of the remedy of reviewing legislation, the Court of Appeal in that country took the fact that the Act is silent as to other remedies as permitting the creation of such remedies, and granted compensatory damages for breach of the Act in *Simpson v Attorney-General* (*Baigent's* case).[274] Damages may often be an appropriate remedy for breaches of a Bill of Rights, and the prospect of an award of damages would be an incentive to the executive to ensure that its servants acted in accordance with the Constitution. Interestingly, in *Kruger v Commonwealth*,[275] Australia's High Court declined to recognise a private right of action for damages arising out of a breach of the Constitution; however, there is every reason to think that, if we had a Bill of Rights which left the courts at large to determine the issue if remedies, the remedy of damages is one which the courts would be very likely to add to their armoury.

2.8.2 Standing

Finally, in relation to enforceability, some attention must be paid to the issue of standing. As a general rule, a person wishing to bring an action must have standing, in other words, must be able to show that they had a sufficient personal interest in the issues involved to give them grounds to bring the action. A related factor which may also provide a barrier to a litigant is that the High Court has interpreted the provisions of Chapter III of the Constitution, which gives it jurisdiction in relation to various 'matters', as preventing it from giving advisory opinions.[276] In other words, the courts will not hear cases in the abstract – there must be a real dispute between the plaintiff and a defendant. Questions of standing and matter are of particular importance in public interest litigation,

273 *Bivens v Six Unknown Federal Narcotics Agents* 403 US 388 (1971).
274 *Simpson v Attorney-General* (*Baigent's* case) [1994] 3 NZLR 667 (CA).
275 (1997) 190 CLR 1.
276 *Re Judiciary and Navigation Acts* (*Advisory Opinions* case) (1921) 29 CLR 257.

where a person seeks to bring an action on behalf of a large group wishing to challenge the legality of the actions of a private person, or the government, on the grounds of some harm which is diffuse rather than affecting any particular individual. One way of overcoming these difficulties, which has long been recognised by the common law, is for the litigants to approach the Attorney-General and seek permission to bring an action in the Attorney-General's name. Such an action, called a 'relator' action, relies on the fact that, under the common law, the Attorney-General has standing to bring actions to enforce the law generally. The private litigants control and fund the action, but technically it is brought in the name of the Attorney-General.

Leaving aside the rather inconvenient expedient of the relator action, there has been some liberalisation of the law relating to standing and matter in Australia: thus in respect of standing, in *Onus v Alcoa of Australia Ltd*[277] the High Court found that an Aboriginal group had sufficient standing to bring an action to restrain a breach of a statute preserving relics of cultural importance to Aboriginal people, simply by virtue of the fact that they were the descendants of the Aboriginal people who had inhabited the area where the relics were located. A liberal approach relating to whether a 'matter' existed was adopted in *Croome v Tasmania*,[278] where the High Court held that a 'matter' did exist where the appellant, who was homosexual, sought a declaration that a State law which criminalised homosexual conduct was invalid for inconsistency with a Commonwealth Act. The court found that there was a matter subsisting between the appellant and the State of Tasmania, despite the fact that the State prosecuting authorities had indicated that they would not prosecute him: the court held that the mere fact that the appellant was subject to potential liability sufficed to create a 'matter' which it could determine. Interestingly, three of the Justices in the *Croome* case,[279] explicitly held that the issues of matter and standing could not be separated, and that, therefore, if a person had a sufficient interest in a case to give them standing there must, by virtue of that fact, be a matter subsisting. Similarly, in *Truth About Motorways Pty Ltd v Macquarie Infrastructure Investment Management Ltd*,[280] the High Court held that the Chapter III requirement that there needed to be a 'matter' before its jurisdiction could be activated, was satisfied in a case where a group of activists brought an action in the name of the appellant company which they had formed in order to oppose the construction of a motorway in Sydney. They alleged that the respondents had breached s 52 of the Trade Practices Act 1974 (Cth) by mis-stating the traffic volumes that the motorway would carry. The court upheld the validity of s 80 of the Act which conferred standing on 'any person' to bring an action to enforce the Act. Essentially, the court held that because there was a remedy which could be granted which would secure the objective sought by the appellants, and that remedy had been resisted by the respondents, there was a matter between them.

Notwithstanding the liberalisation that has taken place in relation to standing, it would be preferable if the complexities of the case law discussed above could be avoided. It is true that because a Bill of Rights protects the rights of the individual, a person whose rights had been infringed would undoubtedly have standing to bring an action to enforce

277 (1981) 149 CLR 27.
278 (1997) 191 CLR 119.
279 Gaudron, McHugh and Gummow JJ, 132 and 138.
280 (2000) 200 CLR 591.

the relevant provisions of that part of the Constitution. However, doubts about standing might arise where conduct infringed the rights of a large group, among whom no particular individual could point to any specific interest in the case. Furthermore, since, when seen as a whole, the Constitution forms a compact binding individuals and the State *inter se*, surely any of the obligations contained in it (and not just those arising from the Bill of Rights) should be able to be enforced by any member of the public? The concept of an action brought on behalf of the public is a venerable one – in Roman law the *actio popularis* permitted any individual to bring an action to enforce a public duty.[281] Echoes of this action live on in contemporary Constitutions, most notably in the South African Constitution, s 38 of which provides as follows:

> **38 Enforcement of rights**
>
> Anyone listed in this section has the right to approach a competent court, alleging that a right in the Bill of Rights has been infringed or threatened, and the court may grant appropriate relief, including a declaration of rights. The persons who may approach a court are–
>
> (a) anyone acting in their own interest;
>
> (b) anyone acting on behalf of another person who cannot act in their own name;
>
> (c) anyone acting as a member of, or in the interest of, a group or class of persons;
>
> (d) anyone acting in the public interest; and
>
> (e) an association acting in the interest of its members.

I would argue that a similar provision, but not restricted to the Bill of Rights, should be included in a new Australian Constitution. The conferral of a general right of standing would emphasise the notion of a Constitution as a document in which all members of the public had an interest, and which all members of the public could thus bring an action to enforce.

2.9 CONCLUSION

There is no denying that, by and large, the human rights of Australians are respected. Parliaments and governments, mindful of adverse reaction by the media and by the public, are generally careful not to enact legislation that infringes civil liberties. On the other hand, it is also true that Parliaments do enact statutes which infringe human rights and, even where they enact laws which are beneficial to human rights, such laws sometimes do not provide a sufficient degree of protection by contemporary standards. However, the principal reason why Australia should have a Bill of Rights transcends these practical considerations of human rights protection, important as they are: even if Australia was a country where human rights were never infringed by legislatures and

281 For a discussion of the *actio popularis*, see *Wood v Ondangwa Tribal Authority* 1975 (2) SA 295 (A) 305E–310G.

governments as a matter of practice, it would still be important to have a Bill of Rights simply as an affirmation of human dignity, and as a rejection of the pernicious idea that the sole test for the validity of a law is whether it has been properly enacted by Parliament.

Finally, there is no doubt that including a Bill of Rights in the Constitution would enhance the power of the courts, and thus of the judiciary which staffs them. This in turn gives rise to the argument that there needs to be greater transparency in relation to the manner in which people are appointed to judicial office, an issue which is fully explored in the next chapter. However, in leaving the issue of a Bill of Rights it is worthwhile to remember that, whereas there are countless examples of people being oppressed by dictatorial governments, and even by democratically elected Parliaments, history has yet to record a popular uprising against a tyranny of judges wielding a Bill of Rights.

THE JUDICIARY AND THE COURTS

3.1 THE ROLE AND STATUS OF THE JUDICIARY

Of all the institutions in the Constitution, the judiciary is the most vulnerable. This vulnerability stems from the fact that the courts have no independent coercive power of their own to enforce their judgments, and are, instead, reliant on the organs of the state to do so for them. For this reason, the judiciary was aptly described by Alexander Hamilton as 'the least dangerous' branch of government, because it had neither the sword of the executive branch, nor the purse of the legislative branch.[1] This fact assumes special significance where the state itself is a party to legal proceedings, because if constitutional law is defined as that body of law which defines and limits the power of the state, then the absence of any independent power at the disposal of the courts means that it is upon the state's acquiescence in judgments made against it that the constitutional order depends. This has been starkly illustrated in Zimbabwe, where the government's frequent refusal to comply with decisions of the courts – most recently judgments given in cases ordering an end to government sponsored illegal land occupations[2] – has led to a breakdown of constitutional order.

The courts' defencelessness against attack by the government means that they are reliant on support by the organs of civil society – the press, the legal profession and the general public – for the maintenance of their independence and respect for their judgments. This does not mean that the judiciary should be beyond criticism. Development of the law is often furthered through comment and debate on the merits of judicial decisions in editorial comment and in academic journals. However, a disturbing trend in recent years has been criticism of the judiciary not taking the form of arguments on points of law, but, rather, manifesting itself as challenges to the judiciary's discharge of the roles given to it under the common law and under the Constitution, often in intemperate terms. As examples of this, one may cite then Queensland Premier, Rob Borbidge, who, in the wake of the High Court's decision in *Wik Peoples v Queensland*,[3] described members of the court as 'self-appointed kings and queens',[4] the statements of Chief Justice Brennan as 'pathetic'[5] and those of Justice Kirby as 'rantings and ravings'[6] and, in a statement that was perhaps meant to be self-fulfilling, said that the judges of the High Court were held in 'absolute and utter contempt' by many Australians.[7] Most

1 Hamilton, 1990, 373.

2 Angus Shaw, 'State ignores court order on land seizures' (2000) *Associated Press Newswires*, 13 November.

3 (1996) 187 CLR 1.

4 Gervase Greene, 'Senator defies PM in attack on court' (1997) *The Age*, 4 March, 4.

5 *Ibid*.

6 Adrian Rollins, 'Attacks "undermine" role of the High Court' (1997) *Sunday Age*, 9 March, 11.

7 James Woodford, 'Borbidge steps up attack on High Court' (1997) *Sydney Morning Herald*, 1 March, 7.

dangerous from a constitutional perspective was Premier Borbidge's statement that 'at the end of the day, the Parliament is the highest court in the land'.[8] Such utterances ought to be anathema to those committed to constitutional government, because by attacking the role and integrity of the courts, they undermine what is ultimately the only defence the courts have against unconstitutional action by the state.[9] Regrettably, in 1998 the Commonwealth Attorney-General abandoned the long-standing tradition that the holder of that office should defend judges against unwarranted attack.[10] This leaves judges in an exposed position, given their own tradition of avoiding making extra-curial statements in defence of their decisions. The Attorney-General's failure to discharge this supportive role was most recently exemplified by his refusal to defend Justice Michael Kirby against false allegations made by Liberal Senator, Bill Heffernan, a decision which attracted widespread adverse comment.[11]

3.2 INDEPENDENCE OF THE JUDICIARY AND SEPARATION OF POWERS

Apart from solicitude for the judiciary by press and public, the only protections available to this branch of government are legal rules embodied in the Constitution. Of course, such rules ultimately rely for their effectiveness upon acquiescence by the executive and legislature. Thus their usefulness depends entirely on the extent to which the doctrine of constitutionalism is respected.

3.2.1 Independence of judges

In Australia, the independence of judges as individuals is secured by s 72 of the Constitution which provides that, after appointment by the Governor-General in Council, justices of the High Court and other courts created by Parliament cannot be removed except by the Governor-General in Council on an address from both Houses of Parliament, on grounds of 'proved misbehaviour or incapacity'. The remuneration of judges is set by Parliament, but may not be reduced while they are in office. There is a mandatory retirement age of 70 years. The process of appointing justices is discussed later in this chapter. Here, it suffices to say that the provisions of s 72 relating to security of tenure mirror those contained in s 3 of England's Act of Settlement of 1700.[12]

To date, no Commonwealth judge has been removed from office under s 72. The requirement in s 72(ii) that misbehaviour or incapacity be 'proved' suggests that removal requires that Parliament engage in a judicial process. In 1999, Labor and Democrat parliamentarians threatened (but ultimately decided against) voting for an inquiry to be

8 Keith Austin, 'Judging the judiciary' (1998) *Sydney Morning Herald – The Guide*, 25 May, 17.

9 For a discussion of the pivotal role the judiciary plays in the constitutional order and the need for judicial independence, see Campbell and Lee, 2001, 1–6 and 48–52.

10 For a discussion of this issue see Parker, 2000, 62 and 82–85.

11 George Williams, 'Without support, court is fragile' (2002) *The Australian*, 20 March, 11; Inga Gilchrist and Natali Sikora, 'It's a disgrace, says top judge' (2002) *Herald-Sun*, 19 March, 2.

12 12 & 13 Will III, c 2, s 3.

conducted on behalf of the Senate by retired judges into the fitness of Justice Callinan to hold office.[13] There is clearly a need for the Constitution to specify precisely what process is to be used in such circumstances. Part of the controversy involving Justice Murphy in the 1980s related to the procedure that should be adopted under s 72(ii).[14] A suitable process was proposed by the 1988 Constitutional Commission, which recommended that the Constitution be amended so as to provide for a Judicial Tribunal, staffed by superior court judges (both State and federal) to hear cases, and to make recommendations to the legislature.[15] The Constitution should also specify that evidentiary rules guaranteeing a fair hearing would also be applicable. It should also be made clear that 'misbehaviour' refers to the judge's conduct while in office, rather than to conduct prior to appointment, as some argued it did in the case of Justice Callinan.[16] It would clearly be inconsistent with the doctrine of security of tenure if a judge was able to be dismissed for conduct engaged in before being appointed to office.[17] On the other hand, 'misbehaviour' should be interpreted as involving not just misconduct in the performance of judicial duties, but also serious breaches of the law and other behaviour of a type which demonstrates unfitness to hold office, engaged in while a judge,[18] which could be achieved through the inclusion of the word 'unfitness' in the relevant Constitutional provision. Finally in this regard, the Constitution should also make provision for the suspension of judges while an inquiry is in progress, as continued discharge of judicial duties while a hearing is in progress would obviously impinge upon public confidence in the integrity of the courts. However, in order to avoid suspension being used as *de facto* removal from the bench, it would be advisable that suspension be permitted only if the Judicial Tribunal had made a preliminary finding that there was a *prima facie* case which was of sufficient seriousness to warrant suspension.[19]

The protection afforded judges against reduction in remuneration could be made more secure by means of a constitutional provision to the effect that the Constitution's establishment of judicial salaries was itself sufficient authorisation for the payment of those salaries without parliamentary authorisation – in other words, the payment of judicial salaries from the Consolidated Revenue Fund should occur automatically, and as an exception to the rule (currently contained in s 83) that no appropriation is lawful unless authorised by an Act of Parliament. Making judicial salaries a permanent charge on the Consolidated Revenue Fund would simply constitutionalise what has already been put into ordinary legislation by all Australian legislatures.[20] Of course, at the end of the day, the security of judicial remuneration depends entirely upon the willingness of the executive to pay it, but it is, nevertheless, worthwhile to include every possible support

13 Gervase Green, 'Callinan set to face Senate legal probe' (1999) *The Age*, 26 June, 12; Stephen Spencer, 'Callinan inquiry dead as Democrats get cold feet' (1999) *Australian Associated Press*, 2 August.

14 Blackshield, 2000, 41–20.

15 Constitutional Commission, 1988, 6.180–203.

16 Blackshield, 2000, 424–25.

17 I would argue that vesting the responsibility for the selection of judges in a Judicial Services Commission (as recommended later in this chapter) would substantially diminish the likelihood of the appointment of candidates who had engaged in pre-appointment conduct which would diminish the reputation of the bench if discovered post-appointment.

18 Campbell and Lee, 2001, 110–11.

19 *Ibid*, 111–14.

20 Winterton, 1995(a), 21 n 178.

for judicial independence in the Constitution. It would also be useful to include in the Constitution reference to the entitlement of judges of a particular court to equal remuneration, so as to avoid the compromise of judicial independence which would arise if some judges of a court were paid more than others.[21] Finally in this regard, some attention should be paid to the issue of the quantum of judicial salaries, and the potential for them to be eroded by inflation. Since, as is argued below, judges should be appointed from nominees of an independent Judicial Services Commission, it would seem appropriate that the same body be vested by the Constitution with the task of determining judicial salaries, subject to the basic requirement that judicial salaries must increase each year by at least as much as the consumer price index.[22] This would not involve any drastic change from current practice, as the salaries of judges are already set by remuneration tribunals in the case of the Commonwealth and all States bar Tasmania.[23]

The independence of judges is also furthered by a rule of the common law that superior court judges – in other words, judges of courts of inherent general jurisdiction – are immune from personal liability for anything done in the course of their judicial office,[24] unless it can be shown that they acted outside their jurisdiction and *mala fide*.[25] The rule has been applied by the High Court[26] and by other courts in Australia.[27] The rationale for this rule is that judges would be deterred from acting fearlessly and impartially if subject to the threat of a lawsuit by the losing side in a case – the judge might instead decide the case on the basis of assessing which party was most likely to bring a suit if dissatisfied with the outcome.[28] The proper remedy for a litigant who believes that a judge has made an error is to appeal. Recent academic comment has been to the effect that the principle of immunity in all circumstances, bar a *mala fide* action beyond jurisdiction, should extend to all judicial officers.[29] That, indeed, has been made the position through legislation in the United Kingdom,[30] and in most Canadian jurisdictions.[31] Given the importance of the rule to the preservation of judicial independence, it would be useful to include it expressly in the Constitution, and to state that it applied to all members of the judiciary in the exercise of the judicial power of the Commonwealth.

21 *Ibid*, 4–5.

22 See the discussion of the quantum of judicial salaries in *ibid*, 26–27.

23 For an overview of the work of such bodies, see *ibid*, 43–75.

24 *Sirros v Moore* [1975] 1 QB 118.

25 *In re McC* [1985] 1 AC 528.

26 See, eg, *Gallo v Dawson* (1988) 82 ALR 401, *Gallo v Dawson* (1992) 66 ALR 859; and *Re East ex parte Nguyen* (1998) 196 CLR 354.

27 Most recently, in *Wentworth v Wentworth* (1999) 46 NSWLR 300.

28 This point was made in *Taylor v Canada (Attorney-General)* (2000) 184 DLR (4th) 706, 714, *per* Sexton JA.

29 Hogg and Monahan, 2000, 198.

30 Courts and Legal Services Act 1990 (UK), s 108.

31 Hogg and Monahan, 2000, 199.

3.2.2 Separation of powers

Apart from the protection that judges enjoy as individuals, the independence of the judiciary as an institution is furthered by the doctrine of separation of powers. The classic formulation of the doctrine by the French political philosopher, Montesquieu, was that tyrannical government could be avoided only if the three branches of government were separated both functionally and physically.[32] Functional separation requires that no branch should control either of the others in their performance of their functions, and that no branch should be able to perform the functions of any other. Physical separation requires that no individual be able to hold office in more than one branch simultaneously. Despite the fact that the doctrine is nowhere explicitly mentioned in the Commonwealth Constitution, the High Court has long held the doctrine to be implicit in the document, at least in so far as the judicial branch is concerned.[33] Two dimensions of the rule have been recognised: that only courts should exercise the judicial power of the Commonwealth, and that courts should not be vested with non-judicial functions.

In *New South Wales v Commonwealth* (*Wheat* case),[34] it was held that where s 71 of the Constitution confers the judicial power of the Commonwealth on the High Court, other federal courts created by Parliament and such other courts as Parliament chooses to vest with the judicial power, that conferral is exclusive – in other words, the judicial power cannot be conferred on any body other than a court. Furthermore, a body would be a 'court' within the meaning of s 71 only if its members enjoyed the security of tenure provided by s 72. The High Court has re-affirmed this principle in a number of cases,[35] but has also recognised a number of exceptions, such as those involving military courts hearing cases involving breaches of defence force discipline,[36] Parliament's jurisdiction to hear cases involving breach of privilege[37] and the judiciary's delegation of their powers to other court officers.[38]

The courts have also considered a number of cases in which the independence of the judicial branch has been threatened, not by the purported conferral of judicial power on another body, but rather by the enactment by Parliament of legislation directing the courts in the manner of their exercise of the judicial power. Legislation which reduced the court to the role of a mere cypher acting under the direction of Parliament would have as deleterious an effect on the independence of the judiciary as would the transfer of judicial power to another body. Thus the High Court has held that an Act of Attainder (legislation in terms of which a named person or persons was stated to be guilty of an offence) would

32 Montesquieu, 1949, 151.

33 By contrast, there is no separation of powers between the executive and legislature, as the Constitution incorporates the system of parliamentary government, which actually requires that Ministers be members of Parliament and be answerable to it. This fusion of powers was acknowledged by the High Court in *Victorian Stevedoring and General Contracting Co v Dignan* (1931) 46 CLR 73. Relations between the executive and the legislature are addressed in Chapter 4.

34 (1915) 20 CLR 54.

35 See, eg, *Waterside Workers Federation of Australia v JW Alexander Ltd* (1918) 25 CLR 434; *Australian Communist Party v Commonwealth* (1951) 83 CLR 1; and *Brandy v Human rights and Equal Opportunity Commission* (1995) 183 CLR 245.

36 Most recently re-iterated in *Re Tracey ex parte Ryan* (1989) 166 CLR 518.

37 *R v Richard ex parte Fitzpatrick and Browne* (1955) 92 CLR 157.

38 *Harris v Caladine* (1991) 172 CLR 84.

breach the doctrine of separation of powers, as the determination of guilt or innocence is unquestionably a judicial function,[39] and has also held unconstitutional legislation which conferred upon an administrative officer the power to make a conclusive legal determination as to the status of a refugee, and which ousted the jurisdiction of the courts to inquire into that determination.[40] On the other hand, it has been held that legislation which directs the courts to convict a person for an offence once the elements of the offence have been proved, or impose a mandatory sentence once guilt has been ascertained, does not breach the doctrine.[41] The judicial function is left unimpaired in those circumstances, because it is still up to the court to determine the issue of guilt or innocence.

The second dimension of separation of powers, namely that courts exercising the judicial power of the Commonwealth should not be vested with non-judicial functions, is less easily explained than the first. Whereas the rationale for the rule that judicial power should not be given to non-judicial bodies is obvious, it is less easy to understand why the courts should have interpreted the doctrine of separation of powers as prohibiting courts being vested with non-judicial functions. In *R v Kirby ex parte Boilermakers' Society of Australia* (*Boilermakers'* case),[42] the High Court held that it was impermissible to vest the Commonwealth Court of Conciliation and Arbitration with the power to settle industrial disputes through conciliation and arbitration, and to set working conditions. The reasoning of the court was based solely on what they said was an implication of the text of s 71, namely that the preservation of the independence of the judiciary required that it be interpreted as being exhaustive in relation to the powers of the judicial branch, and that by stating that the courts were vested with judicial power, it had been intended to exclude any other type of power being vested in them. However, it is by no means obvious that s 71 requires a restrictive rather than a permissive reading. Nevertheless, commentators generally explain the *Boilermakers'* decision on the ground that by making it, the High Court was seeking to protect the judiciary from becoming vested with powers which would involve them in policy-making, and would attract the political controversy that inevitably follows thereupon.[43] The accuracy of this analysis is borne out when one considers the further history of the doctrine: the High Court recognised exceptions to the rule, holding that it was permissible for the courts to exercise such non-judicial powers as were incidental to the judicial function[44] (a good example of which might be the courts' power to make rules of court), and for Parliament to repose non-judicial powers in judges in their individual capacity, as distinct from reposing such powers in the courts as an institution – the so-called *persona designata* exception.[45] However, in *Grollo v Palmer*[46] the *persona designata* rule was itself held to be subject to the exception that judges, even acting

39 *Polyukhovich v Commonwealth* (1991) 172 CLR 501.

40 *Chu Kheng Lim v Minister for Immigration, Local Government and Ethnic Affairs* (1992) 176 CLR 1. The legislation in *Lim* was unconstitutional not only because it attempted to make a determination as to a legal question binding on the courts (thus breaching s 71), but also because it infringed the constitutional guarantee of reviewability of the acts of a Commonwealth servant (thus breaching s 75(v)).

41 *Wynbyne v Marshall* (1997) 117 NTR 11.

42 (1956) 94 CLR 254.

43 Joseph and Castan, 2001, 133–34.

44 *R v Joske ex parte Shop Distributive and Allied Employees' Association* (1976) 135 CLR 194.

45 *Hilton v Wells* (1985) 157 CLR 57.

46 (1995) 184 CLR 348.

in their individual capacity, could not be vested with functions which were incompatible with their judicial role, and which would lead to a diminution of public confidence in the courts. A good example of such incompatibility was provided by the case of *Wilson v Minister for Aboriginal and Torres Strait Islander Affairs*,[47] in which it was held to be incompatible with the judicial functions of a Federal Court judge to vest him with the task of reporting to the Minister on the question of whether areas should be classified as Aboriginal heritage sites. It was held that this breached the doctrine of separation of powers because it involved the judge giving political advice to the executive, and that this gave rise to a risk of a diminution of public confidence in the judiciary through the involvement of that branch in political matters.

The doctrine of separation of the judicial power has arisen wholly from an inference from the Constitution by the courts, and has been developed through case-law. Should the doctrine be included in the text of the Constitution? The parameters of the doctrine, including the question of precisely what a judicial function is (which has led to its own not inconsiderable body of case-law),[48] are dependant upon the facts of the specific cases that come before the courts. For that reason, it is best that the scope of the doctrine be left to the courts to determine, rather than being spelled out in the constitution (if, indeed, that were possible). However, given the importance of the doctrine, it might nevertheless be advisable at least to mention it in the Constitution, if only to give textual recognition to the difference in the relationship between the judiciary and the other branches, as compared with that between the executive and the legislature. I would, therefore, recommend that in conferring the judicial power of the Commonwealth on the courts, the Constitution state that this was done 'in accordance with the doctrine of separation of powers'. The new Constitution would then simply be read in light of the case-law that had developed under the old.

3.2.3 Separation of powers and State Courts

Although State Supreme Courts have, in interpreting State Constitutions, found that the doctrine of separation of powers is not contained within those documents,[49] the High Court's decision in *Kable v Director of Public Prosecutions (New South Wales)*[50] has made the federal doctrine applicable to State courts in certain circumstances. In *Kable* the court invalidated a New South Wales statute which provided that the New South Wales Supreme Court could impose a six-month detention order on Mr Kable (the only person to whom the legislation applied) after the expiry of a prison sentence he was serving, if presented with evidence that he posed a threat to public safety. The High Court held that the system of courts exercising federal jurisdiction in Australia was an integrated whole,

47 (1996) 189 CLR 1.

48 See, eg, *Huddart Parker and Co Ltd v Moorehead* (1909) 8 CLR 330; *R v Spicer ex parte Australian Builders' Labourers' Federation* (1957) 100 CLR 277; *R v Commonwealth Industrial Court ex parte Amalgamated Engineering Union* (1960) 103 CLR 368; *British Imperial Oil Co Ltd v Federal Commissioner of Taxation* (1925) 35 CLR 422; *Shell Co of Australia v Federal Commissioner of Taxation* [1931] AC 245; *R v Trade Practice Tribunal ex parte Tasmanian Breweries* (1970) 123 CLR 361; *Precision Data Holdings v Wills* (1991) 173 CLR 167; *Brandy v Human Rights and Equal Opportunities Commission* (1995) 183 CLR 245.

49 See, eg, *Clyne v East* (1967) 68 SR (NSW) 385; *Gilbertson v South Australia* [1978] AC 772; and *Mabo v Queensland (No 1)* (1988) 166 CLR 186.

50 (1996) 189 CLR 51.

and that public confidence in courts exercising such jurisdiction required that such courts (be they Commonwealth or State) be perceived to be independent of the other branches of government, and that they not be vested with functions that were incompatible with the judicial function. In the instant case, the vesting of the State court with the power to detain people for what they might do, rather than because of what they had done, was incompatible with the judicial function, and would diminish public confidence in the State court's exercise of federal jurisdiction. In addition, Gaudron,[51] McHugh[52] and Gummow JJ[53] stated that since the existence of State Supreme Courts is presumed by the Commonwealth Constitution, it would be unconstitutional for the States to abolish those courts.

While the rationale for the *Kable* decision was entirely laudable, the ambit of the decision leaves something to be desired. The decision applies to State courts only when they are exercising federal jurisdiction which, in *Kable* itself, was taken to have occurred simply because counsel raised the very argument about the integrity of the judicial system. It seems somewhat precarious to build a constitutional doctrine on the foundation of the arbitrary circumstance of whether counsel happens to raise a federal question. Against this, however, it could be argued that it will usually be readily apparent whether a State court is dealing with matters of federal jurisdiction. A more fundamental criticism of *Kable* is that its *ratio* was unduly narrow: as stated, the *Kable* rule forbids only the vesting of non-judicial functions, or functions incompatible with the judicial function, in State courts exercising federal jurisdiction. As Joseph and Castan point out, there is nothing in the rule preventing judicial functions being vested in non-judicial bodies by the States.[54] In the case of Mr Kable, this would have meant that there would have been nothing to prevent the State from enacting a law giving the executive the power to detain people, rather than vesting that power in the courts. However, this problem would be addressed if Australia had a Bill of Rights, because executive detention would undoubtedly amount to a *prima facie* breach of the right to individual liberty. Finally, the *Kable* decision can be criticised on the ground that the court did not widen it to include other aspects of separation of powers – for example, that State court judges exercising federal jurisdiction should enjoy security of tenure, and should be protected against reductions in remuneration. Although the judiciary in the States do, as a matter of fact, enjoy such protections,[55] albeit generally not in the form of entrenched constitutional provisions,[56] the principle that the integrity of the judicial system exercising federal jurisdiction should be protected surely requires that these and other barriers to interference with the courts be included within the ambit of the *Kable* principle. Although it is to be hoped that, as some commentators have suggested, future case-law developments might see the *Kable* principle extended along those lines,[57] it would clearly be preferable if all State Constitutions were to contain entrenched provisions relating to

51 *Ibid*,103.

52 *Ibid*, 110.

53 *Ibid*, 140.

54 Joseph and Castan, 2001, 146.

55 Campbell and Lee, 2001, 101–02.

56 Although note that the Constitution Act 1975 (Vic), s 85; and the Constitution Act 1902 (NSW), ss 53–55 do entrench judicial security of tenure.

57 Johnston and Hardcastle, 1998, 240–41.

security of tenure and remuneration, similar to those contained in s 72 of the Commonwealth Constitution. However, this is an issue which obviously lies outside the scope of this book.

3.3 SELECTION OF THE JUDICIARY

Given the criticism (noted at the beginning of this chapter) to which judges are subject when discharging the jurisdiction currently given them by the Constitution, what would be the likely reaction to an expanded jurisdiction, of the type that would be needed in order to give effect to a Bill of Rights? How would an expansion of the grounds upon which the courts can review legislation be received? Does such an increase in the powers of the judiciary require that a more open process be adopted in relation to the selection of judges?

An objection frequently raised to vesting the courts with a broader range of grounds for overturning laws enacted by Parliament is that 'unelected judges' should not have the power to the will of the people as expressed through Parliament.

As a preliminary point, it is worth reminding ourselves that the precise purpose of having a Bill of Rights is to act as a check on the popular will – such a document is designed for the specific purpose of protecting a core set of rights from unreasonable infringement even by, or perhaps especially by, the majority. The next point is that the judiciary never can be a 'democratic' branch of government, either in its operation (as that would undermine its independence) or in its selection. As an expert profession, it is no more possible for the judiciary to be representative of the population as a whole than it would for the country's neuro-surgeons. Nevertheless, even accepting the fact that who can be selected for judicial office is restricted to the pool of those who have the necessary qualifications and experience, there are ways in which the selection process can be made more representative, in the sense that a greater range of parties participates in the process than at the moment. This should, in turn, lead to a bench whose members reflect a wider range of backgrounds and experiences, even while still being drawn from the pool of the sufficiently qualified.

At present, s 72 of the Commonwealth Constitution simply states that Federal and High Court judges are appointed by the Governor-General in Council – in other words, by the Governor-General acting on the advice of the government. In practice, what happens when an appointment needs to be made is that the Commonwealth Attorney-General advises the Governor-General whom to appoint. Section 7 of the High Court of Australia Act 1979 (Cth) requires that High Court appointees must have been a federal, State or Territory judge, or must have been a legal practitioner for at least five years. In determining who to select, s 6 of the Act requires the Commonwealth Attorney-General to 'consult with' the Attorneys-General of the States. What this means in practice, and the extent to which State Attorneys-General are able to influence the choice, is unclear. Indeed, it is the very lack of transparency about the process and the obvious opportunity it gives to the cabinet to select incumbents whose views it thinks will mirror its own, that exposes it to adverse public comment.

The very real dangers posed to constitutionalism by leaving the choice of judges solely to the government of the day have been illustrated by events that have occurred in several Commonwealth countries. In South Africa, during the 1950s, after the Appellate Division struck down as unconstitutional the government's attempts to remove coloured voters from the voters' roll as part of its apartheid policies,[58] the government responded by increasing the number of Appellate Division judges from five to 11, and by packing the newly constituted court with judges whom the government thought were likely to be supportive of its ideology.[59] More recently, an even more blatant example of court-packing has occurred in Zimbabwe where, faced with the Supreme Court's rejection of legislation depriving landowners due process where land was expropriated, the government initially ignored the court's rulings, and then forced the Chief Justice to take leave for the remainder of his term, appointing government sympathizers to the bench, who subsequently ruled in favour of the land expropriation measures.[60] The cynicism of this tactic illustrates how, even if the independence of sitting judges is respected in a formal sense, the ability of a government which has a free hand in the appointment process to fill the bench with its sympathizers has the potential to undermine the entire constitutional order.

The unwisdom of having the executive branch in sole control over judicial appointment is an observation that could be made in respect of any constitutional system. However, an additional reason against such a practice comes into play in a federal system such as ours. Surely, given that one of the functions of the courts is to decide disputes between the federal government on the one hand, and the State governments on the other, federal principles require that the appointment of judges not be under the control of any single level of government? Yet in Australia, apart from the non-binding consultation with State Attorneys-General engaged in by the Commonwealth Attorney-General, the States have no input into the selection of judges. Thus, I would argue that in devising a new method by which to select judges, we should ensure that whatever body is charged with that task is under the control neither of the Commonwealth nor of the State governments.

There is no doubt that calls to reform the method of selecting judges would become all the louder were the jurisdiction of the courts to be increased through the inclusion of a justiciable Bill of Rights in the Constitution. How, then, could the selection process be reformed in order to increase public confidence that selections are apolitical, and also result in the selection of candidates who not only have the relevant legal qualifications and experience but, as far as possible, reflect the concerns of society?

3.4 SELECTION METHODS

Proposals for reform of the selection method of judges are not new. The possible options have bee most recently summarised in Australia in a discussion paper published by the

58 See *Harris v Minister of the Interior* 1952 (2) SA 428 (A); and *Minister of the Interior v Harris* 1952 (4) SA 769 (A).

59 Appellate Division Quorum Act 1955.

60 See David Blair, 'Zimbabwe head judge to retire early' (2001) *The Sunday Telegraph*, 4 March, 29; and Richard Williams, 'Seizure of white farms will go on' (2001) *Birmingham Post*, 4 October, 13.

Tasmanian Department of Justice.[61] As the Tasmanian Discussion Paper states, the defects of the current system of unfettered appointment by Attorneys-General is that it is not transparent, there are no published criteria against which qualified persons are assessed, and the process has an unsatisfactory outcome in that women and minorities are under-represented on the bench.[62] Is there a method of judicial selection which would overcome this problem?

3.4.1 Popular election and legislative approval

Essentially, there are three major alternatives available should we replace the current system of judicial selection. The first, that of popular election,[63] is not one to which I propose devoting much discussion. States in the United States of America use popular elections in varying ways as part of the judicial appointment process: in some States judges are elected on an openly party-political basis. This clearly politicises the judiciary in a way which is not consistent with the norms of judicial non-partisanship expected in Australia. In other States, once selected by the executive, and after serving on the bench for a period, judges are required to seek confirmation of their appointment through popular election. This politicises the judiciary in a different way, creating as it does an inevitable tension between deciding cases in a way that will ensure electoral popularity, and deciding them in accordance with the dictates of justice under law. The second alternative is the procedure adopted for the appointment of judges to the United States Supreme Court, which requires confirmation of nominees by the Senate.[64] Recent cases have shown that hearings by the Senate Judiciary Committee have degenerated into attempts to obtain nominees' views on specific legal questions, such as abortion and affirmative action, on which it is clearly inappropriate for potential judicial officers to commit themselves in the abstract, and that the Committee frequently votes on political lines in determining whether to recommend approval to the Senate.[65] The approvals process frequently becomes an inquiry not into whether the nominee has the relevant qualifications for the position and has acted legally and ethically throughout their career, but rather on their political and philosophical beliefs. Clearly, the partisan nature of the body charged with the approval process makes it inappropriate for the selection of judges.

3.4.2 A Judicial Commission

The third alternative, which is far more promising, and which has been adopted by many Commonwealth countries, is the establishment of a Judicial Commission to advise

61 Tasmanian Department of Justice and Industrial Relations, 1999. Although this paper addresses judicial appointments from the perspective of a State Supreme Court, its discussion is relevant to federal judicial appointments because the same procedure of unfettered appointment by the relevant Attorney-General is used at both levels.

62 *Ibid.*

63 *Ibid.*

64 Constitution of the United States 1787, Art II, s 2.

65 See, eg, Bronner, 1989.

government on judicial appointments.[66] The idea received support from Chief Justice Barwick in 1977,[67] and was also canvassed by the 1988 Constitutional Commission, although that body went no further than to say that the establishment of a Judicial Commission was a matter of governmental and legislative policy, upon which it did not wish to comment.[68] The idea did, however, receive positive support from the Australian Law Reform Commission, which recommended the establishment of bodies applying published criteria for judicial appointment to advise Attorneys-General on appointments.[69] Support for the concept has also been expressed by academic writers.[70]

Before discussing the composition and powers of a Judicial Commission, it is necessary to address the issue of 'representivity'. In South Africa, the need for the bench to be representative of society is made explicit in s 174(2) of the Constitution, which states that:

> The need for the judiciary to reflect broadly the racial and gender composition of South Africa must be considered when judicial officers are appointed.

In contrast to this is the argument that appointments should be based on merit alone, and that seeking to make the bench more representative is incompatible with a bench elected on the basis of merit. This view is held by retired High Court Justice Sir Harry Gibbs, who said:[71]

> A more recent heresy is that the bench should be representative and that the sex of the aspirant or perhaps his or her ethnic origin should be a more important consideration than merit.

However, a key issue to bear in mind when discussing 'representivity' of the bench is that what is being argued for is not that the bench mirror the composition of society (as has already been stated, plainly it cannot), but rather that when selecting from the pool of qualified candidates, the concept of 'merit' should be expanded to include not just the current criteria of qualifications and experience in legal practice, but also the experience that is conferred by virtue of belonging to social groups other than that of white males, who form by far the majority of holders of judicial office. This argument is well put by Barnett, who notes[72] 'the failure of traditional concepts of "merit" to encompass the unique experiences of women and those from different ethnic (and economic) backgrounds', that 'differences based on gender and ethnic origin provide unique experiences invaluable to the bench', and that 'What they [women and ethnic minority candidates] have, that white male aspirants do not, is experience of being female or of non-Anglo-Celtic origin'. Similarly, former Chief Justice Sir Anthony Mason stated that:[73]

---

66 See, eg, the Judicial Commission established under the Constitution of the Republic of South Africa Act 1996, ss 174 and 178.

67 Barwick, 1977, 494.

68 Constitutional Commission, 1988, 6.174.

69 ALRC, 1994, 9.3.

70 Barnett, 2000; and Harris, 1993.

71 Sir Harry Gibbs, speech delivered at the opening of the Supreme Court Library's Rare Books Room, Supreme Court of Queensland, Brisbane, 11 February 2000, www.courts.qld.gov.au/publications/articles/speeches/gibbs110200.htm.

72 Barnett, 2000, 148.

73 Mason, 1997, 7.

> A candidate having the requisite professional skills and other qualities who would enhance the representative character of the judiciary should be preferred to another candidate who simply has the requisite skills and other qualities.

All that is being said, then, is that, assuming a pool of candidates who meet the minimum requirements relating to legal practice, the criteria that should be taken into account when selecting judges from among them should be broadened so as to take account of the *whole life experience* of the candidates and, by looking at the candidate as a whole, to ensure that the bench reflects society as broadly as is possible, given that pool. Existing criteria going to make up 'merit' would, therefore, not be abandoned, they would simply be supplemented. Furthermore, I would argue that it is not only experience born of gender and ethnicity that should be taken into account by a Judicial Commission – every aspect of candidates' social identity and experiences would be relevant.

3.4.3 Composition of a Judicial Commission

Given that a Judicial Commission is designed to ensure that the bench is as representative as possible, it follows that the Commission itself should be reflective of a wide range of groups and interests. Most Commissions draw their membership from a range of groups who, apart from having a legitimate interest in the composition of the bench (which, at the most fundamental level, all citizens do), are drawn from sectors of society whose qualifications and experience make it appropriate that they be involved in the selection process.[74]

Obviously the number of ways in which the composition of a Judicial Commission can be arranged is infinite. However, I would argue that an important issue in determining the composition of a Commission is the ratio between those who are appointed by the executive branch of government and those who are not, as well as the ratio between representatives of the executive, the bench and the profession one the one hand, and those who sit on the Commission in order to represent the interest of diversity on the other.

Clearly, if the ratio of executive government appointees to others favours the former, then only the form, and not the substance, of the process would have been changed, as ultimately the government will be doing through representatives what it does directly for itself when judicial appointments lie within the gift of the Attorney-General. For the same reason, it is also important to ensure that members of a Commission who supposedly represent other interest groups are, in fact, appointed by those groups, rather than by the executive branch of government. As a general principle, then, the ratio between government and non-government appointees should favour the latter.[75] In similar vein, it is also important, so far as the balance between representatives of the executive, judiciary

74 Under the South African Constitution, s 178, the Judicial Service Commission in that country consists of 10 parliamentarians (three of whom must be from opposition parties in the lower house), four representatives of the legal profession, four Presidential appointees, three representatives of the judiciary, a government Minister, an academic lawyer, and a judge and premier of a province if the appointment is to a provincial bench.

75 See Meagher, 1993, who criticises the method used in Canada, where each province has an informal Judicial Appointments Advisory Committee consisting of nine members (six non-lawyers, two practising lawyers and one judge) all of whom, with the exception of the judge, are appointed by the executive.

and legal profession on the one hand, and those serving the interest of diversity on the other is concerned, that the first three categories taken together should not outnumber the last, because, otherwise, the Commission would be dominated by the same establishment groups who have traditionally been consulted in relation to judicial appointments.

Who should represent the public interest in ensuring representivity of the bench? There are, conceivably, a wide range of organisations representing women, ethnic minorities, victims' rights groups, the disabled, *et cetera*, who could claim a right to be heard. However, from a practical point of view, there is a limit to how many representatives can sit on a Commission before its size makes it unwieldy. In addition, reference to groups in a Constitution requires that such groups be identifiable either by having statutory existence, or by means of some mechanism to ensure that representatives will be able to be identified and the constitutional provisions always remain operational.

Taking all the above into account, the composition of the Judicial Commission could be as follows: a Commonwealth Minister, the Chief Justice of the High Court, a representative of the legal profession elected from among its number by the Board of the Law Council of Australia, a representative elected from their number by the heads of Australian University Law Schools offering a law degree recognised by a State or Territory Supreme Court, a female member of the House of Representatives selected by the leader of the opposition, and a representative elected from their number by those Senators who are elected by voters on the Indigenous Votes Roll (discussed at 6.5.2, below). Such a Judicial Commission would have only one government appointee, and an equal number of representatives from government, the judiciary and legal profession on the one hand, and from groups which traditionally have not participated in the selection process on the other. Moreover, there would be a guarantee of at least one female and one indigenous member.

3.4.4 Powers of a Judicial Commission

Where the real power to appoint judges is located would largely depend upon whether a Judicial Commission had decision-making or merely advisory powers. In New Zealand, the Judicial Appointments Unit presents a short list with no less than two names to the Attorney-General, who then makes the final decision.[76] In South Africa, when vacancies occur on the Constitutional Court, the Judicial Service Commission must give the President three names more than the number of vacancies that need to be filled, and the President then selects appointees from that list. If the President declines to appoint from that list, he must give reasons why the nominees are unacceptable, whereupon the Commission presents him with a supplementary list from which he must finally choose.[77] In the case of all other courts, the President must appoint incumbents on the advice of the Commission.[78]

Assuming that one wishes to leave some discretion vested in the Attorney-General, there would be nothing objectionable in requiring the Commission to submit two names

76 Tasmanian Department of Justice and Industrial Relations, 1999.

77 Republic of South Africa Constitution Act 1996, s 174(4).

78 *Ibid*, s 174(6).

for each vacancy for the Attorney-General to select from. Having two names would also have the advantage that Commission deliberations might be made easier than they would be if only one name was to be submitted.

3.4.5 Commission procedures and judicial appointment criteria

An important factor contributing to transparency in the judicial appointments process is that vacancies to the bench should be advertised in the press, so that potential appointees are aware of the opportunity for appointment. This would represent an important change from current practice, which simply involves the Attorney-General determining who to consider. Applications should be processed in accordance with normal employment practice – in other words, with applicants being asked to address the appointment criteria in writing, and then appear before the Commission for an interview. It should be made clear to candidates that the Commission had the right to make confidential inquiries about them, a practice which would substantially increase the chances of discovering conduct which would diminish the standing of the courts if discovered only after a candidate had been appointed.

Much work has been done, even in jurisdictions which still have appointment by the Attorney-General, in relation to framing criteria against which potential appointees can be assessed. Certainly, having a legal qualification and admission as a practitioner are obvious basic requirements, as is experience of legal practice. Hitherto, judges of the federal courts and the High Court have been selected almost exclusively from the ranks of judges or senior barristers. However, as was stated in a discussion paper by Michael Lavarch, then Commonwealth Attorney-General,[79] it may well be that other types of legal practice, such as that undertaken by solicitors, academics and government lawyers, also provide suitable experience for judicial appointment.[80] At a minimum, the Constitution should specify that in order to be eligible for appointment to the bench, a person must be a judge of an Australian court or be admitted as a legal practitioner.

So far as criteria relating to personal attributes are concerned, the following qualities, most of which were identified in the Tasmanian Attorney-General's Discussion Paper, would seem to serve the objective of obtaining diversity and social responsiveness in the bench: intellectual and analytical ability relevant to judicial-decision-making, integrity, fairness, breadth of life experience and understanding of people and society.[81] These need not be specified in the Constitution – all that would be necessary would be phraseology indicating that the Commission was to consider a broad range of factors in order to promote a bench that reflected society.

79 Lavarch, 1993, 16.

80 The Commonwealth Attorney-General's Discussion Paper is discussed in the Tasmanian Department of Justice Discussion Paper.

81 Tasmanian Department of Justice and Industrial Relations, 1999.

3.5 THE STRUCTURE AND JURISDICTION OF THE COURTS

The federal structure of the Constitution is reflected in the structure of the courts. There are two parallel systems, State and federal, running side-by side, with the High Court at the apex forming an ultimate court of appeal for both systems. Should we have a single system of courts in Australia? This issue was canvassed in the 1988 report of the Constitutional Commission, which came to the conclusion that the creation of an integrated system of courts was unnecessary,[82] and that such problems as existed could be solved through the enactment of cross-vesting legislation.[83] As the Commission pointed out, the creation of an integrated national system of courts would necessarily mean that that system would fall under the legislative power of the Commonwealth.[84] Clearly, this would arouse opposition on the part of the States. Furthermore, given that one of the advantages of federalism is that it permits regional variation in the law, a natural corollary of this is that each jurisdiction should have its own system of courts, applying its own law. Discussion of reform of the structure of the courts in this chapter will, therefore, be based on the assumption that separate State judicial systems would continue to exist, and that such changes as are recommended would relate only to the judicial power of the Commonwealth.

Before discussing constitutional reform of the allocation of the judicial power of the Commonwealth, mention must be made of the publication in 2001 of the Australian Law Reform Commission (ALRC) *Report on the Judicial Power of the Commonwealth*,[85] hereafter in this chapter referred to as the 'ALRC report'. Although confined to a review of the Judiciary Act 1903 (Cth) and related legislation, the report contains a wealth of information relating to the allocation of judicial power within the Commonwealth, and suggests numerous reforms that could be undertaken in order to enhance the efficiency of the system, and to clarify uncertainties in the law. The terms of reference under which the report was drafted required the commissioners to work subject to existing constitutional limitations on the exercise of the judicial power of the Commonwealth. Thus, in making recommendations for reform, the commissioners were unable to suggest changes to the Constitution.[86] This book is not thus constrained, and so, although reference will be made to the Commission's work, the departure point of this section is a re-examination of the judicial power *de novo*. Perhaps of more relevance to this book is the 1988 *Final Report of the Constitutional Commission*[87] which, as part of its overall brief of advising on Constitutional reform, made several recommendations relating to the judicial power of the Commonwealth. Although published nearly a decade and a half ago, much of that report remains relevant today, and many of its recommendations are adopted in this chapter.

82 Constitutional Commission, 1988, 6.1–6.27.

83 *Ibid*, 6.29–6.38.

84 *Ibid*, 6.18.

85 ALRC, 2001. References to specific parts of the report are to chapter and paragraph numbers.

86 *Ibid*, 1.12.

87 Constitutional Commission, 1988.

3.5.1 A court system for the Commonwealth

Perhaps the simplest way to address this complicated area of the law is to decide what functions the Commonwealth courts need to perform and then to structure a court system accordingly. Stripped to its essentials, the Constitution must, at least, provide for the following: original jurisdiction to resolve cases arising under federal law, a process for appeals arising from cases decided under original jurisdiction, and a process for hearing appeals from State Supreme Courts. It is also advisable for the Constitution to provide for the cross-vesting of jurisdiction between State and federal courts.

For sake of convenience, ss 75–77 of the Constitution which allocate the original jurisdiction of the Commonwealth courts are reproduced here:

75 In all matters–

(i) arising under any treaty;

(ii) affecting consuls or other representatives of other countries;

(iii) in which the Commonwealth or a person suing or being sued on behalf of the Commonwealth, is a party;

(iv) between States, or between residents of different States, or between a State and a resident of another State;

(v) in which a writ of Mandamus or prohibition or an injunction is sought against an officer of the Commonwealth,

the High Court shall have original jurisdiction

76 The Parliament may make laws conferring original jurisdiction on the High Court in any matter–

(i) arising under this Constitution, or involving its interpretation;

(ii) arising under any laws made by the Parliament;

(iii) of Admiralty and maritime jurisdiction;

(iv) relating to the same subject-matter claimed under the laws of different States.

77 With respect to any of the matters mentioned in the last two sections the Parliament may make laws–

(i) defining the jurisdiction of any federal court other than the High Court;

(ii) defining the extent to which the jurisdiction of any federal court shall be exclusive of that which belongs to or is invested in the courts of the States;

(iii) investing any court of a State with federal jurisdiction.

3.5.2 Original jurisdiction of Commonwealth courts

Turning first to original jurisdiction, one needs to determine which are the matters over which the Commonwealth courts should have a constitutionally entrenched jurisdiction (in other words, a jurisdiction that cannot be removed by Parliament), which Commonwealth court (High Court or Federal Court) should be vested with that entrenched original jurisdiction, and then which jurisdiction should be left to be determined by Parliament.

3.5.2.1 Actions between the Commonwealth, States and Territories

A necessary feature of the judicial branch in a federal system is that it must provide a forum for the resolution of disputes between the component parts of the federation. Such jurisdiction is currently exercised by the High Court, as the court sitting at the apex of the judicial system, by virtue of s 75(iii) (which covers cases in which the Commonwealth is a party), as read with s 75(iv) (which deals with actions between States). I would suggest that original jurisdiction in such inter-governmental litigation should remain as part of the original jurisdiction conferred on the High Court by the Constitution. Such cases as arise under these sections generally involve matters of constitutional importance which require speedy resolution, and so it is appropriate that they should be able to be dealt with by the High Court, rather than by the Federal Court. One improvement that could usefully be made is the combination of ss 75(iii) and (iv) into a single section (which would have the benefit of distinguishing the s 75(iii) jurisdiction from that contained in s 75(v) as is discussed below), and the extension of the coverage of the section to the Territories, as recommended by the 1988 Constitutional Commission.[88]

3.5.2.2 Matters arising under the Constitution or involving its interpretation

A strange feature of the 1901 Constitution is its omission from the entrenched s 75 jurisdiction of the High Court of matters arising under the Constitution or involving its interpretation. Such matters appear in s 76(i) as ones in relation to which Parliament may confer original jurisdiction on the High Court. Parliament has, in fact, done this by means of s 30(a) of the Judiciary Act 1903 (Cth). However, as was noted by the 1988 Constitutional Commission, it would be preferable that this important element of federal jurisdiction should be constitutionally entrenched.[89] Furthermore, as was also recommended by the Commission, that that jurisdiction should continue to form part of the original jurisdiction of the High Court, in order to provide a swift avenue for the resolution of constitutional disputes.[90] This would not mean that all cases involving constitutional matters would have to commence in the High Court, only that that avenue would always be available, but no doubt would most often be used (as at present) where some important constitutional provision is at stake. As is noted below, cross-vesting legislation could still be used to vest other courts with jurisdiction to hear constitutional cases.

3.5.2.3 Review of the actions of a Commonwealth officer

The subjection of the government to the rule of law is a fundamental aspect of the doctrine of constitutionalism. From this, it follows that there must be a constitutional guarantee of a remedy where the government has infringed the law. Currently, such jurisdiction is vested in the High Court by virtue of s 75(v). Such jurisdiction may also be said to be conferred by virtue of s 75(iii), although that subsection has generally been understood as conferring original jurisdiction on the High Court to hear matters in which

88 *Ibid*, 6.54–56.

89 *Ibid*, 6.51-3.

90 *Ibid*.

the Commonwealth as a polity is a party to a case (for example, an action between the Commonwealth and a State), as distinct from the situation where a remedy is being sought against a particular officer of the Commonwealth.[91]

The existence of this jurisdiction provides protection from privative clauses which might otherwise be used by Parliament to oust judicial review of executive action. As stated in Chapter 2, the Bill of Rights in the proposed new Australian Constitution would contain an express right to judicial review of administrative action, at Commonwealth, State and Territory level, in which case a provision such as s 75(v) would, strictly speaking, be redundant. However, even if the right to judicial review was included in the Bill of Rights, it would still be necessary for those sections of the Constitution which dealt with the jurisdiction of the Commonwealth courts to indicate under which court's original jurisdiction such matters fell. It is questionable whether original jurisdiction in respect of these matters should be vested in the High Court rather than the Federal Court. The impact upon the High Court's business of the foreclosure by ss 474 and 475 of the Migration Act 1958 (Cth) of most avenues to review the actions of the Commonwealth and its officers arising under that Act was noted by Gleeson CJ and McHugh J in *Abebe v Commonwealth*,[92] where the Justices stated that:

> In the present case, the Parliament has chosen to restrict severely the jurisdiction of the Federal Court to review the legality of decisions of the Refugee Review Tribunal. That restriction may have significant consequences for this Court because it must inevitably force or at all events invite applicants for refugee status to invoke the constitutionally entrenched s 75(v) jurisdiction of this Court. The effect on the business of this Court is certain to be serious.

The adverse impact that even a small increase in s 75(v) cases would have on the workload of the High Court was also adverted to by the Law Council of Australia in its submission to the Senate Legal and Constitutional Legislation Committee, when the Committee reviewed the Migration Legislation Amendment (Judicial Review) Bill 1998.[93] Although the increase in workload arising under the Migration Act 1958 (Cth) arises out of a unique set of circumstances, the example does, nevertheless, illustrate the inappropriateness of the highest court in the land being the first point of call for ordinary matters arising under judicial review of administrative action. I would, therefore, argue that such review should fall within the jurisdiction of the Federal Court, which should be given explicit recognition as a constitutional court, rather than just being a creature of statute as at present.

Finally, in accordance with the recommendations of the 1988 Constitutional Commission,[94] the s 75(v) jurisdiction should be extended to include all types of remedies against Commonwealth officers, as there appears to be no good reason to confine its scope to the named remedies of mandamus, prohibition and injunction.

91 Lane, 1995, 269–70.

92 (1999) 197 CLR 510, 534.

93 Law Council of Australia, Submission J037, 6 April 2001.

94 Constitutional Commission, 1988, 6.61.

3.5.2.4 *Matters arising under laws made by Parliament*

Jurisdiction over cases arising out of laws made by Parliament must obviously vest in a Commonwealth court. At the moment, s 76(ii) empowers Parliament to vest such jurisdiction in whichever court it pleases, and original jurisdiction in most of these matters vests in the Federal Court (which now incorporates the former Industrial Relations Court as the Industrial Relations Division of the Federal Court), the Federal Magistrates Court and the Family Court, by virtue of a variety of Commonwealth statutes. The only significant original jurisdiction vesting in the High Court is jurisdiction in relation to trials for indictable offences against the laws of the Commonwealth, which derives from s 30(b) of the Judiciary Act 1903 (Cth), and the jurisdiction relating to electoral matters arising under ss 354 and 376 of the Commonwealth Electoral Act 1918 (Cth).

The vesting of original jurisdiction in criminal matters in the High Court has little to recommend it. The jurisdiction in relation to electoral matters is different. Section 354 of the Commonwealth Electoral Act confers jurisdiction on the High Court in relation to the validity of elections or returns. The section also provides that such matters may be referred by the High Court to the Federal Court for trial. Under s 376 of the Act, Parliament may refer to the High Court disputes relating to the qualifications of members of either house of Parliament, or relating to vacancies in either house. In so doing, Parliament waives its privilege in respect of such matters. There is much to be said for the crucial matters of the validity of elections, and of the eligibility of members of Parliament to sit in either house, to be de-politicised by having them fall within the jurisdiction of the courts as a matter of law, rather than it being left to Parliament to determine whether the courts will hear such matters. There is also much to be said for having such matters dealt with as expeditiously as possible, and thus of continuing to vest jurisdiction in relation to them in the High Court, as was recommended by the ALRC.[95] I would further argue that because of the importance of these cases, jurisdiction in relation to electoral matters should be removed from the Commonwealth Electoral Act and be put into the Constitution as part of the High Court's entrenched original jurisdiction.

So far as the remainder of the jurisdiction in relation to matters arising under laws made by Parliament is concerned (including original jurisdiction in relation to criminal matters), it would be best if the High Court was protected from an increase in its workload caused by the conferral of a wide original jurisdiction under s 76(ii). Such concerns led the 1988 Constitutional Commission to state that, in its opinion, original jurisdiction should be vested in the High Court only in rare cases.[96] This point was echoed by the ALRC in its 2001 report.[97] For this reason, it would be preferable if the Constitution stated that Parliament could vest jurisdiction in relation to such matters in the Federal Court, rather than in the High Court. As noted above, this is what happens now in any event because, with the exception of the original criminal jurisdiction and the electoral jurisdiction, Parliament has, in fact, not burdened the High Court with additional original jurisdiction. It would, however, be preferable if the law as stated in the Constitution were to reflect this *de facto* position.

95 ALRC, 2001, 3.51.

96 Constitutional Commission Final Report, 6.50.

97 ALRC, 2001, 2.84, 3.20.

3.5.2.5 Other original jurisdiction

Brief mention should be made of other areas of original jurisdiction conferred upon Commonwealth courts by the Constitution. The ALRC commented upon the odd assortment of jurisdictions conferred upon the High Court under s 75.[98] In particular, one should note s 75(i) (matters arising under treaties), s 75(ii) (matters affecting foreign representatives), s 75(iv) (in so far as it relates to the so-called 'diversity jurisdiction' involving matters between residents of different States), s 76(iii) (admiralty and maritime jurisdiction) and s 76(iv) (matters covered by the laws of different States), which the ALRC identified as being inappropriate or little utilised.[99]

The jurisdiction conferred by ss 75(i) and (ii) and s 76(iii) deal with matters that should more properly be subject to allocation by Parliament to the Federal Court, in accordance with the discussion in 3.5.2.4, above. The s 75(iv) diversity jurisdiction arose from a belief that State courts might be biased against the inhabitants of other States, a fear that has not been realised.[100] For this reason, that aspect of federal jurisdiction can also safely be removed from the Constitution. The purpose of the s 76(iv) jurisdiction is opaque, although some commentators suggest that it overlaps to some extent with s 75(iii), and might also refer to matters involving conflicts of law between States.[101] To the extent that the subsection relates to diversity jurisdiction, the same goes for it as for s 75(iii), while jurisdiction over any matters potentially governed by the laws of different States can continue to be governed by conflict of law rules as applied by State courts. Thus, s 76(iv) should be removed from the Constitution.

3.5.2.6 Cross-vesting of jurisdiction

The efficient operation of the judicial system in a federation must take account of the fact that cases often involve matters of both State and Commonwealth law. Massive inconvenience would be caused to litigants if different aspects of the same dispute had to be heard in different courts. For this reason, Parliament enacted the Jurisdiction of Courts (Cross-vesting) Act 1987 (Cth), which conferred jurisdiction over matters which lay within the jurisdiction of the Federal Court and the Family Court on State and Territory Supreme Courts, and purported to accept jurisdiction conferred by the State Parliaments upon the federal courts. In addition, s 39 as read with s 38 of the Judiciary Act 1903 (Cth), confers on State Courts the High Court's s 76 jurisdiction (most importantly, the jurisdiction to hear constitutional matters and matters arising under laws made by the federal Parliament), while jurisdiction on jurisdiction to hear constitutional matters was conferred on the Federal Court by s 39B(1A)(b) of that Act.

In *Re Wakim ex parte McNally*[102] the High Court invalidated that part of the cross-vesting legislation which purported to confer upon the Federal Court jurisdiction received from the States, on the ground that s 77 of the Constitution restricted the Commonwealth Parliament to conferring jurisdiction on the Federal Court only in respect

98 *Ibid*, 2.6–7.

99 *Ibid*, 8–9.

100 *Ibid*, 2.8. Also see the discussion of s 75(iv) in Constitutional Commission, 1988, 6.74.

101 Joseph and Castan, 2001, 128–29.

102 (1999) 198 CLR 511.

of matters listed in ss 75 and 76, in which matters arising under State law were not included. The vesting of federal jurisdiction in State courts was, however, explicitly permitted by s 77(iii). This decision created uncertainty regarding the effect of judgments hitherto granted by the Federal Court in respect of matters arising under State law, and raised the prospect of different parts of the same matter having to be pursued in different courts. The first problem was solved by the enactment by the States of legislation to the effect that previous decisions by the Federal Court on matters arising under State law were to be given the force of decisions of the relevant State Supreme Court.[103] The second problem was solved by the States acting under s 51(xxxvii) of the Constitution to refer to the Commonwealth Parliament the power (which would thus be independent of s 77) to legislate to confer jurisdiction in State matters on the Federal Court.[104]

Clearly, an *ad hoc* solution of the type reached after the *Wakim* case is not ideal. For this reason, a new Constitution should include a provision permitting both the conferral of jurisdiction in respect of matters arising under Commonwealth law on State and Territory courts, and the acceptance by the Commonwealth of such jurisdiction as might be conferred on the federal courts by State Parliaments.

3.5.3 Appellate jurisdiction

Currently, the appellate jurisdiction of the High Court is governed by s 73 of the Constitution. In summary, s 73 confers appellate jurisdiction on the High Court in respect of matters which were heard by the High Court in its original jurisdiction, matters heard by other federal courts, and in respect of matters heard by State Supreme Courts. This jurisdiction is subject to exception by Parliament, save only that s 73 requires that there to be some avenue for appeals from courts from which there was a right of appeal to the Privy Council at the establishment of the Commonwealth – in other words, there must always be some provision (albeit one limited by a requirement to obtain leave), from State Supreme Courts to the High Court.[105] Parliament may also confer appellate jurisdiction on any other federal courts it creates.[106]

In practice, Parliament has significantly limited the appellate jurisdiction of the High Court, primarily by means of the requirement that appellants obtain special leave of the Court itself. Such a requirement is imposed by s 35 of the Judiciary Act 1903 (Cth) in respect of appeals from State Supreme Courts, and by s 33 of the Federal Court of Australia Act (1976) in respect of appeals from that court. Appeals from decisions of the High Court sitting in its original jurisdiction are not so restricted, except with regard to interlocutory decisions.[107] The criteria governing consideration of special leave applications are contained in s 35A of the Judiciary Act 1903 (Cth), and essentially focus on the degree of importance of the legal questions raised by the case.

103 The validity of such State legislation was upheld by the High Court in *Residual Assco Group Ltd v Spalvins* (2000) 201 CLR 213.

104 See, eg, the Corporations (Commonwealth Powers) Act 2001 (NSW).

105 Lane, 1995, 244–45.

106 See the discussion of this issue and the authorities cited in ALRC, 2001, 16.15.

107 Judiciary Act 1903 (Cth), s 34(2).

As the law stands, the appellate jurisdiction of the High Court is at the mercy of parliaments, both Commonwealth and State: the Commonwealth Parliament could, with the exception of appeals from State Supreme Courts, completely block appeals to the High Court, while the State Parliaments could similarly restrict the jurisdiction of their Supreme Courts to prevent those courts from being seized of cases which the States did not want subject to appeal to the High Court.[108] For this reason, there would be merit in adopting the recommendation of the 1988 Constitutional Commission, that the Constitution should state that whereas Parliament can make the appellate jurisdiction of the High Court subject to exceptions and regulations, it should always be possible for an appeal to be made from any court (Commonwealth, State or Territory) to the High Court with the special leave of the latter.[109] It would be open to the High Court to deny such leave where the applicant had not exhausted such avenues of appeal which are open to him or her, but the capacity of the High Court to grant such leave where avenues have been closed by the legislature would ensure that the supervision of the Court could not be avoided.

3.5.4 Territory courts

One of the most vexed areas of constitutional interpretation has been that involving the nature of the judicial power exercised by courts which the Commonwealth Parliament created in the Territories. The origin of the problem lies in the High Court's decision in *R v Bernasconi*,[110] in which it was held that the s 122 Territories power was to be read separately from the rest of the Constitution, and that, therefore, Chapter III did not apply to courts established by Parliament for the Territories. Thus, Territory courts do not exercise the judicial power of the Commonwealth as referred to in s 71,[111] and so judicial officers in the Territories are not covered by the protection relating to tenure and remuneration contained in s 72.[112] This situation is clearly anomalous, and a new Constitution should provide that courts established by the Commonwealth in the Territories are federal courts exercising federal jurisdiction, from which it would follow that the constitutional provisions governing the independence of the judiciary and case-law establishing the doctrine of separation of powers would apply in equal measure to Territory courts, as they do to all other courts exercising the judicial power of the Commonwealth.

108 While some of the Justices in *Kable v Director of Public Prosecutions* (NSW) (1996) 189 CLR 51 held that the Commonwealth Constitution presumes the existence of State Supreme Courts (see Gaudron J, 103 and McHugh J, 110), and a majority (Gaudron, McHugh, Gummow and Toohey JJ) held that State Parliaments could not invest State Supreme Courts with functions that were incompatible with the exercise by those courts of federal jurisdiction, there is nothing in *Kable* to suggest that the States are required to allow appeals to their Supreme Courts.

109 Constitutional Commission, 1988, 6.99–101.

110 (1915) 19 CLR 629.

111 *Capital TV and Appliances Pty Ltd v Falconer* (1971) 125 CLR 591, *R v Governor, Goulburn Correctional Centre ex parte Eastman* (1999) 200 CLR 322.

112 *Spratt v Hermes* (1965) 114 CLR 226.

3.5.5 Summary

To summarise the foregoing, a reformed Commonwealth court structure would see the High Court vested with original jurisdiction in respect of actions between the Commonwealth, States and Territories, matters arising under the Constitution or involving its interpretation, and matters relating to the validity of elections or returns, the qualifications of members of Parliament and parliamentary vacancies. The Federal Court would have original jurisdiction in relation to the review of the actions of a Commonwealth officer. Parliament would have the power to vest additional jurisdiction in the Federal Court in relation to matters arising under laws made by the Commonwealth Parliament. Parliament would be able to vest any of the original jurisdiction of the federal courts on State courts, and would in addition be able to legislate to confer upon federal courts any jurisdiction which State Parliaments wished to confer on them. The High Court would have an appellate jurisdiction to hear appeals from any court in Australia in respect of which it grants special leave, and would otherwise enjoy such appellate jurisdiction from its own original jurisdiction, from other federal courts, and from State courts, as the Commonwealth Parliament chose to confer on it.

THE EXECUTIVE

4.1 THE EXECUTIVE AND THE LEGISLATURE

One of the hallmarks of the Commonwealth Constitution (as well as those of the States and Territories) is that they embody the system of parliamentary government, also sometimes referred to as 'responsible government' or 'the Westminster system'. The term 'responsible government' highlights the fact that the executive is answerable to the legislature, and relies on the support of the legislature for its continuation in office. The term 'Westminster system' acknowledges the English origins of the system, and it is, indeed, a notable feature of comparative constitutional law that most countries that were once British colonies continue to base their Constitutions on this system.

The key features of parliamentary government developed in the United Kingdom following the civil war between King and Parliament in the 17th century. In essence, parliamentary government, both in the United Kingdom and in Australia, operates on the assumption that, although as a matter of strict law executive power vests in the Crown absolutely, by convention power is, in reality, exercised on the Crown's behalf by ministers who hold office so long as they retain the confidence of the legislature. The fact that law and convention diverge so fundamentally shows the importance of the latter to the workings of the Constitution – reading the Constitution at face value would give a completely inaccurate picture of how the system works. The role of convention will be explored in more detail in Chapter 10, which deals with the Head of State. Here, it is only necessary to note that the conventions of responsible government, which developed as power shifted from the monarchy to Parliament, are designed to ensure that government is conducted with the support of Members of Parliament, who represent the voters. The operation of the conventions thus ensures that effect is given to the democratic will. Although conventions are of particular importance, some rules are found in statutory form in Australia: Article 4 of the Bill of Rights 1688 (Eng) states that the government cannot collect revenue without parliamentary approval. Section 83 of the Commonwealth Constitution states that revenue can be appropriated (that is, spent) only with the approval of Parliament, while s 64 of the Constitution requires that ministers be members of the legislature, or be elected within three months of appointment. In some countries, the rules relating to parliamentary government, in particular those relating to the appointment and dismissal of the government, are codified in the Constitution and there is no reliance on convention.[1] Thus, it should be understood that the parliamentary system can operate entirely by convention (as in the United Kingdom), partly by convention and partly in accordance with codified rules (as in Australia), or wholly in accordance with codified rules (as in those countries which have opted for codification).

1 For examples, see the discussion on codification in Chapter 10.

The most important characteristic which serves to distinguish the parliamentary system from that which operates in systems which embody complete separation of powers (such as that in the United States), is that under the parliamentary system, the government (by which, in this context, is meant the Prime Minister and other Ministers administering government departments),[2] must be members of Parliament, and rely for their continuation in office on being able to maintain the support of a majority in Parliament. Thus, in contrast with systems which involve separation of powers between all three branches of government, and prohibit an individual from holding office in more than one branch simultaneously, the parliamentary system actually *requires* fusion of powers between the legislature and the upper level of the executive.

The first issue to be addressed in this chapter is whether there would be any merit in changing from the parliamentary system to one embodying separation of powers. This requires an outline of how each system works, and then an examination of their respective advantages and disadvantages. Before doing so, however, it is important to clarify a matter relating to the types of office being discussed and what they are called.

There is a wide variety of parliamentary systems in operation around the world. All share the common feature that the executive (in other words, the head of government and the cabinet) must be members of the legislature, and must retain the support of a majority in the legislature to remain in office. However, within that broad family of Constitutions, there is a diversity of arrangements relating to the offices of Head of State, to which attaches the role of representing the nation as its first citizen, and that of head of government, to which attaches the task of overseeing the day to day running of the country. In some cases, as in the United Kingdom and in Australia, the Head of State function and the head of government function vest in different persons. The Queen is Head of State of both countries, but is represented in Australia by a Governor-General. In both countries, the head of government is the Prime Minister. The rules for appointing the Prime Minister are implemented by the Queen in the United Kingdom, and on the Queen's behalf by the Governor-General in Australia.

In some countries, however, particularly in Commonwealth countries which have severed their links with the British monarchy, a President performs exactly the same role as does the Queen in the United Kingdom or the Governor-General in Australia, with real power being exercised by a Prime Minister as head of government. In other words, the term 'President' does not necessarily refer to a person who exercises day to day control over the government, still less does it necessarily refer to a person who holds the office of head of government in a system embodying separation of powers, as in the United States. It can simply be a person who performs the same limited figurehead role as does the King or Queen in a constitutional monarchy. A good example of this is India, where the President acts on the advice of the Council of Ministers (in other words, the cabinet),[3]

2 As distinct from the professional public servants who staff the departments of government and whose appointments are not subject to termination on political grounds.

3 Constitution of India 1949, Art 74.

who are responsible to the lower house of Parliament.[4] The same relationships exist between President, Prime Minister and Parliament in Dominica,[5] Malta[6] and Mauritius.[7]

In contrast to those countries just discussed, which separate the roles of Head of State and head of government, some Commonwealth countries have combined both functions into one office, usually that of a President (although there is no reason why the office should not be called that of Prime Minister). A good example of such a country is South Africa.[8] In such countries, the same person exercises both the ceremonial and political roles. The rules governing the appointment of the President or Prime Minister are not administered by an individual (since there is no separate Head of State who appoints the head of government), but are, instead, found in the Constitution, and operate automatically.

As has already been stated, in contrast to parliamentary systems where the head of government must retain the support of the legislature to remain in office, systems embodying separation of powers provide for a head of government to be directly elected by the people separately from the legislature. Such office holders are almost universally given the title of President. It is due to this fact that discussion of constitutional reform in Australia has become confused, with some people believing that the severance of links with the Crown, and the replacement of the Queen and Governor-General with a President, would also mean the replacement of parliamentary government with one based on separation of powers. As shown in the preceding paragraphs, that is not the case. The discussion in this, and the preceding paragraphs, serves to highlight that the important characteristic of an office is its function, and not the nomenclature attaching to it. For sake of clarity, I will use the terms 'Head of State' and 'head of government' when discussing the parliamentary system, out of recognition of the fact that a wide range of titles is used around the world to refer to each, and will also assume that we are dealing with a system of parliamentary government such as that in Australia, where the two offices vest in different people. I will use the term 'President' when discussing the system based on separation of powers, in recognition of the fact that, in such systems, the roles of Head of State and head of government are almost invariably fused under the title of President.

4.1.1 Parliamentary government

The system of parliamentary government operates as follows: after an election, the government is formed, either through the choice of the head of government by a figurehead Head of State, or through automatic operation of the Constitution. In Australia, the choice is made by the Governor-General, who acts on behalf of the Queen as Head of State, in accordance with unwritten conventions, and the head of government

4 *Ibid*, Art 75(3).

5 Constitution of Dominica 1978, Arts 59, 60 and 63.

6 Constitution of Malta 1964, Arts 76, 79, 80 and 81.

7 Constitution of Mauritius 1968, Arts 57, 59 and 60.

8 Constitution of the Republic of South Africa 1996, ss 85, 86, 91 and 92. For a discussion of the interaction between the President and Parliament in South Africa, see Gloppen, 1997, 216–17.

is called the Prime Minister. Irrespective of whether the head of government in a parliamentary system is chosen by the Head of State in accordance with unwritten conventions, or by operation of written rules contained in the Constitution (whether operated by a Head of State or operating automatically), the rule regarding the appointment is the same, namely that to be chosen as head of government one must be able to command a majority in the legislature. Thus, the head of government will be the leader of the party, or coalition of parties, which has a majority in the legislature. Sometimes the person who heads the government does not command an absolute majority, and yet is able to win a confidence vote for his or her minority government, because members of the legislature outside his or her party or coalition undertake to support him or her in votes of confidence.

The head of government then chooses ministers to head the departments of government. The head of government will usually select some of those ministers to form a cabinet, which meets regularly to set government policy. The government remains in office only so long as it retains the confidence of the legislature. Loss of confidence occurs when the government loses a motion of no-confidence tabled by it or by the opposition, fails to secure parliamentary approval for continuing finance of the government (taxation and appropriations bills), or fails to secure passage of important legislation which it (the government) has stated will be taken as indicative of confidence. A head of government who no longer has the confidence of Parliament must either resign, allowing the Head of State to appoint whoever can command a majority as head of government, or must ask the Head of State to dissolve the legislature and call an election, in the hope that the voters will return a legislature that does support the government. However, if the voters return a legislature that does not support the head of government, that person would then certainly have to resign. The head of government has the strategically important power of being able to dissolve the legislature (or, in the case of Australia, in the absence of the conditions satisfying the requirements for a s 57 double dissolution, at least the House of Representatives).

As originally conceived, the parliamentary system was meant to subordinate the executive to the legislature, and the history of the system in the United Kingdom from the late 17th to the early 19th centuries was one of a constant struggle by ministries to retain the support of the House of Commons. Party groupings were loose, and indeed many MPs had no party affiliation. Methods of electing MPs varied throughout the country, and many constituencies were so-called 'rotten' or 'pocket' boroughs, controlled by local landowners. The fluid nature of politics in the House of Commons, lubricated by widespread bribery and corruption, made it by no means certain that a ministry which had a majority after an election would long retain it. In other words, the legislature exercised real control over the executive, and a ministry could not afford to alienate the Commons. However, the combination of electoral reform, and the increasing power of party machines during the 19th century, reversed this relationship. By the 20th century, the individual MP relied on the support of the party for selection as a candidate and for funding and, in return, submitted to the discipline of the party whips in Parliament. The reality now is that the likelihood of a government being toppled by rebellious backbench MPs of its own party is extremely slight, and that the leaders of the party in the cabinet control the remainder of the caucus (the party's representation in Parliament). There is, therefore, a divergence between the 18th century theory (that Parliament controls the cabinet) and 21st century reality (the cabinet controls the caucus, and the caucus of the largest party or coalition controls Parliament).

Such control as there is by Parliament over the executive takes the form of probing by the opposition during question time and, in the case of Australia, on those occasions when the government lacks a majority in the Senate, the use of inquiries by that chamber. In addition, extra-parliamentary surveillance by the press also assists in exposing governmental maladministration or wrongdoing. Given the strength of party discipline, it is only when a government has been sufficiently embarrassed by the exposure of wrongdoing by one of its members, and that person has become a political liability, that he or she is asked to resign. Apart from these political controls, the government is also subject to legal responsibility for the acts of the executive. This raises issues relating to the extent to which the Crown still enjoys immunity, which is addressed later in this chapter.

4.1.2 Separation of the executive and legislature

Systems based on full separation of powers operate differently from parliamentary systems. There are many variations within this broad family, but the classic example is that which operates in the United States, upon which this description is based. The roles of Head of State and head of government are fused in the office of President, who is elected separately from the legislature (which in the United States is called Congress, and consists of the House of Representatives and Senate). Both the President and the legislature are elected for fixed terms. The President chooses his cabinet, whose members then cannot simultaneously be members of the legislature. The President does not have the capacity to dissolve the legislature, nor are the President and cabinet dependant upon the support of the legislature to remain in office. Both the President, who wields executive power, and the Congress, which wields legislative power, enjoy equal political legitimacy, as both have been directly elected by the people.

Looked at on their own, these rules suggest that the system is one in which the branches of government operate in isolation from, and with no influence over, each other; however, the separation of powers is complemented by a system of checks and balances, which permits and regulates the interaction of the branches with each other: the executive has an influence over the legislative branch, in that legislation passed by Congress must receive the assent of the President. However, if the President refuses assent (in other words, vetoes the legislation), that refusal may be overridden by two-third majorities in both Houses of Congress. Although the President is able to choose his or her cabinet, the legislative branch influences that process, in that such choices are subject to confirmation by the Senate. Similarly, the President has influence over the judicial branch through his power to nominate federal and Supreme Court justices, but here, too, the legislature is involved, in that such nominations are subject to approval by the Senate. In addition, treaties signed by the President must be ratified by the Senate. The Supreme Court has the power to review acts of the executive, and legislation passed by Congress, and may declare these unconstitutional. Finally, Congress has the power to impeach members of the executive and Supreme Court Justices. A common misapprehension is that the phrase 'checks and balances' means that the system uses a system of checks (in other words, restraints) to create a balance (in the sense of an equilibrium) between the three branches.

However, this is to misinterpret the word 'balance' as used in the Constitution, where it was meant to refer to a balance in the sense of a mechanical device which operates to restrain the operation of another (such as the balance which prevents a watch wheel from turning at excessive speed). In other words, 'check' and 'balance' essentially mean the same thing, and it is inaccurate to believe that the US system was meant to create an equilibrium between the three branches.[9] In fact, as the above examination of the interaction between the branches reveals, most analysts agree that it is the Congress which enjoys the greatest power, being able to override the Presidential veto, and having ultimate control over the personnel of the other branches through its powers of confirmation and impeachment.[10]

4.1.3 An evaluation

Which of the systems, parliamentary government or separation of powers, is to be preferred? Both systems involve some interaction between the executive and legislative branches. Both attempt to subject the executive to control by the legislature. However, although one might think that the dependence of a Prime Minister in a parliamentary system on legislative support causes the executive to be weaker than that in the separation of powers system, where the President is not dependant upon the support of Congress, the reverse seems to be true.

As we have seen, under the parliamentary system as originally conceived in the 17th and 18th centuries, the executive was very much the creature of the legislature, and had to struggle both to retain office and to secure from Parliament the funding it required to operate the government. Approval for funding was frequently made contingent by Parliament on an undertaking from the government to approve Bills proposed by the Commons. Now, however, the executive uses the discipline of the party machine to control the legislative programme, and to ensure that members of the majority party in the legislature vote for it. There is no doubt that a government in Australia will be able to obtain the assent of the House of Representatives for its taxation and appropriation measures.[11] The cabinet effectively controls how Parliament's time is allocated and what legislation reaches the floor. A Prime Minister can use party machinery to whip MPs into line to a far greater extent than it is possible for the President of the United States to discipline members of Congress, given the weaker party system in that country. Indeed, the strength of federal sentiment in the United States, where members of Congress are truly seen by their constituents as representatives of their particular State, means that attempts by Presidents to intimidate members of Congress are politically risky for the former. The President does have available to him a range of inducements which he can use to obtain the support of members of Congress, such as the offer of personal support during congressional re-election campaigns, and allocation of federal spending to projects in particular congressional districts, but his financial dependence on Congress as a whole limits the extent to which the latter can be used. Congress controls its own programme, and it requires skillful negotiation by the President to secure congressional funding for

9 Lutz, 1998, 92–94, 162–64.

10 *Ibid*, 157–58.

11 The issue of the Senate's power to block supply is discussed in Chapter 9.

the programmes he wishes to implement, part of which often involves the *quid pro quo* of the President's assent for legislation that he does not favour. Certainly, a President must adopt a far more circumspect attitude to Congress than a Prime Minister needs to adopt to Parliament. The power of Congress, and the potential for deadlock with the President, has been demonstrated on numerous occasions during the history of the United States, as an example of which one could cite the failure in 1994 of President Clinton to achieve health care reform in the face of strong lobbying of Congress by medical practitioners and medical insurers. Even more dramatic were the federal government shut-downs in November 1995 and again from December 1995 to January 1996, when the President and Congress failed to reach agreement on a budget for the upcoming fiscal year by midnight of the last day for which the government had authorization to spend money.

So far as the government's tenure in office is concerned, the strength of the party system in countries using the parliamentary system means that the theoretical vulnerability of a Prime Minister to a vote of no-confidence in Parliament is more imaginary than real. In fact, Prime Ministers and cabinets are almost as immune from displacement from office by the legislature as are Presidents in the United States. Of course, in systems based on separation of powers, the executive is, as a matter of law, not dependant on the legislature for continuation in office. However, notwithstanding the President's independent tenure of office, the success or failure of a presidency depends in large measure on the ability of the President to negotiate with Congress in the ways outlined in the previous paragraph, and so, while Congress cannot unseat an administration, it can, nevertheless, significantly influence its effectiveness, and thus the President cannot afford to treat it in a cavalier manner.

The extent to which the executive is subject to scrutiny by the legislature provides another interesting area for comparison between the two systems. In both parliamentary and separation of powers systems, there are well established traditions in terms of which Bills are referred to committees of the legislature for discussion. In a parliamentary system, the government of the day will always have a majority on the committees of the House to which it is responsible, and, to that extent, the fate of Bills is a foregone conclusion. The same is not true in a bicameral system, if structured in such a way as to make it unlikely that the second chamber is controlled by the government, as is the case in Australia. In such circumstances, review by committees will be an effective restraint on the legislature. The same remarks are equally true in so far as the role of committees investigating governmental malfeasance is concerned. Parliamentary Committees have long discharged the function of calling both public servants and Ministers to account – a function which was recently confirmed as lying within the scope of the powers of legislative chambers under the law of parliamentary privilege in Australia, in the cases of *Egan v Willis*[12] and *Egan v Chadwick*.[13] The likelihood of a committee being able to make adverse findings against a Minister are, of course, increased if the committee is drawn from a chamber not controlled by the government. The power of committees is even greater in the United States. As already stated, the party system is much weaker in that country, and so the executive cannot automatically assume favourable treatment from the committees, even if the committees are those of a chamber controlled by the same party

12 (1998) 195 CLR 424.

13 (1999) 46 NSWLR 563.

as the President. In any event, however, separation of powers means that it is exceptional for the same party to control the presidency and both Houses of Congress, so there is always likely to be at least one house whose committees will be controlled by a party hostile to the President. Finally, in this regard, it must be remembered that in the United States the President has to accept the supervisory role by Congress in respect of the confirmation of executive and judicial appointments, and the ratification of treaties.

On balance, it seems that the parliamentary system of so-called 'responsible government' has evolved in a way where the executive is more powerful than it is in systems based on separation of powers. Does this mean that, in the interests of greater control of the executive by the legislature, we should move to separation of powers? On the one hand, parliamentary government has the great advantage that in an election voters are able to elect both a legislature and a government simultaneously, and therefore to know that since the government must by definition have a majority in the House of Representatives, it will be able to enact the legislative programme upon which it fights the election. This avoids the situation which commonly occurs in systems based on separation of powers, where the presidency and one or both houses of the legislature are controlled by different parties, and deadlock arises between them. But if the parliamentary system is worthy of retention because of the connection it makes between government and legislature, how can one avoid the potential dangers of a parliamentary executive which is subject to few political restraints? In Australia, the effect of a powerful executive dominating the chamber to which it is only theoretically responsible is mitigated, to some extent, by the existence of a Senate, in which the government rarely has a majority, and with which it has, therefore, to negotiate to enact legislation, and whose committees it does not control. Although, in Chapter 9, I argue that democratic principle, and the theory upon which responsible government is based, require that the power of the Senate be reduced to that of delaying ordinary legislation for a year, and that it be removed altogether in the case of money bills, the supervisory function of Senate committees would continue unaltered. Senate Committees would still exercise an inquisitorial role, and the Senate could penalise a government's non-co-operation with Senate Committees by threatening to delay the government's legislation. More importantly, however, as was argued in Chapter 2, the inclusion of a Bill of Rights in the Constitution would provide the most effective restraint against the government's abuse of power. A Bill of Rights would have the advantage that, in contrast to restraints imposed by the Senate, which are exercised only if opposition parties find it politically expedient to activate them, restraints deriving from a Bill of Rights are based on principle, and would be able to be activated by any litigant who believed that governmental conduct or legislation had breached his or her rights. Finally, as is argued in Chapter 8, restraint would also be placed on governments if the electoral system for the House of Representatives was changed to one based on proportional representation. In such circumstances, single-party government would be the exception, rather than the norm, and although the government would still have to have a majority in the House of Representatives, that majority would, in all likelihood, be drawn from two or three parties. This would lead to a more consultative and consensual style of government. The dictatorial model of the inner circle of a single-party government, directing its caucus on how to vote, would be replaced by the need for the cabinet to ensure that the parties making up the coalition were happy with the direction it was taking. Although revolutionary on the face of it, electoral reform would, in fact, move the parliamentary system back towards its 17th and 18th century origins, where the opinions of the parties upon which it relied for support actually mattered to the government, and where, in the words of Lijphart, we would have 'a less dominant executive and a more assertive legislature'.[14]

In conclusion, then, I would argue that the great strength of the parliamentary system – that by fusing executive and legislature, it allows voters to choose an effective government – militates against replacing it with a system based on separation of powers, and that such dangers as can arise from executive dominance over the legislature can be adequately safeguarded against by means of the other constitutional devices discussed above.

4.2 EXECUTIVE POWER

An important issue not addressed with sufficient clarity by the Constitution is precisely what the content of the executive power of the Commonwealth is. Section 61 of the Constitution, which confers executive power on the Queen, does not elaborate on what 'the executive power of the Commonwealth' means, other than to say that it 'extends to the execution and maintenance of this Constitution, and of the laws of the Commonwealth'. While it is obvious from the phraseology of s 61 that the executive power certainly includes the enforcement of laws enacted by Parliament under the enumerated powers, the question of what other powers the Crown possesses has been left to the courts to determine.

Under general principles of constitutional law, the powers of the Crown derive from two sources: powers conferred by statute, and powers deriving from the common law. The common law powers are usually referred to as the 'prerogative powers' of the Crown. It should, however, be noted that some dispute exists in relation to this nomenclature: according to Dicey, the prerogative consists of all common law of the Crown.[15] However, according to Blackstone,[16] whose views were adopted by Wade,[17] the prerogative refers only to those powers which, by their nature, are those which the Crown alone can exercise – in other words, the exclusive powers of the Crown. Thus, to take an example, Dicey would have said that the power of the Crown to enter into contracts is part of the prerogative simply because it does not derive from statute, whereas Blackstone would have said that it is not a prerogative power, because an ordinary person can enter into contracts, just as the Crown does. In this article, the broader (Diceyan) definition of the prerogative, adopted by the House of Lords in *Council for Civil Service Unions v Minister of the Civil Service*[18] is used, and a distinction is drawn within the broad class of prerogatives between the exclusive prerogatives of the Crown, and those which it shares in common with ordinary persons (the latter sometimes being referred to as the personal prerogatives).

14 Lijphart, 1999, 61.
15 Dicey, 1959, 425.
16 Blackstone, 1979, Vol 1, 232.
17 Wade, 1988, 241–42.
18 [1984] 3 All ER 935 (HL).

The existence of common law powers of the Crown in Australia has been recognised in the context of a number of cases in which the so-called 'nationhood power'[19] has been identified by the High Court.[20] In the latest of these cases, *Davis v Commonwealth*,[21] the court reaffirmed that the s 61 executive power of the Commonwealth included such prerogatives as were necessary to sustain and advance the nation, examples of which included national security, national symbols and the promotion of the sciences and arts. In addition, a majority (Wilson, Dawson, Toohey and Brennan JJ) held that the s 61 executive power, as read with the s 51(xxxix) incidental legislative power, vested Parliament with the capacity to enact laws in furtherance of that executive power – an interesting reversal of the more usual role, which is that the legislature delegates power to the executive. Some Justices (Mason CJ and Deane and Gaurdron JJ) went further by holding that there was also an implied legislative power to do with nationhood matters independent of ss 61 and 51(xxxix). It is thus clear that the Commonwealth executive does enjoy the prerogative powers of the Crown, although this is, of course, subject to the limitation that these are only those aspects of the prerogative which are required for the exercise of functions of the Commonwealth as the federal government, and that the remainder of the prerogative power vests in the executives of the States.[22]

4.3 CROWN LIABILITY

As noted above, one of the ways in which the executive is controlled is through its liability for breaches of the law. One dimension of this liability is judicial review in accordance with the principles of administrative law. Constitutional protection of that right exists in the form of s 75(v), which currently forms part of the original jurisdiction of the High Court, but which I have argued should be made part of a new entrenched jurisdiction of the Federal Court (see Chapter 3).

Liability can also attach to the executive under the law of contract, and vicariously for the acts of its servants under the law of torts. However, this area of the law is complicated by uncertainty as to the extent to which the common law doctrine of Crown immunity operates in Australia. This was one of the major issues addressed by the Australian Law Reform Commission in its *Report on the Judicial Power of the Commonwealth*[23] (hereafter referred to as the 'ALRC report'). Frequent reference will be made in this section to that report and the useful reform proposals it contains.

Under the common law, various prerogatives – powers, privileges and immunities – attach to the Crown. For our purposes, the most important of these are the immunities enjoyed by the Crown. These are that the Crown is presumed to be immune from the operation of statute law, and that the Crown is immune from civil suit (in other words, from liability in tort and in contract). In addition, the Crown enjoys numerous procedural

19 For a particularly clear exposition of this area, see Joseph and Castan, 2001, 108–17.

20 See, eg, *Australian Communist Party v Commonwealth* (1951) 83 CLR 1; *Barton v Commonwealth* (1974) 131 CLR 477; and *Victoria v Commonwealth and Hayden* (*AAP* case) (1975) 134 CLR 338.

21 (1988) 166 CLR 79.

22 Joseph and Castan, 2001, 117.

23 ALRC, 2001. References to specific parts of the report are to chapter and paragraph numbers.

immunities, such as not being subject to coercive orders in relation to discovery, interrogatories and costs, not being subject to temporary or permanent injunctions or orders of specific performance, and being immune from execution of judgments against its property. The issue of Crown immunity is complicated in a federation by the question of to what extent one level of government (State or Commonwealth) can bind another – often referred to as the 'inter-governmental immunity' issue. Is legislation enacted by the Commonwealth Parliament binding upon the governments of the States, and, conversely, are the State Parliaments able to bind the Commonwealth?

Many of immunities of the Crown have been whittled away by legislation which overrides the common law. Thus, s 56 of the Judiciary Act 1903 (Cth) permits the bringing of actions against the Crown in tort and in contract, while s 64 of that Act states that in an action to which the Commonwealth or a State is a party, the rights of the parties shall be the same as if the action was between subject and subject. Similar legislation establishing Crown liability exists in the case of all the States and Territories. So far as immunity from statute is concerned, here, too, it is common for Parliament to override immunity by including a provision in the legislation expressly stating that the Crown is bound. Furthermore, in *Bropho v Western Australia*[24] it was held that even in the absence of such a statement, the courts will interpret statutes as binding the Crown where the policy underlying the Act indicates that the Crown should be bound. But despite the progress that has been made in this area, the ALRC report noted that significant uncertainty plagues the law in this area, in relation to the interpretation of the statutory provisions (particularly in relation to the extent to which they have removed Crown immunity), and the extent to which the Commonwealth and the States are immune from each other's law.[25]

The immunity of the Crown is clearly incompatible with the doctrine of constitutionalism, which requires that the government be subject to the law.[26] However, it is also true that the Crown must act in the interests of the nation as a whole, and it may, therefore, not be appropriate that it should be fettered by the prospect of liability, particularly civil liability, in its furtherance of the national interest.[27] Clearly, the law needs to strike a balance between these competing concerns.

4.3.1 Crown immunity from statute

A key concern expressed by the ALRC in its Report was the lack of certainty surrounding the question of whether the Crown was bound by statute which, in the absence of a specific provision in the statute concerned, is determined on a case by case basis, in accordance with the test in *Bropho*.[28] For this reason, the Commission recommended that the law be changed to provide that, as a general rule, the Commonwealth executive was bound by legislation enacted by the Commonwealth Parliament, in the absence of an

24 (1990) 171 CLR 1.
25 ALRC, 2001, 22.40 and 22.48.
26 *Ibid*, 22.44.
27 *Ibid*, 22.46.
28 *Ibid*, 22.49.

express exemption clause in the legislation concerned.[29] In other words, the former common law presumption would be reversed, and the Commonwealth Parliament would have to justify why the executive was being exempted from the operation of the statute.[30] The Commission recommended that such a change apply to all legislation enacted after the new presumption came into effect, with a sunset clause applying to all existing legislation, to give Parliament the opportunity of deciding whether it wanted that legislation to bind the Crown.[31] Given the importance of this area of law to the doctrine of constitutionalism, it would be beneficial to put express provisions in a new Constitution incorporating these recommendations. Before proceeding to address these issues in detail, it should be noted that the specific rule prohibiting either the Commonwealth or the States from taxing the property of the other, which currently appears in s 114 of the Constitution, would be reproduced in a new Constitution. That provision is discussed at 5.6.3, below. In this part of the book, I discuss what general principles would govern the subjection of one level of government to legislation enacted by another, leaving aside the specific category of legislation covered by s 114.

4.3.1.1 Commonwealth legislation and State executives

Should the Commonwealth Parliament be able to subject State governments and their instrumentalities to Commonwealth legislation? This is the so-called inter-governmental immunities issue, which has produced important case-law. The basic rule of the Constitution is that although, as was held in *Amalgamated Society of Engineers v Adelaide Steamship Co Ltd* (*Engineers* case),[32] the Commonwealth may legislate to bind the States, that capacity is counterbalanced by the 'implied federal principle' found in *Melbourne Corporation v Commonwealth*,[33] that the Commonwealth may not use its power in such a way as to discriminate against the States by placing special burdens or disabilities on them, or by destroying or substantially curtailing their ability to function as autonomous governments. The parameters of the *Melbourne Corporation* principle are vague, and it has served to restrict the legislative power of the Commonwealth in only a few cases.[34] Its status as a rule governing Commonwealth/State relations is addressed in Chapter 5, in the context of a broader discussion of federalism. But so far as the main issue of State government subjection to Commonwealth statutes is concerned, one must agree with the Commission's recommendation that, out of consideration for the federal relationship, State governments should not be presumed subject to enactments of the Commonwealth Parliament, and that it should, instead, be the case that State governments remain presumptively immune from Commonwealth legislation, in the absence of an express

29 *Ibid*, 22.50 and 26.32–33.

30 *Ibid*, 22.57 and 26.34–36.

31 *Ibid*, 26.41.

32 (1920) 28 CLR 129.

33 (1947) 74 CLR 31.

34 *Queensland Electricity Corporation v Commonwealth* (1985) 159 CLR 192; and *Re Australian Education Union ex parte Victoria* (1995) 184 CLR 188. See also *Victoria v Commonwealth* (*Second Uniform Tax* case) (1957) 99 CLR 575 which, although not decided on the basis of the *Melbourne Corporation* case, is clearly analogous to it, in that the court held that it would be an abuse of the s 51(ii) taxation power if the Commonwealth used it to prohibit the States from collecting taxes.

statement by the Commonwealth Parliament that it was to bind State executives.[35] The Commission believed that the Commonwealth Parliament should be required to apply its mind to the question of whether it was appropriate for its legislation to bind the States in each case. I would argue that, as with the proposed rule regarding the subjection of the Commonwealth executive to Commonwealth statutes, this presumption regarding State executives should also appear in the Constitution.

4.3.1.2 State legislation and the Commonwealth executive

Undoubtedly the most complex area of inter-governmental immunities is the question of the extent to which the Commonwealth is subject to State and Territory statute law. In the *Engineers* case, the High Court stated that, just as Commonwealth legislation could apply to the State executives, there was no reason why State law should not apply to the Commonwealth, subject to s 109 override, and to the Commonwealth's dominance in areas over which it is given exclusive legislative capacity. In other words, the *Engineers* doctrine was meant to be reciprocal. This is, indeed, how it was interpreted in *Pirrie v McFarlane*,[36] in which it was held that State legislation bound a Commonwealth servant acting in the course of his duties, and *Uther v Federal Commissioner of Taxation*,[37] in which it was held that State legislation could deprive the Crown of its prerogative rights as privileged creditor.

Unfortunately, the initial clarity of the decision in the *Engineers* case has been lost, due to subsequent decisions which are conflicting and uncertain. In *Commonwealth v Cigamatic Pty Ltd*,[38] a majority of the court over-ruled *Uther*, and found that State company legislation could not override the prerogative rights of the Crown in right of the Commonwealth as preferred creditor. Dixon CJ held that States may not define or regulate the rights and duties of the Crown in right of the Commonwealth *vis-à-vis* its subjects, or interfere in its fiscal or prerogative rights, but that the Commonwealth could be bound by State law when it entered into a transaction (the example he gave being sale of goods) in relation to which the State had made a general law governing those choosing to enter into the transaction. The first limb of Dixon CJ's statement is clearly incompatible with the previously established view that the *Engineers* case conferred reciprocal rights upon the States and Commonwealth to bind each other (subject only to Commonwealth statutory override under s 109). The second limb of the statement introduces an element of uncertainty, because subjection of the Crown in right of the Commonwealth to a State law of general application relating to a particular activity could well affect the rights of the Crown *vis-à-vis* its subjects, or its fiscal or prerogative rights.

Cigamatic was reinterpreted in *Re Residential Tenancies Tribunal of New South Wales v Henderson ex parte Defence Housing Authority*.[39] In this case, the court had to determine whether the Commonwealth Defence Housing Authority was subject to the jurisdiction of a State Tenancies Tribunal in respect of a lease which the Commonwealth had entered into. In finding that the Commonwealth, as landlord, was subject to the Residential

35 ALRC, 2001, 22.53–54, 27.23–31.
36 (1925) 36 CLR 170.
37 (1947) 74 CLR 508.
38 (1962) 108 CLR 372.
39 (1997) 190 CLR 410.

Tenancies Act 1987 (NSW), a majority of the court distinguished between capacities of the Crown in right of the Commonwealth, which the States cannot limit, and the exercise of those capacities which may be subject to State laws of general application, at least in the case of those activities which the Commonwealth carries out in common with other citizens. A majority of the court found (but for different reasons) that because the State was simply regulating leases entered into by all landlords in New South Wales, the legislation it had enacted did not limit the capacities of the Commonwealth, and that the latter was, therefore, subject to the jurisdiction of the Residential Tenancies Tribunal. However, as McHugh J stated, it is difficult to draw a line demarcating 'capacities' from the 'exercise of capacities'.[40] Surely, by subjecting the way in which capacities are exercised to State law, one also limits the capacities themselves? One cannot discern a coherent principle from *Henderson*, in part because there was no line of reasoning commanding a majority of the court. However, an analysis[41] which might serve to explain the case emerges from the distinction made by Dawson, Toohey and Gaudron JJ[42] between exclusive capacities of the Crown (for example, privileges or immunities), and capacities which it exercises in common with its subjects and on an equal footing (for example, entering into contracts).[43] Was this the same distinction as was made by Dicey (discussed at 4.2, above), who considered that the prerogative (that is, common law) powers of the Crown fell into two categories: the exclusive prerogatives which belonged to the Crown alone (for example, declaring war), and the personal prerogatives relating to activities which it shared in common with its subjects (such as entering contracts)? Were the Justices saying that interference by the States with exclusive capacities of the Crown alters the relationship between the Crown and its subjects, and is therefore not permitted, but that where State legislation applies in a non-discriminatory manner to the Commonwealth executive in its exercise of those capacities that it shares with its subjects, there is no reason why the Crown should be immune from State law? Even if this is the correct way to interpret *Henderson*, this analysis is based on the reasoning of a minority of the court, and so cannot be said to be the law in this area. Indeed, uncertainty has continued to prevail, with the High Court, in *Commonwealth v Western Australia*,[44] rejecting the argument that it should apply the test in *Bropho* (discussed above) to find the Commonwealth bound by the Mining Act 1978 (WA), thus apparently contradicting its finding in *Jacobsen v Rogers*[45] that *Bropho* should be used to determine whether State law bound the Commonwealth executive.

There is clearly a need for reform in this area. The issue which needs to be considered is whether, as a matter of principle, the Commonwealth executive should be presumed bound by State legislation or not. The principle of equality between the Commonwealth executive and other persons before the law of the States, indicates that *prima facie* the Commonwealth should be bound. In its report, the Commission thus recommended that the same principle that it recommended in respect of Commonwealth legislation applying to the Commonwealth executive (namely, that the Commonwealth be bound unless it

40 *Ibid*, 454–55.

41 See Joseph and Castan, 2001, 210–12.

42 (1997) 190 CLR 410, 439.

43 For arguments in favour of this analysis see Joseph and Castan, 2001, 210.

44 (1999) 196 CLR 392.

45 (1995) 182 CLR 572.

expressly stated otherwise in the legislation) should also apply in relation to legislation enacted by State and Territory legislatures – in other words, that the Commonwealth be presumed to be subject to State and Territory law.[46] This would remove uncertainty as to areas such as the subjection of the Commonwealth to State and Territory public health and safety, environmental and planning laws.[47] The Commonwealth executive would not be bound if the State Parliament did not make the legislation applicable to its own executive,[48] or stated expressly that it was not to apply to the Commonwealth executive.[49] It was also noted that, should the Commonwealth wish to exempt itself from State or Territory law, it could easily do so by enacting inconsistent legislation, relying on the s 109 inconsistency provision,[50] or, as the Commission recommended, by means of regulation, so that the Commonwealth could act speedily if it became necessary to exempt itself from State legislation and there was insufficient time for an Act to be passed by the Commonwealth Parliament.[51]

In line with the discussions in 3.1 and 3.1.1, above, I would recommend that a new Constitution contain provisions giving effect to these recommendations.

4.3.2 Immunity from suit

So far as the Crown's immunity from suit is concerned, the Commission noted that disputes over the interpretation of the relevant provisions make it uncertain whether immunity has been removed by s 56 of the Judiciary Act 1903 (Cth), s 64 of that Act, or s 75(iii) of the Constitution, and whether those provisions subject the executive to liability in all areas of the law (as opposed to just contracts and torts).[52] The Commission thus recommended that the Judiciary Act be amended to make this clear. By the same token, it would be useful to include in a new Constitution a provision which expressly stated that the Crown was vested with substantive liability under law, and that a person who had any claim against the Commonwealth could bring an action in the courts to pursue that claim, in the same way as if the claim was being brought against a person of full age and capacity.

4.3.2.1 Liability in contract

Assuming that one accepts that, as a matter of general principle, the Crown should be liable in the same way as is the individual, the question then to be addressed is whether there should be any exceptions to this rule. Under the common law, the principle of 'executive necessity' operates to prevent the Crown from being fettered in the exercise of its powers by liability in contract. This principle derives from the case of *Rederiaktiebolaget 'Amphitrite' v The King*,[53] in which the House of Lords denied damages to a Swedish

46 ALRC, 2001, 22.55–56, 28.42.
47 *Ibid*, 28.33–34.
48 *Ibid*, 28.46.
49 *Ibid*, 28.47.
50 *Ibid*, 28.35.
51 *Ibid*, 28.43.
52 *Ibid*, 23.5–11, 25.30–40.
53 [1921] 3 KB 500.

shipping company whose vessel had been detained by the British government during the First World War, notwithstanding prior agreement by the government that it would be permitted to depart. The basis for the court's decision was that the alleged contract was invalid because the Crown could not fetter its discretion to act in the public interest. The *Amphitrite* doctrine was accepted by the High Court as being part of Australian law in *Ansett Transport Industries (Operations) Pty v Commonwealth.*[54] If applied in all its rigour, the doctrine would have the effect of enabling the Crown to avoid contractual liability whenever it chose, since all contracts affect the exercise of executive power, at least to some extent, in that they impose obligations on the Crown.

The scope of the doctrine is, to some extent, limited by the fact that the courts do not automatically accept that the Crown's abandonment of a contract is justified. Indeed, as was shown by the New Zealand case of *The Power Co Ltd v Gore District Council,*[55] where a contract has been entered into by virtue of a statutorily-conferred discretion, the court may find (as it did in that case) that the conferral of the discretion anticipated its use to enter into contracts, and so that, far from fettering the executive, the contract actually *furthered* its policy objectives.[56]The same principle was applied in Australia in *L'Huillier v Victoria.*[57] Furthermore, in practice, the Crown does not take advantage of the doctrine, and, indeed, commonly includes in its contracts termination for convenience clauses, in which it undertakes to pay compensation (albeit in a lesser amount than could be recovered in damages) should it find it necessary to terminate the agreement.[58] (Although it could be argued that, since the executive necessity doctrine is to the effect that contracts binding the Crown are void, the termination for convenience clause could itself be evaded.)[59] In the final analysis, however, the real deterrent to the Crown availing itself of the doctrine is the loss of reputation it would suffer in the commercial world if it did not comply with its contractual undertakings.[60] Furthermore, one can easily conceive of circumstances in which overriding public interest should permit the Crown to be able to evade contractual obligations without being deterred by a potential damages claim. For these reasons, it is probably sufficient to leave the issue of executive necessity as it is – in other words, essentially under the control of the courts in their development of the common law of contract. This exception to the provision on Crown liability which I recommended for inclusion in a new Constitution in paragraph 3.2, above, could be accommodated by including a phrase stating that the liability of the Commonwealth existed 'under law'.

Thus far, we have examined the ability of the executive to evade contractual liability by virtue of the common law. But can the same also be achieved by means of intervention by the legislature? First, it is clear that a contractual provision purporting to bind a Parliament not to legislate in a certain way,[61] or making the validity of legislation

54 (1977) 139 CLR 54.

55 [1997] 1 NZLR 537.

56 In similar vein, see also the decision in *ABC Containerline NV v New Zealand Wool Board* [1980] 1 NZLR 372.

57 [1996] 2 VR 465.

58 Seddon, 1999, 171.

59 *Ibid*, 173.

60 *Ibid*, 169.

61 *Rothmans of Pall Mall (NZ) Ltd v Attorney-General* [1991] 2 NZLR 323.

conditional upon the approval of a contracting party,[62] would be of no effect. It is also established that the legislature may enact legislation overriding a contract,[63] but in that event, the question arises as to whether, if it extinguished contractual rights, the Commonwealth would be required to pay just terms compensation under s 51(xxxi), which would, of course, nullify the advantage it had gained by extinguishing the contract. To the extent that legislative override of a contract would amount to an acquisition of a chose in action, it would seem that the right to compensation would attach in such circumstances, under the precedent of *Geordiadis v Australian and Overseas Telecommunications Corporation*.[64] On the other hand, some argue that extinguishment of contractual rights does not always amount to 'acquisition' within the meaning of s 51(xxxi),[65] and it is certainly the case that, as was noted in Chapter 2, the law in this area is subject to great uncertainty. I would argue that it would be best to leave this area of the law to development by the courts in their interpretation of the law of contract, and the limits of the constitutional right to compensation. Finally, note that, as was discussed in Chapter 2, the right to just terms compensation for deprivation of property would be subject to the reasonable limitations clause contained in the Bill of Rights. There would, therefore, be no irreconcilable tension between that right and the occasional necessity of the Commonwealth to nullify contractual obligations without paying compensation. Everything would simply depend upon whether, in the circumstances of the case, the limitation of the right to compensation was permissible under the reasonable limitations clause.

4.3.2.2 Liability in tort

Assuming that one accepts, as a general principle, the removal of the liability in tort, a plaintiff who alleges the commission of a tortuous act by a servant of the Crown can sue both the servant and the Crown, the former directly, the latter under common law principles of vicarious liability.[66] It is clearly of benefit to the plaintiff to be able to sue the Crown, rather than only the individual servant. In addition, the vicarious liability of the Crown is of obvious benefit to the Crown servant, who would otherwise face the suit alone. In some jurisdictions, legislation immunizes the individual servant from liability, where the servant acted in good faith and not in wilful excess of authority, and preserves the vicarious liability of the Crown.[67] Such is the case in New South Wales,[68] which also prohibits the Crown as employer from seeking indemnity from the employee.[69] The immunization of individual Crown servants from liability has the advantage that it removes the tendency, which would otherwise exist, for Crown servants to shrink from

62 *Commonwealth Aluminium Corporation Pty Ltd v Attorney-General (Qld)* [1976] Qd R 231; *West Lakes Ltd v South Australia* (1980) 25 SASR 389.

63 *Perpetual Executors and Trustees Association of Australia Ltd v Federal Commissioner of Taxation* (1948) 77 CLR 1.

64 (1994) 179 CLR 297.

65 Seddon, 1999, 181–82.

66 Hogg and Monahan, 2000, 114–17.

67 *Ibid*, 191–92.

68 Law Reform (Vicarious Liability) Act 1983 (NSW), s 10.

69 Employees Liability Act 1991 (NSW), s 3.

vigorous discharge of their duties for fear of civil liability.[70] As Hogg and Monahan state, negligence by public servants in the performance of their duties is more appropriately dealt with through internal disciplinary procedures than through exposure to liability.[71]

A particular doctrine of the common law in Australia which limits the tort liability of the Crown is that found in the decision in *Enever v The King*,[72] which is to the effect that the Crown's vicarious liability for the acts of its servants is excluded where the servant is exercising an independent statutory discretion, as distinct from acting under the direct control of the relevant Minister. The *Enever* principle was recently re-affirmed in *Cubillo v Commonwealth*.[73] The principle has been entirely removed from the law in New South Wales by the Law Reform (Vicarious Liability) Act 1983 (NSW), and in respect of police officers in some other Australian jurisdictions, including the Commonwealth.[74] Although, as was noted by the Commission, the Commonwealth does indemnify Ministers and public servants against personal liability,[75] the fact remains that the *Enever* rule stands as an inappropriate and anomalous exception to the principle that the Crown should be liable in the same way as an individual would be. For this reason, the Commission recommended that the *Enever* rule be removed from the law.[76] So far as the Constitutional provision suggested in 3.2 of this chapter, above, is concerned, appropriate drafting would need to be used to ensure that there was no doubt that the Commonwealth was vicariously liable for the acts of its servants, even where the latter were exercising an independent discretion.

A somewhat broader common law rule which serves to limit the tort liability of the Crown is that which draws a distinction between the 'planning' or 'policy' functions of the Crown, and its 'operational' functions.[77] The effect of this rule is to immunise the Crown from liability in tort where the damage caused by a decision it has made is as a result of a policy decision – to take a simple example, a decision to re-route a highway which resulted in economic loss to businesses situated on the old route ought obviously not lead to liability on the part of the Crown, even though the loss was foreseeable and causally connected with the Crown's decision. This rule is very similar to the one operating in the law of contract under the *Amphitrite* principle, in that, like the *Amphritrite* principle, this rule of tort law seeks to prevent the Crown's discretion being fettered by the prospect of civil liability. The rule serves to exclude the courts from determining whether decisions which are policy-laden (for example, because they involved the allocation of scarce resources) were unreasonable or not, a matter which it is obviously for the executive, rather than the judiciary, to decide. By contrast, once the Crown has moved beyond policy to the implementation phase of its operations, which is governed by legal rather than political standards, negligent conduct towards those to whom it owes a duty

70 Hogg and Monahan, 2000, 191.

71 *Ibid*, 127–28.

72 (1906) 3 CLR 969.

73 (2000) 174 ALR 97.

74 See Australian Federal Police Act 1979 (Cth), s 64B(1).

75 ALRC, 2001, 25.14–15.

76 *Ibid*, 25.20.

77 For a comprehensive discussion of the rule, see Hogg and Monahan, 2000, 163–66.

of care should obviously be actionable. The rule has been accepted into Australian law in cases such as *Sutherland Shire Council v Heyman*,[78] where Mason J stated that:[79]

> The distinction between policy and operational factors is not easy to formulate, but the dividing line between them will be observed if we recognise that a public authority is under no duty of care in relation to decisions which involve, or are dictated by, financial, economic, social or political factors or constraints. The budgetary allocations and constraints which they entail in terms of allocations of resources cannot be made the subject of a duty of care. But it may be otherwise when the courts are called upon to apply a standard of care to action or inaction that is merely the product of administrative direction, expert or professional opinion, technical standards or general standards of reasonableness.

The principle has subsequently been re-affirmed in a number of Australian cases.[80] The exclusion of Crown liability in such circumstances is obviously necessary in order to permit the executive that freedom of action which it requires in the formulation of policy. As in the case of the limitations of liability in respect of contract, this area of the law, and, in particular, the distinction between policy and operational decisions, can safely be left to control by the courts.

What of the situation where Parliament legislates to exempt the Crown from vicarious liability? In such circumstances, the plaintiff would be left with an action only against the Crown servant, which might be worth very little, or might be left with no right of action at all where legislation also gives the servant individual immunity. The use of statute law to give immunity to the Crown has been criticised on the ground that it is obviously incompatible with the principle that the Crown should be in a no more advantageous position than any other defendant.[81] One might argue that different considerations apply in the field of tort to those operating in the field of contract – after all, parties choose whether to assume obligations imposed by the law of contract, whereas the obligations imposed by the law of tort apply irrespective of choice. Why should the Commonwealth be able to 'opt out' of tort law by means of statutory immunity? Although one can see the logic of this argument, it must, nevertheless, be recognised that because of the sheer scale of its operations, there may well be instances in which it is necessary to immunise the Crown from liability, or at least to subject it to a ceiling, in order to preserve the fiscus from being drained by claims in tort, to the detriment of the broader public interest. Thus, despite the fact that differential treatment between the Crown and other defendants is not consistent with the doctrine of constitutionalism, it would be inadvisable to put into the Constitution any prohibition against the enactment of legislation by Parliament limiting the tort liability of the Commonwealth. Finally, it should be remembered that in light of the constitutional guarantee of a right to review of the actions of Crown servants (discussed in Chapter 3), there will always be a range of legal actions, other than one for damages, available to someone who is aggrieved by abuse of power by the executive.

---

78 (1985) 157 CLR 424.

79 *Ibid*, 469.

80 See, eg, *Pyrenees Shire Council v Day* (1998) 192 CLR 330; *Crimmins v Stevedoring Industry Finance Committee* (1999) 200 CLR 1; and *Cubillo v Commonwealth* (2000) 174 ALR 97.

81 Hogg and Monahan, 2000, 120–23.

4.3.3 Procedural immunities

So far as immunity from orders during the course of litigation are concerned, the Commission noted that although s 64 of the Judiciary Act 1903 (Cth) has been interpreted by the courts as having removed the Crown's immunity from discovery (except in so far as public interest immunity under the law of evidence is concerned), interrogatories and temporary injunctions, the fact that the section did not explicitly mention the Crown's subjection to remedies required that the law be clarified to reflect that principle.[82] Similarly, in so far as coercive remedies such as injunctions and specific performance were concerned, the Commission recommended that the law make explicit what has been taken as implied by s 64, namely that the Crown is subject to such remedies.[83] The Commission did, however, note that, in certain circumstances, it might be necessary for the Crown to retain the benefit of an immunity, and that, therefore, once the law had been altered to establish the general principle that immunity was removed, Parliament should be given the power to re-confer immunity,[84] subject to the inviolability of those remedies which are necessary for the enforcement of the Constitution itself. The Commission made specific mention of the public interest immunity (which can be pleaded by parties other than the Crown) as an area of immunity which should remain available to the Crown.[85]

The Commission also recommended that State and Territory executives should, in relation to the federal law jurisdiction of the courts, be liable to the same extent as is the Commonwealth – in other words, that immunities should also be removed from the States and Territories in matters falling within the federal jurisdiction of the courts.[86]

The final procedural immunity to be considered is the Crown's immunity from execution against its property, which is expressly mentioned in s 65 of the Judiciary Act 1903 (Cth). The immunity is, however, counterbalanced by s 66 of the Act, which imposes upon the Minister of Finance or the Treasurer an obligation to satisfy judgments given against it. As noted by the Commission, there are good policy reasons why Crown property should be immune from execution, chief of these being that intolerable disruption to public services could be caused if defence, transport educational or health facilities could be seized.[87] If accompanied by an obligation to provide monetary satisfaction for judgments, there is thus good reason for executive immunity from execution to be retained. As noted by the Commission, there have been no examples in Australia where governments have refused to pay damages under s 66 or equivalent provisions. A constitutional issue does, however, arise in that, under s 83 of the Constitution, the executive may not spend money without the authority of appropriations legislation passed by Parliament. In other words, a government could use its majority in Parliament to frustrate a judgment against itself by failing to include an appropriation for damages in its budget. A collision between the executive's submission to decisions of the courts (a fundamental aspect of the doctrine of constitutionalism), and the requirement

82 ALRC, 2001, 23.16.

83 *Ibid*, 23.23.

84 *Ibid*, 23.34.

85 *Ibid*, 23.35.

86 *Ibid*, 23.47–49.

87 *Ibid*, 24.12.

that the executive obtain legislative authorisation for the expenditure of money (a fundamental aspect of the doctrine of parliamentary government), has never occurred.[88] However, such circumstances could arise. The only way to avoid that would be to include in the Constitution a provision which both directed the Treasurer to satisfy judgments, and authorised him to draw upon the Consolidated Revenue Fund in order to do so. That, indeed, is the case in a number of Australian jurisdictions, where the relevant statutory provision requiring that the Treasurer satisfy the judgment itself contains wording authorising the necessary appropriation.[89] I would, therefore, argue that express terms dealing with the issue of the satisfaction of judgments in the manner outlined in this paragraph be put into the Constitution.

88 *Ibid*, 24.11 and 24.18.

89 See, eg, the Crown Proceedings Act 1992 (ACT), s 13(6). Similar provisions exist in the legislation in the Northern Territory, South Australia, Victoria and Tasmania.

FEDERALISM

5.1 FEDERALISM IN AUSTRALIA

A basic definition of federalism is that it is a system of government in which the Constitution of the nation-state allocates legislative authority to the national government and to regional governments, and in which any amendment of the Constitution in such a way as to alter that division cannot be effected by either the national or the regional governments acting on their own.[1] Australia fits this definition because ss 51, 52, 90, 114 and 115 of the Commonwealth Constitution 1901 allocate certain legislative powers to the Commonwealth, by implication leaving all others to the States, and because amendment of the Constitution requires not only legislation by the federal Parliament, but also the approval of the voters both nationally, and in a majority of States considered as separate entities.

An important element of the definition of federalism at the beginning of this paragraph is that in a federal system the legislative authority of regional governments is derived *from the Constitution* – in other words, regional governments enjoy original authority. By contrast, in unitary systems, only the central government is granted *original* authority by the Constitution, while regional and/or municipal governments enjoy *delegated* authority, which may at any time be revoked by the central government. In the case of Australia, the conferral of original authority is found in s 106, which provides that, subject to the Constitution, the Constitutions of the States remained in force after federation, and s 107, which states that, with the exception of the exclusive legislative powers of the Commonwealth, the Parliaments of the States enjoy the same legislative power as they had prior to federation. Some might argue that, because after federation the State parliaments continued to draw their authority from the State Constitutions just as they had done prior to federation, the States do not derive their authority from the Commonwealth Constitution. However, this is to miss the point that, at federation, the States underwent an alteration in their sovereign status, and became subordinate to a new entity called the Commonwealth of Australia, whose Constitution can reduce, or even extinguish, the legislative competence of the States, if amended in such a way as to achieve that result. Of course, that is unlikely to happen, as the States took care to build into the s 128 amending procedure a requirement to obtain the assent of the voters in a majority of States. This puts in place one of the requirements of a true federation that has already been mentioned – namely that the assent of the States as separate entities must be required for an alteration of the Constitution. Nevertheless, the legal position is as was stated by Barwick CJ in *Victoria v Commonwealth* (*Payroll Tax* case),[2] namely, that at federation, the former colonies were replaced as separate entities by the Commonwealth,

1 Burgess, 1993, 5.
2 (1971) 122 CLR 353, 370–71.

and the States of the Commonwealth henceforth derived their existence from the Commonwealth Constitution.

The reasons why the founders of Australia decided upon a federal form of government are familiar to all with a knowledge of the standard works dealing with constitutional history published during the 20th century.[3] This history was revisited in the many academic writings which were published in the years leading up to the centenary of federation in 2001.[4] To re-state the familiar, most authorities agree that, having accepted the need for the colonies to unite in order to co-ordinate defence of the continent and to create a single economic entity, federalism was chosen, in preference to outright union, in order to preserve as much State autonomy *vis-à-vis* the central government as possible – in other words, that federalism was selected in preference to a unitary system in order to curb what was feared might be the overweening authority of the national government.[5] Indeed, a unitary system was hardly given any consideration during the period of constitution-making.[6] Thus, as Crommelin notes,[7] the opening resolution put to the first National Australasian Convention in 1891 established as a basic principle that:

> ... the powers and privileges and territorial rights of the several existing colonies shall remain intact, except in respect to such surrenders as may be agreed upon as necessary and incidental to the power and authority of the National Federal Government.

Similarly, Quick and Garran stated:[8]

> The problem to be solved in the case of the Australian colonies desiring to federate was similar to that which had to be solved by the framers of the American Constitution; it was – how to reconcile the creation of a strong national government with the claims and susceptibilities of separate, and, in their own eyes, quasi-sovereign States.

That federalism is to be explained by reference to an essentially negative sentiment is not to deny the legitimacy of the fears of those colonial politicians. It was quite obviously reasonable for them to apprehend the likelihood that, in a unitary system, regional governments might soon lose authority to the central government.

Does the preservation of State autonomy, in and of itself, continue to provide a satisfactory justification of federalism today? Although the continued existence of a federal system has not achieved prominence in public debate, it is possible to discern three basic positions that have been articulated: the first is that the federal system should be maintained as it is. This position commands broad public support: in its assessment of public attitudes to the Constitution, the Constitutional Centenary Foundation found that, while there was some dissatisfaction with the way in which the federal system operated, there was little support for centralisation of powers, and, indeed, that there was support for greater decentralisation of functions.[9] Furthermore, as was the case when the

3 See, eg, La Nauze, 1972.
4 These include Irving, 1997; Irving, 1999; and Hirst, 2000.
5 See Craven, 1992, 51; and Federal-State Relations Committee, Parliament of Victoria, 1998, 1.17.
6 Galligan and Walsh, 1992, 195.
7 Crommelin, 1992, 34.
8 Quick and Garran, 1976, 414.
9 Constitutional Centenary Foundation, 2000, 30.

Constitution was drafted, support for federalism appears to be motivated primarily by a negative sentiment towards the power of the Commonwealth, rather than by a perceived positive characteristic inherent in federalism itself. The second position is also supportive of federalism, but argues that we need more federalism rather than less.[10] Supporters of this position propose a variety of measures in pursuit of their goals, including a reduction in the powers of the Commonwealth, an increase in the number of States through their division into smaller units, and/or the recognition of local governments in the Constitution complied with an express grant of power to them. The third position is anti-federalist. Its supporters call for the abolition of State governments as repositories of original legislative power. They argue that for its small population, Australia is over-supplied with legislatures (15 chambers in all, counting federal, State and mainland Territory legislatures), and that a unitary system, with regional governments exercising delegated powers, would be less costly to administer.[11]

I would argue that a proper analysis of the federal system calls for a more thorough consideration of the benefits of that system than it has heretofore received. I would also argue that the disconnection that exists between Australian people and their Constitution, a disconnection which stems from widespread ignorance of our system of government, perpetuates that view of the Constitution as something 'out there' that distributes power between governments, rather than as something that is 'of the people', and which distributes power between them and all governments of whatever level. What if we analysed federalism from the perspective of the individual citizen? Would we arrive at a justification of it that is more satisfying than one based on State chauvinism and a suspicion of the Commonwealth government?

5.2 FEDERAL THEORY

5.2.1 The genesis of modern federalism in the United States

For an appreciation of the benefits of federalism as considered from the vantage point of the individual citizen, one could do no better than refer to *The Federalist* papers, which were penned during the period when the various States of the American confederation were deciding whether to approve the federal Constitution, which had been produced by the Philadelphia Constitutional Convention of 1787. Written primarily for the benefit of the citizens of New York, a State whose assent to the proposed Constitution was seen as crucial to its success, *The Federalist* presented a justification of the proposed federal Constitution founded upon the idea of civic republicanism, then current in America.[12] Crucial to an understanding of civic republicanism, and its impact on American constitution-making, is the idea of the Constitution as a covenant – in other words, as an agreement between the members of a particular society which was taken to have been entered into with God as witness.[13] Indeed, the word 'federal' is derived from the Latin

10 See, eg, Crommelin, 1992, 46–47.

11 Hall, 1998.

12 The background to *The Federalist* papers is concisely summarised in Schechter, 1990, 291–304. The most important *Federalist* letters justifying the proposed federal system are Nos 10, 37, 39 and 51.

13 Elazar, 1998, 7–10.

word *'foedus'* meaning covenant or compact.[14] The habit in the American colonies of entering into covenants relating to the structure of government long pre-dated the Revolution. The Protestant churches in America had an established tradition of setting the framework of church government by means of communally agreed upon rules.[15] This experience, combined with disinterest on the part of the British government in American colonial affairs, meant that both the knowledge and opportunity existed in the colonies to apply these ecclesiastical habits in the civil sphere, and so the history of the colonies reveals a multitude of examples of covenants establishing organs of government – in other words, a process which we would now call constitution-making.[16] By the time of Revolution, the process had become secularised, and so Constitutions of that era are better described as compacts, which are similar to covenants, but lack the religious element of a promise made before the deity.[17] However, the key feature shared by covenants and compacts is that they are formed by mutual agreement between the citizens or their representatives, and this element is apparent both in the Declaration of Independence of 1776[18] and in the Constitution of 1787,[19] the latter of which, significantly, begins with the words 'We the people'.

From the above, one can deduce that a key element of American federalism was that it was the product of a 'bottom up' view of the direction in which constitutional authority flowed: Constitutions were made by a process of agreement between the people or their representatives, rather than being imposed from above. For this reason it is unsurprising that, when called upon to draft a Constitution in 1787, the representatives of the States chose a federal rather than a unitary system – the States were seen as the representatives of the people, and as parties to a compact in which they retained their identity, and agreed to form a national government for certain limited purposes. Later in this section, I will explore further the issue of whether the federal compact in the United States should be seen primarily as one between several million people or between the 13 States. For the moment, it is necessary to focus only on the fact that an agreement, or covenant, formed the foundation of the federal system.

The second important feature of American constitutional practice which made it likely that federalism would be adopted as a form of government, was the fact that under the colonial Constitutions, a large number of public offices were filled by election, rather than being within the control of the executive, which was usually very weak. Public service through office-holding was thought to promote civic virtue. By voting for office-holders, the citizen became informed about public affairs. By holding office himself, the citizen assumed his share of the burdens of government, and prevented the concentration of power in a few individuals, thereby serving the community and preventing tyranny. The authors of *The Federalist* papers sought to demonstrate how proposed federal

14 Elazar, 1984, 3.

15 Elazar, 1988, 15–18 and 31–34.

16 Elazar, 1984, 17–43. The earliest of these proto-Constitutions was the Mayflower Compact of 1620, entered into by the (male) members of the group of settlers who arrived in North America on the vessel of that name; however, there are many other examples of covenants of this type entered into by the members of colonial societies during the 17th and 18th centuries – see Lutz, 1988, 23–49.

17 Elazar, 1988, 91; Lutz, 1998, xxvii-xxxvi.

18 Elazar, 1998, 47–71.

19 *Ibid*, 75–96.

Constitution served civic republicanism. From their arguments, and others current at the time, we can identify classic arguments in favour of federalism which continue to be advanced to this day, both overseas and in Australia.[20]

5.2.2 Advantages of federalism

The first major advantage of federalism is that, by diffusing legislative and executive authority, federalism prevents the concentration of power in the hands of a single government. At the outset, one must recognise that diffusion of power does not necessarily guarantee that the *content* of the laws made by the various governments will be just, or that those laws will be applied in a just manner. As I have already argued, that result is far more likely to be achieved by having a Bill of Rights. Thus, federalism is neither a necessary nor a sufficient condition for just government. That lesson was one to which the founders of the United States Constitution subsequently gave explicit recognition through the enactment of the first ten Amendments forming the Bill of Rights. Nevertheless, even in the absence of a Bill of Rights, diffusion of power confers several obvious advantages: by creating a multitude of locations of competition for political power, the energy of an individual or party which seeks to monopolise power must be brought to bear at several places, and this makes it more difficult to obtain absolute control of power than would be the case if there was but one game that needed to be won.[21] Furthermore, if elections in those various locations are held at different times, it becomes extremely unlikely that a party will be able to control all of them at any given time.[22]

The second major advantage of federalism is that, by dividing the polity into a number of smaller units, government is made more accessible to citizens. This, in turn, means that citizens are more easily able to hold government accountable through direct contact with their representatives. Furthermore, State politicians are, at least in respect of those matters which fall under State government authority, directly answerable to the electorate, and cannot blame adverse outcomes on the vagaries of national political forces over which they can say they have no control. So far as the individual citizen is concerned, making government more accessible increases the opportunity that citizens have for participation in government, not just as voters, but also as office-holders, the hoped-for consequence being that the more offices there are to fill, and the greater the number of citizens who take their turn at filling them, the lesser the likelihood that a particular party will be able to monopolise power.

The third major advantage of the diffusion of authority in a federal system is that by permitting a degree of regional autonomy, the system allows experimentation in social policy, and gives regions an opportunity to diverge from the rest of the country, again, at least in respect of those matters falling under State control.

20 See de Q Walker, 2001; Evans, 2001, 7–8; Galligan, 1995, 39–46; Craven, 1992, 52; and Galligan and Walsh, 1992, 196–202.

21 As was stated by de Tocqueville, 1969, 162: 'Political passions, instead of spreading like a sheet of fire instantaneously over the whole land, break up in conflict with individual passions of each state.'

22 Lutz, 1988, 163.

I would suggest that these arguments not only provide a cogent defence of federalism, but also provide a positive, citizen-focused justification of that system, by emphasising the benefits conferred upon society by having a politically involved citizenry. These arguments incorporate, and yet go far beyond, those anti-central government sentiments which, as we have already seen, commonly form the basis of a defence of federalism in Australia.

5.2.3 Arguments against federalism

In opposition to all this, those who reject federalism argue that the cost of having State governments does not justify the benefits obtained from federalism, and that governmental efficiency would be better served if the second tier of government was eliminated.[23] Is a unitary system inevitably more efficient than a federal one? The anti-federalists' argument is that unitary systems will be more efficient simply because of the economies of scale that are offered by having one bureaucracy delivering government services (instead of the eight we have in Australia), and because a unitary system avoids certain costs inherent in federalism, such as costs arising out of inter-governmental negotiation, communication and co-ordination, and costs involved in resolving inter-governmental disputes. One recent estimate of the costs of duplication and overlap as a result of having a federal system of government concluded that federalism cost Australia between 0.5% and 1.0% of total Commonwealth government expenditure,[24] which on the 2000-01 figure of a $162 billion Commonwealth budget, represents the sum of between $0.8 and $1.6 billion. The anti-federalists also argue that two of the major benefits of federalism – bringing government closer to the people, and increasing the opportunity for people to hold public office – can just as easily be achieved by delegation of power to States in a unitary system, as it is through the conferral of original power on the States in a federal system.

The counter to this economic argument is two-fold: first, other data indicate that federalism may, in fact, not be more costly than a unitary system. de Q Walker notes that overall expenditure on government as a percentage of GDP is lower in the federal countries of Australia (32.7%) and the United States (30.5%), than it is in the unitary countries of New Zealand (39.6%), the United Kingdom (40.1%) or France (52.4%).[25] Furthermore, the 1994 Australian Federalism Conference concluded that there was no persuasive argument based on economic efficiency which impelled a change to a unitary system.[26] The second counter to the argument based on economics is that, even if it were true that unitary systems were inherently more efficient than federal ones, the key advantage of federalism is that under a federal system, the inability of either level of government to amend the Constitution on its own protects the sub-national units from having power withdrawn from them. Furthermore, although it might be possible to

23 See Hall, 1998.

24 Federal–State Relations Committee, Parliament of Victoria, 1998, 12, n 24.

25 de Q Walker, 2001, 41.

26 Parliament of Victoria, 1994, 5.

attach a dollar value to the cost of having a federal system, the intangible political benefits of federalism (already discussed) are not measurable on an empirical basis.

Looking at the question from a technical perspective, the advantage of changing to a unitary system is that the whole body of law relating to the federal – State balance would disappear from the law. Courts would not need to spend time determining issues such as the scope of the Commonwealth's legislative powers, the circumstances in which State legislation was overridden by that of the Commonwealth, and the difficult question of whether agents of one level of government are subject to the laws of the other when discharging their duties (usually referred to as the inter-governmental immunities issue, which was discussed in Chapter 4). But however great the temptation to sweep the federal system away may be, it is important to realise that the attachment Australians have to the current system – even if that attachment is sentimental rather than rational – in itself provides a powerful argument for the retention of the federal system. The loyalty people have to their States as institutions performs the important function of fostering public support for the institutions of constitutional government. I have already mentioned, in Chapter 1, how vital this factor is in strengthening democracy. Given that, in general, the public has little awareness of, or even interest in, constitutional issues, it is, I believe, important to build upon such institutional loyalty that exists. Indeed, if anything, people want the federal system strengthened and invigorated, and oppose what they see as the progressive slide of power to the Commonwealth government. In light of this, it would seem unwise to abolish a system of government which strikes a chord among most Australians. Furthermore, as I also indicated in Chapter 1, the approach adopted in this book has been to advocate constitutional change only where that change remedies a significant constitutional defect or omission. The arguments for and against the retention of the federal system are too finely balanced for one to be able to say that there is a pressing need to convert to a unitary system, and so, based on the principle of avoiding change for its own sake, I would conclude that the federal system should be retained. The real challenge is to find ways to improve the system – particularly in relation to the fiscal imbalance which exists between the States and the Commonwealth, which is discussed at length later in this Chapter. The object should be to reform and re-invigorate Australian federalism, so as to retain its advantages while, at the same time, minimising such inefficiencies as it may cause.

5.2.4 Federal Constitutions – State compacts or peoples' charters?

Before moving on to an analysis of particular provisions of our Constitution, an important question relating to federal theory must be addressed. Put simply, that question is whether a federal Constitution should be viewed primarily as securing the rights of the States which are parties to it, or whether it should be viewed as a compact defining the rights of all the inhabitants of the country. In posing this question, I do not mean to suggest that a federal Constitution will be wholly of one character or the other. Clearly, all federal Constitutions perform both these functions. Nevertheless, as will be shown below, an analysis of a federal Constitution sometimes reveals instances where the tension which exists between these two ways of viewing a Constitution has affected the design of the Constitution and the inter-relationships of the institutions it created.

Commentators on federalism have noted that agreement by the people lies at the basis of many democratic Constitutions, both federal and non-federal. However, as King states:[27]

> What is distinctive about federations is not the fact that 'the people' are viewed as sovereign, but that the expression of this sovereignty *is tied to the existence and entrenchment of regional, territorial entities*. In federations, 'the people' are taken as a single entity in one sense, but as a plurality of entities in another. The people are represented as a whole (the nation) and as parts (the distinct reasons comprising the nation). [Emphasis added.]

In other words, it is not only the people as citizens, but also the territorial units, that are seen as the parties to the federal compact. The communitarian nature of the federal Constitution of the United States has often been noted. As Lutz states:[28]

> It was as a developing nation of communities rather than of individuals that Americans first formed their constitutions at the state and national levels.

Furthermore, as Elazar states, the fact that America federalism was based upon a compact between the States meant that it conformed to the rule that:[29]

> In polities founded by covenant or compact, the process of constitution-making involves a convention of the partners to the pact or their representatives ... As a pact among equals, or the political expression of such a pact, the constitution can only be changed through the consent either of all the partners or a majority thereof if it has been so agreed.

The significance of this analysis is that it reveals that American constitutionalism is founded upon dual citizenship: individuals are citizens of the nation as a whole, and enjoy rights as such, but are also citizens of the individual States.[30] Furthermore, although it is true that the major feature which distinguishes a federation from a confederation is that the central government has a relationship with the individual citizens in the former, which is lacking in the latter, it is also true that in a federal system, the central government has a relationship with the States, and that it is the States, as well as the individual citizens who make up the nation, who are parties to the compact that is the Constitution. Whether the overall impression given by any specific federal Constitution is one of being primarily a compact between the States, or primarily one between the individual citizens and all levels of government, is obviously a matter of degree. However, in the case of the United States Constitution, there are a number of factors which weigh heavily towards the impression that the document places its major emphasis on the Constitution as a compact between the States: each State was given equal representation in the Senate irrespective of population.[31] The key issue of how the Constitution was to be amended was decided by requiring not the assent of a majority (even a special majority) of the people as individuals, but rather a special majority of the States, again irrespective of population.[32] Of course, it is true that the Constitution opens with the words 'We the people', which suggests that the people as individuals were

27 King, 1993, 96.

28 Lutz, 1988, 71.

29 Elazar, 1985, 244.

30 Lutz, 1988, 116

31 Constitution of the United States of America 1787, Art 1, s 3.

32 *Ibid*, Art V.

parties to the Constitution; however, that phrase is equally capable of being interpreted as meaning that the drafters were referring to the people formed into the 13 polities represented at the 1787 constitutional convention. Furthermore, although the Constitution does contain a Bill of Rights, it is important to remember that that was an Anti-Federalist mechanism originally designed to restrain the power of the federal government *vis-a-vis* the States, rather than to confer rights on the people *vis-à-vis* government, both State and federal, and was appended to the Constitution as an afterthought.[33] Moreover, the extension of the application of the Bill of Rights to the States occurred only through an expansive interpretation of the 'due process' clause in the Fourteenth Amendment in the 20th century, and was, in many instances, bitterly resisted by the States.[34]

What is the position in Australia? On the one hand, the preamble to our Constitution begins with the phrase '*Whereas the people* of New South Wales, Victoria ... have agreed to unite in one indissoluble Federal Commonwealth' (emphasis added), which suggests that the federal compact was between the people as individuals. This view is bolstered by the fact that the Constitution was assented to by referenda held in the separate colonies in 1898 and 1899.[35] Furthermore, constitutional amendment in Australia requires majorities of the *voters* nationwide and in a majority of the States, rather than the assent of the State *legislatures*, as in the United States. On the other hand, evidence for the view that it is the States, rather than their individual citizens, who are parties to the Australian federal compact, is provided by statements from the Constitutional Conventions, such as this one by Sir Richard Baker:[36]

> A federation, as it appears to me, consists in the fact that the compact made between the constituent States who want to enter into that federation provides that not only shall the legislatures of the different states be supreme concerning the powers which have been delegated or left to them, but that they shall also have a voice as states concerning the powers which are left to the federal government ...

Further evidence for this is provided by the fact that that the Constitution contains special provisions designed to entice specific States to enter the federal compact – s 7 allowing Queensland to elect its Senators from divisions within the State, s 95 relating to Western Australian customs duties and s 111 anticipating the desire of South Australia to surrender the Northern Territory to the Commonwealth.[37] Most important, however, is what the Constitution prescribes in relation to the Senate and to constitutional amendment. Under s 7, each State is entitled to equal representation in the Senate irrespective of population, and under s 128, not only the assent of a majority of the people, but also the assent of separate majorities in a majority of the States, is required for constitutional amendment. I would thus argue that the Constitution gives the dominant impression of being a treaty between the States, rather than a document designed to secure the rights of individual citizens *vis-à-vis* governments of whatever level. I would

33 Lutz, 1988, 15; Kaminski and Bernstein, 1990, 425–26.

34 Rossum and Tarr, 1999, 420–29.

35 Galligan, 1995, 25–27.

36 National Australasian Convention Debates, 1891, 111 – see Crommelin, 1992, 39.

37 These provisions are mentioned by Irving, 1997, 199–203 in the context of her discussion of competing views on this issue during the 1890s. She concludes that whereas the view of a federal Constitution as a compact between States was prevalent in the early 1890s, by the end of the decade the idea of it being a compact between the people had 'at least co-equal claim'.

also argue that this, in turn, means that the Constitution is something 'out there', which distributes powers between governments, rather than something that is 'of the people', and which distributes power between them and the governments.

In my view, the elevation of the State to the position of fundamental unit in both American and Australian federalism is unsatisfactory from the perspective of democratic theory, because if, to take an extreme example, the population of one of the States withered away to a few thousand people, that State, and thus the small group of people resident in it, would nevertheless retain the same equal status *vis-à-vis* all the other States as it had done before. In fact, one does not even have to posit that extreme example for this criticism to be valid – it has been valid in respect of the Australian federation right from its inception, given the disparities in population between the States. The implications of this criticism will become evident later in this book. In 5.8, below, I focus on what changes should be made to the Constitution in relation to procedures required for amendment. In Chapter 9, I discuss what reforms ought to be made in relation to the powers of the Senate, in light of the fact that the equality of representation given to the States results in profound inequality in the value of individual votes.

5.3 THE LEGISLATIVE POWER OF THE COMMONWEALTH UNDER THE AUSTRALIAN CONSTITUTION

There are a variety of ways in which the allocation of legislative powers in a federation can be structured. One could specify the legislative powers of the federal government and leave the residuum to the States. Or one could list the States' powers, leaving the residuum to the federal government. Another option is to put three lists of powers in the Constitution, listing exclusive powers of the federal government, exclusive powers of the States, and a residuum lying within the capacity of either the federal or the State legislatures, but with one government overriding the other in the event that both had entered the field and had legislated inconsistently. An even more complex federal model is one which allocates legislative power between three tiers of government – federal, State and local. Although some commentators have canvassed the adoption of such a system in Australia,[38] and the 1988 constitutional referendum contained a proposed constitutional provision which would have required the States to establish a system of local government, a three-tier federal system is not recommended in this book. Adding a third tier to the federal system would make it significantly more complex than it already is, would require the specification of the legislative powers of at least two of the branches, and would make the law on inconsistency of legislation more difficult to apply. This chapter thus proceeds on the basis that the fundamental division of original powers between only two levels of government should not be departed from in a new Constitution.

In Australia, the legislative powers of the Commonwealth are specified, and thus legislation enacted by the federal Parliament is valid only if it falls within a power appearing in the Constitution. This arrangement may be contrasted with that in Canada,

38 Advisory Council for Inter-Government Relations, 1980, 9–10; Chapman and Wood, 1984, 174–75.

where s 92 of the Constitution Act 1867 specifies provincial legislative powers, leaving all others to the federal Parliament.[39]

It is usually argued that whichever powers – federal or State – a Constitution defines, it thereby limits, and so that Constitutions, such as those of Australia and the United States, which define the powers of the federal government, are federations in which the States are dominant. Conversely, it is often argued that a Constitution such as that of Canada, which defines the power of the Provinces and leaves all other matters to the federal government, sets the balance in favour of the federal government. However, this is to ignore the effect of judicial interpretation. In both Australia and the United States, the courts have used canons of statutory interpretation to give a generous meaning to federal powers, and to read them as being supported by implied incidental powers which have vastly expanded their scope. In Australia the 'reserve powers' doctrine (the theory that the drafters of the Constitution were presumed to have intended that Commonwealth powers be interpreted restrictively, in order to give pre-eminence to the residual powers of the States) was overthrown by the High Court in *Amalgamated Society of Engineers v Adelaide Steamship Co Ltd*,[40] and replaced by a rule of statutory interpretation that Commonwealth powers were to be given a broad and generous interpretation. This laid the way open for an ever more expansive interpretation of Commonwealth powers at the expense of the States.[41] This has been particularly true with respect to the economy, where the expansion of Commonwealth powers over the economy has occurred primarily through a number of key enumerated powers. Thus the Commonwealth's s 51(i) power over inter-State and overseas trade and commerce was interpreted as carrying an implied power, which legitimated Commonwealth regulation of purely intra-State conduct, where such regulation was seen as being necessary in order to give effect to the regulation of the inter-state or overseas activity.[42] An even greater contribution to the expanding role of the Commonwealth has been made by the s 51(xx) corporations power, which has been interpreted as permitting Commonwealth regulation of any of a trading or financial corporation's[43] activities,[44] the activities of its officers[45] and even the activities of third parties *vis-à-vis* corporations[46] (although there is a limit to how many degrees of separation from a corporation a person may be in for their activities to be regulable by the corporations power).[47] Since business activity in Australia is overwhelmingly undertaken by corporations, the s 51(xx) power gives the Commonwealth effective control over the economy. In addition to these, one should also

39 Although s 91 of the Constitution Act does list certain federal legislative powers, these are expressly stated not to cut down the generality of the residue left to the federal Parliament.

40 (1920) 28 CLR 129.

41 Craven, 1992, 55–56.

42 See, eg, *O'Sullivan v Naorlunga Meat Ltd* (1954) 92 CLR 565; and *Airlines of New South Wales v New South Wales (No 2)* (1965) 113 CLR 54.

43 A corporation may be found to be a trading or financial corporation either because it is formed for such a purpose (*Fencott v Muller* (1983) 152 CLR 270) or because trading or financial activities form a 'sufficiently significant' part of its activities, without necessarily having to be the dominant activity (*R v Federal Court of Australia ex parte National Football League Inc* (1979) 143 CLR 190; and *Commonwealth v Tasmania* (1983) 158 CLR 1).

44 *Strickland v Rocla Concrete Pipes Ltd* (1971) 124 CLR 468.

45 *R v Australian Industrial Court ex parte CLM Holdings Pty Ltd* (1977) 136 CLR 235.

46 *Actors and Announcers Equity Association of Australia v Fontana Films Pty Ltd* (1982) 150 CLR 169.

47 *Re Dingjan ex parte Wagner* (1995) 183 CLR 323.

mention that the s 51(ii) taxation power provides the Commonwealth with a tool to encourage or deter particular economic activity, either by exempting it from, or subjecting it to, a tax.[48] Finally, in this regard, one should mention the s 51(xxix) external affairs power, which has been used in controversial circumstances, and which, no doubt, carries yet untapped potential. It has enabled the Commonwealth to enact into domestic law measures designed to further international treaties. The power was used to prevent Tasmania constructing the Franklin Dam, the area of the State where the dam was to be built having been declared a World Heritage site by the Commonwealth, under legislation enacted to give effect to an international environmental treaty,[49] and was also used to enact the Racial Discrimination Act 1975 (Cth), enacted in order to give effect to the International Convention on the Elimination of all forms of Race Discrimination.[50]

A number of commentators take the view that the expansion in Commonwealth powers has undermined the federal principle, and have anchored the blame for this in what they see as the High Court's overly-expansive interpretation of the enumerated powers.[51] To some extent, this is unfair – it is the pervasive nature of corporate operations in the modern economy, rather than interpretation by the High Court, that gives the corporations power its reach, and the Commonwealth would be unable to comply with international obligations in the absence of a power enabling it to enact treaties into domestic law. Nor is Australia unique in this regard: the courts in the United States went even further in interpreting the equivalent inter-State commerce power under that country's Constitution, and have virtually obliterated the distinction between inter- and intra-State commerce by finding that all economic activity (even that occurring wholly within the confines of one State) ultimately has some effect on inter-State commerce.[52] Without such an interpretation of the inter-State trade and commerce power, Congress would have had no means of enacting legislation on matters of broad economic policy as, unlike the Australian Constitution, the United States Constitution contains no corporations power.

The only effective means of limiting Commonwealth legislative power, and/or expanding that of the States, would be to re-configure the distribution of powers so as to curtail their scope or remove them from the list of enumerated powers. However, neither the corporations power nor the external affairs power are candidates for restriction, given

48 *Murphyores Incorporated Pty Ltd v Commonwealth* (1976) 136 CLR 1; and *Northern Suburbs General Cemetery Reserve Trust v Commonwealth* (1993) 176 CLR 555.

49 *Commonwealth v Tasmania* (1983) 158 CLR 1.

50 *Koowarta v Bjelke-Peterson* (1982) 153 CLR 168.

51 Barwick, 1995.

52 Thus, in *Wickard v Filburn* 317 US 111 (1942) the Supreme Court upheld a federal law regulating the cultivation of wheat which the farmer was going to sell wholly intra-State on the ground that any production of wheat within a State added to the entire amount produced nationally and thus had an impact on inter-State trade. Another example of his approach is provided by *Heart of Atlanta Motel v United States* 379 US 241 (1964), in which the inter-State commerce clause was held to support a provision of the Civil Rights Act 1964 prohibiting racial discrimination in restaurants on the ground that inter-State travellers might use the restaurant. However, there are limits to how tenuous a connection with inter-State commerce the courts will accept as justifying a law under the Constitution – in *United States v Lopez* 515 US 549 (1995) the Supreme court invalidated a federal law purportedly based on the inter-State commerce clause which prohibited the carrying of guns by school students. The court rejected the federal government's argument that the law related to inter-State commerce because if schools were unsafe young people would fail to become educated and this would affect the national economy.

that a uniform corporations law is required for the efficient operation of the economy, and that the Commonwealth must, as a sovereign state at international law, have some means of engaging in, and ensuring national compliance with, international obligations. In short, I would argue that, unfortunate for federalism as the expansive interpretation of the key powers discussed in the above paragraphs may have been, they are, by their very nature, effective only if given a broad interpretation. Since any attempt to adjust the balance between Commonwealth and State legislative powers would be of little use if those powers were not curtailed, I would argue that the scope of the Commonwealth's powers should be accepted for what they have become, and that a new Constitution should not restrict federal powers. Indeed, as is discussed later on in this chapter, there are persuasive arguments in support of an expansion of some Commonwealth powers, and the conferral of a few new powers on the Commonwealth Parliament. In my view, the most effective means of enhancing the role of the States in the Australian federation would be to address the fiscal imbalances from which the system suffers, and it is to this issue that I now turn.

5.4 REDRESSING THE FISCAL IMBALANCE IN AUSTRALIAN FEDERALISM

Disputes over revenue-allocation are a key feature of the politics of federations, the essential question being how much of the revenue raised by the central government should be allocated to the States for them to spend? Until the introduction of the General Sales Tax (hereafter referred to as the GST), a regular feature of Commonwealth-State relations was a disputatious Premiers' conference, at which the Commonwealth, States and Territories attempted to reach agreement on what proportion of Commonwealth revenue would be given (or, as the States might say, returned), to the States. The States' capacity to raise their own revenue is limited by the fact that, since the Second World War, the Commonwealth has had a *de facto* monopoly over the levying of income tax,[53] and s 90 prohibits States[54] and Territories[55] from imposing excises (in other words, taxes on goods). This means that the States are left with a narrow range of revenue sources, such as business licence fees, motor-vehicle registration fees, taxes on transactions (such as gambling) and stamp duties on land registration. The narrow revenue base of the States

53 Prior to 1959, Commonwealth legislation denied grants to any State which levied income tax. Since then the matter has been addressed politically – the Commonwealth indicating that the levying of State income taxes would see the State(s) concerned lose their Commonwealth grants. Of course, from the perspective of the State governments, introducing income tax would be politically damaging both because no new tax is popular and because the Commonwealth grants would be lost.

54 The most recent case on State excises (*Ha v New South Wales* (1997) 189 CLR 465) adopted a strict (but correct) interpretation of s 90 to the effect that the States could not impose taxes on goods indirectly by dressing them up as fees for licences to trade in the goods *pro rata* to the amount of goods sold in a previous tax period. This decision led to the enactment of Commonwealth legislation in terms of which the Commonwealth collects an excise uniformly across Australia (so as to comply with the s 51(ii) prohibition against taxing States unequally) but then refunds it (using its s 96 power to grant money to the States) on condition that the States then refund to wholesaler and retailers the excess amount over and above what they would have raised before the *Ha* decision. The net effect, from the consumer's point of view, is that taxes on products such as petrol vary from State to State.

55 The Territories are bound by s 90 as was held in *Capital Duplicators Pty Ltd v Australian Capital Territory (No 1)* (1992) 177 CLR 248.

has caused what theorists refer to as 'vertical fiscal imbalance', with the Commonwealth receiving approximately 71% of all government earnings collected in Australia, and the States raising only 56% of the income they need for the services they provide, being reliant on Commonwealth grants for the other 44%.[56]

5.4.1 State revenue sources

What moneys do the States receive from the Commonwealth? Prior to the introduction of the GST in 2000, the States' major source of revenue from the Commonwealth took the form of general purpose grants. These were usually referred to as Revenue Replacement Grants, as they provided each State with a lump-sum, justified as compensation paid to the States for their not levying income tax since the Second World War. These grants could be spent as the States pleased. In addition, the States received (and still do receive) specific purpose payments (SPPs) – funds that are tied to specific projects, such as health, education and welfare, as mandated by the Commonwealth. The GST legislation put Commonwealth–State fiscal arrangements on a new footing. Under the Intergovernmental Agreement on the Reform of Commonwealth-State Financial Arrangements (the IGA), entered into by the Commonwealth, State and Territory Governments in June 1999, the revenue raised by the GST is distributed to the States, and the States no longer receive general purpose Revenue Replacement grants. However, as was the case with Revenue Replacement grants, the basis upon which the GST revenue is distributed between the States and Territories is determined by the Commonwealth Grants Commission. The Commission applies what is called the horizontal fiscal equalisation principle, in terms of which the pool of available money is distributed to the States in accordance with adjusted *per capita* relativities. In other words, the distribution is not done in direct proportion to each State and Territory's population, but is adjusted in order to ensure that:[57]

> State governments should receive funding from the Commonwealth such that, if each of them made the same effort to raise revenue from its own sources and operated at the same level of efficiency, each would have the capacity to provide services at the same standard.

This requires the Commission to take into account factors such as the capacity of each State and Territory to raise revenue, its demography and the additional costs imposed caused by the need to provide services to populations in remote areas. The end product of these calculations is a factor by which the States' and Territories' populations will be adjusted. Thus, on this model, in 2000 New South Wales received 0.90 of a crude *per capita* entitlement per inhabitant, while Tasmania received 1.51 and the Northern Territory 4.16.[58] The same system of adjusted *per capita* relativities is used to determine how SPPs granted to the States and Territories for health care are distributed among those polities.

While the adjusted *per capita* relativities method ensures that such Commonwealth revenue as is distributed to the States and Territories is distributed equitably, it, of course,

56 These figures are based on data contained in Australian Bureau of Statistics, 2000; and Department of the Treasury, 2001.

57 For a statement of the principle and the factors taken into account in applying it, see Commonwealth Grants Commission, 2000, 4–6.

58 *Ibid*, 17.

does not address the fact that the States are financially dependant upon legislation enacted by the Commonwealth Parliament. As is shown by the following table, the States are dependant upon Commonwealth grants for a significant proportion of their income:[59]

	NSW	VIC	QLD	WA	SA	TAS	ACT	NT
Own taxes	47.6%	44.1%	28.3%	35.3%	35.4%	26.6%	35.9%	18%
Commonwealth funds	31.7%	33.1%	35.6%	37.9%	39.5%	46.7%	34.1%	67.2%
Other (including interest and dividends)	20.7%	22.9%	36.1%	26.8%	25.1%	26.7%	30%	14.8%

Some commentators find this dependence unhealthy, arguing that the 'vertical fiscal imbalance', by which they mean that there is a disjunction between what governments raise in revenue and what they spend, is inimical to democratic accountability:[60] As stated above, the State and Territory governments raise 56% of what they spend, with the shortfall coming from the Commonwealth. Conversely, the Commonwealth spends 68% of what it raises, the remainder going to the States. The consequence of this is that one level of government (the Commonwealth) decides what taxes to impose while another (the States) decides how to spend the money (or, at least, that portion of Commonwealth revenue they receive), whereas ideally in a democracy the same level of government should be accountable for both decisions. Against this, however, one can say that the basic principle of parliamentary government that taxation and expenditure should be approved by the legislature is, nevertheless, preserved, in that the Commonwealth Parliament approves the taxation, while the State Parliament approves the expenditure. Furthermore, perfect fiscal balance is probably unattainable in a federal system, and it may be inevitable that one level of government will collect more than it needs, while the other will collect less, with the result that some system of revenue-transfer will be required. However, it must surely be possible to re-order fiscal affairs in Australia in such a way as better to reflect the principles of federalism, for it is inconsistent with federal principles that the financial security of the States should depend upon the whim of the federal Parliament. Surely if federalism requires that the Constitution distribute legislative powers between the federal government and those of the States, and that that distribution should not be able to be altered by the federal government or the States acting unilaterally, the Constitution should also seek to guarantee the States the income required to discharge the financial responsibilities that go with their legislative capacity, and that that guarantee should also not be able to be tampered with unilaterally? What mechanism could be included in the Constitution to ensure fiscal balance in the federation?

59 The source of this data is Australian Bureau of Statistics, 2000.

60 See, eg, Mathews, 1980, 10–11. For a concise discussion of fiscal imbalances in Australian federalism, see Galligan, 1995, 214–32.

5.4.2 Fiscal relationships in other federations

Two recent analyses of federal-State relations, including fiscal relations, provide useful material for answering this question. These analyses are a report, *Federalism and the Role of the States*, published in 1999 by the Federal-State Relations Committee of the Victorian Parliament,[61] and a study on Commonwealth-State fiscal relations, undertaken by the Review of Commonwealth-State Funding, commissioned by the governments of Victoria, New South Wales and Western Australia.[62] Both studies examined fiscal relations in other federations, and it is worthwhile examining this comparative material.

In Germany,[63] although the federal, State and local governments all have the authority to levy their own taxes,[64] in practice personal income, corporate and sales tax are all levied by the federal government, and at uniform rates throughout the country. The Constitution requires that revenue from personal and corporate income tax must be divided between the federal, State and local governments, in accordance with a formula which specifies that the federal and State governments must receive equal shares of what is left after a portion is given to local governments.[65] The portion given to local governments is determined by federal legislation, which can be altered only with the assent of the Bundesrat (the upper house of the federal Parliament).[66] Since the members of the Bundesrat are nominated by the State governments,[67] this means that any alteration in the share of the local governments, and thus the equal shares of the federal and State governments, can be effected only with the assent of the States. Revenue from the sales tax is distributed somewhat differently: the federal legislature can enact legislation determining the formula by which this tax is distributed, but in so doing, the Constitution requires that the legislature take into account various factors, including the need to ensure that each level of government has sufficient revenue to meet expenditures, and that living standards are equal in each State.[68] In practice, adjustments to the sales tax distribution formula are re-negotiated by the federal and State governments, as this legislation, too, requires the assent of the Bundesrat. Because of the Constitutionally-mandated sharing of revenue, there is little need for fiscal equalisation beyond that which is effected by the distribution of the income and sales taxes,[69] although some grants are still given by the federal government and wealthier State governments to poorer ones, under an agreement negotiated between the federal government and the States designed to ease the fiscal strains imposed by the unification of the former East and West Germany.[70]

In Canada,[71] provincial governments derive significant revenue from taxes they levy themselves, which include personal income, corporate and sales taxes, levied at different

61 Federal-State Relations Committee, 1999.

62 Review of Commonwealth – State Funding, 2002.

63 The position in Germany is discussed in the Federal-State Relations Committee, 1999, 3.41–56.

64 Constitution of Germany 1949, Art 105(2).

65 *Ibid*, Art 106(3).

66 *Ibid*, Art 106(5).

67 *Ibid*, Art 51.

68 *Ibid*, Art 106(3).

69 Federal-State Relations Committee, 1999, 3.91.

70 *Ibid*, 3.92–96.

71 *Ibid*, 1.22–44.

rates by each Province. In the case of all Provinces except Quebec, the actual collection of provincial income taxes is effected by the federal taxation agency, acting as an agent for the Provinces. Apart from the income they receive from their own taxes, the Provinces also receive lump-sum equalisation grants from the federal government. These grants are usually unconditional, and are distributed to Provinces in accordance with a formula designed to provide assistance to the poorer provinces – in other words, those whose revenue-raising capacity fall below a certain *per capita* level, determined with reference to the average revenue-raising capacity of five selected provinces.[72]

The position in the United States[73] is similar to that in Canada, except that State governments collect their taxes directly, rather than relying on the federal government as their agent. Also as in Canada, States receive federal grants which contribute an aggregate 18% of their revenue. Such grants are almost always conditional.

In seeking to address the fiscal imbalance in the Australian federation, the Victorian Parliamentary Committee noted that the Commonwealth's fiscal dominance undermines the position of the States as equal partners in the federal system.[74] It also noted that s 94 of the Constitution contemplates the distribution to the States of the surplus revenue of the Commonwealth – presumably, such revenue as is surplus to that which is needed by the Commonwealth for the achievement of its purposes.[75] However, in this regard it should also be stated that s 94 is merely permissive, and leaves it to the Commonwealth to determine how much (if indeed any) of its surplus it will distribute. Drawing on its comparative study, the Committee noted that there were essentially two means of increasing the level of fiscal equality within a federal system: the establishment of a Constitutionally-mandated revenue-sharing scheme (such as that which exists in Germany), or the exercise of significant autonomous revenue-raising powers on the States (as is the case in Canada and the United States). The Australian Constitution makes no provision for revenue sharing. So far as the independent revenue-raising capacity of the States is concerned, this is restricted by s 90 of the Constitution, which prohibits the States from imposing taxes on goods. Furthermore, the Committee stated that the desire for uniformity in the conduct of business across Australia militates against the States imposing corporate tax (which would, in all likelihood, differ in its rates from State to State), and the imposition of income taxes by the States would require a reduction in Commonwealth income tax rates, a step which the Commonwealth has always refused to take, and which would, of course, result in a reduction in Commonwealth grants to the States.

5.4.3 Federal-State financial relations and the GST

Subsequent to the publication of the Victorian Parliamentary Committee's report, the GST system (which was discussed in the report as a likely future development)[76] was

72 *Ibid*, 1.45–50.
73 *Ibid*, 2.25–26.
74 *Ibid*, 11.1.
75 *Ibid*, 11.2.
76 *Ibid*, 11.23–31.

introduced.[77] The GST scheme involves the levying of a 10% goods and services tax by the Commonwealth. As stated earlier in this chapter, under a political agreement between the Commonwealth and the States, the entire proceeds of the GST are allotted to the States, in consideration for which the States were required to abolish a number of indirect taxes they levied. The States also no longer receive Financial Assistance Grants, or Revenue Replacement Grants, from the Commonwealth. The allotment of GST revenue to the States is effected by the Commonwealth Grants Commission, using its fiscal equalisation formula. Although the federal government argued that the GST established a revenue sharing system (on the grounds that the States now have an entitlement to the proceeds of a specific tax), the GST system falls far short of a true revenue-sharing arrangement, such as that which exists in Germany: The GST legislation is not constitutionally entrenched, and the provisions allocating the revenue to the States are subject to change by the Commonwealth Parliament in the same way as is any other legislation. The much-vaunted protection supposedly afforded to the States by the fact that their agreement is required for any alteration to either the base upon which, or the rate at which, the tax is levied, is insubstantial – as a mere political agreement between the Commonwealth and the States, there is nothing to prevent its being overridden by the Commonwealth Parliament. It is also disingenuous for the Commonwealth to represent that the GST amounts to an enhancement of the revenue-raising capacity of the States, and to omit them from its annual accounts, which it does on the ground that the GST is 'a States' tax'.[78] The GST is levied under the authority of Commonwealth legislation. Furthermore, it did not result in an overall enhancement of State revenues – the removal of Financial Assistance Grants and Revenue Replacement Grants had the result that the States' financial position was much the same after the GST as it had been before: to take fiscal year 2002–02 as an example, the States' projected income from the GST and from Budget Balancing Assistance (refunded by the Commonwealth, which collects former State petrol, alcohol and tobacco excises) was $32 billion, whereas under the pre-GST system the States would have received $19 billion in Financial Assistance Grants, $7 billion in Revenue Replacement Payments, and would have raised another $5 billion in indirect taxes themselves, which meant that the States lost $31 billion in order to receive $32 billion.

5.4.4 Revenue-sharing as a means of securing the fiscal position of the States

If the GST system does not amount either to a true revenue-sharing scheme, or enhance the revenue-raising capacity of the States, how could those objectives be achieved? In answering this question, the Victorian Parliamentary Committee concluded that either the Constitution could be amended so as to include a revenue sharing scheme,[79] or the States could be given an autonomous source of revenue.[80] The Commission did not

77 A New Tax System (Goods and Services Tax) Act 1999 (Cth).

78 See Department of the Treasury, 2001, 12, where it is expressly stated that GST revenue is excluded from calculations of Commonwealth revenue.

79 Federal-State Relations Committee, 1999, 11.46.

80 *Ibid*, 11.47.

pursue the first of these options, but focused on the second. It rejected the strategy of the States levying either sales taxes[81] or corporate taxes, on the ground that such taxes would be inconsistent with recent macroeconomic liberalisation in Australia. The Committee's recommendation was that the Commonwealth reduce its rates of personal income tax, and that instead of the States receiving Financial Assistance Grants, they be given the opportunity to levy personal income tax themselves.[82] Such a recommendation, if implemented, would essentially return the fiscal situation to that which obtained prior to the Second World War.

The Commission's apparent reluctance to pursue the option of revenue-sharing via constitutional reform is disappointing, although no doubt understandable in light of the pessimism which most people have in relation to the chances of effecting constitutional change in Australia. In my view, irrespective of whether revenue-sharing or an enhancement of independent revenue collection by the States is used as the avenue by which a more equitable federal fiscal balance is achieved, it is vital that the system be given a basis within the Constitution. Anything less than that leaves the States with the same vulnerability to the Commonwealth as they have always suffered.

In order to determine which device (revenue-sharing or dedicated State revenue allocation) would be most suitable for Australia, it is necessary to examine the fiscal position of the States and the Commonwealth in more detail. Looking at State and local governments, their fiscal position in 2000–01 was as follows:[83]

Source	Amount	Percentage
Tax revenue	$49 billion	41
Sales and service fees	$14 billion	12
Non-tax income (such as interest)	$3 billion	3
GST revenue transferred from Commonwealth	$30 billion	25
Budget Balancing Assistance from Commonwealth	$2 billion	2
SPP's from Commonwealth	$20 billion	17
Totals	$118 billion	100

The Commonwealth's fiscal position is as follows:[84]

81 Which would of course require a repeal of s 90 of the Constitution.

82 Federal-State Relations Committee, 1999, 11.32–44.

83 Statistics are based on Australian Bureau of Statistics (ABS), 2000. However, note in place of the $33 billion recorded in the ABS statistics as Commonwealth grants, I have substituted the $30 billion in GST revenue and the $2 billion in Budget Balancing Assistance which replaced these grants with the introduction of the GST in the following year. In addition, I have included the $20 billion that States receive from the Commonwealth in specific purpose payments (that is, tied grants) from the Commonwealth.

84 Statistics are derived from Department of the Treasury, 2001, adjusted to reflect the $31 billion collected from the GST as Commonwealth rather than State revenue. Note that the Commonwealth also receives about $15 billion per annum in non-tax income, which is not reflected in these figures.

Source	Amount	Percentage
Personal income tax	$72 billion	44
Corporate income tax	$24 billion	15
Other income tax	$6 billion	4
GST Revenue	$30 billion	19
Other indirect taxes (excises, duties)	$25 billion	15
Other taxes	$5 billion	3
Totals	$162 billion	100

Thus, the State governments raise only 56% of what they need, and rely on the GST and excise duties imposed by the Commonwealth Parliament and other conditional grants from the Commonwealth (called specific purpose payments, or SPPs) for the remaining 44% of their expenditure. These Commonwealth allocations to the States total $52 billion, and represent 32% of the $162 billion in revenue collected by the Commonwealth.

If the dedicated State revenue option was chosen, the Constitution would have to include a provision allocating particular types of tax to one or both levels of government. In light of the above figures, one could say that in order to ensure that the States received the same total income from the Commonwealth as they do at present, the Constitution would have to give them exclusive power over tax revenues worth $52 billion, which would be achieved if, for example, the Constitution stated that corporate income tax and 'other' indirect taxes (that is, all indirect taxes other than the GST) were to be made over to the States. However, the dedicated revenue model suffers two significant drawbacks: first, it assumes that the revenue generated by whichever tax or taxes are earmarked for the States will remain in the same proportion to all revenues as exists at the moment. There would, therefore, be a risk that States might suffer a shortfall if those particular revenue sources dropped in proportion to all others, and a windfall if they increased. Secondly, the system is one in which the problem of inter-State equalisation is difficult to solve. As already noted, the allocation of GST to the States is done in accordance with a formula designed to ensure that each State is able to deliver the same level of services to its residents. In order for the same result to be achieved under a system where State Parliaments were levying and collecting the particular tax or taxes allocated to them by the Constitution, either the taxes would have to be imposed at different rates from State to State, or they would have to be imposed at a uniform rate, and then redistributed by some system of inter-State transfers. This could only be done by means of a provision in the Constitution permitting some central inter-State or federal agency to take a portion of their revenue from some States and to give it to others.

I would argue that matters would be far simpler if Australia took the option of a revenue-sharing system similar to that used in Germany. The Constitution would give to the Commonwealth exclusive authority to levy personal and corporate income taxes, the GST and other indirect taxes at uniform national rates. This would simply give formal recognition to what happens at the moment. All other taxes currently collected by the States and by local governments would, by default, remain within the authority of the State Parliaments. The Constitution would require that the revenue raised from all those

Commonwealth taxes be divided between the Commonwealth, on the one hand, and the States and Territories on the other, in a fixed ratio of 68:32. This reflects the current division of all Commonwealth revenue as stated above. The 32% allocated to the States would then be distributed between them by a Grants Commission, mandated by the Constitution to distribute the money as at present – in other words, in such a way as to achieve equalisation in the provision of services within the States.

The 68:32 ratio is derived from current patterns of revenue-raising. It is also based on the current allocation of legislative authority, and thus current responsibilities for the provision of government services, between the Commonwealth and the States. It is reasonable to assume that patterns of revenue-raising are not subject to significant change over time. In addition, as the discussion later in this chapter of Commonwealth legislative powers will show, although I recommend some broadening in the scope of existing Commonwealth legislative powers, the only completely new powers I would include in a new Constitution are those relating to scientific research and nuclear energy. The new Constitution would thus not significantly enhance the matters in respect of which the Commonwealth had responsibility for expenditure. One could, therefore, safely assume that the allocation of Commonwealth revenue between it and the States in a 68:32 ratio would be as appropriate under the new Constitution as it would be if revenue-sharing was introduced under the current Constitution, and that the ratio can, therefore, safely be set in the Constitution. As a part of the Constitution, the ratio would be subject to amendment by the normal procedures required for constitutional amendment (discussed later in this chapter). But should there be some additional, less time-consuming way of amending the formula, so as to accommodate unexpected and significant changes to patterns of revenue-raising and/or Commonwealth or State expenditure? It will be recalled that in Germany, amendments to the fiscal distribution formula requires the assent of the Bundesrat. However, the Bundesrat is a very different creature from the Australian Senate. Unlike the Senate, which is not a true 'States' House, and whose members vote along party lines, the Bundesrat consists of members appointed by the State governments, and voting on their instruction. If we were to create an analogous procedure for the amendment of a revenue-sharing provision in the Australian Constitution, it would be necessary to give that power to a body which was recognised in the Constitution, and whose membership consisted of representatives of the Commonwealth and State governments. No such body exists at present. However, there are some institutions which might provide suitable models. The annual Conference of State Premiers, which is attended by the Premiers of the States, the Chief Ministers of the Territories and the Commonwealth Prime Minister, holds periodic meetings at which the heads of the Australian governments discuss matters of mutual concern. Before the introduction of the GST, the Conference was notable for the often acrimonious discussions that occurred on the issue of how much Commonwealth revenue would be passed to the States, and how it would be distributed among them. A similar forum is the Council of Australian Governments (COAG), at which the heads of government and the President of the Australian Local Government Association meet to exchange views. Neither of these bodies have any status within the Constitution. I would, therefore argue that, as an additional avenue to the normal one for amendment provided in the Constitution, the 68:32 ratio be able to be amended by a two-thirds majority of a meeting of a constitutionally-recognised Council of Australian Heads of Government, the members of which would be the Prime Minister of the Commonwealth, the State Premiers and the Chief Ministers of the ACT and the Northern Territory. The ability of such a body to amend this provision in the Constitution would provide a safety valve in times of national emergency. In addition, the recognition of the Council in the Constitution might foster federal co-operation in respect of other matters of mutual interest.

One issue that would need to be addressed if such a system was adopted would be that of whether the Commonwealth would be able to impose conditions on the States and Territories in respect of any of the 32% transferred to them. It will be recalled that of the $52 billion currently transferred to the States each year, $20 billion takes the form of SPPs, which are granted on condition that they are used for specific projects.[85] These projects are associated with matters such as health, education, social welfare, transport (including roads) and local government – in short, a wide variety of other programmes relating to matters which do not fall within the legislative power of the Commonwealth, but for which it provides funding. Surprisingly, it is often the largest grants, such as those associated with health and education, that have the fewest conditions attached to them.[86] Should a revenue-sharing provision in a new Constitution allocate some of the States' and Territories' entitlement as untied grants and some as tied? On the one hand, it might be argued that there is no need to tie any of the allocation given to the States and Territories, because their governments will suffer the electoral consequences of failing to maintain services such as health, education and welfare. It could also be argued that leaving the States' and Territories' portion of national revenues untied is consistent with the overall philosophy of State fiscal autonomy, which is surely what revenue-sharing is designed to achieve. On the other hand, it might be argued that there will sometimes be legitimate reasons for conditions to be attached to funds received by the States, as, for example, where a matter such as environmental protection, which falls within the legislative capacity of the States, needs expenditure as a result of international obligations assumed by the Commonwealth. Perhaps the best solution to this question is to analyse how SPPs are currently distributed and then to determine which are the categories in respect of which the Commonwealth should be able to impose conditions. Specific purpose payments for 2001–02 were allocated as follows:[87]

Education	$6.6 billion
Health	$7.5 billion
Social welfare	$1.6 billion
Housing	$1.1 billion
Transport	$1.3 billion
Local government	$1.4 billion
Other	$0.8 billion

Within the broad category of SPPs, a distinction is made between SPPs 'to' the States (for programmes they administer themselves), and SPPs 'through' the States, which they pass on to other bodies (primarily to non-government schools and to local governments). Of

85 The nature and scale of SPP's is discussed in Review of Commonwealth – State Funding, 2002, 25.

86 *Ibid.*

87 *Ibid*, 23.

the total of $20 billion in SPPs, $5 billion takes the form of SPPs 'through' the States ($3.6 billion of the education funds, $0.1 billion of the housing funds, and the $1.4 billion for local government). In addition, the $800 million in 'other' SPPs will contain many programmes (for example, the environmental programmes mentioned above), in relation to which it is legitimate for the Commonwealth to impose conditions. Even if we assumed that most of the $1.3 billion for transport was dedicated to federal highways, that would mean that only $7.3 billion of the $20 billion were funds which should be tied. That $7.3 billion represents 14% of the $52 billion transferred from the Commonwealth to the states or, to express it differently, 4.5% of the overall Commonwealth tax revenues of $163 billion. Integrating this data into the proposed constitutionally-mandated 68:32 division of Commonwealth tax revenue between the Commonwealth and the States, one would conclude that the Commonwealth's legitimate interest in subjecting some of the funds to conditions would be satisfied if the Constitution provided that Commonwealth tax revenues be divided in the following ratio: 68% to the Commonwealth, 27% in unconditional transfers to the States, and 5% to the States which could be subject to conditions imposed by the Commonwealth. This would mean a radical reduction in the proportion of money subject to conditions as compared to the current situation, but, as was stated above, increased fiscal independence for the States would be subject to State accountability to their electorates in relation to how the untied money is spent.

A discussion of fiscal relationships in a federation would be incomplete without mentioning some of the debate that has taken place on the question of how best to achieve equality of outcomes from the perspective of the inhabitant of a particular State or States. Some have argued that the complex formula of *per capita* relativities used by the Commonwealth Grants Commission does little to further the objective of equal living standards within each State and Territory, and that other models, or even the allocation to the States of whatever revenue was raised within their borders, would achieve the same outcome.[88] That is a debate that lies beyond the scope of this book. For present purposes, it is simply necessary to note that all that needs to be included in the Constitution is a requirement that, in distributing revenue among the States and Territories, the Grants Commission does so in a way which achieves reasonable equity in the provision of services throughout Australia. The precise method used to do that is a technical issue for Parliament or the Grants Commission to determine. The constitutional mandate will have been fulfilled if it can be shown that whatever distribution system is used is reasonably adapted towards the stated objective.

5.5 THE LEGISLATIVE POWERS OF THE COMMONWEALTH IN A NEW CONSTITUTION

It is now necessary to consider what powers should be given to the Commonwealth Parliament in a new Constitution. As a preliminary point, I would recommend that, in drafting a new Constitution, the opportunity be taken to revise the rather haphazard listing of powers in s 51, and to group the powers into three broad categories – exclusive

88 Harding, Warren, Beer, Phillips and Osei, 2002.

powers of the Commonwealth (most of which relate to the operation of the Commonwealth as a national government); powers which ought to fall within the authority of the Commonwealth Parliament because they relate to matters which should be subject to uniform national regulation, but which are open to legislation by the States in the absence of Commonwealth enactments; and those powers which relate to the Constitution itself. Many of the powers within each of these broad categories relate to topics which are already contained in s 51 of the current Constitution. In some cases, the power as currently formulated could simply be reproduced in the new Constitution. In others, the existing power would need to be reworded, and in such instances I discuss in the accompanying footnotes what the relationship between the old and the new would be. The categories also contain some new powers which do not have analogues in the existing Constitution. I also address the question of which powers appearing in the current Constitution should be omitted from a new one, either because they are redundant, or because they should fall within the preserve of the States.

5.5.1 Exclusive powers of the Commonwealth

The first category to be discussed are the exclusive powers of the Commonwealth. The following points should be made in relation to these powers.

First, it will be noted that, the proposed exclusive powers are far more numerous than in the current Constitution. However, I would argue that in many instances, powers which were not formally made exclusive in the 1901 Constitution are exclusive powers *de facto*. Many of the supposedly non-exclusive powers contained in the current Constitution, which relate to the functions of the Commonwealth as the national government, are ones which one cannot imagine it being appropriate for the States to exercise. In this group are external affairs; borrowing money on the credit of the Commonwealth; expenditure of money for Commonwealth purposes; the granting of money to the States and Territories; naturalisation, immigration; aliens and defence. One should also include here the powers relating to the service and execution of judicial process throughout the Commonwealth, and the recognition throughout the Commonwealth of laws and proceedings of the States. A new power in this area, recommended by the Constitutional Commission, is a power in relation to principles of choice of law.[89] As the Commission concluded, the choice of law issues that arise in a multi-jurisdictional environment such as that in Australia can lead to 'forum shopping', particularly in torts cases.[90]

The most significant addition to the exclusive powers, and one which marks a departure from the existing Constitution, is that relating to taxation. As stated in the discussion of federal-State financial relations earlier in this chapter, the new Constitution would vest in the Commonwealth an exclusive power to levy all personal and corporate income taxes, and all indirect taxes. This would make the power markedly different from how it is at present. Furthermore, in light of the new version of s 99 which would be included in the new Constitution (see 5.6.2, below), and which would prohibit

89 Constitutional Commission, 1988, 10.326.

90 *Ibid*, 10.338 and 10.347.

discrimination or preference in regard to laws relating to trade, commerce or revenue, there would be no need to include in the taxation power a qualification prohibiting geographic discrimination in the application of laws imposing taxation.

The following would be the exclusive powers of the Commonwealth:

- taxes on the income of any person or corporation, and taxes on goods and services including duties of customs and excise;
- the borrowing of money on the credit of the Commonwealth;
- the appropriation of money for such purposes as the Commonwealth Parliament sees fit;[91]
- the granting of assistance to any State or Territory on such conditions as Parliament deems fit;[92]
- defence, including the raising of defence forces;[93]
- external affairs;
- aliens, naturalisation, citizenship and migration;[94]
- currency;[95]
- the service and execution throughout the Commonwealth of legal process, and of the judgments of Commonwealth and State and Territory courts;[96]
- the recognition throughout the Commonwealth of State and Territory laws, State and Territory public records and State and Territory judicial proceedings;[97]
- principles of choice of law;
- the seat of government of the Commonwealth, and all places acquired by the Commonwealth for public purposes;
- the Commonwealth public service.[98]

---

91 This would replace the appropriations clause currently found in s 81 of the Constitution with a formulation recommended by the Constitutional Commission at 11.296. The substitution of the qualifying words 'for the purposes of the Commonwealth' in s 81 with the words contained in the text above would remove doubt over the question of whether the Commonwealth was restricted, when appropriating funds, to doing so only for such purposes as appear in the enumerated powers. Although in *Victoria v Commonwealth and Hayden* (*AAP* case) (1975) 134 CLR 338 a majority of the High Court either stated or assumed that the Commonwealth was not so restricted by the text of s 81, a re-formulation would bring certainty to the question.

92 This puts into the enumerated powers the provisions currently contained in the Constitution, s 96.

93 This re-drafting of the defence power and its inclusion in the list of exclusive powers of the Commonwealth effectively incorporates the prohibition against States raising military and naval forces, currently contained in the Constitution, s 114.

94 Currently covered by the s 51(xix) 'Naturalization and aliens' power and the s 51(xxvii) 'Immigration and emigration' power. The addition of the word 'citizenship' was recommended in Constitutional Commission, 1988, 4.177–189 in order to remove any uncertainty on the question of whether citizenship was an implied aspect of naturalisation.

95 The term 'currency' covers 'currency, coinage and legal tender' referred to in the current s 51(xii) power. Including the power relating to currency in the list of exclusive powers of the Commonwealth would obviate the necessity for the prohibition on the States coining money contained in s 115.

96 This is a re-wording of the s 51(xxiv) power so as to include Commonwealth process as well as those of the States, and to make it clear that the power extends to the service of process within the State where it was issued – see Constitutional Commission, 1988, 10.302–04.

97 This is a re-wording of the s 51(xxv) power so as to make it clearer. This power gives the Commonwealth the means to give effect to the 'full faith and credit' provision in s 118.

98 This is a more succinct way of expressing what is currently contained in s 52(ii).

5.5.2 Concurrent Commonwealth powers

The second category of powers are those relating to matters in respect of which it is desirable that there be national uniformity, but which there is no reason the States should not be able to legislate on in the absence of legislation enacted by the Commonwealth. Many of these powers would simply be carried over from the current Constitution,[99] but there are some which have been significantly altered, or which are wholly new, and it is useful to discuss these before listing all the powers. In this regard, specific reference needs to be made of three powers relating to macro-economic legislation: corporations, trade and commerce, and conciliation and arbitration. Reform is also recommended in relation to marriage, divorce and other family proceedings, in relation to the races power, and in relation to air and sea navigation. New powers relating to scientific research and nuclear energy are also discussed.

Although many would oppose any expansion of Commonwealth powers and (indeed, a theme of this chapter has been to explore ways of evening the federal balance to the advantage of the States), there is no denying that economic activity is an area in relation to which the Commonwealth should have the legislative power to achieve nationwide uniformity, in order to ensure that the economy operates efficiently and that a common regulatory framework governs anyone engaging in economic activity in Australia. Thus, I would agree with recommendations of the 1988 Constitutional Commission that the corporations, trade and commerce and conciliation and arbitration powers be broadened.

The Commission recommended that the corporations power be redrafted so as to allow the Commonwealth to legislate not just for the activities of corporations, but also for their formation.[100] At present, the Commonwealth's power to enact legislation relating to the formation of corporations relies upon a temporary reference of this matter to the Commonwealth by the States under s 51(xxxvii). This was necessitated by the fact that the previous co-operative scheme became inoperable following the High Court's finding in *Re Wakim ex parte McNally*,[101] that the legislation providing for the cross-vesting of jurisdiction between State and Commonwealth courts, upon which the scheme depended for its enforcement, was invalid. A reformulation of the power so that it conferred on the Commonwealth a broad and unqualified power with respect to corporations would eliminate this long-running problem.

Along with a broadening of the corporations power, the 1988 Constitutional Commission report also recommended an expansion of the trade and commerce power to cover intra-State trade.[102] To some extent, such a reform is almost unnecessary, given that the Commonwealth has the corporations power available to it, and that most business in Australia is conducted by corporations. However, an expansion of the trade and commerce power would allow the Commonwealth to extend laws relating to matters such as competition, consumer protection and industrial relations to businesses which are not corporations, and whose activities were contained wholly within one State. This

99 Minor changes to the wording are discussed in footnotes following.

100 Constitutional Commission, 1988, 11.87.

101 (1999) 198 CLR 511.

102 Constitutional Commission, 1988, 11.11

would, in turn, permit uniform regulation of all trade and commerce – that conducted by corporations and by other forms of business, and that conducted both inter-State and wholly within individual States.[103] This would also obviate the necessity of States having to enact parallel legislation on matters such as trade practices so as to ensure that businesses which are not corporations, and which operate wholly intra-State, are subject to the same regime as are corporations and businesses operating inter-State.[104] I would, therefore, recommend that the Constitution confer a general power over trade and commerce on the Commonwealth.

The third power relating to the economy is the s 51(xxxv) power, which gives the Commonwealth legislative authority with respect to the conciliation and arbitration of inter-State industrial disputes. The fact that this power is limited to the conciliation and arbitration of disputes (as distinct from permitting the regulation of industrial disputes generally), and requires an element of inter-statedness, severely limits is usefulness. In order to enable the Commonwealth to use the power effectively, the courts have given it an increasingly strained interpretation, finding that matters such as the registration of unions, which, on the face of it, might appear not to relate to the conciliation and arbitration of disputes, fall within the implied incidental aspect of the power.[105] Similarly, the courts have found that disputes which appeared to have only a tenuous inter-State element,[106] or were mere 'paper disputes',[107] fell within the ambit of the power. Ultimately, however, the Commonwealth has found that the corporations power provides a far more useful way of circumventing the restrictions contained in the conciliation and arbitration power, as the courts have approved the use of the corporations power as a vehicle for the general regulation of labour relations matters pertaining to corporations.[108] Thus, as in the case of the inter-State and overseas trade power, the conciliation and arbitration power found itself overshadowed by the corporations power. Given the Commonwealth's *de facto* power in the area of labour relations, it would seem that considerations of uniformity of treatment of labour relations, both in the corporate and non-corporate environment, and the desirability of sweeping away highly technical case-law required by 'constitutional distinctions that are unrelated to the object of settling disputes or the broader purposes of industrial relations policy',[109] give force to the

103 This and other reasons justifying a broadening of the power were canvassed by the Constitutional Commission, 1988, 11.39–60.

104 Federal-State Relations Committee, 1999, 4.28–32.

105 *Jumbunna Coalmine v Victorian Coal Miners Association* (1908) 6 CLR 309.

106 *R v Ludeke ex parte Queensland Electricity Commission* (1985) 159 CLR 178; *Re Australasian Meat Employees' Union ex parte Aberdeen Beef Co Pty Ltd* (1993) 176 CLR 154.

107 *Burwood Cinema Ltd v Australian Theatrical and Amusement Employees' Association* (1925) 35 CLR 528, *Attorney-General (Queensland) v Riordan* (1997) 192 CLR 1.

108 See *Actors and Announcers Equity Association of Australia v Fontana Films Pty Ltd* (1982) 150 CLR 169, where the High Court held that the corporations power could be used to control not just the activities of employees of corporations, but also secondary picketing against corporations by union members who were not its employees. There is, however, a limit to how remote a connection the courts are prepared to accept as satisfying the requirement that a law must be with respect to corporations, as is shown by *Re Dingjan ex parte Wagner* (1995) 183 CLR 323, where the High Court held that a sub-contract between a person and another person who had a contract with a corporation was not a matter which fell within the ambit of the corporation's power.

109 Constitutional Commission, 1988, 11.135.

Constitutional Commission's recommendation that the conciliation and arbitration power be replaced by a power to legislate with respect to labour relations generally.[110]

It is true that the redrafted trade and commerce, corporations and labour relations powers would sweep away the last vestiges of restraint on the Commonwealth's legislative capacity in the field of broad economic management. Yet I would argue that in an economy that is already nationally integrated, and becoming increasingly so internationally, the interest of economic efficiently provides a powerful argument in favour of such an arrangement.

The s 51(iii) power of the Commonwealth to grant bounties is of little practical importance today. It was made an exclusive power of the Commonwealth because s 90 prohibits the States from conferring bounties on the production or export of goods, subject only to the s 91 exemption permitting bounties in relation to mining, and any other categories expressly permitted by the Commonwealth Parliament. The power was made exclusive to the Commonwealth in order to ensure free trade, but this rationale is not persuasive: free trade is not impeded if one State uses its resources to give a bounty to a particular industry, even if that results in an advantage being conferred over competitors in other States. Indeed, States frequently do bid against each other in order to attract business, by offering tax holidays and other favourable treatment. While the Commonwealth should continue to have a power to confer bounties, there seems to be no good reason why the power should be exclusive.

A feature of the constitution which has caused significant problems for litigants in the area of family law is the fact that, although s 51(xxi) gives to the Commonwealth the power to legislate with respect to marriage, and s 51(xxii) the power to legislate with respect to divorce and matrimonial causes and 'in relation thereto, parental rights, and the custody and guardianship of infants', the courts have interpreted these provisions as not going so far as to allow the Commonwealth to legislate in such a way as to provide for the custody of children who were not children born of the marriage of the parties disputing their custody.[111] A broadening of the power to cover family law generally would eliminate such problems, and would allow the Commonwealth courts to deal with all matters arising out of family law disputes.

The history of the s 51(xxvi) races power is notorious. The power was included in the Constitution in order to provide the Commonwealth with the means to make special provision for migrant groups which the government wished to legislate for separately – and usually adversely.[112] The power expressly excluded Aboriginal people from its ambit, and thus legislation in respect of them fell within the preserve of the States. The constitutional amendment of 1967 removed this restriction, thus allowing the Commonwealth to enact legislation securing equal rights for Aboriginal people. Would a races power be required in the new Constitution? As is discussed later in this chapter, the new Constitution would confer upon the Commonwealth a new power to enact laws giving effect to provisions contained in the Constitution. The Bill of Rights contained in the new Constitution would protect the right to equality and, as was discussed at 2.5.11,

110 *Ibid*, 11.119.

111 *In Marriage of Cormick* (1984) 156 CLR 170; *R v C ex Parte C* (1985) 156 CLR 249; *Re F ex parte F* (1986) 161 CLR 376.

112 Blackshield and Williams, 2002, 181; Irving, 1997, 116.

above, would permit the enactment of affirmative action measures for the benefit of disadvantaged groups. The Bill of Rights would also recognise the rights of people to protect and develop their culture. Finally, as is discussed in Chapter 6, a new Constitution would recognise customary law, and would make provision for indigenous self-government. It may, therefore, be argued that the races power would be redundant. However, there are areas of Australian law affecting indigenous people which might not be covered by the categories already mentioned in this paragraph. One such area is native title, which the High Court, in *Mabo v Queensland (No 2)*,[113] recognised as a doctrine within the common law of property. Although any attempt to deprive indigenous people of their native title rights would breach equality rights,[114] legislation on native title itself might not be characterised as relating to the right to equality. Similarly, although it could plausibly be argued that native title is an aspect of indigenous culture, or, alternatively, is a matter relating to indigenous self-government, this, too, is a matter which would be subject to interpretation. I would therefore recommend that, in order to remove any uncertainty in this regard, the new Constitution should confer on the Commonwealth Parliament a power analogous to the race power, but that the new power simply refer to 'indigenous people', so as to make it clear that the power extended both to Aborigines and to Torres Strait Islanders. Note that because the Bill of Rights would protect the right to equality, there would be no question of the power being able to be exercised in a discriminatory way against indigenous people, an issue which the court in *Kartinyeri v Commonwealth* (*Hindmarsh Bridge* case)[115] left open in its interpretation of the s 51(xxvi) race power.

Currently, the Commonwealth has no express power relating to air and sea navigation. Section 51(vii) of the Constitution refers only to 'Lighthouses, lightships, beacons and buoys'. A power which referred to air and sea navigation would cover s 51(vii) as well as air navigation, currently within the Commonwealth's legislative power only because in the High Court found that that topic falls within the incidental power to the inter-State and overseas trade and commerce power.[116] The 1988 Constitutional Commission also recognised the need for an express power covering Admiralty and maritime matters,[117] as the s 76(iii) power to confer jurisdiction on the High Court has been interpreted as relating to the enforcement of Admiralty and maritime law as it existed when the Constitution was drafted, rather than to the enactment of new laws in this field.[118]

An area which calls out for comprehensive and, I would argue, uniform, regulation is that of scientific research. In particular, one can think of matters such as reproductive technology and genetic engineering,[119] which were topics not contemplated by the framers of the Constitution, and which need to be regulated by laws with national coverage, in order to avoid unscrupulous practitioners taking advantage of omissions

113 (1992) 175 CLR 1.

114 *Western Australia v Commonwealth* (*Native Title* case) (1995) 183 CLR 373.

115 (1998) 195 CLR 337.

116 *Airlines of New South Wales Pty Ltd v New South Wales (No 2)* (1965) 113 CLR 54.

117 Constitutional Commission, 1988, 10.130.

118 *Owners of SS Kabilia v Wilson* (1910) 11 CLR 689.

119 Brennan, 2001, 21.

from the law in different jurisdictions. Similarly, nuclear energy ought also to be given express recognition within the Commonwealth Parliament's heads of power, as recommended by the 1988 Constitutional Commission.[120]

The non-exclusive powers of the Commonwealth would, therefore, be as follows:

- trade and commerce;[121]
- corporations;[122]
- banking, excluding the operation of banks by State governments;[123]
- insurance other than the operation of insurance schemes by State governments;[124]
- negotiable instruments;[125]
- bankruptcy and insolvency;
- intellectual property;[126]
- bounties on the production or export of goods;
- marriage and family relationships;[127]
- social welfare benefits and services and also pensions;[128]
- indigenous people;[129]
- telecommunications;[130]
- air and sea navigation, including Admiralty and maritime matters;

120 Constitutional Commission, 1988, 10.110.

121 As discussed in the text above, this power would not be restricted to inter-State and overseas trade and commerce, as is the case in the current s 51(i).

122 As discussed in the text above, this is an unqualified power relating to corporations.

123 This is a re-draft of the current s 51(xiii) banking power. The exclusion of 'State banking' from the ambit of the Commonwealth's power by s 51(xiii) is somewhat ambiguous. The re-draft makes it clear that what is meant is the operation of banks by State governments, not the relationships that State governments might have with other banks. Section 51(xiii) qualifies the exception in relation to State banking by conferring on the Commonwealth the power to legislate on State banking taking place beyond the limits of the State concerned. This provision is inconsistent with the purpose of the exclusion of State banking from the ambit of the power, which is surely to protect an instrumentality of the State government from interference by the Commonwealth, and should therefore be omitted. Furthermore, s 51(xiii)'s conferral of power in relation to the incorporation of banks would be covered by a corporations power which extended to the formation of corporations and is thus also unnecessary. Finally, the clause in s 51(xiii) relating to paper money is covered by the power relating to currency and can therefore be omitted.

124 The current formulation of the insurance power in s 51(xiv) refers to 'Insurance other than State insurance; also State insurance extending beyond the limits of the State concerned'. The same arguments can be made in support of a re-drafting of this power as are made in relation to the banking power in the preceding footnote.

125 This would replace the terms 'bills of exchange and promissory notes' contained in 51(xvi) with a more generic term.

126 This would replace the s 51(xxviii) 'copyrights, patents of inventions and designs, and trademarks' power with a more generic formulation.

127 This power would replace the existing s 51(xxi) marriage power and the s 51(xxii) divorce and matrimonial causes power. The new formulation is discussed later in the text.

128 This power would cover all matters currently contained in the unwieldy s 51(xxiiiA) welfare power and the s 51(xxiii) power relating to invalid and old-age pensions.

129 This replaces the s 51(xxvi) races power, as discussed in the text above.

130 Currently defined in s 51(v) as the power with respect to 'Postal, telegraphic, telephonic, and other like services'. 'Telecommunications' is a broader term which would cover future developments in this area.

- census and statistics;
- astronomical and meteorological observations;
- scientific research;
- nuclear energy;
- quarantine;
- fisheries beyond three nautical miles of the shore-line;[131]
- weights and measures;
- the deprivation of property from any State or person for public purposes.[132]

5.5.3 Powers pertaining to the operation of the Constitution

The third category of powers can best be described as those relating to the operation of the Constitution itself. Most of these appear in the current Constitution, and could therefore be adopted unaltered, except in such a way as to make their wording clearer. The only changes that should take place are the addition of an express power to give effect to the provisions of the Constitution, which, to take some examples, would be used to enact legislation giving effect to the provisions of the new Constitution relating to the Bill of Rights (discussed in Chapter 2), direct democracy (discussed in Chapter 7) and the electoral system (discussed in Chapter 8). Such a power would incorporate the existing s 51(xxxvi) power relating to matters for which the Constitution provides until Parliament provides otherwise. The other change would be the removal of the s 51(xxxviii) power, which empowers the Commonwealth Parliament to legislate, with the consent of the States, in any way that the Parliament of the United Kingdom could have legislated at the commencement of the 1901 Constitution. This power would obviously be rendered redundant with the enactment of a new Constitution.

The third category of powers would therefore cover the following topics:

- the giving of effect to the provisions of the Constitution;
- any matter referred to the Parliament of the Commonwealth by the Parliament or Parliaments of any State or States, but so that the law shall extend only to States by whose Parliaments the matter is referred, or which subsequently adopt the law;
- matters incidental to the execution of any power vested by this Constitution in the legislative, executive or judicial branch of the Commonwealth.[133]

---

131 The exclusion of the power of the Commonwealth to legislate with regard to fisheries from the area within three nautical miles of the coast would constitutionalise the political agreement reached between the Commonwealth and the States in 1979 in the wake of the decision in *New South Wales v Commonwealth* (*Seas and Submerged Land Act* case) (1975) 135 CLR 337, in which the High Court held that the s 51(xxix) external affairs power enabled the Commonwealth to legislate on all matters from the shore-line of Australia. That political agreement, now contained in the Coastal Waters (State Title) Act 1980 (Cth), involved a withdrawal of the Commonwealth from legislating for the area within three nautical miles of the coast, and thus a cession of authority in relation thereto to the States.

132 For a discussion of the formulation of this power and its interaction with the Bill of Rights, see 2.5.15, above.

133 This is a more succinctly phrased version of the express incidental power contained in s 51(xxxix).

5.5.4 Redundant s 51 powers

A number of powers contained in the 1901 Constitution were arguably redundant when that Constitution was drafted, and appear to have been included from an abundance of caution: thus the s 51(xxvii) power relating to the influx of criminals was an unnecessary power, as its subject matter was covered by the s 51(xxviii) power relating to immigration and emigration. Similarly, the s 51(xxx) power relating to relations with the islands of the Pacific was covered by the s 51(xxix) external affairs power.

The 1901 Constitution contains three powers relating to railways: s 51(xxxii) relating to the control of railways for defence purposes; s 51(xxxiii) relating to the acquisition of railways from a State by agreement with that State; and s 51(xxxiv) relating to the construction of railways in a State with the agreement of that State. The first of these is redundant in that it is, arguably, already included in the s 51(vi) defence power. The second does not augment Commonwealth powers, but, rather, acts as a restraint on the s 51(xxxi) acquisitions power, in that the Commonwealth can acquire railways from the States only with the assent of the latter. There would seem to be no good reason to have different rules apply to railways as compared to other State assets which might be acquired by the Commonwealth, in which case this restriction should be removed. Finally, the s 51(xxxiv) power relating to the construction of railways would seem to be redundant in light of the availability of the grants power to the Commonwealth, which it already uses to construct highways in co-operation with the States. The net effect is that all the railways powers can safely be removed from the Constitution, and this would be consistent with current reality, which is that railways are legislated on by the States rather than the Commonwealth.

Finally, I have already noted in the text and accompanying footnotes in 5.5.1 and 5.5.2, above, that a number of existing powers would be subsumed within redrafted powers in a new Constitution.

5.5.5 Commonwealth powers and the *Melbourne Corporation* principle

A doctrine with important ramifications for the legislative power of the Commonwealth, and, indeed, a key doctrine of Australian federalism, is the *Melbourne Corporation* principle, which takes its name from the case of *Melbourne Corporation v Commonwealth* (*State Banking* case),[134] in which the principle was first recognised. In that case, the High Court held that because of the federal nature of our Constitution, it was implicit in the Constitution that the Commonwealth could not use its powers in such a way as to discriminate against the States by singling them out as the subjects of legislation, or so as to threaten the continued existence of States, or substantially curtail or interfere with the ability of their governments to function. The case is important, because it established that even if Commonwealth legislation is *prima facie* within s 51, if the effect of the legislation is to interfere with the functioning of a State government, the legislation will be invalid. Furthermore, the principle was held to be reciprocal – in other words, the States, too, are barred from destroying or substantially curtailing the powers of the Commonwealth. Before discussing the *Melbourne Corporation* principle, it should be noted that it

134 (1947) 74 CLR 31.

supplements other specific restrictions on Commonwealth legislative power designed to ensure the continued functioning of State governments, such as the prohibitions on Commonwealth legislation on State banking and insurance contained in s 51(xiii) and (xiv) respectively, and the s 114 prohibition on either the Commonwealth or State governments taxing the property of the other.

Whether a law enacted by one level of government goes so far as to substantially curtail the functioning of another is a matter of degree, and in practice the High Court has not often found that this has occurred.[135] However, the principle was re-affirmed in *Queensland Electricity Commission v Commonwealth*,[136] in which the court held that the implied federal principle prohibited any Commonwealth legislation which discriminated against a State or States by placing special burdens or disabilities on them, or which destroyed or curtailed the continued existence of the States or their capacity to function as governments. This case involved a challenge to legislation enacted by the Commonwealth, using its s 51(xxxv) conciliation and arbitration power, which made special provision for a dispute between Queensland electricity providers and employees. The court held that the legislation infringed the first limb of the prohibition, in that it discriminated against Queensland by singling out disputes in the electricity industry to which the Queensland government was a party, and by subjecting them to a legislative regime which differed from that governing other industrial disputes in the industry. The principle was also applied in *Re Australian Education Union ex parte Victoria*.[137] There, the Commonwealth had used the Industrial Relations Act 1988 (Cth) to make an award covering public servants in Victoria. The High Court held that the Commonwealth had interfered with the operation of the State government to an extent that infringed the second limb of the rule, and that the Commonwealth could not use its s 51(xxxv) power to regulate the number and identity of persons a State wanted to employ or make redundant, their qualifications, or the terms of their employment or redundancy, although the Commonwealth could make awards regulating minimum wages and working conditions. However, in the case of holders of high office, including ministers, ministerial assistants and advisors, high level statutory office holders, and judges, even this limited Commonwealth power would not apply, as it was necessary for the States to have complete control over employment conditions at this level. Finally, mention should be made of *Victoria v Commonwealth* (*Second Uniform Tax* case)[138] which, although not a case in which the *Melbourne Corporation* principle was applied directly, relied on similar reasoning. In this case, the court held that the federal nature of the Constitution precluded the Commonwealth from using its s 51(ii) power to prohibit taxpayers from paying their

135 The High Court rejected arguments that the Commonwealth had breached the *Melbourne Corporation* principle in *Victoria v Commonwealth* (*Payroll Tax* case) (1971) 122 CLR 353 (where the Commonwealth had legislated to impose payroll tax on State governments in respect of workers in their employ); *Commonwealth v Tasmania* (*Tasmanian Dam* case) (1983) 158 CLR 1 (where the Commonwealth had legislated so as to prevent the State of Tasmania from developing an area which had been declared a World Heritage site); *State Chamber of Commerce and Industry v Commonwealth* (1987) 163 CLR 329 (in which the Commonwealth taxed States on the value of fringe benefits they provided to their employees); and *Richardson v Forestry Commission* (1988) 164 CLR 261 (in which the Commonwealth imposed a freeze on development of an area within a State pending an investigation as to whether the area was a World Heritage site).

136 (1985) 159 CLR 192.

137 (1995) 184 CLR 188.

138 (1957) 99 CLR 575.

tax liability to States before they had discharged their liability to the Commonwealth. It was also stated *obiter* that the taxation power could not be used to enact legislation prohibiting the States from imposing taxes. Although such legislation would fall into the field of taxation, the use of s 51(ii) in such a way would obviously terminate the States' ability to function effectively.

The *Melbourne Corporation* principle is but one rule of law pertaining to the broad area of the application of Commonwealth and State law to each other's governments. This issue has already been discussed in Chapter 4, where, it may be recalled, it was argued that a new Constitution should contain a provision expressly stating that the Crown in right of the Commonwealth should be presumed bound both by its own statute law and that of the States, but that the States should be presumed not to be bound by Commonwealth law. In either situation, these presumptions could be overridden: in the cases where it was desired to free the Commonwealth government from subjection to State law, this would be done by means of the Commonwealth enacting legislation which was inconsistent with State law. In the case where it was desired that Commonwealth law should not apply to State governments, this could be done by the Commonwealth legislation expressly stating that it did not apply to the States. However, this analysis reveals the vulnerability of each level of government to an impertinent exercise of legislative power by the other: the Commonwealth's ability to escape State law would depend upon whether that State law related to a topic which fell within the enumerated powers of the Commonwealth Parliament, because only then would the Commonwealth be able to override the legislation enacted by the State. Admittedly, instances where the Commonwealth would be unable to find a head of power to legislate under would be few and far between. Indeed, perhaps in all instances State legislation binding the Commonwealth would be able to be characterised as affecting the Commonwealth public service or Commonwealth places, and so would be able to be overridden by the Commonwealth Parliament. However, the position of the States would be much different: since the only way of their being exempted from Commonwealth legislation would be by the Commonwealth choosing not to make the legislation applicable to the States, there would be nothing the States could do to avoid being subject to Commonwealth legislation against the will of the Commonwealth. In other words, there is clearly a need for the *Melbourne Corporation* principle to act as a long-stop in cases where either level of government (but particularly the States) is unable to evade the other's legislation, in circumstances where the legislation, if effective, would undermine the subject government's ability to function.

In drafting a new Constitution one would therefore need to address the question of whether to try to incorporate the *Melbourne Corporation* principle in the text, or whether to leave it as an implied doctrine. The doctrine is somewhat nebulous in its terms, and thus it is not entirely clear as to precisely what type of action it prohibits one level of government engaging in *vis-à-vis* the other. Some might argue that the vagueness of the doctrine makes it impossible to put into the text of the Constitution. However, it could also be argued that a doctrine which places an important restraint on the dealings of each level of government with the other, and which, therefore, has a key role to play in the distribution of power within the system, should not be left in limbo. If the doctrine was to be incorporated into the text of the Constitution, what provision would capture its essence? Here it is important to distinguish between the two limbs of the *Melbourne Corporation* principle. The rationale for the second limb, which prohibits either level of government from using its legislative power in such a way as to threaten the continued existence of the other, or substantially to curtail or interfere with the ability of the other's government(s) to function, is easy to divine: a Commonwealth law on taxation which prohibited States from levying taxes, or a Commonwealth law on corporations which prohibited State governments from entering into contracts with corporations, to choose two examples, would certainly destroy the capacity of State governments to function and, practically speaking, would thus destroy the federal system. Judicial formulations of the second limb of the *Melbourne Corporation* principle would form a satisfactory basis for an express provision in the Constitution – perhaps formulated in terms of a prohibition against any law of the Commonwealth or of a State which substantially interferes with the existence of the other as an autonomous entity within the federation. Such a formula would ensure that the second limb of the doctrine was established as a permanent feature of the Constitution, while leaving it to the courts to determine precisely what legislation crossed the boundary of tolerance, as is the case at present. The rationale for the first limb of the *Melbourne Corporation* principle is less easy to fathom: in the absence of any threat to the autonomy of a particular level of government, a law which applied only to that level of government would seem to be unobjectionable. Furthermore, even subsequent to the application of this aspect of the doctrine in *Queensland Electricity Commission v Commonwealth*,[139] the High Court in *Richardson v Forestry Commission*[140] noted that the first limb of the doctrine is infringed only when the Commonwealth 'invalidly' discriminates against a State or States, and that there will, in fact, be many occasions (such as, for example, the designation of a particular area as a World Heritage site) where the Commonwealth legislation must perforce apply only to a particular State or area within a State. The key issue, therefore, is not whether the Commonwealth has legislated in relation to a matter pertaining only to one State (one could think of many examples where this might legitimately be done), but what the concept of 'invalidly' so doing means. Practically speaking, is there really any reason other than interference with State autonomy to label legislation as having an 'invalid' application to the States? If this is the case, then surely the first limb of the *Melbourne Corporation* principle is redundant, as legislation which interferes with the autonomy of a State is in any event captured by the second limb? In other words, I am arguing that because it will often be necessary for legislation to apply to a particular State, the first limb of the *Melbourne Corporation* principle cannot be interpreted literally, and should, instead, be read as prohibiting legislation which discriminates against a State or States only when that legislation contravenes the second limb. For this reason, the *Melbourne Corporation* principle would be satisfactorily incorporated into the Constitution by using the formulation of the second limb described earlier in this paragraph.

5.6 OTHER FEDERAL PROVISIONS

There are a number of provisions in the 1901 Constitution which can be said to serve a 'federal' purpose, in that they address issues which arise from the fact that Australia is a

139 (1985) 159 CLR 192.
140 (1988) 164 CLR 261.

federation. How some these matters would be treated in a new Constitution is addressed in this section.

5.6.1 Free trade and freedom of movement

A key issue engaging the attention of delegates to the Constitutional Conventions was the need to ensure free trade within the Commonwealth. From this was derived s 90, which gives to the Commonwealth the exclusive power to impose duties of customs and excise (to prevent the erection of internal customs barriers), and s 92 which prohibits either the Commonwealth or the States from impeding inter-State trade, commerce and intercourse.

So far as s 90 is concerned, the proposed granting of exclusive powers to the Commonwealth over all indirect taxes and duties as a corollary to the revenue-sharing scheme discussed earlier in this chapter, would cover the prohibition contained in s 90. Thus, a separate provision like s 90 would not be required. The rights currently conferred by s 92 would be protected by provisions in the Bill of Rights protecting freedom of commercial activity, freedom of movement and freedom of expression.

5.6.2 Equality of treatment of States

The drafters of the Constitution also wanted to ensure equality of treatment of the States by the Commonwealth. This purpose is served by s 99, which prohibits the Commonwealth from giving of preference in respect of laws of trade, commerce and revenue to States or parts thereof. A similar purpose is also served by the limitation on the s 51(ii) taxation power prohibiting the Commonwealth from discriminating between States or parts of States in its enactment of taxation laws. There is an obvious overlap between s 99 and s 51(ii) – indeed, if one takes the view that preference and discrimination are but different sides of the same coin,[141] it is arguable that the rider to s 51(ii) is redundant because of the coverage of s 99. Any uncertainty in this regard could be eliminated in a new Constitution by drafting a section in the same terms as the existing s 99, but covering both discrimination and preference.

The interpretation of the geographic element in s 99 has been problematic: in *Elliott v Commonwealth*[142] it was held that legislation requiring that seamen seeking employment in five named ports (Sydney, Newcastle, Brisbane, Melbourne and Port Adelaide) be licensed did not offend s 99, even though it did not apply in other ports in those States, and did not apply to any port in Western Australia or Tasmania. This was a highly formalistic interpretation of the section, because it effectively meant that to fall foul of s 99, legislation must have as an explicit criterion either (named) States, or localities within States *referred to as parts of States* – for example, as 'ports in New South Wales', which the challenged legislation did not! This problem could be addressed by framing the s 99

141 One should note that in *Elliott v Commonwealth* (1936) 54 CLR 657 the High Court stated that discrimination, in the sense of targeting a certain class, does not necessarily involve conferring a preference or benefit on that or any other class. However, the court did not cite any examples to illustrate its reasoning. I would argue that surely preference towards one involves discrimination against those not favoured, while discrimination against one involves preference towards those not discriminated against.

142 (1936) 54 CLR 657.

equivalent in such a way as to make it applicable to States or parts of States 'however defined'. This would make it quite clear that the section could not be evaded by drafting technicalities of the type permitted in *Elliott*.

5.6.3 No taxation of Commonwealth or State property

An important rule protecting the federal nature of the Constitution is contained in s 114, which prohibits the Commonwealth and the States from taxing each other's property. This provision disables either level of government from enhancing its revenue at the expense of the other. Along with the prohibitions on the Commonwealth legislating in relation to State banking and insurance, it also serves to protect the continued autonomous existence of the State governments. This provision should thus be reproduced in a new Constitution. The effect of this provision on the broad area of inter-governmental relations (addressed in Chapter 4), should also be noted. There, it was recommended that a new Constitution provide that, as a general rule, the Commonwealth should be presumed to be bound by State laws, but that the States be presumed not to be bound by laws of the Commonwealth. The prohibition against one level of government taxing the property of the other would stand as a specific exception to these general presumptions.

5.6.4 Equality of treatment of residents of States

The drafters of the Constitution were also concerned to protect the residents of any State from discrimination by the Commonwealth or any other State. This objective was secured by including in the Constitution the s 117 prohibition against discrimination on grounds of residence in a State. The rights conferred by s 117 would be protected in a new Constitution by including place of residence as a ground of prohibited discrimination in the section in the Bill of Rights protecting the right to equality. This issue has already been discussed at 2.5.11, above.

5.6.5 Full faith and credit

Section 118 of the Constitution provides that 'full faith and credit' shall be given throughout the Commonwealth to the laws and judicial proceedings of the States. The purpose of this provision, which is closely modelled on one contained in the United States Constitution,[143] is to ensure mutual recognition throughout Australia of the status of State laws, public records and judicial proceedings. Section 118 is supported by s 51(xxv) which gives the Commonwealth the power to enact laws in order to ensure that such recognition takes place. The need for such a provision in a federal Constitution is self-evident.

143 Constitution of the United States of America 1787, Art IV, s 1.

5.6.6 State Constitutions

As discussed at the beginning of this chapter, the States were subsumed into a new entity called the Commonwealth of Australia at federation and, by virtue of s 106, their Constitutions became subject to the Commonwealth Constitution. Similarly, under s 107, the powers of the State Parliaments continued in existence unless given exclusively to the Commonwealth or withdrawn from the States. The subordination of both the federal and State parliaments to the federal Constitution is an important feature of federal systems, and, like the current Constitution, a new Constitution should explicitly state that this is the case in similar terms.

5.6.7 Inconsistency

Any federal Constitution must contain a provision addressing inconsistency between federal and State laws. This function is performed by s 109 of the Constitution, which provides that where a State law is inconsistent with a law of the Commonwealth, the latter shall prevail, and the State law shall be invalid to the extent of the inconsistency. A number of tests for inconsistency have been developed by the courts in interpreting s 109. This area of the law is well settled, and there would be no reason to change the wording of the section in a new Constitution.

5.7 THE TERRITORIES

Under s 122 of the Constitution, the Commonwealth Parliament has the power to make laws for the Territories, and to determine their representation in the Commonwealth Parliament. The courts have interpreted this as a plenary power, entitling the Commonwealth to legislate on any Territory-related matter,[144] including with extra-territorial effect provided that the law was sufficiently connected to the Territory.[145] However, it is still unsettled as to whether this means that s 122 is 'disjoined from the rest of the Constitution',[146] or whether the Commonwealth is bound by restraints found elsewhere in the Constitution when legislating under s 122 (the integrationist approach). Unfortunately, the response given by the High Court on this question has been inconsistent: in *R v Bernasconi*,[147] it was held that the phrase 'law of the Commonwealth' in s 80, which confers a right to jury trial for indictable offences against the law of the Commonwealth, should be interpreted differentiating between Commonwealth (that is, nationwide) law, and the laws of the States, and that, since the former category did not embrace laws made for the Territories, such laws were not covered by s 80. By contrast, in *Kruger v Commonwealth*,[148] a majority of justices either stated or assumed that the s 116 right to freedom of religion applies when the Commonwealth exercises its s 122

144 *Spratt v Hermes* (1965) 114 CLR 226.

145 *Lamshead v Lake* (1958) 99 CLR 132.

146 This was the separationist approach adopted by Dixon J in *Australian National Airlines v Commonwealth* (1945) 71 CLR 29.

147 (1915) 19 CLR 629.

148 (1997) 190 CLR 1.

Territories power. In *Newcrest Mining (WA) Ltd v Commonwealth*,[149] three Justices held that even though the s 122 Territories power confers plenary power on the Commonwealth in respect of the Territories, the Commonwealth was still obliged to pay just terms compensation as required under s 51(xxxi) when it acquired property in a Territory.

These difficulties could be overcome simply by including the Territories power within the general list of enumerated powers of the Commonwealth Parliament, all of which would be prefaced by the words 'subject to this Constitution' (as is the case in the current Constitution). There would then be no doubt that the Territories power, like all others, should be read subject to restraints on Commonwealth legislative power contained elsewhere in the document.

5.8 CONSTITUTIONAL AMENDMENT

The amendment provision in a Constitution is of crucial importance. We have already seen, in the discussion of Bills of Rights in Chapter 2, that the effectiveness of a Bill of Rights depends upon its being entrenched – in other words, being protected from override by ordinary legislative enactment. Similarly, one of the hallmarks of a true federation is that the Constitution is not able to be amended by the central government or the sub-national units acting on their own.

Currently, s 128 of the Constitution requires that amendments be approved by a majority of voters nationwide, as well as by majorities in a majority of States. In addition, s 128 States that any amendment which alters the representation of the States in either House of Parliament, or the limits (in other words, the borders) of any State, must obtain the assent of a majority of voters in the State(s) concerned. The 'double majority' requirement (of a majority nationwide plus majorities in a majority of States) was seen as fulfilling the federal requirement that the consent of the States, as well as that of the country as a whole, be obtained for amendments to the Constitution. Furthermore, in the context of a population distribution which favoured New South Wales and Victoria, the double majority requirement was seen as necessary to protect the States with smaller populations from override by the larger States.

In Chapter 2, I referred to the various ways in which Constitutions in other jurisdictions are entrenched. These include requiring special legislative majorities, referenda, or combinations of both to effect amendment. The system contained in s 128 has the advantage that constitutional amendment cannot be effected by legislatures acting on their own – each step, both in relation to the national majority, and the State majorities, must be achieved by popular vote. This may be contrasted with the United States, for example, where amendments are effected by a two thirds majority of each house of Congress, followed by majorities in the legislatures of three-quarters of the States – at no stage is there direct involvement by the people.[150]

Assuming that we wished to retain direct involvement by the people, the next question to be addressed is whether, in relation to the first of the double majorities, s 128

149 (1997) 190 CLR 513.

150 Constitution of the United States 1787, Art V.

sets the bar too low in requiring only a simple majority of voters nation-wide to approve amendments. An important theme of the chapter on a Bill of Rights was the danger of using majorities, be they legislative or electoral, to determine the content of human rights. I argued that a Bill of Rights often performs a counter-majoritarian function of protecting individual rights from majority override. I also argued that the concept of human rights, as an entitlement deriving from human dignity, was one based on a system of objective truths, and that, at best, majority opinion could provide only indirect and uncertain evidence of that truth. On the other hand, it was recognised that in a rationalist system, no-one can claim conclusively to have discovered the truth. What implications does this have for drafting a provision governing amendments to a Constitution containing a Bill of Rights? First, it would obviously be inconsistent with a rational system to make the Constitution immutable. Recognition of the fact that human understanding of the truth changes over time requires that there be some procedure for change, even of the provisions contained in a Bill of Rights. The question, then, becomes whether a simple majority of voters should suffice to effect such changes. I would argue not. The importance of decisions regarding constitutional matters, and, in particular, questions regarding human rights, indicates that constitutional change should require a greater degree of consensus than that represented by 50% + 1 of the voters. Setting a special majority – such as that of two-thirds of voters – would ensure that proposed changes enjoyed a substantial degree of support. Of course, it is true that either a simple majority or a two-thirds majority of voters are capable of being actuated by prejudice and a desire to deprive individuals and majorities of their rights. However, setting the bar higher than a simple majority does at least make it more difficult for the Constitution, and thus the Bill of Rights, to be amended. Furthermore, if one accepts the idea that majorities do at least provide evidence (however flawed) of truth, then it follows that a two-thirds majority is more likely than a simple majority to produce an objectively correct outcome.

The next question to be addressed is what majority, additional to a two-thirds majority nationwide, should be required for constitutional amendment in accordance with the federal principle? At present, s 128 does not distinguish between those provisions in the Constitution that affect the balance of power between the Commonwealth and the States, and those that do not. It is simply assumed that, because Australia is a federation, it is legitimate for the States (through separate majorities of their voters) to have a say in determining whether any constitutional amendment should be passed. However, this is to ignore the proper balance that should be maintained between the rights of the States as parties to the federation, and the right of each citizen to have an equal influence in relation to constitutional amendment.

I have already touched upon this issue in 5.2.4, above, where I noted that federal Constitutions manifest a tension between the equal rights of States and the equal rights of individuals. The requirement in s 128 that the consent of a majority of voters in a majority of votes be obtained for all constitutional amendment effectively gives a minority of voters a veto over change simply on the basis of where those voters happen to live. In cases where a particular amendment does not differentially affect the rights of residents of a State *qua* residents of that State, as distinct from their rights as residents of Australia, the principle that every citizen's vote ought to be of equal weight dictates that the fact that they live in a particular State should not give their vote any greater power than that cast by any other voter. Matters are different where a proposed amendment would differentially affect the rights of all the States *vis-à-vis* the Commonwealth, or the rights of particular State or States. In those circumstances, it is legitimate for the Constitution to require that the assent of the States concerned be separately manifested. I would, therefore, argue that the amending provision in a new Australian Constitution should distinguish between three categories of constitutional amendment:

- those not affecting the balance between the States and the Commonwealth or the position of any particular State, which should require the assent of a two-thirds majority of voters nationwide;
- those affecting the balance of power between the States and the Commonwealth, which should require the assent of two-thirds of the voters nationwide, and of a majority of voters in a majority of States; and
- those affecting the rights or boundaries of a particular State or States, which should require the assent of two-thirds of the voters nationwide, of a majority of voters in a majority of States and of a majority of voters in the specific State(s) affected.

Certain types of amendment would obviously fall into the category of those which affect the balance of power between the States and Commonwealth. Amendments affecting the representation of the States in the Commonwealth Parliament, the 68:32 ratio for the distribution of Commonwealth revenues between the Commonwealth and the States (although note that an alternative avenue for the amendment of this 68:32 ratio would be by a two-thirds vote of the Council of Australian Heads of Government, as discussed earlier in this chapter), or the legislative powers of the Parliament of the Commonwealth or of the States, being obvious examples of these. Similarly, as examples of amendments affecting the rights of an individual State or States, one could think of amendments which would alter the boundaries of a State or States. These specific cases should be expressly mentioned in the constitutional provisions relating to amendments falling within each category, but the provisions ought to be drafted in sufficiently general terms as to make it clear that their scope extends to any amendments which would affect the federal balance in the case of the second category of constitutional amendment, or of affecting the position of a specific State or States in the case of the third.

These arrangements pertaining to constitutional amendment would ensure that in all cases of constitutional amendment there was agreement by a substantial majority of voters in the whole country, and that the federal balance in the Constitution would require the assent of the States, but without allowing a minority of voters to block the will of a two-thirds national majority in relation to amendments that did not differentially affect individual State interests.

These arrangements pertaining to constitutional amendment would ensure that in all cases of constitutional amendment there was agreement by a substantial majority of voters in the whole country, and that the federal balance in the Constitution would require the assent of the States, but without allowing a minority of voters to block the will of a two thirds national majority in relation to amendments that did not differently affect individual States.

INDIGENOUS AUSTRALIANS

6.1 INDIGENOUS PEOPLE AND COLONISATION

The relationship between the broader Australian society and its indigenous minority is one which has engaged public attention under the broad heading of 'reconciliation'. Reconciliation has a variety of dimensions. Many of these, such as the recognition of land rights and the provision of remedies for the harm suffered by a stolen generation, lie outside the scope of a book on constitutional law. Here, we need to consider the discrete issue of what impact, if any, the status of indigenous Australians, as the first inhabitants of the country, should have on the Constitution.

A legitimate question that can be asked is why special consideration should be given to indigenous Australians as a specific ethnic group. Why not for other, equally well defined groups, such as Australians of British, Irish, Greek or Italian descent? The answer to this is that of all the ethnic groups who have come together to form the Australian people, only the indigenous inhabitants were involuntary participants in the union of cultures: true, the initial settlers from Britain were convicts transported to Australia against their will, but they brought their law and culture with them. All subsequent migrants came to Australia voluntarily, and did so accepting that, although there was no impediment to their continuing to practice cultural traditions in their new country, they would, nevertheless, become members of a broader Australian culture, of which their own specific culture would form a small, and perhaps changed, component. Indigenous Australians, on the other hand, had no choice as to whether to accept settlers and their imported culture, and within a century of colonisation, indigenous people found that their culture had been displaced as the dominant culture, and that their success (indeed survival) as a group was tied to adaptation to the colonisers' culture. From a legal point of view, colonisation had the significant consequence that indigenous law was displaced as the law of the land, and that both the content of the law, and the way infractions of it, or disputes arising under it, were mediated, was determined by the rules of that 'imported' law. From an historical point of view, there is thus a clear difference between indigenous Australians and others, in that the former were the only participants in the melting pot transaction whose law and culture were surrendered involuntarily. This chapter explores the means by which the status of indigenous people be recognised in the Constitution.

6.2 HOW ARE INDIGENOUS PEOPLE DEFINED?

A host of issues arise whenever a legal system distinguishes between people of different ethnic groups. How are the groups to be defined? Is the allocation of a person to a group determined by the law through the application of an objective test, by the individual concerned, or by the group itself? If the law makes special provision for a particular group, does it thereby discriminate against other groups?

A number of fundamental principles are relevant in this regard. First, the compulsory allocation of persons to groups through legislation, as occurred under apartheid in South Africa,[1] is inconsistent with the individual's freedom of association. Furthermore, if the allocation is coupled with discrimination, in the sense that the enjoyment of legal rights is made contingent upon allocation to a particular group, then it is also *prima facie* inconsistent with the right to equality. Secondly, it follows that if compulsory allocation to racial groups by law is impermissible, freedom of association implies that the individual should be entitled to state whether they choose to associate with a particular group for legal purposes. However, the third consideration is that because association contains an element of mutuality (in other words, both the individual, and the group with which that individual wishes to associate, have an interest in the relationship), the individual's claim of membership is not enough – the group itself must accept the individual's claim before the individual can be said to be a member of the group. However, one should also note that the prohibition of forced association applies to groups as much as to the State – where a group derives benefits by increasing its membership, it might be tempted forcibly to 'claim' individuals as members. This, too, is clearly inconsistent with freedom of association.[2]

In light of the above, we can deduce a rule regarding identification of individuals with groups for legal purposes: membership of a racial or ethnic group may be referred to in legislation, provided that the individual is not compulsorily categorised by the legislation, but rather chooses voluntary association with the group, and is accepted by the group. To some extent, this rule is already recognised in Australia: although there is no statutory definition of an Aborigine or Torres Strait Islander, even in legislation mentioning members of those groups, two court decisions give some guidance as to the position. In *Mabo v Queensland (No 2)*,[3] Brennan J (as he then was) held that:

> Membership of the indigenous people depends on biological descent from the indigenous people and on mutual recognition of a particular person's membership by that person and by the elders or other persons enjoying traditional authority among those people.

Similarly, in *Shaw v Wolf*,[4] the Federal Court heard a challenge to the validity of the election of certain regional members of the Aboriginal and Torres Strait Islander Commission (ATSIC) elected in Tasmania. One of the issues raised in the case was whether certain successful candidates were Aborigines. Merkel J held that a person was an Aborigine if they (i) were objectively of Aboriginal descent, (ii) *bona fide* identified themselves as an Aborigine, and (iii) were regarded as an Aborigine by the relevant Aboriginal community. Note that the objective element of descent was not in itself sufficient to lead to the legal consequence that a person was an Aborigine – there could be

1 Allocation to racial groups was mandated by the Population Registration Act 1950.

2 Although the primary evil of apartheid resided in its treatment of non-white South Africans, apartheid legislation such as the Prohibition of Mixed Marriages Act 1949 (which prohibited marriage between persons of different races) and the Immorality Act 1957 (which prohibited sexual relations between members of different races), which were designed to 'preserve' the white race, sacrificed the individual freedom of whites to marry whom they chose.

3 (1992) 175 CLR 1, 70.

4 (1998) 83 FCR 113.

no compulsory designation based on biological factors, and both self-identification and group acceptance were also necessary.[5]

Assuming the correctness of this tri-partite test for membership of an ethnic group, the next important question to address is in what circumstance such legal identification should operate, and what implications racial or ethnic identification has for the right to equality. Is it ever permissible to distinguish between ethnic groups? In answering this question, one needs to progress in two stages. First, assuming that group identification is not used as a factor in determining whether a person is entitled to government services, and is done only for the purpose of providing the same rights or services as other people but separately, is the very fact of separate treatment racist? This question has frequently been the subject of debate in societies where members of ethnic groups have sought separate schools, for example, in pursuit if their right to preserve their culture. In that debate, reliance has often been placed on the United States Supreme Court decision in *Brown v Board of Education of Topeka*,[6] in which it was held that the provision of separate but equal educational facilities by a State was discriminatory (and thus unconstitutional) because, as the court said:[7]

> To separate [children] from others of similar age and qualifications solely because of their race generates a feeling of inferiority as to their status in the community that may affect their hearts and minds in a way unlikely ever to be undone … We conclude that in the field of public education the doctrine of 'separate but equal' has no place. Separate education facilities are inherently unequal.

However, the key factor to remember about *Brown* is that it dealt with an education system in which classification by race and assignment to separate schools was *compulsory* – in other words, was not one in which there was any option as to whether to send children to mixed or separate schools. Where such a choice does exist, the mere availability of a separate institution for persons of particular ethnic groups does not in itself raise problems relating to inequality. This must, however, be subject to a caveat: in the context of public (as opposed to private) institutions, it would arguably be discriminatory for an institution, such as a school established for a particular group, to do so on an *exclusive* basis. In other words, while it is permissible for the state to provide separate facilities for those who want them, it would be racially discriminatory to prohibit members of groups other than that for which the institution was provided from attending that institution, should they wish to be educated in the cultural milieu it provided.[8]

5 Interestingly, Merkel J had cause to re-visit the issue of group identification in *Commonwealth v Yarmirr* (1999) 168 ALR 426, 496–98, which related to a native title claim to the sea and sea-bed off Croker Island. In this case, he drew the distinction between identification with a race, on the one hand, and with a group or community on the other, noting that whereas biological descent was always a requirement of the former, one could belong to a community or group without a biological link because, eg, the group or community's rules regarding descent might have the effect that persons of a different race marrying into it would be taken as becoming members of the group or community.

6 347 US 483 (1954).

7 *Ibid*, 494.

8 As noted in the discussion of Bills of Rights in Chapter 2, this issue was a live one in South Africa during constitutional negotiations in the 1990s. In order to avoid the right to freedom of association being used as a cover for *de facto*, or 'privatised', apartheid, s 31(2) of the Constitution expressly qualifies this right so as to prohibit its use to establish private institutions which provide services on grounds of racial or other exclusivity.

Assuming that the three criteria relating to descent, self-identification and communal acceptance provide a satisfactory meaning for identifying indigenous people, and that making separate provision for ethnic groups in non-exclusive institutions does not offend against the right to equality, what specific constitutional mechanisms could be used to protect the distinct identity of indigenous people?

6.3 INDIGENOUS SOVEREIGNTY AND TREATIES

Perhaps the most controversial aspect of the debate on indigenous rights is the proposal that indigenous sovereignty be recognised in Australia. The concept of sovereignty is a nebulous one, and used in different senses. In its purest sense, sovereignty refers to the capacity of one political entity to act without subjection to any other entity. Thus states are sovereign at international law. However, the term has also come to be used in relation to the status of specific groups within the state, specifically by indigenous peoples seeking self-determination. The right to self-determination is recognised by the United Nations in numerous Declarations.[9] In Australia, the call for indigenous sovereignty is often been coupled with a call for a treaty to be negotiated between Aboriginal peoples and the Commonwealth, as a means of giving effect to such sovereignty.[10] The use of the terms 'sovereignty' and 'treaty', carrying as they do a meaning associated with interactions between states at international law, suggests (whether intentionally or not) that indigenous claims pose a threat to Australia's identity as a single nation. Is this fear well grounded? In answering this question, it is useful to investigate what the term 'indigenous sovereignty' means in other jurisdictions, and to examine that concept (as understood in those jurisdictions) against the test for location of sovereignty provided by Kelsen's theory of legitimacy, in terms of which the validity of a rule of a law is determined by discovering what the ultimate source of authority of that law is.[11] That ultimate authority can be described as the sovereign within that legal system. Thus, to take an example, a city ordinance imposing a fine for a traffic violation would draw its authority from an enactment by the city council, which in turn exercised authority conferred by a local government Act, which in turn drew its authority from an Act of Parliament, which in turn drew its authority from the Constitution. The person or entity under whose authority the Constitution was established would be the source of sovereignty within that legal system. The validity of laws thus ultimately depends upon a political fact (which Kelsen called the *Grundnorm*), coupled with the acquiescence (and note, not necessarily the agreement), on the part of the population to obedience to the authority established by that political fact. In the case of Australia, both the Commonwealth and State Constitutions draw their authority from the fact that the British

9 See, eg, the International Covenant on Civil and Political Rights, Art 1; and the International Covenant on Social and Economic and Cultural Rights, Art 1 (GA Res 2200A (XXI), 16 December 1966)), both of which recognise the right to self-determination on the part of 'peoples', as well as the draft Declaration on the Rights of Indigenous Peoples, Arts 3 and 31, which specifically makes the right applicable to indigenous peoples.

10 See, eg, ATSIC, 1995, 3.27–3.31 and 4.79–4.87.

11 Kelsen, 1945, 116–22.

Crown established sovereignty over Australia.[12] Kelsinian analysis is of particular use when discussing the status of indigenous people, because one can discover whether indigenous groups enjoy sovereignty (in the true sense) by inquiring whether such executive and/or legislative power as such groups exercise derive their authority from a sovereignty which antedated colonisation (in which case, the indigenous group in question can be said to be truly 'sovereign'), or whether that power is exercised by virtue of authority ultimately traceable back to the legal order which came into effect at colonisation (in which case, the indigenous group is not 'sovereign', although it may well enjoy a degree of autonomy delegated to it by the post-colonial legal system).

6.3.1 The United States of America

In the United States, indigenous tribes are said to enjoy limited sovereignty as 'domestic dependent nations'. As was explained by the United States Supreme Court in *United States v Wheeler*,[13] this means that such authority as is wielded by Indian tribes is not delegated by the United States government, but is, rather, traceable back to the sovereignty that they enjoyed prior to colonisation. However, the court also stated that such residual authority that remains in the tribes can be removed by Congress, because Indian territory was incorporated into the United States. From a Kelsinian perspective, the tribes occupy an interesting position: the legitimacy of tribal governments, and the laws they apply, is clearly sourced in a surviving sovereignty whose existence is quite independent of the United States government. In many instances, the ambit of this continuing sovereignty is defined in treaties with the United States. On the other hand, because that sovereignty is vulnerable to erosion by Congress, its continued existence is reliant upon the restraint of Congress, and so it is also true to say that indigenous sovereignty is potentially extinguishable by that of the United States.

12 Recent statements by the High Court to the effect that the legitimacy of the Constitution is now to be found in the consent of the Australian people are, with respect, not compatible with Kelsinian theory. Thus, while Mason CJ stated in *Australian Capital Television Pty Ltd v Commonwealth* (1992) 177 CLR 106, 138 that the enactment of the Australia Act 1986 'marked the end of the legal sovereignty of the Imperial Parliament and recognised that ultimate sovereignty rested in the Australian people', and Deane J stated in *Theophanous v Herald & Weekly Times* (1994) 182 CLR 104, 171 that the legitimacy of the Constitution now derived 'exclusively [from] the original adoption (by referenda) and subsequent maintenance (by acquiescence) of its provisions by the people', this ignores the fact that, as was noted by Gummow J in *McGinty v Western Australia* (1996) 186 CLR 140, 274, the people are not free to amend the Constitution as they please, being bound by the terms of s 128. Clearly, the acquiescence of the Australian people is important because it constitutes evidence of the effectiveness of the current constitutional order, which Kelsinian theory would acknowledge as being lost if, eg, the Australian people were to acquiesce in the authority of a coup leader who seized power. However, while such acquiescence exists, the validity of the Australian Constitution is clearly traceable back to an Act of the British Parliament, which was accepted as being binding on Australia because of Britain's acquisition of sovereignty. Whereas power may be divided between the two levels of government, sovereignty is not. It is also not correct to say (as, eg, does Coombs, 1994, 206–07) that sovereignty in Australia is 'divided' between the States and the Commonwealth. Both levels of government ultimately draw their authority from Britain's acquisition of sovereignty over Australia.

13 435 US 313 (1978), 322–28.

6.3.2 Canada

The status of indigenous people in Canada is complex. There are three indigenous groups – North American Indians (sometimes called First Nations people), Métis (persons of mixed Indian and European descent) and Inuit. North American Indian tribes (or bands, as they are also known) enjoy differing status depending upon whether they are Treaty Indians (in which case, they enjoy rights conferred under Treaties signed pre- or post-confederation), Status Indians (whose rights are regulated by the Indian Act 1985) or Non-Status Indians (who do not meet the criteria for Indian Act status). From a Kelsenian perspective, even those tribes which negotiated treaties prior to confederation in 1867 do not enjoy sovereignty, as the treaties (most important of which was the Royal Proclamation of 1763) included an explicit statement of the Crown's acquisition of sovereignty. However, these early treaties, as well as those entered into in more recent times, certainly recognise rights, within the received legal system, in respect of land ownership and self-government.

The Royal Proclamation contained both an assertion of the Crown's sovereignty and protection of Indian land rights. Court decisions such as *Guerin v The Queen*[14] and *Delgamuukw v British Columbia*[15] have confirmed the fact of the acquisition of sovereignty by the Crown, and also the principle that acquisition of sovereignty did not, in the absence of any other positive lawful act, extinguish native title. Although, in the case of some Indian peoples, native title was extinguished by treaties entered into post-1763 in exchange for annuities, hunting and fishing rights and allocation of land and resources,[16] in the case of other groups, land was unlawfully taken, and this has led to the lodgement of native title claims, some of which are being addressed through litigation, while others have been settled through negotiation.

The issue of self-determination has come to the fore in Canada in recent years. In its 1993 report,[17] the Royal Commission on Aboriginal People stated that, in its opinion, indigenous people in Canada had a right to self-government which was:

> ... *inherent* in its source, in the sense that it finds its origins within the Aboriginal communities, as a residue of the powers they originally held as autonomous nations. It does not stem from constitutional grant, that is, it is not a derivative right ... According to the 'derivative' viewpoint, Aboriginal peoples have no right of self-government other than those the written constitution creates or that the federal or provincial governments choose to delegate. By contrast, under the 'inherent' doctrine Aboriginal people are the bearers of ancient and enduring powers of government that they carried with them into confederation and retain today.

As a matter of law, this view is incorrect. Certainly the *existence* of indigenous institutions of government and indigenous law can be traced back to pre-colonial times, but that is not to say that the *sovereignty* which originally produced those institutions and laws continues to exist, as the above statement implies – this, indeed, is the key difference

14 (1984) 13 DLR (4th) 321, *per* Dickson J, 335–41.
15 (1993) 104 DLR (4th) 470.
16 See Brennan, 1994, 137.
17 Royal Commission on Aboriginal People, 1993, 36.

between the status of indigenous people in the United States and in Canada.[18] According to Kelsinian analysis, the ultimate legal authority in Canada is now the received legal system, which was established as a consequence of the Crown's acquisition of sovereignty. The Royal Commission's statement does, however, serve to highlight the willingness of the Canadian system to satisfy indigenous claims to self-government. Many argue that the legal system has already recognised such a right through the inclusion in the Constitution Act 1982 of s 35 which, under the heading 'Rights of the Aboriginal Peoples of Canada', provides as follows:

> 35 (1) The existing aboriginal and treaty rights of the aboriginal peoples of Canada are hereby recognized and affirmed.
>
> (2) In this Act, 'aboriginal peoples of Canada' includes the Indian, Inuit and Métis peoples of Canada.
>
> (3) For greater certainty, in subsection (1) 'treaty rights' includes rights that now exist by way of land claims agreements or may be so acquired.
>
> (4) Notwithstanding any other provision of this Act, the aboriginal and treaty rights referred to in subsection (1) are guaranteed equally to male and female persons.

The term 'aboriginal rights' in sub-section (1) is clearly capable of an interpretation broad enough to include the right to self-determination, and the insertion of sub-section (3) confers constitutional protection not only upon rights which can be shown to have been recognised historically, but also those that may be acknowledged under treaties negotiated after 1982. Land claims are often accompanied by claims to political self-government, and this has led to agreements between the federal and provincial governments, on the one hand, and Indian tribes on the other, in terms of which the latter are given self-government in lands which have been successfully reclaimed.

Finally, it is relevant to note that the legal status of Inuit has recently undergone an important change with the establishment in 1999 of the Territory of Nunavut as a new political entity formed from part of the Northwest Territory. Although the population of the Nunavut Territory is ethnically diverse, the Inuit form 85% of the total, and so the creation of the Territory can be seen as advancing indigenous self-determination. Under the Nunavut Act,[19] the Nunavut Territory enjoys substantial legislative autonomy as a delegate of the Canadian government.[20]

6.3.3 New Zealand

In New Zealand, the status of indigenous people is ambiguous. On the one hand, Article 1 of the Treaty of Waitangi, entered into between the Crown and a number of Maori chiefs in 1840, recognises the Crown's acquisition of 'sovereignty' (English version) or

18 According to the common law, the Crown's acquisition of sovereignty over a territory did not automatically displace the law then applying in that territory (see *Campbell v Hall* (1774) 1 Cowper 204). That law carried on in force until displaced by some positive act performed under the authority of the new sovereign. However, that did not mean that the old sovereignty survived. Rather, its laws became the laws adopted by the new sovereignty.

19 1993, c 28.

20 For a discussion of the establishment of Nunavut, see Jull and Kajlich, 2001, 267. For an overall discussion of Nunavut and indigenous self determination, see Hicks and White, 2000.

'kawanatanga' (Maori version). But Art 2 of the Treaty also preserves the 'undisturbed possession' (English version) or *'rangatiratanga'* (Maori version) enjoyed by Maori over their 'Lands Estates Forests Fisheries and other properties' (English version) or their *'taonga'* (Maori version). These linguistic differences are important, because the term *'rangatiratanga'* itself has a meaning which is closer to 'sovereignty' than to mere 'possession', and the term *'taonga'* has a broad meaning of 'treasures' (both tangible and intangible), rather than only those types of property mentioned in the English version.[21] The existence of two versions of the Treaty, and the difficulty of translating the key Maori terms, has led to keen debate on the issue of the precise degree of sovereignty preserved to indigenous people under the Treaty, in so far as the sovereignty ceded under Art 1 is apparently preserved under Art 2. However, the current legal position can be summarised as follows: as a document that was assented to by the Crown upon colonisation, but which has not been enacted by the New Zealand Parliament, the Treaty is not part of that country's statute law. However, the *principles* of the Treaty are important, in that under the Treaty of Waitangi Act 1975, the Waitangi Tribunal was established to consider, and then give to the government non-binding recommendations on, claims that the government has infringed Treaty principles. Although the English and Maori versions of the Treaty appear as schedules to the Act, this has not made the Treaty itself part of New Zealand law.[22]

Furthermore, in *New Zealand Maori Council v Attorney-General* (*Maori Council* case),[23] the Court of Appeal did recognise that there is a presumption of statutory interpretation that Parliament does not intend to legislate contrary to Treaty rights. In addition, while affirming that under the received legal system the Crown acquired sovereignty from the Maori tribes, the court held that the Treaty imposed upon the Crown a continuing fiduciary duty to consider Maori interests in its making of executive decisions.

The Waitangi Tribunal has not confined itself to hearing and advising the government only on claims relating to land. Thus it interpreted the Treaty requirement that Maori be preserved in possession of their 'treasures' as requiring the Crown to allocate a portion of frequencies in the radio spectrum to Maori broadcasters, in order to preserve the Maori language.[24] Subsequently, in *New Zealand Maori Council v Attorney-General* (*FM Frequencies* case),[25] the Court of Appeal affirmed that the Crown was obliged to take Treaty rights into account when allocating radio frequencies. Similarly, in *Bleakley v Environmental Risk Management Authority*,[26] the High Court held that, in exercising statutory powers, government agencies had to take into account the preservation both of tangible and intangible Maori 'treasures', among which were Maori spiritual beliefs.

21 In general, on the legal status of the Treaty of Waitangi, see McDowell and Webb, 1995, 183–223.

22 *Ibid*, 204–05.

23 [1987] 1 NZLR 641 (CA). The same principle was enunciated in *Huakina Development Trust v Waikato Valley Authority* [1987] 2 NZLR 188 (HC).

24 *Report of the Waitangi Tribunal on Claims Concerning the Allocation of Radio Frequencies* (1990) (Wai 26 and Wai 150).

25 [1992] 2 NZLR 576 (CA). The Court of Appeal's decision was affirmed by the Privy Council in *New Zealand Maori Council v Attorney-General* [1994] 1 NZLR 513 (PC).

26 [2001] 3 NZLR 213 (HC).

6.3.4 South Africa

The position in South Africa differs from that in the United States, Canada and New Zealand in that because indigenous people are in the majority in South Africa, the political struggle in that country was presented as a struggle for majority rule and equal voting rights, and not as one for self-determination of an indigenous minority against a settler majority.[27] Nevertheless, it is clear that following colonisation, no residual sovereignty remained with indigenous authorities, and that their authority became subordinate to that of the colonial governments that later amalgamated to form South Africa. Subsequent political struggles by black South Africans had the objective of capturing control of the post-colonial entity, rather than in seeking autonomy within it. The fact that indigenous sovereignty had been extinguished meant that any post-conquest power exercised by indigenous authorities was exercised under the authority of the colonial legal system. Such authority as indigenous rulers (kings, chiefs and headmen) continued to enjoy was delegated to them by colonial authorities as part of a policy of 'indirect rule', necessitated by the small number of colonial administrators relative to the subject population.[28] That this remained the position after the Union of South Africa was formed in 1910 is most starkly illustrated by s 1 of the Black Administration Act 1927, which vests the President of South Africa with the title of 'Supreme Chief' of all tribes, and by 2(7) of that Act, which empowers him to recognise and appoint chiefs of tribes, and to make regulations prescribing their duties, powers, privileges and conditions of service. Furthermore, the President may depose such chiefs as have been recognised or appointed.[29] The power to appoint and depose – which is not constrained by customary laws of succession to chieftainship[30] – gives to the received legal system control over the most fundamental institution of indigenous society, and serves to emphasise the completeness of the loss of indigenous sovereignty. The post-apartheid legal system continues to recognise indigenous political authorities as part of the received legal order, as is shown by s 211(1) of the Constitution, which recognises the institution, status and role of traditional leadership, according to customary law, but subject to the Constitution.

6.3.5 Conclusion

What conclusions can one draw from the above? First, classic Kelsinian sovereignty survives only in the case of indigenous people whose sovereignty was to some extent

27 Indeed, there is some irony in that the term 'self-determination' was a euphemism frequently employed by the white minority government when referring to apartheid, their argument being that an ethnically diverse country such as South Africa required separate government for each ethnic group, rather than majoritarianism which causes domination of minorities by the majority. Of course, the reality of apartheid was that the white ethnic minority controlled the central government through a racially exclusive franchise, and such 'self-determination' as was granted to black South Africans took the form of autonomy for economically marginal rural 'homelands' in which only a small percentage of the black population lived. During negotiations on a new Constitution some white political groups continued to demand special protection as an ethnic minority, and, although under the Bill of Rights minorities can avail of the protection of cultural rights, as was noted in Chapter 2, the right is formulated in such a way as not to permit it to be used as a vehicle for racially-exclusive institutions, public or private.

28 Bennett, 1991, 55–56.

29 Black Administration Act 1927, s 2(7) bis.

30 *Mathibe v Union Government* 1925 AD 81; *Minister of Native Affairs v Buthelezi* 1961 (1) SA 766 (D).

preserved by treaties entered into at the time of colonisation – in other words, among our examples, only in the case of North American Indians living in the United States. Although it is true that whatever quantum of residual sovereignty there is relies for its continued existence on the non-intervention of the received legal system, I would argue that that sovereignty still has its own *grundnorm*, because in answer to the Kelsinian question of what is the ultimate fact upon which indigenous authority rests in the United States, one would have to give the unqualified answer of 'the historical acceptance of the assumption of power by tribal leaders'. The fact that such sovereignty could, in theory, be further eroded by the organs of national government does not mean that indigenous authorities derive their powers from the national government, any more than the fact that prior to colonisation indigenous peoples were vulnerable to removal of their authority through external invasion meant that, until that event occurred, they were not sovereign. Secondly, the mere existence of 'a treaty' does not constitute conclusive proof of continuing sovereignty. Treaties entered into at colonisation may, in fact, have provided for a surrender of sovereignty, and have left indigenous people with a degree of autonomy, the ambit of which can be determined by the coloniser's legal system. This is the position in New Zealand and Canada. Treaties entered into well after a loss of sovereignty – such as some of the treaties entered into in Canada – may confer substantial autonomy on indigenous people, but under the Kelsinian analysis, whatever law-making capacity is thereby conferred draws its legitimacy from the received legal system, and no 'sovereignty' in the true sense is conferred by such a treaty. Thirdly, and perhaps most importantly, whether there is a treaty in place bears no necessary relation to the degree of self-determination enjoyed by indigenous people. Notwithstanding the existence of a treaty, indigenous law is not recognised as a source of law in New Zealand, whereas in South Africa, where there is no treaty, indigenous law has long been recognised as a source of law within the overall legal system.

6.4 ABORIGINAL SOVEREIGNTY IN AUSTRALIA

In Australia, continuance of indigenous sovereignty is not recognised by the legal system. In *Coe v Commonwealth*,[31] *Mabo (No 2)*,[32] *Coe v Commonwealth (No 2)*,[33] *Walker v New South Wales*;[34] and most recently, in *Thorpe v Commonwealth (No 3)*,[35] the courts affirmed that the Crown's acquisition of sovereignty over Australia was not open to challenge in the courts, and that no vestiges of indigenous sovereignty remain. Such limited self-determination as is enjoyed by indigenous people in Australia, or which might in future be conferred, would thus be under the authority of the received legal system.

However, for some indigenous leaders, the question of sovereignty and a treaty has assumed great symbolic importance, perhaps even greater importance than the question of what actual benefits could be derived from arrangements relating to indigenous

31 (1979) 53 ALJR 403, 408 and 409.
32 (1992) 175 CLR 1, 69.
33 (1993) 118 ALR 193, 199–200.
34 (1994) 182 CLR 45, 47–50.
35 (1997) 71 ALJR 767.

autonomy which might be entered into with the Commonwealth and State governments. This is evident from the following remark in a report to the Commonwealth by the Council for Aboriginal Reconciliation in 1995:[36]

> Models for regional agreements leading to autonomy and localised forms of self-government ... should not be confused with the issues of and discussion about the concept of sovereignty for Aboriginal or Torres Strait Islander peoples. Regional agreements are separate from the issue of sovereignty and involve ceding by the Commonwealth and the relevant State and Territory Government of powers to an indigenous structure within the framework of the present Constitution. It was also made clear ... that, as with other constitutional issues, regional agreements were discussed on the basis that they did not prejudice the right of Aboriginal or Torres Strait Islander peoples to pursue sovereignty issues in other contexts.

I would argue that this line of reasoning is flawed both as a matter of theory and of practice: Under Kelsinian theory, the sovereignty horse has well and truly bolted the stable, given that the legal system regards indigenous sovereignty as having been extinguished. Non-acknowledgment by indigenous peoples of loss of sovereignty[37] is irrelevant from a legal point of view, because whether sovereignty has been lost or not is determined simply by reference to historical facts, and in particular, to whether the coloniser succeeded in establishing its authority, which patently was the case in Australia. Any arrangement entered into now must, therefore, involve a transfer of power to indigenous people only 'within the framework of the present Constitution'. It is simply not possible to resurrect a sovereignty that no longer exists.[38]As was stated by the Senate Standing Committee on Constitutional and Legal Affairs in its 1983 report on indigenous rights:[39]

> ... sovereignty is not now vested in the Aboriginal peoples except in so far as they share the common sovereignty of all peoples of the Commonwealth of Australia. In particular, they are not a sovereign entity under our present law, and so they cannot enter into a treaty with the Commonwealth.

Furthermore, even those United Nations documents which recognise the right of peoples to self-determination (and which are frequently relied upon by those seeking to advance indigenous rights), do not require a surrender of national sovereignty – accommodation of indigenous self-determination within the nation-state being recognised as an entirely appropriate vehicle for that purpose.[40] What *can* certainly be done under Australian

36 Council for Aboriginal Reconciliation, 1995, 47–48.

37 For statements of this nature, see ATSIC, 1995, 4.82.

38 See Brennan, 1994, 18, 22 and 153–55.

39 Senate Standing Committee on Constitutional and Legal Affairs, 1983, 50.

40 See, eg, the Declaration of Principles of International Law Concerning Friendly Relations and Co-operation Among States in Accordance with the Charter of the United Nations GA Res 2625 (XXV), 24 October 1970, which states that:

> Nothing in the foregoing paragraphs shall be construed as authorising or encouraging any action which would dismember or impair, totally or in part, the territorial integrity or political unity of sovereign and independent States conducting themselves in compliance with the principle of equal rights and self-determination of peoples as described above, and thus possessed of a government representing the whole people belonging to that territory without distinction as to race, creed or colour.

In support of the argument that internal constitutional arrangements relating to self-determination satisfy the international obligations in this regard, see Daes, 1993.

constitutional law is for the existing sovereignty to transfer some of its own authority to indigenous institutions. For this reason, and in contrast with the point of view reflected in the Council for Aboriginal Reconciliation's report, some Aboriginal leaders have abandoned the pursuit of 'indigenous sovereignty' on the ground that it is unrealistic and not productive of any tangible advantage.[41]

Next, so far as the issue of a 'treaty' is concerned, although that term raises the implication of an agreement between sovereign nations, and is, to that extent, inappropriate in the context of internal constitutional arrangements, the reality is that the issue of its use or non-use is of relatively little importance, given the fact that, because indigenous sovereignty is extinguished, the term 'treaty' in this context could, from a legal point of view, never carry that international law implication. This was made quite clear by Prime Minister Hawke, during the furore which arose after his commitment in the Barunga Statement of 1988 to negotiate a treaty recognising indigenous rights.[42] As stated above, it is against the background of that same understanding that treaties have been negotiated in Canada between the government and indigenous peoples well after the latter lost sovereignty as a result of colonisation. The only importance the issue has in Australia is whether using some other term (such as '*makarrata*',[43] 'charter' or 'compact') would enhance the chances of achieving broad public support for indigenous self-determination.

From a constitutional law perspective, however, it is questionable whether a treaty or other document of that type, however labelled, would be the best vehicle for securing indigenous rights. Indeed, it was uncertain what status the document the Hawke government proposed signing with Aborigines would have had. A treaty which was merely a political agreement would have no status at law – at the very most it might establish an administrative law right to review on the basis that failure to consider treaty obligations would amount to a failure to take into account all relevant considerations. Of more benefit would be the situation where a treaty had the status of a contract between the government and those with whom it was entered into, but even that would provide no protection against legislative override. The same would apply if the treaty itself was embodied in ordinary legislation – later inconsistent legislation could be used to override whatever was contained in the earlier legislation which gave legal effect to the treaty. The only step that will provide a secure foundation for indigenous rights is not a treaty, but rather recognition of indigenous rights in the Constitution. The focus on the issue of sovereignty and a treaty over the past two decades has, I would argue, elevated symbol over substance, and has drawn attention away from the 'main game', which should be to secure indigenous rights within the Constitution. This is the issue which should engage our attention when considering constitutional reform. How, then, could indigenous rights to self-determination be acknowledged in Australia?

---

41 See, eg, Pearson, 1993.

42 Brennan, 1994, 103.

43 The word '*Makarrata*' is a word in the Yolngu language which signifies an agreement promoting harmony between parties formerly in dispute. Its use as a name for a national document recognising indigenous rights was proposed by the National Aboriginal Conference (a fore-runner of ATSIC established by the Fraser government) – see Brennan, 1994, 60.

6.5 RECOGNISING INDIGENOUS RIGHTS IN AUSTRALIA

The concept of self-determination is broad, but a useful working definition is that proposed by Roberts, who states that there is broad agreement that:[44]

> ... self-determination is the right of indigenous Australians to make decisions on issues relating to them and to manage their own affairs,

even though there are differences on the details of that definition and on the strategies that should be adopted in order to achieve it. Self-determination has several dimensions – political autonomy, recognition of indigenous law, and preservation of indigenous culture being obvious ones. In the following sections of this chapter I discuss various aspects of self-determination, and suggest ways in which they might be given effect to in a new Constitution.

6.5.1 Self-government

Perhaps the most important aspect of self-determination is political autonomy, or self-government. The increasing recognition given to ethnic minority rights during the last century led to the development of theories justifying the right of such groups to autonomy within the State, and the construction of various constitutional mechanisms whereby that might be achieved.[45]

Political autonomy can be implemented in a variety of ways. In countries where ethnic divides are geographically based, ethnic groups can achieve autonomy through federalism. In Australia, geographic autonomy could form only part of the solution – although there are areas of Australia which are designated as Aboriginal reserves, most people classifying themselves as indigenous live outside those areas and among the general community. To what extent does indigenous self-government exist in Australia, and how could existing institutions be reformed and/or new institutions be set up to enhance self-government?

6.5.1.1 Community self-government

Turning first to those areas of Australia which are either under indigenous ownership, or are classified as Aboriginal reserves, self-government is to some extent facilitated by local government structures established under State and Territory law, because to the extent that indigenous communities are the seat of local government entities, such communities exercise self-government in respect of those local government functions. Thus, under s 97 of the Local Government Act 1993 (NT), indigenous communities may apply for recognition of a community government scheme, which is administered by a Community Government Council. Once the scheme is approved under s 105, the Council may exercise delegated legislative power over such local government matters as have been put within its jurisdiction under the scheme. In Queensland, s 42 of the Community Services (Aborigines) Act 1984 (Qld) and s 40 of the Community Services (Torres Strait) Act 1984

44 Roberts, 1994, 212.

45 See, eg, Hannum, 1990; and Horowitz, 1985.

(Qld), authorise Aboriginal and Torres Strait Island councils to make by-laws applying to any person within their communities,[46] and provide for the establishment of courts, presided over by indigenous justices of the peace, to try breaches of by-laws and 'disputes concerning any matter ... governed by the usages and customs of that community'.[47] The Aboriginal Councils and Associations Act 1976 (Cth) makes provision for the incorporation of local Aboriginal associations and councils with the power to make by-laws,[48] and several associations have been incorporated, mostly in the Northern Territory.[49]

Some progress has been made towards indigenous self-determination on a regional level. In 1994 the Aboriginal and Torres Strait Island Council Act 1989 (Cth) was amended to establish the Torres Strait Regional Authority, to which functions formerly discharged by ATSIC were transferred. As is noted in the discussion on ATSIC below, these functions are essentially administrative, and involve the delivery of Commonwealth-funded services to the indigenous population. In 1997, the House of Representatives Standing Committee on Aboriginal and Torres Strait Islander Affairs published a report recommending greater autonomy for Torres Strait Islanders,[50] and consultation with Torres Strait Islander communities has subsequently been held on this issue, although no policy decision has been made by the government as yet.

Although these institutions do confer a level of autonomy on indigenous communities (those established under local government legislation by accident, institutions like the Torres Strait Island Regional Authority by design), none of them contemplate the possibility of recognising, or vesting power in, institutions which are authentically indigenous. This is the real challenge in giving effect to indigenous self-government: vesting power in bodies which are autochthonous, in the sense that they spring from indigenous society itself. A primary objective of the process of giving indigenous people control over their own affairs should, therefore, be to recognise the desire on the part of indigenous communities for self-government, and where that desire is manifested, to negotiate with the communities what functions (legislative, executive and judicial) would be delegated to them. In the case of some communities, it may be found that existing structures (such as units of local government and associations set up under State, Territory and Commonwealth legislation), are satisfactory vehicles for that purpose, in which case it is to them that powers would be delegated. The important point is that in deciding to which institutions powers should be delegated, governments would have to be take cognisance of indigenous ways of decision-making. In view of the preference shown by some communities for a high level of autonomy, it is clear that a genuine policy of conferring self-government requires an approach which allows indigenous people themselves to take the initiative, and to identify which units they see as requiring autonomy, which may well mean that autonomy will come to be devolved

46 See the Community Services (Aborigines) Act 1984 (Qld), s 25; and the Community Services (Torres Strait) Act 1984 (Qld), s 23.

47 Community Services (Aborigines) Act 1984 (Qld), ss 42 and 43; and Community Services (Torres Strait) Act 1984 (Qld), ss 40 and 41.

48 Aboriginal Councils and Associations Act 1976 (Cth), s 30.

49 For a discussion of incorporated associations which some communities have formed to manage their affairs, see Coombs, 1994, 173–74.

50 House of Representatives Standing Committee on Aboriginal and Torres Strait Islander Affairs, 1997.

down to the level of individual clans.[51] I would suggest that, as a minimum, self-government would require that such bodies be vested with the power to develop indigenous law, and to settle disputes arising under it (see 6.5.2, below), and the power to determine how governmental services are to be delivered in their communities, including the power to appropriate government funding (a role currently discharged at a national level by ATSIC). That such an arrangement might, depending upon the traditions of individual communities, mean that legislative, executive and judicial functions were wielded by the same body is, I would argue, no need for concern.[52] The objective is to give effect to indigenous self-government, not to replicate imported notions of government in indigenous communities. These arrangements would have the advantage in that, by conferring a high degree of autonomy on communities, and restricting the national body only to such representative functions as the communities choose to give it (what Coombs called 'bottom-up federalism'),[53] maximum responsiveness to the needs of specific communities would be achieved.[54]

Given that the achievement of self-government would involve negotiation between Commonwealth, State and Territory governments, on the one hand, and individual communities on the other, on the precise model(s) to be used, flexible language would need to be employed when formulating the right in the Constitution. As has already been noted, indigenous groups in Canada now argue that the inclusion of a broad reference to 'indigenous rights' in s 35(1) of that country's Constitution casts an obligation on the government to negotiate self-government with indigenous peoples. The right to self-government would have to be stated as a right to negotiate on self-government, simply because it is difficult to see how the right could be formulated any more precisely, given the need to avoid being prescriptive on the question of exactly what form self-government should take. Practically speaking, it is likely that negotiations on community self-government would be likely to lead to devolution to indigenous communities of matters such as health, education, public facilities, welfare and business licensing, as these are matters in relation to which communities have a legitimate interest in establishing a legal regime which differentiates them from other communities and the general legal system. Ultimately, however, success in giving life to this right will depend upon the spirit in which political negotiations are entered into.

---

51 See Coombs, 1994, 174–76. See also Sterritt, 2002, who emphasises the need to ensure that indigenous self-government institutions remain focused at community level. Other papers delivered at the same conference as this paper are available at the conference website: www.reconciliationaustralia.org/act_governance.html.

52 This very issue was addressed in the South African case of *Bangindawo v Head of Nyanda Regional Authority* 1998 (3) BCLR 314 (Tk), in which it was held that indigenous courts which did not adhere to the doctrine of separation of powers (as they were presided over by chiefs who wielded legislative and executive powers within their tribes) were not invalid under s 96(2) of the 1993 Constitution, which provided that courts be presided over by an independent judiciary. The court held that to impose the Western concept of separation of powers on indigenous courts would be to erode customary law in the face of clear indications in the Constitution that it be preserved. The court did, however, invalidate a provision in the legislation governing indigenous courts which forebade legal representation to those appearing before them, holding that this infringed the rights of access to courts and a fair trial contained in ss 22 and 25(3) of the 1993 Constitution.

53 Coombs, 1994, 182–83.

54 The need for models of self government which are 'tailored to the unique social and cultural features and the geographical [*sic*] location of the Aboriginal people concerned' is emphasised in ATSIC, 1995, 4.72.

6.5.1.2 Indigenous people in urban areas

Accommodating self-government on the part of indigenous people not resident in defined communities – for example, those in major urban areas – would be more problematic. Self-government of the type that could operate in indigenous communities would obviously be impractical, because there is no geographic basis upon which authority could be delineated, and because, in many instances, indigenous people are no longer able to identify the original community from which they came. However, even if indigenous people in urban areas were unable to enjoy self-determination in a political sense, a degree of control over their own affairs could be realised through the mechanism of the right to cultural autonomy. This is discussed below. Urban indigenous people would also participate in elections to the national representative body mentioned in the next section.

6.5.1.3 National representation

The Aboriginal and Torres Straits Islander Commission (ATSIC) is commonly, but erroneously, thought to be a representative body for indigenous people. This impression doubtless stems from the fact that indigenous people who are registered as voters in ATSIC elections elect members of 60 regional councils, and 17 zonal commissioners, who sit on the national body. However, when one looks at the functions of ATSIC, it becomes clear that it exists essentially for the purpose of administering services which the Commonwealth provides for indigenous people. Its representative dimension was put in place in order to ensure that indigenous people have some control over how ATSIC distributes these resources. ATSIC is accountable to the Minister for Aboriginal Affairs, who can direct it in the discharge of its functions. For this reason, many Aboriginal leaders have denied that ATSIC carries any authority to negotiate on behalf of indigenous people in relation to issues of self-determination.[55] Furthermore, once community self-government had been implemented, ATSIC's role would increasingly diminish (to the point where the organisation might eventually become redundant), because the function of management of the administration of government programmes in communities would, as I have already stated, be a component of community self-government

There is clearly a need for a new national body which is specifically established to represent indigenous people, which is elected by them, and which would for the first time provide a national forum both for discussion of indigenous affairs, and for making representations to the government in relation thereto. In addition, that body itself, or a tribunal appointed by it, could discharge the general function of evaluating government legislation and policies with regard to their impact on indigenous rights,[56] as well as the function of assessing native title claims, and making recommendations on them to the government in a less adversarial environment than is provided by the courts, in much the same way as does the Waitangi Tribunal in New Zealand.[57] Indigenous voters would be entitled to vote in elections for the national body, and so the voice of rural indigenous communities and urbanised indigenous people would be heard. I would suggest that

55 Coombs, 1994, 183–86.

56 As was recommended in ATSIC, 1995, 3.67–69.

57 For arguments in favour of such a tribunal, see Brennan, 1994, 157.

such a body should be given constitutional recognition, and that the eligibility of persons registering on an indigenous voters' roll to elect its members should also be stated in the Constitution. Since the role of such a body might evolve over time (for example, if it was given the power to recommend settlements of native title claims), it would be best to define its functions in general terms, and to vest Parliament with the power to increase them.

6.5.2 Reserved seats

Putting in place structures which allow indigenous self-government would secure for Aboriginal people a substantial measure of control over their own affairs within the Australian legal system. But what of representation in national institutions? If, as was discussed at the beginning of this chapter, the status of Aboriginal people as the original inhabitants of Australia justifies their specific recognition by the Constitution, is there not an argument for Aboriginal people being given the option of specific representation in Parliament?

Reservation of seats for Maori voters has been used in New Zealand since 1867, and has also been adopted in other countries.[58] Under the current New Zealand system,[59] voters who identify themselves as Maori can choose to be entered on the Maori voters roll. The number of seats in Parliament to be elected by voters on the Maori roll is proportionate to the number of voters choosing the Maori option relative to all voters. When the allocation was done under the 1993 legislation, there were sufficient voters on the Maori voters' roll to give an entitlement of five out of 120 seats in Parliament.[60] The chief advantage of separate representation in New Zealand has been that, although political differences exist between indigenous representatives as much as between other members of Parliament (in other words, one cannot expect there to be a unanimous 'Maori view'), there has, at least, always been the guarantee of a voice representing indigenous interests.

The idea of reserving seats for Aboriginal members in the House of Representatives has been mooted by several commentators.[61] Brennan has advocated the representation of indigenous people in the Senate, arguing that, given that the Senate's electoral system is unrepresentative in any event, it should be reformed to accommodate Aborigines, on the ground that they are an interest group which is of equal or greater relevance to modern-day Australia than was State-identity at the time of federation.[62]

In Chapter 8, I argue for electoral reform and the introduction of proportional representation in elections for the House of Representatives. The system advocated there is one which involves supplementing seats based on electoral divisions with those elected

58 See, eg, the Constitution of India 1949, Art 330, which requires that seats be reserved for Scheduled Castes in the House of the People (the lower house of Parliament), and Art 332 which requires that seats be reserved for Scheduled Tribes in State legislatures. See also the Constitution of Fiji 1997, s 51 which creates four voters' rolls for people of Fijian, Indian, Rotuman and other descent.

59 See the Electoral Act 1993, ss 45 and 76–78.

60 Palmer and Palmer, 1997, 12. Since Maori form approximately 12% of the New Zealand population, this allocation of seats indicates that just over one-third of Maori voters choose to go on the separate roll.

61 See ATSIC, 1995, 4.27; and Council for Aboriginal Reconciliation, 1995, 41–43.

62 Brennan, 1995, 201.

on a State-wide basis from party lists. The reservation of seats for indigenous people would be possible in a proportional representation environment, as is shown by the case of New Zealand. However, there are reasons why representation of indigenous people in the House of Representatives would be problematic. In the first place, the fact that indigenous Australians comprise 2.2% of Australia's population would mean that, even if all people who were entitled to do so chose to go on a separate indigenous voters' roll, there would be a maximum of five representatives in a House expanded to 225. In the event that less than one-fifth of those entitled to be registered took that option, separate representation would not occur. The benefit of separate representation might, therefore, be more apparent than real. Furthermore, the fact that the number of reserved seats would necessarily fluctuate according to the number of indigenous people choosing to go on the separate roll would add a significant degree of complexity to the system of proportional representation proposed in Chapter 8. Since, under the proposed system, list seats would be allocated to each State in proportion to its population (unlike in New Zealand, where there is a single national list), and there is no State in which the indigenous population is sufficiently large to entitle it to even one seat, the only way in which separate indigenous representation could be achieved would be by designating the appropriate number of list seats as indigenous seats on a nationwide basis, and then allocating the remainder in proportion to the non-indigenous population of each State. This would, however, mean that there were two elements of disproportionality in a supposedly proportional system: the first would stem from the fact that there would be an element of disproportionality caused by the fact that one third of seats in the House elected on the basis of party lists would be chosen from State and Territory lists rather than from national lists, thus resulting in fractions of quotas. The second element of disproportionality would arise from the allocation of some of those list seats to indigenous voters, because that, too, would require the creation of yet another category of list seats, thus further distorting the proportionality of the overall electoral outcome. Of course, in a proportional representation environment, there would be nothing to prevent a political party which drew its votes primarily from indigenous people from obtaining representation in the House, and this might, indeed, occur.

The structure and powers of the Senate is given detailed treatment in Chapter 9. The conclusion reached there (consistent with Brennan's argument) is that because individual votes vary in strength in Senate elections (because an equal number of seats is allocated to each State, irrespective of population), considerations of equality of representation could not be raised as an objection to the creation of a new category of Senate seats reserved for indigenous people. The details of the representation system are discussed in Chapter 9. Here, it is necessary simply to note that what is envisaged is the allocation of 12 Senate seats to be elected on a nationwide basis by voters who chose to go on a separate indigenous voters' roll. That number would ensure an adequate representation of indigenous people relative to their status as a distinct community within Australian society. It would also ensure that there was a sufficient number of indigenous parliamentarians to spread their workload among Senate Committees.

An issue which would need to be addressed if reserved seats were set aside for indigenous members of Parliament would be the relationship between such parliamentarians and the national indigenous representative body discussed in 6.5.1.3, above. To which group should the government pay heed when soliciting the opinion of the indigenous community? What if the views of the national representative body were at variance with those of indigenous parliamentarians? I would argue that the role of the national representative body would be entirely distinguishable from that of the indigenous parliamentarians. The former would have the task of presenting a coherent 'indigenous voice' to government in relation to matters differentially affecting indigenous people. The latter would exist to provide an identifiable indigenous voice in *deliberations affecting Australia as a whole.* They would not have a role which related specifically to indigenous affairs. In addition, one could not expect them to discharge the role of providing a united voice for indigenous people because, as is the case with other parliamentarians, one would expect that they would represent different political parties.

6.5.3 The right to culture

Cultural rights are protected by Art 27 of the International Convention on Civil and Political Rights 1996 (ICCPR), which provides that:

> In those States in which ethnic, religious or linguistic minorities exist, persons belonging to such minorities shall not be denied the right, in community with the other members of their group, to enjoy their own culture, to profess and practice their own religion, or to use their own language.

The draft Declaration on the Rights of Indigenous Peoples expands on this right in respect of indigenous peoples in several of its Articles.[63] This right has already been discussed in the chapter on a Bill of Rights, where it was noted that protecting such a right gives to ethnic groups the freedom to preserve and develop their culture. Since this right would be enjoyed by all groups, both indigenous and non-indigenous, it would (assuming that the other measures towards indigenous self-determination recommended in this chapter were also put into the Constitution), make redundant a separate 'indigenous Bill of Rights' which some commentators have advocated.[64] I also suggested that a practical example of that right would be the entitlement of cultural or ethnic groups to receive public funding to support educational institutions established by them, in order to preserve their culture. Here, the example of schools teaching through the medium of the Maori language in New Zealand is an obvious one to follow.[65] Clearly, the right to preservation and development of culture would be of special value to indigenous people, given their minority status, and one could envisage that in addition to the establishment of educational institutions, indigenous people might wish to avail of specifically targeted health services or to run their own health-delivery services. As in the case of any right which cast a positive obligation on the state, the extent and mode of compliance with this right by the state would be dependant upon the availability of resources, and so, for example, compliance might take the form of governmental subsidy to institutions established by indigenous people, rather than the state's establishment of separate institutions for them.

---

63 See Arts 4, 12, 13 and 14.

64 See, eg, Council for Aboriginal Reconciliation, 1995, 43.

65 Bishop and Glynn, 1999, 63 and 72–96.

6.5.4 Recognising indigenous law in Australia

There is some irony in the fact that, while recognition of indigenous or customary law is considered by its opponents to be among the most radical and dangerous of claims that is made by supporters of indigenous rights, such recognition has long been extended to customary law by legal systems which were, by any measure, far more conservative than that of Australia. In South Africa, for example, statutory recognition has long been enjoyed by tribal courts which hear civil matters arising under customary law, and exercise limited criminal jurisdiction.[66] Indeed, the acknowledgment of customary law was the norm in Africa even in colonial times, and has remained a feature of most African legal systems since decolonisation.

6.5.4.1 The current position

Before discussing how customary law might be accorded recognition in Australia, it is useful to give an overview of its current constitutional position. Under English law, a colony could be acquired by settlement, conquest or cession. Settlement applied where the territory was uninhabited, and had the consequence that the settlers brought English law with them. Conquest applied where territory was inhabited. According to the common law, as stated in *Campbell v Hall*,[67] local law survived until it was overridden by incompatible law enacted by the conquering power. Cession occurred where the territory was inhabited and sovereignty was ceded to the United Kingdom. The applicable law would be determined by the terms of the agreement of cession, but the usual term was that local law would continue to apply. Prevailing legal doctrine is to the effect that Australia was acquired by settlement, even though the continent was inhabited by Aborigines at the time the British arrived. The fact of prior Aboriginal occupation was reconciled with the theory of settlement because the common law included within the definition of 'uninhabited' lands those places which were inhabited by people who were 'uncivilised' according to 18th century norms. Australia was thus considered to be *terra nullius* (uninhabited land) and to have been acquired by settlement rather than conquest. It therefore followed that English law applied upon the foundation of the colony of New South Wales.

However, in *Mabo v Queensland (No 2)*,[68] the High Court, while affirming Britain's acquisition of sovereignty (and the extinguishment of indigenous authority), rejected the *terra nullius* doctrine, stating that native title rights in land continued in existence after settlement, in so far as they had not been extinguished by introduced law. It should, however, be noted that the scope of the ruling in *Mabo* was quite narrow: the court did not say that Australia had been acquired by conquest, which would have led to the inevitable conclusion that all Aboriginal law not displaced by a positive act under the received law had survived. Instead, the court maintained the position that Australia had

66 See the Black Administration Act 1927, ss 12 and 20 of (which recognise the jurisdiction of Chiefs' and Headmen's courts) and the Law of Evidence Amendment Act 1988, s 1 (which empowers other courts to take judicial notice of customary law). In addition, note that the Constitution of the Republic Of South Africa 1996, s 211 recognises traditional authorities and customary law.

67 (1774) 1 Cowper 204.

68 (1992) 175 CLR 1.

been acquired by settlement, and that English law had become the general law, but held that in the specific case of land, the common law now recognised that title held under Aboriginal customary survived, unless extinguished by the received legal system. This outcome is unsatisfactory, in that it mixes a consequence of acquisition by conquest (survival of indigenous law), with a consequence of acquisition by settlement (reception of the settlers' law), and also because only indigenous rights in respect of land have been accorded recognition under the common law native title doctrine.

I have already noted the point that in several decisions, the courts have stated that the Crown's acquisition of sovereignty over Australia is not subject to legal challenge. This means that such indigenous law has been recognised (at the moment, only native title) exists *as part of the common law* contained in the *Mabo (No 2)* decision. Thus, any future developments in indigenous law would, given the rule about sovereignty, have to occur through further rule-making within the received legal system. In addition, it should be noted that, as was held in *Coe v Commonwealth (No 2)*[69] and *Walker v New South Wales*,[70] no aspects of indigenous law, other than native title, are recognised by the contemporary legal system, it being held that indigenous law was wholly overridden by laws enacted after colonisation. It thus appears that recognition of indigenous law as part of the Australian legal system would require legislative action or recognition through the Constitution.

The most comprehensive study of the status of indigenous law in Australia is the Australian Law Reform Commission's 1986 report on *The Recognition of Aboriginal Customary Laws*[71] (hereafter in this chapter referred to as the 'ALRC report'). The Commission's major recommendations were that recognition should be extended to Aboriginal law,[72] but that no single method of recognition would suit all circumstances.[73] Of the methods of incorporation canvassed, the Commission favoured incorporation by reference,[74] functional recognition of indigenous institutions as the equivalent of institutions in the received law,[75] and accommodation of indigenous law in the administration of the received law.[76] The Commission recommended against wholesale codification of indigenous law (because of the danger that codification would be unable to accommodate variations between Aboriginal communities, and would also take development of the law out of the hands of the communities), or the exclusion of the received law from Aboriginal areas (because this would deprive Aboriginal people of

69 (1993) 118 ALR 193, 199–200.

70 (1994) 182 CLR 45, 47–50.

71 ALRC, 1986.

72 *Ibid*, 194.

73 *Ibid*, 199–207.

74 By which is meant the enactment of a statute which incorporates indigenous law, either generally or in relation to a specific issue, without stating what that law is, thus leaving it to the courts progressively to discover and apply that law.

75 Eg, by recognising traditional Aboriginal marriages as amounting to marriage for the purposes of the received law (one instance of this being the Family Provision Act 1979 (NT), s 7(1A), which accords traditional marriages the same status as marriages under the Marriage Act 1961 (Cth) for purposes of claims for maintenance made against a deceased estate).

76 Eg, by interpreting statutes in such a way as to take account of Aboriginal values (as was done in *R v Bara Bara* (1992) 2 NTLR 98, or by the courts using their discretionary powers in relation to court procedures and the rules of evidence to take account of Aboriginal sensibilities).

rights under the received law).[77] Although 12 years have elapsed since the Commission's report, little has been done to implement it, nor did the decision in *Mabo (No 2)* spur legislative action to accord recognition to indigenous law in areas other than native title.[78] In 1994 the Commonwealth government published a report on the extent to which steps had been taken to implement the Commission's recommendations.[79] Lack of progress in implementing the Commission's recommendations was also a consistent theme adopted by speakers at the 1995 Indigenous Customary Law Forum,[80] yet recognition of indigenous law remains an important but unfulfilled dimension of the recognition of indigenous rights generally.

6.5.4.2 Conflict of law rules

The most important technical issue to be resolved (assuming that recognition was accorded to indigenous law), is how to determine when indigenous law should apply and, in cases where more than one system of indigenous law is potentially applicable, which one of these should be chosen. Mechanisms allowing such jurisdictional problems to be addressed are a common feature of countries which acknowledge legal dualism, and essentially involve devising a body of internal conflict of law rules.

How in practice might such a system work in Australia? An important issue to recognise is that, whereas for some indigenous people, customary law is a vital component of every day life within their communities, for others who have left such communities, or who may, indeed, be the descendants of those who left communities decades ago, such law has no impact at all. Even more difficult is the case of those whose lives are spent partly in indigenous communities and partly in urban Australia (in particular, in rural towns), and who reject traditional authority without feeling accepted in mainstream society. What law would apply to them? As Brennan notes, while their rejection of traditional authority, and their refusal to accept its jurisdiction, certainly undermines customary law, the application of such law to them would be inconsistent with their evident preference for the general law.[81] In the case of people who no longer identify themselves as indigenous, application of indigenous law to them as though they were still part of the indigenous community would be inconsistent with the test for aboriginality discussed at the beginning of this chapter. But should people be able to 'opt out' of the indigenous legal system, and how would one prevent the self-identification component of aboriginality being cynically used by individuals seeking to bring themselves within the jurisdiction of whichever legal system best suited them at any given time?

Perhaps the most useful analysis of how customary law might be accommodated within the broader legal system was that provided by Coombs, who canvassed the views of the Yirrkala community of East Arnhem Land on the question.[82] The proposal put by

77 ALRC, 1986, 208.

78 For an overview of the potential offered by *Mabo (No 2)* for the recognition of indigenous law, see Amankwah, 1994.

79 Office of Indigenous Affairs, 1994.

80 Indigenous Customary Law Forum, 1996.

81 Brennan, 1995, 140–48.

82 Coombs, 1994, 118–30.

that community was that the administration of law within Yirrkala lands would be under the control of a law council composed of clan elders. The council would name members of the community to form a community court to resolve alleged infractions of the law. On the key issue of the jurisdiction of the law council, the Yirrkala proposed that geography would be the essential criterion of jurisdiction, and that anyone resident in or visiting Yirrkala territory would be subject to its laws, and that submission to jurisdiction would be a requirement to obtain a permit to enter the territory. However, the Yirrkala proposal also accepted that in some instances (not precisely defined, but certainly including homicide), State or Commonwealth law would govern, albeit preceded by a preliminary hearing by an indigenous court, which would then advise the magistrate or judge hearing the case under received law.

Although geography cannot be the sole determinant of jurisdiction, the Yirrkala proposals point to the type of solution that the legal system should be working towards. Clearly, what is needed is a set of rules which can be applied to determine whether indigenous law is applicable (where that point is put in issue). In cases where indigenous law councils claim jurisdiction, there would have to be some mechanism by means of which parties who dispute the jurisdiction of an indigenous authority could apply to the general court system for a determination of which legal system was applicable. In many, perhaps most, cases arising on indigenous lands, the parties would be quite satisfied to have their dispute regulated by customary law, but in some instances, for example, where a person of Aboriginal ethnicity no longer chooses to identify themselves as Aboriginal, the opportunity must be given for such a person to adduce evidence as to why Aboriginal law should not be applicable. Clearly, much will depend upon what presumptions as to the applicability of indigenous law are in force, and upon whom the onus should rest in arguing that one or other legal system should apply.

At this point, it is useful to refer to the example of South Africa, where, over the past 50 years or so, a large body of law, both statutory and judicial, has been built upon the question of which law – indigenous or received – should be applied in particular cases. In South Africa, s 20 of the Black Administration Act[83] confers jurisdiction on courts presided over by Chiefs and Headmen (which each have authority over a specific geographical area) to hear cases involving crimes at common, statutory and customary law, other than crimes listed in the third Schedule of the Act (essentially, serious crimes such as murder, rape, culpable homicide, robbery and assault with intent to do grievous bodily harm). Civil jurisdiction is governed by s 12(1), and is limited to claims arising out of customary law. A general limit on jurisdiction restricts the courts to hearing civil cases between blacks, and criminal cases in which blacks are the accused. Who is a 'black' South African for the purposes of the Act is defined by s 35 as 'any person who is a member of any aboriginal race or tribe of Africa'. Here, then, one can see that the application of indigenous law is restricted by geographic location, the branch of law that the case arises under, and the ethnicity of the parties to the case.

In addition to the above, courts established under the received legal system have a statutory discretion to apply indigenous law should they think it appropriate.[84] How that discretion should be applied was discussed in the case of *Ex parte Minister of Native*

83 1927.

84 Law of Evidence Amendment Act 1988, s 1.

Affairs: In re Yako v Beyi,[85] in which it was held that the legislation did not require that a Commissioner consider either common law or customary law as *prima facie* applicable,[86] but, rather, that the discretion was an open one, and that a Commissioner should 'determine which system of law it would be fairest to apply in deciding the case between the parties',[87] and similarly should bear in mind that 'the dominant consideration is his own reasoned view as to the best system of law to apply in order to reach a just decision between the parties'.[88] Quite apart from its general vagueness,[89] this formulation presents the fundamental problem in that, while inviting presiding officers to answer the choice of law question in such a way as to achieve what they conceive of as a 'fair' or 'just' outcome, it offers no guidelines as to what 'fairness' and 'justice' means in this context.

Bennett, one of the leading South African authorities on customary law, suggests that the choice of law discretion should be guided by the fundamental principle underlying legal pluralism, which is that the members of each community are entitled to have their own law applied to them, and that, therefore, 'their expectations must be accommodated by application of the system of law which they could reasonably have anticipated [would apply] in the circumstances of the case'.[90] In this process, the techniques of private international law are useful, but only to a limited extent, as they are employed in the context of choice of law between jurisdictions, whereas the issue at customary law is which of a number of *personal law systems within a jurisdiction* is applicable.[91] Furthermore, private international law techniques involve the characterisation of a legal issue, followed by the use of the relevant connecting factor – for example, if the validity of a marriage is the issue, the connecting factor is the *lex loci celebrationis*, which will lead to identification of the *lex causa*. By contrast, in the case of choice of law between customary and the received law, the appropriate legal system is indicated by factors associated with the parties themselves, rather than by reference to the branch of substantive law involved, and so a contractual dispute, for example, might be decided under customary law between litigants A and B, but under common law between litigants C and D, because of their differing personal circumstances.[92] Thus, internal conflict of law rules operate by taking into account factors such as the identity of the protagonists, the geographic location of their transaction, and the nature of the transaction to determine which legal system should regulate the relationship between them.

According primacy to the intention of the parties is unproblematic where the parties have entered into an express choice of law agreement.[93] However, such cases are rare,

85 1948 (1) SA 388 (A).

86 *Ibid*, 397.

87 *Ibid*.

88 *Ibid*, 400–01.

89 Olivier, 1995, 206; and van der Vyver, 1982, 312–14.

90 Bennett, 1985, 105.

91 Sanders, 1990, 58.

92 Bennett, 1985, 106–08.

93 *Ibid*, 108–09; and *Mbonjiwa v Scellam* 1957 NAC (S) 41. See also *Sompetu v Kolisi* 1976 BAC 8 (S), where the applicable system was agreed at a pre-trial conference. Note, however, that the court is still exercising its discretion – it has been made clear that the parties do not by their agreement oust the discretion of the court (*Moima NO v Matladi* 1937 NAC (N & T) 40, *Lebona v Ramokone* 19467 NAC (C & O), *Ciya v Malanda* 1949 NAC 154 (S)).

and the courts are more usually confronted with a situation where only one of the parties indicates which legal system he or she expects to be applied – usually this is apparent from the way in which the plaintiff presents his or her summons[94] (or the defendant his or her defence).[95] In such instances it is clear that the court cannot allow an expression of preference to be determinative,[96] as the choice of law question may be the very issue in dispute in cases where a litigant seeks to have applied whichever system of law favours him or her. In the absence of an agreement between the parties, their expectation should, Bennett suggests, be discovered by taking into account as many connecting factors as are relevant in the circumstances of the case,[97] with the courts basing their decisions on the aggregate impression thus created.[98] Thus the courts have paid attention to factors such as 'lifestyle'[99] (by which is meant the litigants' cultural orientation, which is, in turn, indicated by a number of factors, such as whether the person resides in a rural area and with the tribal community), the nature of the transaction (where the transaction is known only to one system of law),[100] the form a transaction takes,[101] and the place in which an event or transaction occurs.[102]

I stated earlier in this section that the key factors in a choice of law regime are what presumptions are put in place with regard to the applicability of a legal system, and who is to bear the onus of proving that one or other legal system is applicable. Bearing in mind the ALRC's recommendation that, even after recognition of indigenous law, Aborigines should retain rights under the general law (for example, to enter into marriages under the received law),[103] and that the the key factors to be considered are the intention of the parties, the identity of the parties, the place where an event or transaction occurs, and the nature of the event or transaction, I would suggest that the following choice of law rules should govern the applicability of indigenous law:

- In light of the argument in favour of recognition presented in this chapter, there would be a rebuttable presumption that indigenous persons intend indigenous law to apply in cases arising between indigenous parties on indigenous lands (such as Aboriginal reserves).
- The above presumption would be rebutted in cases where a party is able to discharge the onus of showing that there was no common intention between all parties that indigenous law should apply. This may be proved by reference to an express agreement that indigenous law should not apply, or may be implied from the lifestyle of a party, or the form or subject matter of the transaction.
- Where the parties agree that indigenous law is to apply, but disagree as to which community's law applies, neither community's law would enjoy a presumption of

94 See, eg, *Mkize v Makatini* 1950 NAC (NE) 207; *Mvemve v Mvemve* 1950 NAC (NE) 284; *Ngidi v Ciya* 1965 BAC (NE) 50.

95 See, eg, *Moima NO v Matladi* 1937 NAC (N & T) 40.

96 *Ciya v Malanda* 1949 NAC 154 (S).

97 Bennett, 1985, 108.

98 *Ibid.*

99 *Ibid*, 74–75 and 109–10.

100 *Ibid*, 74 and 110.

101 *Ibid*, 110.

102 *Ibid*. See also *Mokoba v Langa* 1952 NAC (S) 76.

103 ALRC, 1986, 157.

applicability, and the court would decide the issue after hearing arguments from both parties.

- Indigenous law would be presumed not to have been intended to apply in cases involving indigenous people outside indigenous lands, or between non-indigenous people and indigenous people wherever they arise. This presumption would be rebutted where a party discharged the burden of showing that there was common intention that indigenous law would apply, such intention again being inferred from an express agreement or being implied from the lifestyle of the parties or the form or subject matter of the transaction.
- Indigenous law would not apply in cases involving serious criminal offences or offences in relation to which there is clearly no indigenous law (for example, revenue offences). Which offences those would be would need to be negotiated with indigenous communities prior to the enactment of statutory rules governing the applicability of indigenous law. The Yirrkala study shows that there is a recognition among Aboriginal communities that certain issues lie beyond what they themselves see as the proper ambit of contemporary customary law. There should, however, be a formal process whereby members drawn from local communities sit as assessors when such offences are tried in magistrate's courts or State Supreme Courts.

The practical effect of applying such rules would be that, with the exception of the excluded criminal offences, indigenous law would be the default system in cases between indigenous people arising within areas designated as Aboriginal or Torres Strait Island lands. An indigenous person (defined according to the tripartite test discussed earlier in this chapter) seeking not to have indigenous law apply to them would have the option of seeking an order from a magistrate's court that the general law, rather than received law, was applicable to the case, but would have the burden of proving the facts indicating the inappropriateness of the applicability of indigenous law to them. By contrast, a non-indigenous person would not be subject to indigenous law in respect of any event (whether giving rise to civil or criminal liability), even if occurring on Aboriginal lands, unless, if the matter was put in issue by any party, a magistrate's court held that indigenous law was applicable (for example, because the person had expressly or impliedly agreed that they should be subject to indigenous law, either generally or in respect of the specific event or transaction). Indigenous people outside indigenous lands could regulate their legal relations according to indigenous law (for example, succession to property), but agreement to have that law apply would have to be proved by the party asserting it.

How would recognition of indigenous law be given effect to in the Constitution? The Constitution should, at the very least, recognise indigenous law as a source of law in Australia. The jurisdictional issues discussed in the above paragraphs could be satisfactorily dealt with by stating that indigenous law should be applied 'where appropriate', leaving it to Parliament to amplify the concept of appropriate application of the law (in other words, to draft conflict of law rules such as those suggested above) in separate legislation. In the absence of such legislation, it would be up to the courts to interpret the Constitution in such a way as to set similar bounds to the concept of appropriate application.

6.5.4.3 *Interaction between indigenous law and a Bill of Rights*

One of the most contentious issues that arises in jurisdictions which confer recognition of indigenous law is the compatibility of that law with human rights. In particular, adverse public comment has been aroused over the issue of corporal punishment inflicted in accordance with indigenous law. As a preliminary point, it may be noted that concern in respect of the incompatibility of indigenous law with human rights has not been matched by equal concern by governments that received common and statute law should be invalid if incompatible with human rights. Be that as it may, the issue is an important one which must be faced by those arguing for the recognition of indigenous law.

The potential for conflict between indigenous rights and other internationally protected rights was noted by the Law Reform Commission's 1986 report,[104] and by the Commonwealth in its 1994 report.[105] Although finding that recognition of indigenous law involved some measure of acceptance of cultural difference, the Law Reform Commission also asserted that certain of the rights protected by the ICCPR (the examples given by the Commission being the right to life, the right not to be tortured and the right to an interpreter), were of universal application. Furthermore, Art 1 of the draft Declaration on the Rights of Indigenous Peoples states that indigenous peoples have the right to the enjoyment of all rights and freedoms protected by the Charter, the Universal Declaration and international human rights law, while Art 33 states that customary law must be developed 'in accordance with internationally recognised human rights standards'.

As stated above, the issue of the relationship between fundamental rights and indigenous law assumes particular importance in respect of traditional punishments, such as spearing. There might also be rules of indigenous law which are incompatible with the protection afforded to equality on the basis of gender by human rights law. Focusing for the moment on the issue of traditional punishments, legal scholars in Australia have adopted a variety of positions: in his comment on the issue, Zdenkowski[106] acknowledged, but did not resolve, the issue of the conflict between such an approach and human rights doctrines. Although noting that limits might be placed on what customary punishments would be recognised, he also noted that such restrictions would, in turn, raise the issue of paternalism. The only writers to address the issue squarely were McLaughlin[107] and Blay,[108] who reached opposing conclusions. McLaughlin adopted an unambiguously universalist approach, stating that:[109]

> ... it is unconscionable to place indigenous rights under the banner of human rights, but then to exclude the operation of those human rights within customary law.

By contrast, Blay argued that, whereas the principle contained in Art 7 of the ICCPR that no-one be subject to 'torture, cruel, inhuman or degrading treatment or punishment' may be universal, what amounts to such punishments may be culturally-specific, and that, for

104 *Ibid*, 179–93.
105 Office of Indigenous Affairs, 1994, 7.
106 Zdenkowski, 1994.
107 McLaughlin, 1996.
108 Blay, 1986.
109 McLaughlin, 1996, 9.

example, imprisonment may be seen as more cruel by an Aborigine than would spearing in the thigh.[110] Certainly the theory of punishment underlying Yirrkala law, for example, is that more damage is done both to the offender and to the community by imprisonment than by corporal punishment.[111] Blay further argued that the exclusion of 'pain or suffering arising only from, inherent in or incidental to lawful sanctions' from the definition of torture in Art 1 of the Convention against Torture can, because of the ambiguity inherent in the term 'lawful sanctions', be interpreted as excluding from the definition of torture punishment which is lawful under indigenous law,[112] and that, therefore, such punishments should be granted recognition, even in the light of the international documents.[113] It is suggested that this line of reasoning be rejected: reading the exclusion provision in the definition of torture in such a way as to exclude from 'torture' whatever is lawful within a jurisdiction, undermines the entire purpose of the document, and amounts to a virtual invitation to parties to enact legislation legalising torture. Clearly, sense can be made of the exclusion only if it is interpreted as covering only such pain or suffering arising from lawful sanctions *other than torture* – in other words, it is recognised that even lawful sanctions falling short of torture might contain an element of pain or suffering,[114] but that once such pain or suffering reaches a certain threshold, the punishment *becomes torture in itself,* and is thus prohibited by the Convention, even if that punishment is valid the legal system of the jurisdiction. Seen in this light, the Convention cannot possibly be seen as permitting punishments which amount to torture (or, it follows, to cruel, inhuman or degrading treatment or punishment).

How, then, do we resolve the conflict between the universalist's rejection of indigenous punishments which offend international human rights instruments, and the cultural relativist's acceptance of them as a manifestation of the right to self-determination? In the first place, while disagreeing with Blay's conclusions on the issue of 'lawful sanctions', his point that what constitutes 'cruel and inhuman punishment' is to some extent indeterminate is well made, and it may be that, taking into account both the physical and psychological effects of punishments imposed under indigenous and the received law, the former may, in fact, not be cruel and inhuman, notwithstanding its corporal nature. This is a question best answered by criminologists and anthropologists. However, what does one make of punishments which are found to impose physical or psychological pain to an extraordinary degree – in other words, where it is the severity of the punishment, rather than its type, that is problematic? Once severity becomes an issue, the question which must be addressed is what are the limits of consent by a member of a culture to punishment imposed by that culture? This is an issue which remains to be settled, as the leading common law decision in *R v Brown*[115] shows. The answer must, however, depend on some test relating to the seriousness of the injury inflicted, taking

110 Blay, 1986, 207–08.

111 Coombs, 1994, 125–36.

112 *Ibid*, 209–10, 214–15.

113 *Ibid*, 217–19.

114 Eg, limited periods of solitary confinement used as a disciplinary measure.

115 [1993] 2 All ER 75. For academic comment on the case highlighting the court's failure to enunciate a clear rule on the question of what level of injury may be consented to, see Thompson, 1994; Giles, 1994; and Bix, 1993.

into account the risk it poses to life, the permanence of its effects and whether it requires medical attention.[116] Assuming, then, that, assessed on some objective – probably medical – standard, a particular punishment is found to be excessive, one will then (and only then) finally have to make the choice between conflicting rights posited at the beginning of this paragraph. The answer one arrives at ultimately depends upon one's stance in relation to the question of whether there are any rights that are universal. In the author's opinion, universality lies at the heart of the entire concept of human rights, whereas cultural relativism leads ultimately to the justification of any human rights breach, no matter how egregious, on the basis of differing cultural values. For that reason, the clash would have to be resolved in favour of human rights obligations, and I would, therefore, argue that indigenous law, like all other sources of law in Australia, would need to be made subject to the rest of the Constitution, including the Bill of Rights.

It may, however, be found that the conflict on this issue is more apparent than real: indigenous law is not positivist, being, rather, understood by Aborigines as a body of rules forming part of an established moral order.[117] However, this does not mean that indigenous law is static, as is shown by the fact that while death was reportedly imposed as a punishment by some indigenous communities in the 19th century and even into this century,[118] nowadays such is rarely, if ever, the case.[119] Certainly under Yirrkala law, for example, the death penalty has been abrogated by disuse, and that group also averred that they would be willing to abandon other forms of corporal punishment which are, in any event, usually nowadays being replaced by compensation.[120] Although human modifications of a naturally-ordained order would seem to be a contradiction in terms, evolution in indigenous law can be explained as a *new understanding* by Aborigines of the rules ordained by that natural order, just as a natural lawyer would argue that, while natural law is immutable, human understanding of that law is progressive. It may, therefore, be that indigenous authorities themselves reach the conclusion that such physical punishments that inflict serious injury are inconsistent with human dignity.

6.5.5 Indigenous Australians and a preamble to the Constitution

At a purely symbolic level, prominent indigenous leaders have called for some recognition to be accorded to indigenous people as the first inhabitants of Australia in the preamble of the Constitution. Thus, as Lois O'Donoghue stated, the concept of self-determination includes 'appropriate recognition of our status as First Australians being enshrined in the Australian Constitution'.[121] The precise formula to be used in such a statement of recognition attracted much controversy during the period prior to the

116 In the course of his dissenting judgment in *Brown*, Slynn LJ suggested that seriousness of injury should be the criterion by which capacity to consent was determined (at 121j–122d), and, in reaching a conclusion on the facts of the case, took into account the fact that the injuries were not of such a nature as to require medical treatment (at 122j). In the wake of the *Brown* decision, the United Kingdom's Law Commission recommended that 'serious injury' should mark the point beyond which consent should not be permitted – see United Kingdom Law Commission, 1994, 32.5.

117 Maddock, 1984, 212–13.

118 *Ibid*, 224.

119 Debelle, 1983, 63 and 68.

120 Coombs, 1994, 125 and 128.

121 O'Donoghue, 1992. See also Council for Aboriginal Reconciliation, 1995, 36–37.

referendum on the proposed new preamble in 1999. Although the proposed preamble would have referred to Aborigines and Torres Strait Islanders as the 'nation's first people', the government refused to include any reference to indigenous people as the 'custodians' of the land, preferring, instead, to state that indigenous peoples had 'deep kinship with their lands'.

How much is included in a preamble is, to some extent, affected by the status a preamble is to have. Under the rules of statutory interpretation, reference may be had to a preamble in order to ascertain the meaning of the actual body of the statute.[122] Obviously, the more loose and general the wording of the preamble is, the greater the scope that the preamble could influence the body of the Constitution in ways not anticipated by the drafters of the Constitution. On the other hand, a preamble which says little of substance would have little impact on the interpretation of the body of the Constitution, even if the normal rule of statutory interpretation was allowed to operate. However, if it is to serve any purpose, a preamble should at least contain a statement of historical facts and contemporary aspirations. Some argue that, in the case of Australia, whose history is disputed, a preamble which refers to historical facts which disclose dispossession and oppression of one sector of the community by the organs of government could affect the interpretation of the Constitution in such a way as to either create or increase legal liability. The preceding parts of this chapter have indicated how the rights of indigenous people could be recognised and protected in the body of the Constitution. If that is done, and the balance between indigenous rights and those of the rest of society is satisfactorily struck, there would seem to be a good argument for not allowing that balance to be affected by broad statements in a preamble. How, then, should one address the call by many indigenous people that the preamble should acknowledge not only that they were the original inhabitants of the country, but also that they were the original owners of the land and that they suffered both dispossession and oppression?

There are two ways of achieving this: one could insert into the Constitution an express statement that the preamble is to have no legal effect. The proposed preamble put to referendum in 1999 would have been accompanied by a new section in the Constitution expressly denying it any legal force. The other option would be to include in the preamble the qualifying phrase 'subject to law' (which would, of course, include law deriving from the Constitution itself). With either of these safeguards in place, the preamble could contain a full statement of the country's history, an acknowledgment of past wrongs and a commitment to strive to achieve common aspirations in the future, but with it being clear that the preamble was to be read subject to substantive law.

6.5.6 An apology and the Constitution

One final point should be made in respect of indigenous Australians and the Constitution: a consistent demand by many indigenous activists is that an apology be made on behalf of the Australian government for past injustices towards indigenous people, in particular for instances of unjustified removal of Aboriginal children from their parents. One ground upon which the present government has refused to make an

122 *Wacando v Commonwealth* (1981) 148 CLR 1.

apology is that such an act might amount to an admission of liability by the government, and thus expose it to claims for damages.[123] Assuming that an apology was made by the Prime Minister from the floor of Parliament, no such liability could arise, as it is beyond doubt that it would be protected by parliamentary privilege.[124] Indeed, the head of every State and Territory government has tendered such an apology from the floor of their legislatures without attracting liability to the Crown. There is no reason in law why the Prime Minister, as head of the Commonwealth government, should not do the same.

6.6 ASSIMILATION OR SEPARATION?

Much energy continues to be expended on the debate as to whether the interests of indigenous Australians are best served by assimilation or by separation, and, indeed, on which of these social forces is favoured by indigenous people themselves. That is a social and political question which cannot be answered in a Constitution, and on which the Constitution should be neutral. It may be that, even if presented with the possibility of self-government within their own communities, indigenous people will prefer to have governmental services provided by existing local, State and Commonwealth agencies, to have their disputes regulated by received law and, where they move out of communities, to avail of mainstream education and health services, rather than ones provided specifically for indigenous people. Nothing in the recommendations made above compels one outcome or the other. The role of the Constitution should be facilitative, not prescriptive – providing options for self-determination for those who choose it. The institutions such as community self-government, reserved seats in Parliament and separate social services may be availed of by many, some or none of Australia's indigenous population. That is not important. What is important is that the Constitution should provide indigenous people with these options.

123 Michael Gordon, 'The great divide' (1997) *The Australian*, 31 May, 21.

124 See the Parliamentary Privileges Act 1987 (Cth), s 16, which re-enacts Art 9 of the Bill of Rights 1688 (Eng) and provides that 'freedom of speech and debates or proceedings in Parliament ought not to be questioned or impeached in any court or place outside Parliament'. Courts in Australia have repeatedly confirmed that this provision prevents statements made in Parliament being tendered as evidence in court or even having inferences drawn from them in court – see *Sankey v Whitlam* (1978) 142 CLR 1; *Amman Aviation (Pty) Ltd v Commonwealth* (1988) 19 FCR 223; and *Hamsher v Swift* (1992) 33 FCR 545.

DIRECT DEMOCRACY

7.1 THE CITIZEN AS LAWMAKER

As originally practised in Ancient Greece, and in particular in Athens, democracy involved the direct participation of those with citizenship rights[1] in the legislative process. Although democracy manifested itself in different forms in different city-states and at different periods, the classic period of Athenian democracy in the fourth century BC put direct democracy at the centre of the political order, in that the citizens' assembly, the *ekklesia*, was the ultimate source of legal authority in the state. To what extent would it be either desirable or feasible to introduce an element of direct democracy into our modern Constitution? If we did do that, what form should direct participation take?

A genuine commitment to a citizen-centred constitution surely requires that the idea of citizen as law-maker be given serious consideration. Direct democracy confers – or if one takes a long enough historical perspective, perhaps one should say restores – the citizen's right to participate in law-making. This has the advantage that measures which enjoy broad popular support can be enacted into law even though they do not have the support of the governing party or coalition in Parliament. Even though the proportional representation system advocated in Chapter 8 would increase the likelihood that smaller parties could get some of their legislative agenda accepted by major parties as the price for entering into coalition, there will inevitably be instances where the negotiation process requires parties to abandon initiatives which are popular with their supporters. Direct democracy gives voters an alternate avenue by which to have such measures enacted and to circumvent the dominance which parties have over the political process.[2] The disaffection that many Australians have with their political leaders has often been noted, and the suspicion with which voters greet proposals for change put forward by political leaders has been cited as the reason why constitutional reform is so difficult to achieve in Australia. Might not the availability of direct legislation serve as an antidote to alienation from the political process?

Before addressing direct democracy, we should pause to consider the concept of 'popular sovereignty' as it exists in Australia. Despite statements by judges of the High Court to the effect that sovereignty resides in the people of Australia,[3] the ultimate source

1 Women were not accorded political rights in Athens. Furthermore, approximately 50% of the population in Athens were slaves, who had no rights, and whose labour was part of the reason why those who did have citizenship rights had the time to engage in public affairs. For an overview of Athenian democracy, see Hansen, 1991, 90–93 and 129.

2 de Q Walker, 1987, 46–50.

3 Thus in *Australian Capital Television Pty Ltd v Commonwealth* (1992) 177 CLR 106, 138, Mason CJ stated that the enactment of the Australia Act 1986 (Cth) 'marked the end of the legal sovereignty of the Imperial Parliament and recognised that ultimate sovereignty rested in the Australian people', and Deane J stated in *Theophanous v Herald & Weekly Times* (1994) 182 CLR 104, 171, that the legitimacy of the Constitution now derived 'exclusively [from] the original adoption (by referenda) and subsequent maintenance (by acquiescence) of its provisions by the people'. However, this ignores the fact that, as was noted by Gummow J in *McGinty v Western Australia* (1996) 186 CLR 140, 274, the people are not free to amend the Constitution as they please, being bound by the terms of s 128.

of governmental authority in Australia derives from the fact that the Crown of the United Kingdom acquired sovereignty over this country. However, while from this purely *jurisprudential* point of view sovereignty undoubtedly vests in the Crown, it is also true that, from a *political* point of view, the people of Australia are seen as forming the base of the legislative process, and as having the ultimate say in what laws are enacted, by virtue of their ability to elect the government.[4] Furthermore, as will be noted in Chapter 10, the theoretical powers that the Crown has under our Constitution are substantially modified by conventions which originated in the 17th and 18th centuries, and which serve to ensure that the government of the day represents the democratic will. For these reasons, there is good reason to consider whether a mechanism should be put in place to allow more direct expression to be given to the political sovereignty of the people.

7.2 PLEBISCITES, REFERENDA AND INITIATIVES

Direct citizen involvement can take a variety of forms. A plebiscite is a non-binding indicative poll designed to show the government whether citizens approve of a particular law or policy, or which of a number of law or policy options they prefer. A referendum, on the other hand, involves the citizen in law-making in that, if the matter placed before voters is approved, it becomes law automatically, by virtue of already enacted legislation which provides that the change will come into effect in the event of the measure passing the referendum. Referenda can be classified either as legislative referenda, used to enact ordinary legislation, or as constitutional referenda, used to amend the Constitution. An important distinction should be between referenda which can be called only by the legislature or the government, and those which can be initiated by citizens themselves (often called 'initiatives' for this reason). A distinction can also be made among initiatives between direct initiatives, which can be put to the people by citizens without any participation by the legislature, and indirect initiatives, which are put to the voters only if the legislature fails to enact the proposed law within a specified period.[5]

In this chapter the focus will be on referenda rather than on plebiscites, as the fact that the latter do not change the law means that their major significance is political rather than legal. Furthermore, while it may be useful that Parliament be given the power to put ordinary legislation to the people in the same way that it can call a constitutional referendum under s 128, the really important reform that will be considered is giving to the people themselves the opportunity of initiating direct legislation, both ordinary and constitutional.

---

4 See, eg, *West Lakes Ltd v South Australia* (1980) 25 SASR 389, 396, where King CJ held that a requirement that the assent of the voters be obtained in a referendum before entrenched legislation could be amended would not amount to the abdication by Parliament of its legislative authority to an outside body because, ultimately, it is the voters who the legislature represents.

5 For a useful analysis of the terminology in this area, see de Q Walker, 1987, 10–13. Mention should also be made of another institution often associated with plebiscites and referenda – that of recall, which enables voters to vote to terminate the tenure of a holder of public office. That institution is not addressed in this book. Recall is possible only in constitutional settings which embody separation of powers between the legislature and the executive. In that circumstance, where members of the executive are directly elected, an argument can be made for an opportunity to 'dis-elect' them. Recall would, however, not be compatible with the system of parliamentary government which we have in Australia, where the executive owes its tenure to the legislature rather than to the voters directly.

In the vast majority of jurisdictions that use referenda, the proposal to hold a referendum must be approved by the Head of State, the government, or the legislature. Governments frequently use referenda as a tool to validate their policies. They are somewhat more reluctant to call referenda where measures are controversial, and voter approval is less certain. Italy, New Zealand, Switzerland, and various States of the United States are notable in that they provide for citizen-initiated referenda.[6]

Little attention needs to be paid to the situation in Italy, as the power that citizens have to initiate referenda can be used only to repeal rather than enact laws, and cannot be used in respect of international treaties, taxation or budgetary laws, or amnesties.[7]

In New Zealand, the Citizens Initiated Referenda Act 1993 enables voters to initiate referenda by circulating a petition which receives the support of at least 10% of enrolled voters. Referenda are indicative only, and so the results are not binding on the government. They ought, therefore, more correctly to be termed 'plebiscites'. So far, three referenda have been held under the legislation. The first referendum, held in 1997, was on the question of whether a compulsory superannuation savings scheme should be introduced. The proposal was defeated by a massive margin, with 92% of voters voting against it. In 1999, a referendum on the proposal of reducing the number of MPs from 120 to 99 was held, resulting in 82% of voters voting in favour of the proposition. Parliament has, however, not moved to enact the proposal into law, a major consideration against doing so being that it would undermine the proportionality of the electoral system, proportional representation having been introduced in 1993.[8] A second referendum, in 1999, held in conjunction with that relating to the number of members of Parliament, was on the broad proposition that the criminal justice system be reformed so as to place more emphasis on the rights of victims (including their receiving compensation), and to impose mandatory imprisonment with hard labour on those convicted of offences involving serious violence. That proposal won the approval of 92% of voters. Clearly, such a proposal amounted to a call for a general shift in legislative policy, rather than the enactment of a single specific piece of legislation, and thus really falls outside the realm of direct legislation.

Switzerland is the only country in Europe in which citizens may enact new laws by referendum. Referenda are regularly held at the federal, cantonal and local levels.[9] At the federal level, referenda to amend the constitution may be called at any time at the instance of the federal government, while citizens may call a referendum to amend the constitution by collecting the signatures of 100,000 voters. The amendment passes if it receives a majority nationally, and majorities in a majority of the 26 cantons. Citizens may also initiate referenda to negative an ordinary law, by obtaining 50,000 signatures on a petition. However, citizens cannot initiate their own positive changes to ordinary law, and must resort to constitutional amendment to effect positive change. This has resulted in the federal Constitution containing provisions on a range of matters not usually addressed in

6 See Butler and Ranney, 1994, 26–27.

7 Abrogative citizen initiated referenda are provided for by the Constitution of the Republic of Italy 1947, Art 75. For a detailed discussion, see Bogdanor, 1994, 62–69.

8 See the discussion of the implications of reducing the number of MPs in New Zealand Parliament, 2001, 34–38.

9 For a comprehensive discussion of the use of referenda in Switzerland, see Kobach, 1994, 98–151.

Constitutions. Where a referendum succeeds in changing the law, the change can be overridden only by another referendum. The frequent use of referenda at the federal level has meant that political parties are of lesser importance than they might otherwise be, as public sentiment on issues put to referenda tends to cut across party loyalty lines.

Direct democracy has a long history in the United States, having become established during the Progressive Era of the first two decades of the 20th century. As part of their programme of redressing social imbalances, the Progressives promoted direct democracy as an antidote to the powerful alliance, which had been built in the final decades of the 19th century, between powerful corporations and political machines.[10] The political strength enjoyed by the Progressives in the western States accounts for the fact that it was mostly there that voters were successful in effecting constitutional change permitting direct legislation. Direct democracy enjoyed a resurgence in the 1970s among the left, following the general decline in faith in governmental institutions caused by the Vietnam war and Watergate, and in the 1980s among the right, who sought to reduce the role of government, and who found in direct democracy a useful tool to achieve tax cuts.

Direct democracy takes a variety of forms in the United States.[11] In all States (barring Delaware) the legislature must refer constitutional amendments to the people for approval in a referendum. In addition, a total of 27 States provide for either the initiative or popular referendum; of these, 21 permit both, three permit only the initiative and three permit only the popular referendum. The term 'initiative' has already been defined. The term 'popular referendum' has a particular meaning in the United States, and refers to the ability of voters to subject a law enacted by the legislature to popular approval.[12] The law is held in abeyance pending the referendum, and comes into force only if approved by the voters. Of the 24 States permitting the initiative, 15 permit it in respect both of both constitutional amendments and ordinary statutes, three in respect of constitutional amendments only and six in respect of ordinary statutes only. Where initiatives are permitted, the direct initiative is far more common than is the indirect initiative: of the 18 States permitting constitutional amendment initiatives, 16 allow direct initiative. Similarly, of the 23 States permitting ordinary statute initiatives, 16 allow the direct initiative. Constitutional amendments effected through the initiative process can be reversed only by adhering to the requirement for a constitutional amendment which, in the case of all but one of the States, requires a referendum. Ordinary statutes enacted by means of the initiative are less secure: in all but five of the States permitting such initiatives, there is some process open to the legislature to enable it to reverse the popular legislation. The statutory initiative has been used to legislate on a wide variety of topics – from tax cutting and deficit spending limitation measures in the 1980s, to term limits in the 1990s, which saw voters in 24 States enact laws limiting the number of terms State

10 For an account of the Progressive roots of direct democracy, see Allswang, 2000, 8–31; Magleby, 1984, 20–25; and Bowler and Donovan, 1998, 4–5.

11 For an overview of direct democracy at the State level in the United States, see Magleby, 1994, 218–57. Statistics relating to the availability of direct democracy in the United States are derived from the Initiative and Referendum Institute, whose website address is www.iandrinstitute.org/.

12 For a discussion of the popular referendum, see Zimmerman, 2001, 195–222. A notable difference in relation to procedural matters governing initiatives and popular referenda is that usually petitioners have a very short time – usually 60–90 days – after the enactment of a statute to have its operation suspended pending the holding of a referendum.

legislators might serve.[13] It would be impossible to mention all the topics in relation to which popular initiatives have been used, but as examples of their variety, one can cite issues such as gambling, environmental protection, assisted suicide, gun control and the medicinal use of marijuana, to name but a few.[14]

Finally, it should be noted that in most States the legislature may itself place proposals before the people for approval. This is often done where the legislature is proposing some major piece of public expenditure, in relation to which it wishes to ensure there is broad popular support. Indeed, in some States the law requires that some measures, most frequently public bond issues (in other words, borrowings by the State government) be approved in a referendum.[15]

7.3 AN EVALUATION OF DIRECT DEMOCRACY

The arguments in favour of direct democracy made at the beginning of this chapter can be succinctly restated: direct citizen participation in the legislative process increases citizen interest in, and knowledge of, political matters, and enhances the legitimacy of the law. The prevailing theory under which representative government operates is founded on the Burkean model of the representative as trustee, who is elected to bring his or her own discretion to bear on questions before the legislature, rather than upon the model of the representative as delegate, who is required to defer to the wish of his or her constituents in relation to each question.[16] This, coupled with the strength of party discipline in the legislature, can lead to the will of the people being frustrated where parties are unwilling to introduce measures into the legislature. Direct democracy allows the people to circumvent this obstacle.[17] Giving legislative power to the voters may thus counter the alienation from the political process which many feel.

However, despite the obvious appeal that direct legislation has for democrats, there are a number of powerful arguments that can be made against it. The most predictable of these is that voters lack the knowledge required to make competent choices about complex matters. According to this line of argument, legislation is an expert field of endeavour, best left to representatives who, it is stated, have both the ability and the time needed to evaluate proposed laws. Leaving aside the fact that this argument may presume too much about the intellectual calibre of elected politicians, and the degree of deliberation they engage in in a parliamentary system dominated by a rigid party system,[18] it appears that the underlying assumption that voters are incompetent is false. In their analysis of voter behaviour in the United States, Bowler and Donovan[19] show that, in fact, voters:

13 Bowler and Donovan, 1998, 131.

14 Zimmerman, 2001, 160–87.

15 *Ibid*, 25–28 and 126–30.

16 For a discussion of the delegate and trustee theories, see Cronin, 1989, 26–27

17 In this regard, see Budge, 1996, 105–32.

18 In fact, it is clear that very often, elected representatives are ignorant of the detail of what they are voting on and operate under the instruction of party managers – see Haskell, 2001, 99.

19 Bowler and Donovan, 1998, 42.

> ... vote in predictable ways, in ways that respond to information demands, and in ways that often are consistent with their ideology and (our conceptions of) their interests. At a basic level, then, direct democracy voters appear sufficiently competent to make informed choices.

Furthermore, surveys in the United States indicate that, although voters complain that they find referendum questions confusing, they feel they have insufficient information to make a choice. Even though they are confronted with too many questions, they nevertheless also state that they favour the direct legislation device – in California (a State where initiatives are particularly common) by 70% of respondents to a survey in 1988, 68% in 1990 and 69% in 1996.[20] It is thus clear that, whatever the drawbacks voters perceive in relation to direct democracy, they find the institution enormously appealing. An important factor which acts as a deterrent to voters approving measures which they do not understand is the fact that, faced with a proposition about which they feel insufficiently informed to make a rational choice, voters always have available to them the option of simply abstaining, or of voting 'no'. Indeed, a substantial body of evidence indicates that voters are inherently risk-averse, and that, far from impetuously validating measures put to them, they tend to abstain when faced with highly technical questions which they feel they do not understand,[21] to vote 'no' when a proposition is comprehensible but is perceived to be controversial and to carry the risk of adverse consequences[22] (particularly in times of poor economic performance),[23] and to vote affirmatively only when confident that they have been provided with enough information to enable them to understand what is being put to them, to feel secure that the measure is risk-free and, of course, that it serves their personal or ideological self-interest, which surveys also indicate they are entirely capable of identifying.[24] The inherent bias towards negative voting on initiatives has the result that, far from providing an easy avenue for activists to enact radical measures, initiatives are, in fact, difficult to pass: during the period 1898–1992 only 36% of the 1,091 voter-initiated referenda held in the United States were approved, the approval rates for the two States with the largest number of initiatives (Oregon, with 274 and California, with 236) being 32% and 33% respectively.[25]

Some argue that direct democracy carries with it a substantial risk that tyrannical majorities might use the device to discriminate against vulnerable minorities. As examples of this, one might cite the success in California, in 1994, of Proposition 187 – that illegal migrants be denied access to welfare and education facilities funded by the State government, and the 1992 referendum in Colorado, in which a majority of voters struck down a law prohibiting discrimination on the ground of sexual orientation. While it may, indeed, be true that majorities could use the referendum process to undermine the rights of minorities, this is no more true than is the statement that a majority of legislators might do the same thing. To take examples from just one year, 1996, State legislatures enacted

20 Bowler and Donovan, 1998, 445–46.

21 *Ibid*, 54.

22 *Ibid*, 54.

23 *Ibid*, 68–83.

24 *Ibid*, 99–102.

25 Magleby, 1994, 251.

laws extending the range of anti-sodomy laws, subjecting teachers who taught evolution as fact rather than theory to dismissal, and prohibiting recognition of same-sex marriages. Clearly, it cannot be said that indirect democracy is any less capable of producing oppressive legislation than direct democracy. The remedy in each case is surely the same: to have a justiciable Bill of Rights, to which all law – that enacted as a result of direct democracy, as well as that enacted by conventional legislative procedures – is subject to review by the courts. In fact, there are several examples of laws enacted by referendum being declared unconstitutional by the courts: a California initiative repealing a law prohibiting discrimination in the sale or lease of real property was struck down by the US Supreme Court in *Reitman v Mulkey*,[26] and the 1992 Colorado initiative repealing laws prohibiting discrimination on grounds of sexual orientation was ruled unconstitutional in *Romer v Evans*[27] in 1996. Provided that a Bill of Rights is in place, the initiation of legislation by citizens poses no greater danger to freedoms than does legislation enacted by a Parliament.

A different, but related, objection to direct legislation is that, despite its supposed virtue of reflecting the popular will, the processes of direct legislation can be abused by a well funded minority to enact legislation which the majority of voters do not want, but are apathetic in opposing. In other words, 'referendum fatigue' may enable a proposal supported by 20% of the voters, but rejected by 15%, to become law, even though the remaining 65% of the voters would have opposed the measure, had they bothered to vote. Empirical studies in Switzerland, where voting is not compulsory, and where the turnout in some referenda in the 1980s dropped below 35%, have shown that in some instances there was a marked disparity between the level of support obtained by proposals in referenda, and the level of support they enjoyed among voters as a whole, although only in one case did it appear that a proposal which succeeded at referendum would have been defeated if all voters had participated.[28] The risk of this occurring would be particularly strong if compulsory attendance at the polls was dispensed with and, as noted in Chapter 2, there is a strong argument that it should be, on the ground that it is incompatible with the citizen's right of political non-participation. However, even in the context of compulsory attendance at the polls, there is a possibility that, confronted with a multiplicity of referendum questions, many voters might decline to vote on some of them, and this might lead to a well organised minority succeeding in having the measure enacted. A remedy against this would be to require that for a referendum to succeed, it would have to secure not just a majority of votes cast, but a majority equal to 50% + 1 of voters enrolled to vote. This would ensure that no measure could be enacted without the support of a majority of the electorate.

Another argument frequently advanced against direct democracy is that it would place too much power in the hands of wealthy individuals or pressure groups. The fear is that such groups would win referenda with expensive media campaigns which lie beyond the resources of their opponents. Arguments which seek to restrict political rights on the grounds that voters need protecting from viewpoints simply because those viewpoints are backed by lavish campaign spending, are inherently suspect because they

26 387 US 369 (1967).

27 517 US 620 (1996).

28 Kobach, 1994, 139–40.

cast the state in a paternalistic role and suggest that voters' minds are malleable. As such, they have been implicitly rejected by the United States Supreme Court when it struck down campaign funding limitations in *Buckley v Valeo*[29] and *First National Bank of Boston v Bellotti*,[30] and by Australia's High Court when it invalidated restrictions on access to television airtime in *Australian Capital Television Pty Ltd v Commonwealth (No 2)*.[31] However, even leaving aside theoretical objections, in practice there is little evidence to suggest that lavish funding of referenda campaigns determines the outcome on polling day. There are numerous examples where measures backed by powerful lobby groups have failed to obtain voter approval[32] – indeed, there is substantial evidence that lavish spending in favour of a proposition frequently alienates voters, who deduce that an attempt is being made to buy their support.[33] In short, the empirical evidence indicates that it is virtually impossible to buy victory in a referendum. Spending on campaigns *against* a proposition has more of an effect on the outcome,[34] but even here the resulting increase in the likelihood that the proposal will be defeated (usually because opponents of a measure focus their campaign on arguing 'If in doubt vote "No"') is marginal,[35] and there are many examples of expensive campaigns by corporations and other wealthy interest groups failing to defeat popular measures, notwithstanding the fact that the wealthy interest groups vastly outspent their opponents, in one instance by a ratio of 40:1.[36] The conclusion to be drawn from this is that it is simply not true to say that the referendum process delivers law-making into the hands of those with the resources to run expensive campaigns.

The wave of tax cutting and tax limitation measures enacted in the United States since the famous Proposition 13, enacted in California in 1978, highlights one of the arguments most commonly advanced against giving citizens initiative power – namely, that successful initiatives imposing budgetary constraints may, at worst, be mutually inconsistent (as, for example, would be initiatives requiring a simultaneous reduction in taxes and a balanced budget), or may, at best, place government finances under severe stress.[37] Interestingly, however, Proposition 13 itself, which required an immediate reduction in property taxes, and thereafter capped increases, was certainly not an example of fiscal irresponsibility: property taxes had in some instances trebled in the past five years, the State had accumulated a vast surplus of US$5 billion which it refused to spend, and the tax cut did not lead to a massive reduction in public services.[38] The State government responded to the passage of the initiative by rewriting its budget, which it did within the space of three weeks.[39] Although some States followed suit with similar tax cutting or expenditure-limiting measures, in others, where there were no large

29 424 US 1 (1976).
30 435 US 675 (1977).
31 (1992) 177 CLR 106.
32 Bowler and Donovan, 1998, 148–49.
33 de Q Walker, 1987, 89; and Bowler and Donovan, 1998, 153.
34 Cronin, 1989, 109.
35 Bowler and Donovan, 1998, 148.
36 de Q Walker, 1987, 87–88.
37 For a discussion of Proposition 13, see Allswang, 2000, 105–10.
38 de Q Walker, 1987, 77–79.
39 Schmidt, 1989, 133.

surpluses capable of absorbing a diminution in State income, such measures were defeated.[40] Indeed, in California itself, voters rejected Proposition 9 in 1980, which would have cut taxes further, this time in the absence of a surplus to compensate for the loss of State income.[41] In the words of David Schmidt, the record of tax-cutting initiatives across the United States following Proposition 13 shows a 'cautious, rational, judicious approach to tax reform',[42] which saw voters approve only one-third of tax-cutting measures put to them in the period 1968–86. Despite the potential that exists for initiatives to imperil governmental finances, it is worth remembering the importance that the people's assent to taxation has in the history of Western democracy. It was this issue that lay at the root of the struggle between King and Parliament in 17th century England, and there is a strong argument for saying that, far from being an abuse of direct democracy, initiatives on taxation and expenditure are, indeed, the most appropriate ones to be available to citizens. It may, of course, occur that voters act irresponsibly in this regard, but two points can be made in response to that argument: first, there is nothing to prevent voters electing representatives who promise irresponsible fiscal policies (in other words, the risk of fiscal irresponsibility exists both in the context of direct and representative democracy), and secondly, if it does occur that directly legislated measures lead to adverse consequences, such as an excessive deficit, increased government borrowing or a cut-back in government services, then the citizens themselves have to live with the consequences, or accept whatever measures are necessary to remedy the situation. In other words, although direct democracy places power in the hands of voters, it also imposes an obligation on them to accept the responsibilities that attach to the process, chief among which is that of living with the consequences of their actions.

7.4 PROCEDURAL ISSUES

Assuming that provision was made in the Constitution for citizen-initiated legislation, a number of procedural issues would need to be considered.

Perhaps the most important of these procedural matters is the relationship between direct democracy and the parliamentary process. Should Parliament be able to overturn a law enacted directly by the people? If a measure voted into law by the people was able to be repealed by ordinary legislative enactment, there would seem to be little purpose to permitting direct legislation. Given that direct legislation is often resorted to by citizens precisely because the legislature refuses to enact the measure in question, it would be senseless to give the people the right to legislate directly if the legislature could simply overturn what the people have enacted. On the other hand, entirely removing from the legislature the capacity to amend or repeal laws enacted by the people, and permitting such amendment or repeal to take place only through another referendum, might place the legislature in the position where, faced with some emergency requiring the immediate repeal of the enactment, it was legally unable to respond, and a referendum would take too long to organise. Various solutions have been adopted in different jurisdictions. In

40 Schmidt, 1989, 133.

41 *Ibid*, 134.

42 *Ibid*, 144.

some States of the USA, the legislature is prohibited from overturning direct legislation for a fixed number of years. However, this would still leave the legislature unable to respond to an emergency during the prescribed period. A far preferable mechanism, adopted in yet other States, requires a two-thirds majority of both chambers of the legislature to amend or repeal a law enacted by referendum. The requirement of a two-thirds majority ensures that popular initiatives can be overridden only under conditions of bipartisan agreement – in other words, operates on the assumption that if circumstances are truly urgent, bipartisan support for override will be able to be obtained.

Another crucial issue is the level of voter support for a proposition that should have to be demonstrated before the measure can be put on the ballot. The most common threshold requirement imposed on citizens who wish to have a proposition put to the people is that they obtain the signatures of a certain number of voters in support of having a referendum. That number can be expressed as a percentage, as an absolute number of registered voters or, as is common in the United States, as a percentage of the number of votes actually cast in a preceding election, varying from a low of 2% in North Dakota to a high of 15% in Wyoming, with a median of 8% for non-constitutional initiatives.[43] Bearing in mind that a voter turnout of around 40% of the voting age population would not be uncommon in a State election,[44] a threshold set at 8% of votes actually cast is the equivalent of just over 3% of those entitled to be registered. A balance needs to be struck between setting a low threshold, which might result in a multiplicity of frivolous questions being put to the voters, and setting a high threshold, which would make it difficult for all but the wealthiest, and best organised, groups to avail of direct legislation. Bearing this in mind, a threshold of 3% of registered voters seems reasonable. The law would need to specify the time limit within which those proposing an initiative must obtain the required number of signatures on their petition. In the United States, this varies from the brief 90 days required in Oklahoma to the generous four years allowed in Florida.[45] The law would also need to specify the manner in which signatures on petitions are verified – in most States in the USA, this is done by a process of sampling.

Should those wishing to have a proposal put to referendum be required to present voters with a full draft of the proposed legislation when soliciting signatures for the petition, or should it be sufficient for them to state what the objectives of the referendum will be at the petition stage, and to present the full text bill only once the threshold has been cleared? In most jurisdictions, proponents must present the voters with the text of the proposed bill even at the petition stage, and if errors are discovered after the collection of signatures has started, the process has to begin again from scratch.[46] This, then, leads to the question of who should draft the bill to be put to referendum – obviously, the more professional the drafting, the less likely it is that errors will occur. Groups who are proposing a referendum, and who can afford it, might, therefore, retain legal advisers to do the drafting. However, in many cases, those who have initiated the referendum may not have the money to engage lawyers. I would, therefore, argue that proponents should

43 Magleby, 1994, 225–26.

44 Note that registration as a voter is not compulsory, and so, in the 1998 State elections in California, eg, 72% of the voting age population actually registered to vote, and 58% of these voted, which means that 41% of the voting age population (who would be entitled to sign an initiative petition) cast a vote.

45 Zimmerman, 2001, 35–37.

46 de Q Walker, 1987, 138.

be able to avail of the services of parliamentary counsel to draft proposed bills. This might, however, lead to the parliamentary drafting office being inundated with requests to draft proposed bills which might not even meet the threshold required before they can be put to referendum. A solution to this problem might be to have two thresholds: the law could state that if the proponents of a measure gather a certain number of signatures in support of a proposal which simply states the objectives of the proposed law – perhaps 1% of registered voters – the proponents will then be entitled to receive the assistance of parliamentary counsel in drafting the full text, summary and title of the bill. This process would avoid the litigation which has often ensued in the United States, where proponents dispute the content of the summary and title of the bill drafted by electoral officials for the ballot paper. After the drafting process has been completed, the proponents will be required to seek the additional number of signatures to meet the 3% threshold required to have the bill put to referendum.

There is no reason why citizen-initiated legislation should be available both as a means for enacting ordinary legislation, and also as an avenue for constitutional amendment. Australians are already familiar with constitutional referenda, required by s 128 of the Constitution. It would, therefore, not be too radical a step to permit constitutional referenda to occur upon the initiative of citizens, rather than only on the initiative of Parliament, as at present. However, assuming that popular initiatives could be used both for ordinary legislation and for constitutional amendments, it would obviously be necessary that the latter type of initiative would have to satisfy whatever special procedures were prescribed in the Constitution for its amendment – in other words, given that an initiative put into the Constitution will be to be reversed only by means of a constitutional amendment, effecting a constitutional amendment through popular initiative should be no less easy than amendments effected by any other means.

Should proponents of a measure be able to put it directly on the ballot (once they have obtained the required number of signatures on a petition), or would it be preferable to adopt the indirect initiative, in which the legislature is given the chance to enact the proposal before it can be put to the people? A disadvantage of limiting the initiative to the indirect variant is that, having mustered the support to satisfy the threshold requirement, the supporters of a proposal then have to wait while the legislature considers whether to enact the proposal.[47] If the legislature decides not to enact legislation, the proponents will then have to restart their campaign for the referendum itself. There seems no good reason why the legislature, which could enact legislation whenever it chose, should be able to delay a popular initiative.

In many States of the United States, there are provisions which seek to prevent procedural abuses of the initiative process. Thus in California, the initiative cannot be used to vote an individual into public office, and the law requires that initiatives must deal with one subject only. The latter requirement is designed to avoid the drafting of omnibus measures dealing with a wide range of completely unrelated subjects, often used by proponents of a particular measure as a tactic to win the support of a large coalition of groups.[48] This requirement is enforced by vesting a power in an official to

47 *Ibid*, 137.

48 Magleby, 1994, 227–28.

determine whether the proposal addresses only one subject, and litigation sometimes ensues where a determination of that nature is challenged. Whether such a restriction is necessary is open to debate. After all, legislatures often enact omnibus bills dealing with a variety of topics, and so there would seem to be no necessary reason for restricting direct legislation in this way. In addition, the inherent difficulty of determining how closely related the provisions of a measure must be for it to be said that they form one 'subject', provides a recipe for unnecessary dispute and litigation, if the experience of jurisdictions which impose such requirements is anything to go by.[49]

Finally, provision would have to be made for the circumstance where mutually inconsistent proposals are put before voters on a single occasion. This often occurs where groups who oppose an initiative put forward their own proposal on the same topic. This problem could be addressed either by providing that, in such circumstances, the legislature shall have the power to combine the initiatives into one, with voters being able to vote preferentially between opposing propositions or, as is the case in California,[50] by stipulating that where proposals conflict, the one which received the greatest number of affirmative votes is adopted.

7.5 CONCLUSION

In this chapter, I have sought to argue that direct democracy provides a route for the enactment of legislation which accords practical, rather than merely theoretical, acknowledgement of the role of the people in the Constitution. Although legislation by initiative would mark a radical departure from current constitutional arrangements, the preceding material has indicated that the disadvantages of direct democracy are less substantial than critics of the institution would have one believe. I would, therefore, propose that a new Australian Constitution provide for direct legislation, subject to the procedural safeguards mentioned in this chapter.

49 Zimmerman, 2001, 90–94.

50 Constitution of California 1849, Art 2, s 10(b).

FAIR REPRESENTATION

8.1 FAIR REPRESENTATION

I stated early in this book that one of the fundamental principles upon which a Constitution ought to be based is fairness. This is of particular importance in so far as the electoral system is concerned, because the casting of votes constitutes the basic, and, for most people, the only, way in which the individual citizen participates in the law-making process. I have already discussed (at 2.5.5.1, above) the necessity for a Bill of Rights to include express acknowledgement of the right to vote. What this chapter addresses is the necessity, implied by the principle of equality, that every vote be an equal vote.

8.2 REPRESENTATION AND THE COMMONWEALTH PARLIAMENT

To what extent is the principle of fair representation upheld by the Constitution? The first, and most obvious, point to be made is that the requirement in s 7 – that each original State shall have equal representation in the Senate – embeds *inequality* of representation in our system of government. For example, given that New South Wales has 4,148,000 voters, and Tasmania has 325,000 voters, yet each State elects 12 senators, it is true to say that the Tasmanian voter has nearly 13 times the influence over the composition of the Senate as does a voter in New South Wales. I address the question of the Senate in Chapter 9, in the context of reform of the structure and powers of Parliament. This chapter focuses on representation in the House of Representatives.

Representation in the House of Representatives is not tainted by inequality in the same way as that in the Senate; indeed, s 24 of the Constitution requires that members shall be 'directly chosen by the people' and that 'the number of members chosen in the several States shall be in proportion to the respective numbers of their people'. There are, however, factors which cause every vote not to have the same value.

The first is that s 24 of the Constitution also mandates that each original State shall choose at least five members of the House, and so, even if a State's entitlement on the basis of population were to fall below that number, it would continue to have that minimum level of representation, causing voters in the other States to be under-represented.

The second factor is that, so far as the method of electing members within the various States is concerned, the phrase 'directly chosen by the people' has not been taken to require a system of proportional representation. The preferential voting electoral system contained in the Commonwealth Electoral Act 1918 (Cth) never produces a House that reflects the distribution of first preference votes between parties (an inevitable consequence of having a system based on single member electorates), and not infrequently produces an outcome in which the party which wins the most first preference votes fails to obtain a majority in the House, as the table in 8.3.2 of this chapter, below, shows

Furthermore, it is unlikely that a legal challenge would be successful in invalidating the current electoral system. In the case of *Attorney-General (Cth); ex rel McKinlay v Commonwealth*,[1] which did not involve a challenge to the fundamentals of the geographic basis of the electoral system, but only to the 10% deviation in population which the Commonwealth Electoral Act 1918 (Cth) permits electorates to have from the average, the High Court held that the deviation was not inconsistent with the requirement that members be 'directly chosen by the people'. The majority was of the opinion that a wide variety of electoral systems were in use in different jurisdictions which were accepted as having a democratic form of government, and that it could, therefore, not be said that being 'directly chosen by the people' forbade a deviation in electorate populations of that order of magnitude. It follows from the result in this case that a challenge to the more fundamental principles underlying the system would be even more unlikely to be successful.[2]

The most recent attempt to change the Constitution to provide for equality of representation (in the sense of an equal number of voters per electorate) occurred in 1988, when a proposed Constitutional amendment, which would have put into the Constitution an upper limit of 10% on deviations from the mean number of voters in each electorate, was rejected 66% to 32% nationally, and failed to obtain a majority in any State. Nevertheless, the failure of this proposal (and of the others presented for approval at the same time) has been ascribed to political factors relating to the timing of the referendum, and the government's failure to explain and campaign in favour of the proposals, rather than to any virulent opposition to them on the part of the electorate.[3]

8.3 ELECTORAL REFORM – PROPORTIONAL REPRESENTATION

Assuming the principle of equality of representation – that each vote should have equal value, and should have equal influence on the outcome of elections – is accepted as a democratic ideal, it is clear that the electoral system for both the House and the Senate are in need of reform. The remainder of this chapter focuses upon various electoral systems, and how their application to elections for the House would affect representative government in Australia. Given that fundamental changes are recommended in Chapter 9 in respect of the powers of the Senate, which changes make it unnecessary to change the electoral system used to choose its members, this chapter focuses on the House of Representatives.

The essential question involved in discussions of electoral reform is which, among the many possible electoral systems, best serves representative government? A key

1 (1975) 135 CLR 1.

2 In a similar case to *McKinlay*, the High Court held in *McGinty v Western Australia* (1996) 136 CLR 140 that the principle of representative democracy, which was implied in the Western Australian constitution (as in that of the Commonwealth), did not require absolute equality in voting strength as between electorates for the Western Australian Parliament.

3 Blackshield and Williams, 2002, 1309.

consideration in answering this is the recognition of the duality of purpose which elections serve in a system of responsible government such as ours. The first purpose voters have in electing a member of the legislature is to send a delegate to speak in Parliament on their behalf, and to make representations to government departments. This purpose was served by the English Parliament from its inception in the 13th century. The second, and more recent, function served by elections is to take a national poll to determine which party, or coalition of parties, has a mandate from the country as a whole to form a government. This purpose became important from the 18th century, which saw the acceptance by the monarchy of the principle of responsible government – that the Prime Minister and cabinet had to maintain the support of Parliament to stay in office.

There are a large number of electoral systems that have been devised with the objective of ensuring that the composition of a legislature accurately reflects the will of the voters.[4] What follows is an overview of the various systems, designed to assist answering the question of which system would preserve the benefits of the current system (representation of the inhabitants of an electorate by a specific member of Parliament), while eliminating its major defects, namely, failure to reflect in Parliament parties' relative nationwide share of their first preference votes, and the frequent award of government to a party or coalition with less than majority national support among voters.

8.3.1 The first past the post, single member electorate system

The problem with electoral systems based on geographically defined electorates returning a single member is that, whereas they serve the purpose of personal representation well, they frequently serve the purpose of governmental selection very badly. This is most dramatically shown by the example of the United Kingdom, which combines single member electorates with a 'first past the post' voting system, in terms of which all one needs to win the electorate is a plurality – in other words, just more votes than any other candidate, but not necessarily an absolute majority of votes cast in an electorate.[5] The effect of this is shown by the following table of results from general elections held in the United Kingdom since 1974, which illustrates how the geographic basis of the system disadvantages parties whose support is spread across the country.[6]

4 There is a good summary of electoral systems on the Australian Electoral Commission website at http://aec.gov.au/pubs/electoral_systems.htm.

5 Thus, eg, in an electorate with four candidates A-D standing for election, A will win with 29% of the vote if B gets 27%, C 26% and D 8% even though 71% of the voters in the electorate voted against A.

6 United Kingdom Government, 1998, para 78.

	CONSERVATIVES		LABOUR		LIBERAL/LIB-DEM	
Year	% vote	% seats	% vote	% seats	% vote	% seats
1974	37.9	46.8	37.1	47.4	19.3	2.2
1974	35.8	43.6	39.2	50.2	18.3	2.1
1979	43.9	53.4	36.9	42.4	13.8	1.7
1983	42.4	61.0	27.6	32.0	25.4	3.5
1987	42.3	57.8	30.9	35.2	22.6	3.4
1992	41.9	51.6	34.3	41.6	17.9	3.1
1997	30.7	25.0	43.2	63.6	16.8	7.0

In the first election of 1974, the party which gained most seats received less votes than its major opponent, while in every election, the system favoured both the Conservatives and Labour, with awards of seats in excess of their share of the national vote, while prejudicing the Liberals/Liberal-Democrats, who received paltry representation after reasonably substantial success nationwide. Note, also, that the election of 1983 saw a decrease in the Conservatives' share of the vote coupled with an increase in the number of seats that party won!

Clearly, while the 'first past the post' system serves the purpose of giving each geographic electorate an identifiable representative, it fails dismally in reflecting the will of the country as a whole.

8.3.2 The alternative vote system

Like the United Kingdom, Australia has a single member electorate system for elections for the House of Representatives. However, the system in Australia differs from that in the United Kingdom in that to be elected, a candidate needs to obtain an absolute majority (in other words, 50% + 1) of votes cast in an electorate. Voting is by alternative vote (AV), which means that the voter is required to indicate preferences among the candidates. Should no candidate achieve an absolute majority after the first round of counting, the ballot papers of the least popular candidate are distributed according to the second preferences indicated by voters. Redistribution of lowest candidate's preferences continues until a candidate has achieved an absolute majority. The 'alternative vote' system has several advantages over the plurality 'first past the post' system. By requiring successful candidates to obtain at least 50% + 1 of the votes cast (after distribution of preferences), it does, at least, avoid the possibility, inherent in the plurality system, that a candidate who is overwhelmingly unpopular in the electorate might be elected – under AV such a candidate would be unlikely to obtain election because, to be successful, a candidate must obtain some cross-party support. The AV system also avoids the absolute irrelevance of votes cast for defeated candidates under the plurality system, which, effectively, disenfranchises the voter who votes for loosing candidates. Under AV, a voter's ballot continues to have effect through transfers, even if the first-choice candidate fails to get elected. Finally, AV gives smaller parties some influence within individual electorates, by means of leverage over the policies of the larger parties seeking transfer of their preferences. This, in turn, encourages cross-party co-operation.

However, as is shown in the following table, because the system is still based on single member electorates, it not infrequently produces a nationwide result where the party which wins the most number of seats (and thus government) obtains fewer first preference votes nationally than does the party with the second highest number of seats (which finds itself in opposition). The table also shows that minor parties receive far fewer seats than their first preference votes would entitle them to.

	LABOR		**LIBERAL**		**NATIONAL**		**DEMOCRATS**		**OTHERS***	
Year	% vote	% seats	% vote	% seats	% vote	% seats	% vote	% seats	% vote	% seats
1977	39.6	30.6	38.1	54	10	15.3	9.4	0		
1980	45.1	40.8	37.4	43.2	8.9	16	6.6	0		
1983	49.5	60	34.4	26.4	9.2	13.6	5	0		
1984	47.5	55.4	34.4	30.4	10.6	14.1	5.4	0		
1987	45.8	58	34.6	29	11.5	12.8	6	0		
1990	39.4	52.7	35	37.2	8.4	9.5	11.4	0	1.4	0
1993	44.9	54.4	37.1	33.3	7.2	10.9	3.8	0	1.9	0
1996	38.8	33.1	38.7	50.7	8.2	12.1	6.8	0	1.7	0
1998	40.1	45.2	33.9	43.2	5.2	10.8	5.1	0	10.5	0
2001	37.8	43.9	37	46.6	5.6	8.7	5.4	0	9.3	0

* 'Others' refers to Greens from 1990–96 inclusive, and to the combined vote of Greens and Pauline Hanson's One Nation in 1998 and 2001. Votes and seats won by non-party affiliated independents are not reflected in this table.

Some of these results are striking in their disproportionality: in 1977 and 1996, the Liberals on their own were able to win a majority of the seats in the House with only 38% of the first preference vote, while in every election from 1983 to 1993 inclusive, the Australian Labor Party won a majority of seats while winning only a minority of votes. Minor parties have never achieved representation since 1977, despite the fact that the Australian Democrats obtained 9.4% and 11.4% of the vote in 1977 and 1990 respectively, while One Nation obtained 8.4% in 1998.

8.3.3 List systems

The purest form of proportional representation would be one where there are no geographic electorates, and where each party is allocated the same percentage of seats in the legislature as it receives in a nationwide vote. This system is used in Israel.[7] Under

7 See Basic Law 1958, Art 4. For a description of the system, see Shugart and Wattenberg, 2001, 124–25.

this system, voters vote for parties rather than for candidates, and parties fill their entitlement to seats from ordered lists of candidates, published prior to the election. The outcome is absolute fairness of representation as between parties, but at the cost of depriving voters of an identifiable representative. There are many possible ways in which list systems can vary from the pure (some might say crude) proportional representation used in Israel.

One of the most important factors in determining how proportional the outcome of list system elections is, is the way in which the number of votes required to be won for each list seat is calculated, usually referred to as the quota. Of the various ways in which quotas can be calculated (the mathematical complexities of which are beyond the scope of this book),[8] it is generally agreed that the largest remainder system using a Hare quota produces the most proportional outcome,[9] followed by the largest remainder system using a Droop quota, and then highest average systems in the following order: the Sainte-Lague, the modified Sainte-Lague and then the d'Hondt.[10]

Another way in which list systems can be varied is by requiring parties to reach a threshold (for example, 5% of the votes cast nationally) before it is entitled to representation. The higher the threshold, the less proportional the outcome, but the less likely it is that 'micro-parties' will obtain representation.

Party list systems can also be modified in such a way as to have the lists operate at a regional, rather than a national, level. Voters still vote for a party rather than for individual candidates, but for a list of candidates vying for seats assigned to a particular region. This reduces the proportionality of the outcome somewhat, but does, at least, mean that members on each party's list are identified with a specific region.

Finally, some list systems differ in relation to the extent to which they permit voters to determine to which of the candidates on a party's list that party's list seats should be awarded. As was stated above, the lists are closed in Israel – in other words, the party alone determines the order in which its candidates will be put, and thus which candidates will fill the party's list seats. However, some list systems, such as that in Austria, Norway, Sweden and Belgium,[11] have flexible party lists, which permit the voter to vote for a specific candidate appearing on the party's list or, alternatively, to indicate preferences among the candidates from a particular party. Seats are still allocated in proportion to the total number of votes the party obtained for all its members, but the voters have the ability to affect the order in which they are elected. It would, of course, still be necessary for each party to register an ordered list, which could be used to determine who was elected in the circumstance where voters gave to some specific candidates a number of votes which exceeded the quota needed for election, and the party was entitled to more seats than could be filled by only those candidates.

The defect of pure list systems (even those permitting voters to influence the order in which candidates are elected), is that they make no provision for the voter to have an identifiable representative drawn from their specific locality. How, then, can one combine

8 For an excellent discussion of ways in which remainders can be dealt with when allocating seats to parties in proportion to their share of the national vote, see Farrell, 1997.

9 Farrell, 1997, 62–64 and 67. See also Lijphart, 1994, 23–24 and 153–59.

10 See Farrell, 1997, 65; and Newland, 1982, 49.

11 For a discussion of flexible list systems, see Marsh, 1985, 367.

the advantage of proportionality conferred by list systems, with that of an identifiable representative conferred by single member electorate systems? Two types of system, the mixed member proportional (MMP) system, and the multi-member electorate single transferable vote (STV) system, attempt to accommodate both objectives, but in different ways.[12]

8.3.4 The mixed member proportional system

The mixed member proportional (MMP) system – sometimes referred to as the Additional Member system – involves the election of half the total number of members of the legislature in single member electorates, and the other half from ordered party lists, from which each party is entitled to draw an additional number of members, so that its overall representation in the legislature is proportional to its national party vote.[13] Thus, half the legislature is selected according to the 'first past the post system' as used in the United Kingdom, while the other half is selected according to the list system. Germany has used the MMP system since 1949, but of late it has been adopted by countries with well established democratic traditions, such as New Zealand, Venezuela, Scotland and Wales, as well as by a large number of countries in Latin America and Eastern Europe, where democracy has recently been (re)established.[14]

The most commonly cited example of the MMP system is that which operates in the Federal Republic of Germany.[15] Under the German system, of the 656 seats in the Bundestag (the lower house of the legislature), 328 are elected in single member electorates and 328 are selected from regional party lists. Each voter fills out two ballot papers – one for their electorate and the other for a political party. After all votes are counted, the law requires that the final composition of the Bundestag reflects each party's nationwide share of the list votes and so, depending on how many electorate seats each party has won, the total number of members each party is entitled to is calculated by reference to the percentage of the list vote they obtained, using the highly proportional largest remainder system with a Hare quota,[16] and however many seats a party has won in the electorates is 'topped up' from its lists. In the rare event (which has happened only twice in Germany since 1949), that a party gains more seats in electorates than its percentage of the nationwide vote entitles it to, it retains those seats and the number of members of that Parliament is increased.[17] Each party is required to publish an ordered list of candidates for each region prior to the election, and the specific identity of its candidates who fill its list seat allocation in the legislature is decided in accordance with how its list votes were distributed between the regions. The only qualification to this is that, in order to be eligible for an allocation of seats, a party must win at least three electorate seats or 5% of the national vote. This threshold requirement is not a necessary feature of MMP systems, and, indeed, makes the system less proportional than it might

12 For an overview of proportional representation systems, see Newland, 1982.

13 For a concise explanation of the MMP system, see Shugart and Wattenberg, 2001, 9–24.

14 *Ibid*, 2.

15 The German system is discussed in detail in Farrell, 1997, 86–109.

16 *Ibid*, 89.

17 *Ibid*, 93.

otherwise be. In the case of Germany, it was the product of the history of that particular country, specifically of a perceived need to avoid the high level of political fragmentation that had occurred during the Weimar Republic, whose electoral law was one of pure proportional representation, which had resulted in a large number of minor parties being represented in the Reichstag, and which had, in turn, contributed to the inability of governments to maintain stable majorities.[18] Independents are considered as being one-person parties for purposes of the electoral system. If a vacancy occurs in the Bundestag through the resignation or death of a list seat member, the vacancy is filled by the next available person on the party's list. The following worked hypothetical example shows how the system operates:

Assume that one has a 100 seat legislature, with 50 seats filled from electorates and 50 from party lists. The following table demonstrates how, after the results of the electorate seats are counted, parties are allocated list seats, so that the total number of seats they have in Parliament (electorate seats + list seats) gives them the same proportion of seats in Parliament as their nationwide percentage of the list vote entitles them to:

	Electorate seats	**Percentage of national party vote**	**List seat entitlement**	**Final number of seats in Parliament**
Party A	30	40	10	40
Party B	17	30	13	30
Party C	3	25	22	25
Party D	0	5	5	5
TOTALS	50	100	50	100

The MMP system was adopted in New Zealand in 1993.[19] The New Zealand system falls slightly short of absolute proportionality, because of the existence of Maori seats elected on a separate voters' roll, and because (as in Germany), parties are entitled to list seat representation only if they reach a 5% threshold on the party list ballot, or if they succeed in winning at least one electorate. Two elections (in 1996 and 2000) have been held under MMP. In the 1996 election parliamentary representation was achieved by the long-established moderate right-wing National party and the moderate left-wing Labour party, as well as by four minor parties (the centrist New Zealand First and United New Zealand parties, the left wing Alliance party and the libertarian ACT party). The results were as follows:

National	44
Labour	37
NZ First	17
Alliance	13
ACT	8
United NZ	1

18 For an analysis of the German system, see Scarrow, 2001, 55–69; and Kasase, 1984, 155–56.

19 Electoral Act 1993. For a detailed discussion of the system in New Zealand, see Palmer and Palmer, 1997, 21–37.

The New Zealand First party emerged as king-maker, choosing to forming a coalition with the National party, giving the government a majority of 61 in the 120 seat house. In practice, the government was also able to count on the support of MPs representing ACT and United New Zealand.[20] In the 2000 election the results were as follows:

National	39
Labour	49
NZ First	5
Alliance	10
ACT	9
Greens	7
United NZ	1

Labour formed a minority 59 member coalition with the Alliance party. The government was supported on matters of confidence by the Greens (who could ensure the survival of the government either by voting with it or merely abstaining). The government survived through the life of the Parliament.

A provision in the legislation establishing MMP required that a parliamentary review of the system be held in 2000.[21] The MMP Review Committee (a select committee of the New Zealand Parliament) published its report in 2001.[22] The Committee's report was disappointing in that its members failed to reach consensus on the key issues of whether the MMP system should be retained, whether the 5% threshold should be retained, or even on whether there should be another referendum on the electoral system. To some extent, members of the Committee adopted positions that were dictated by their partisan interests. Thus members from the larger Labour, National and Alliance parties supported the retention of the 5% threshold, whereas representatives from the smaller parties argued for its reduction. More significant, perhaps, were the results of public opinion surveys commissioned by the Committee, which indicated that voters have little interest in the electoral system, that few understand the mechanics of MMP, that support for MMP stood at 40% while the old 'first past the post' system obtained a 47% approval rating, that there was strong support for MMP among ethnic minorities (whose experience was that MMP has increased the number of minority members in Parliament) and, perhaps most tellingly, that respondents' attitudes to the electoral system were heavily dependant on their current views about politics and politicians generally. Despite the lukewarm support for MMP evidenced by the survey, it is questionable whether, if put to the test, the system would be rejected by voters in a referendum. The system has caused no instability in government in New Zealand, but has delivered substantially enhanced representation for women (up from 21% of Parliament under the last first past the post election in 1993 to 31% in 1999), and for Maori, Pacific Islanders and Asians (whose representation climbed from 8% to 17% during the same period). Given the importance New Zealand society has placed on gender equality and indigenous rights, it is difficult

20 For an account of the 1996 election and the history of the government it produced, see Vowles, 1998; and Barker, 2001, 297–322.

21 Electoral Act 1993, s 264.

22 New Zealand Parliament, 2001.

to imagine that country reverting to an electoral system which disadvantaged women and ethnic minorities, the slight preference expressed for the old system in the opinion poll notwithstanding.

There are variants of the MMP system, differing essentially on the question of the respective percentages of the seats in a legislature which should be elected in geographic electorates and on party lists, and on the question of what percentage threshold should apply before a party is entitled to list representation. Obviously, the more the electorate: list seat ratio is set in favour of list seats, the greater the extent to which the legislature will reflect nationwide voter sentiment. Similarly, the lower the threshold is set for parties to receive list seats, the more representative the outcome will be. The 50:50 electorate/list seat split used in Germany and New Zealand has produced legislatures which very closely reflect the relative national strengths of the parties (as reflected by the percentage of party list votes they obtained), even with a 5% threshold imposed in respect of party list representation.

Some argue that a drawback of the MMP system is that it divides members of Parliament into two classes and, more significantly, deprives voters of a choice in respect of who the list representatives will be (because that is determined by how the parties order their lists). This problem can, to some extent, be addressed formally by dividing the country into regions, each of which has a number of electorate seats and a number of list seats proportional to its population, the result being that there is, in effect, a separate election for each region, thus identifying the list MPs elected from that region with its inhabitants. This, indeed, is what is done in Germany, where the system still produces a highly proportional result, despite the fact that some degree of proportionality is lost due to the addition of a geographic element into the election of the list seats. Furthermore, as stated above, MMP systems can operate with flexible lists, where voters are given the choice of determining the order in which a party's candidates will be elected, but with the party's registered list operating as a default ordering mechanism.

The MMP system found favour in the 1998 report of the United Kingdom's Independent Commission on the Voting System (the Jenkins Report), which was charged by the government with the task of assessing whether the United Kingdom's first past the post electoral system should be reformed and, if so, which system should replace it. The report recommended the adoption of MMP, but with some variations from how it operates in Germany: The major compromise that the Commission recommended was to reduce the ratio of constituency MPs to list MPs from 50:50, as in Germany, to 80:20, in deference to the tradition of MPs being responsible to an electorate.[23] This would not only reduce the number of MPs without a constituency link, but would also make coalitions somewhat less likely.[24] However, it was acknowledged that such reduction in the number of list MPs would result in a loss of proportionality.

The Commission also proposed that the regions from which the additional or list members would be selected should be relatively small, returning at most two list MPs, so as to increase the likelihood of list MPs performing a constituency service role, albeit at the level of a region rather than that of an individual electorate.[25] The Commission also

23 United Kingdom Government, 1998, 118 and 151–59.

24 *Ibid*, 122.

25 *Ibid*, 133–35.

recommended that the party lists should be open – in other words, that voters should have the choice either of voting in accordance with a party's ordered list or of voting for a specific candidate on the list.[26] Finally, the Commission found that having list MPs chosen from small regions would render redundant the requirement under the German system that parties would have to reach a 5% threshold before being entitled to list representation.[27]

Although the likelihood of electoral reform occurring in the United Kingdom remains slight, given the huge vested interests that the two major parties have in maintaining the current system, the report of the Commission is, nevertheless, useful in so far as it provides us with a reasoned choice between electoral systems produced by a country with a long history of democratic government. Although, as will become apparent below, I would suggest that more radical electoral reform is needed for our House of Representatives, the recommendations contained in the Jenkins Report have found some support in Australia.[28]

8.3.5 The single transferable vote system

The other major family of list system is that which is based upon the single transferable vote in multi-member electorates. Common to such systems is the division of the polity into geographic electorates which return several members to the legislature. A quota is set for election, being the total number of votes cast in the electorate divided by the number of members to be elected plus one. Under such systems, the voter has a *transferable* vote. Such systems are often referred to as single transferable vote (or STV) systems, because the voter can, by indicating ordered preferences, cause their vote to be transferred down the list of candidates.[29] The advantage of such systems is that voters are able not only to vote for the party that most represents their point of view, but also to determine which of that party's candidates in the electorate should occupy the seats it is entitled to, rather than having that choice determined in accordance with a list dictated by the party. Furthermore, because they can rank individual candidates, voters can also vote in such a way that their vote contributes to the election of members of more than one party. Voters may indicate an ordered preference among all candidates standing in the multi-member electorate. If a candidate reaches the quota, then his or her surplus votes are distributed among the other candidates in accordance with the second preferences expressed by that candidate's voters.[30] If no candidate reaches a quota on the first round, or after the transfer of votes from a candidate who has reached the quota, then the candidate with the least votes is eliminated, and their votes distributed according to the preferences indicated by the voters. The process of transferring the votes of each candidate who

26 *Ibid*, 139–41.

27 *Ibid*, 144.

28 Bartlett, 1999, 116–17.

29 For an explanation of the system in the context of Ireland, see McKee, 1983, 168–77.

30 Note that this is not done randomly. To take an example, if a candidate needed only 1,000 first preference votes to be elected, but received 1,500 – in other words, an excess of one-third – then instead of 500 votes being randomly selected for redistribution according to second preferences, all that candidate's ballot papers are re-examined and votes distributed to the second preferences at a value of 0.33 per vote.

obtains a quota (or eliminating the candidate with the lowest number of votes if a round of counting fails to put a candidate over the quota), continues until all seats are filled.

In Australia, the STV is used in elections for the Senate, as well as for elections for the lower house of the Tasmanian Parliament and for the ACT Legislative Assembly. The system used for Senate elections differs from that used in Tasmania and the ACT. Voters in Senate elections have the choice of voting in accordance with a particular party's preference as to the order in which votes should be distributed down the entire list of candidates standing in the electorate. This is commonly referred to as voting 'above the line', a reference to the fact that the ballot paper contains two sections – one above a line, which the voter can use to choose a political party's box (and, by implication, that party's decision as to how preferences should be distributed), and the other below the line, consisting of a box for each of the candidates in the electorate, which the voter can order in accordance with his or her personal preferences. The opportunity to vote above the line carries the advantages of relieving voters of the burden of filling in individual preferences, and of permitting them to give force to their preferred party's political strategy without the necessity of following a 'how to vote card'. However, the legislation goes further than provide an opportunity for above the line voting, and, in fact, biases the process towards that practice, because a voter choosing to vote below the line has to indicate preferences for at least 90% of the candidates for the vote to be ruled formal (in other words, for it not to be treated as spoiled). This clearly prejudices the voter who wishes to exercise their own choice as among candidates, but only in respect of those candidates about whom he or she has a positive opinion. Being forced to express a preference down the list, and beyond the extent to which the voter desires, seems not to be defensible in principle, and has the effect of causing the overwhelming majority of voters (94.9% of voters in the 1998 federal election) to vote above the line.

The particular variant of the STV system used in the ACT and Tasmania, usually referred to as the Hare-Clark system after its progenitors,[31] is essentially the same as that used for the Senate, but with the differences that there is no provision at all for 'above the line' voting – the names of the candidates nominated by each party are listed randomly on ballot papers rather than being determined by the party,[32] and vacancies are filled by re-counting the ballot papers (rather than by nomination, as under the Senate electoral system). Of these aspects, the absence of above the line voting is particularly odious. As was stated by the Jenkins Report in the United Kingdom:

> Some people want to be able to choose between candidates of the same party, but many are interested only in voting for parties, and would not appreciate being forced into choosing between candidates of the same party about each of whom they know little.

Compulsory preferential thus tends to encourage voters to behave randomly. Indeed, given that multi-member electorates are a *sine qua non* of the STV system, and that it is only the most diligent of voters who has either the time or the inclination to discern the differences between candidates of the same party, randomisation is virtually guaranteed.

31 The system combines the ideas of the English lawyer, Thomas Hare, and the Tasmanian Attorney-General, Arthur Inglis Clark.

32 This system of random placement of candidates' names (with the result that ballot papers differ from each other) is called Robson Rotation.

Single transferable vote systems have the advantage that every member of the legislature is identified with a specific geographic electorate. They also offer a more proportional outcome than does the single member electorate system, because each multi-member electorate operates as a proportional system in miniature. However, their disadvantage is that, because they are based on geographically delineated electorates, they do not lead to as proportional an outcome between parties as does the MMP system, as is shown in detail in the next section of this chapter.[33] Obviously, the greater the number of seats allocated to each multi-member electorate, the greater the proportionality of the outcome nationwide, and the better the chance smaller parties have of electoral success. On the other hand, the larger each electorate is, the more tenuous becomes the link between elected representatives and a specific population of voters – which proponents of the system advertise as its chief virtue. In Ireland, the number of representatives from each electorate is either three, four or five. In the ACT, there are electorates with five and seven members, while in Tasmania, electorates for the lower house each have five members (down from seven after the reduction in the size of the House from 35 to 25 as of the 1998 elections). In the case of the Commonwealth Senate, each State, as an electorate, sends six representatives to Parliament (12 on the rare occasion that there is a full Senate election after a double dissolution).

An analysis of STV elections indicates that it does not perform well against the criterion of representivity: Indeed, the case of Ireland shows that, under STV, it is still possible for a result to be sufficiently disproportionate as to allow a government to win a majority of seats in the legislature while winning a minority of votes, as occurred in the elections of 1965 and 1969, when the Fianna Fail party won 47.7% and 45.7% of the vote, but in excess of 50% of the seats on each occasion.[34] Although one might argue that such a result could be expected, given that some of the electorates in Ireland return only three or four members, results from the ACT and Tasmania, which have electorates returning up to seven members (in the case of Tasmania until the 1996 elections), are only marginally better.

The following table shows election results in Tasmania from 1982–98 inclusive. (Percentages of votes refer to first preference votes):

	Labor		**Liberal**		**Others***	
Year	% vote	% seats	% vote	% seats	% vote	% seats
1982	36.8	40	48.5	54	14.4	6
1986	35	40	54	54	10.5	6
1989	34.7	37	47	48.5	18.3	14
1992	28.8	31.4	54	54	17	14
1996	40	40	41	45.7	19	14
1998	45	56	38	40	17	4

* Greens, Australian Democrats, Independents.

33 Catt, Harris and Roberts, 1992, 60 and 97.

34 Bogdanor and Butler, 1983, 11–12.

In all of these elections, the larger parties were over-represented, while smaller parties and independents were under-represented. In some instances, under-representation of independents was quite significant, as in the case of the elections of 1986 and (to a spectacular degree) in the election held in 1998 after the seat reduction of 1996. In both 1982 and 1998 a party won more than 50% of the seats while winning less than 50% of the first preference vote.

The next table shows election results in the ACT since it adopted STV in 1995. Here, too, the percentage of votes refers to first preference votes:

	Labor		**Liberal**		**Others***	
Year	% vote	% seats	% vote	% seats	% vote	% seats
1995	31.6	35.2	40.4	41.1	27.9	23.4
1998	27.1	35.2	37	41.1	29	23.4
2001	41.7	47	31.6	41	26.6	11.6

* Greens, Australian Democrats, Independents

Here again, the larger parties were over-represented. In 1998 the Australian Democrats obtained nearly 6% of the vote but no seats, while in 2001 over-representation of larger parties and under-representation of smaller groupings was particularly striking, with independents receiving no seats for their aggregate 9.5% of the vote, and this despite the fact that independents frequently received the benefit of each other's preferences.

Finally, it bears repeating that what these figures show is that even when seven member electorates are used (thus attenuating the supposed advantage that system has over MMP of every parliamentarian being accountable to voters in an electorate), proportionality is still not achieved under STV. The degree of proportionality is, of course, even less where three or four member electorates are used. In general, it can be said that STV does not strike a satisfactory balance between proportionality and electorate representation. This conclusion is, indeed, supported by the empirical evidence generated by studies in which the representivity of electoral systems is compared, a topic to which I now turn.

8.3.6 An electoral system for Australia

In light of the above survey of major electoral systems, we now arrive at a point where we are able to make a comparison between them, and thus a choice as to which best serves the objectives of allowing voters a choice of an identifiable representative at electorate level, coupled with overall representivity of party strengths at a national level.

It is readily apparent that both the first past the post system and the alternative vote system fail the test of achieving proportionality at a national level. Conversely, proportional representation based purely on elections by party list provides voters with no identifiable local representative to whom they can address their concerns. The choice thus lies between MMP and STV. MMP and STV both provide a result which is more proportionate than do FPP (first past the post) and AV, and a less proportionate result than does the pure list system. But which of these two provides a more proportionate result?

The most recent empirical research on the issue of comparative representivity of voting systems clearly indicates that MMP provides a more proportionate result than does STV. This emerges from Farrell's study of voting systems used in 59 democracies, published in 2001,[35] which used an indicator of electoral disproportionality[36] (in other words, an index which increases in value the greater the disparity there is between a party's seat entitlement and the votes it actually received) to rank electoral systems. Farrell's study also compared the average number of parties which achieved representation in the countries' legislatures over a number of past elections, as well as the average percentage of members of the legislature who were female. Unsurprisingly, pure list systems (such as that used in Israel) took the first 13 positions in the table, because they had the lowest disproportionality indices. On average, proportional systems based on lists using the lowest remainder Hare quota system had a disproportionality index of 2.13 while systems using STV had an average of 5.39. For our purposes, the relative rankings of selected countries using MMP, STV, Alternative Vote and FPP are of most interest, and produced the following results:

Ranking	Country	Electoral system	Disproportionality index	Number of parties	% female representatives
14	Germany	MMP	3.38	3.31	30.9
27	Ireland	STV	5.39	3.22	12
38	Australia (HoR)	AV	10.31	2.46	22
44	United Kingdom	FPP	15.19	2.2	18.4

Several observations can be made in relation to he above data: first, Germany's MMP system delivers substantially better proportionality than does Ireland's STV system, and would, indeed, have yielded an even lower disproportionality index, had it not been for the 5% threshold imposed on parties before they are entitled to representation. It has already been noted that the degree of disproportionality that may occur in an election conducted under STV can lead a party to win a majority of seats without achieving 50% of the vote (as occurred in Ireland in 1965 and 1969 and in Tasmania in 1982 and 1998). Secondly, the enhanced proportionality of MMP is achieved without a substantially increased number of parties represented in the legislature. This is an important counter-argument to that presented by opponents of proportional systems, who allege that it causes party fission and thus unstable coalition government. The issue of coalitions is addressed separately below. Here, it is only necessary to note that the proportionality delivered by MMP is at the cost of an average of only one more party achieving representation as compared with the other electoral systems. Finally, the significant level of representation achieved by women under the German system (which, as we have seen, was replicated in relation to both women and indigenous people in New Zealand), provides an added bonus when compared with other systems.

If MMP is provides significantly better nationwide proportionality than does STV, what of the criterion of voter contact with a personal representative? As has already been stated, in Germany and New Zealand MMP provides personal representation in the form

35 Farrell, 2001, 157–59.

36 Farrell uses 'Gallaghan's least squares' index – for an explanation of the way the index is calculated, see *ibid*, 145.

of the 50% of members of Parliament who are elected in single member electorates. A consistent criticism levelled against MMP is that the 50% of parliamentarians who are not reliant on an electorate for their tenure in the legislature form a body of persons who do not participate in service of voters in electorates, and who are accountable to party machines rather than to voters. For this reason, some proponents of proportional representation favour STV over MMP on the ground that the lower degree of national representivity achieved by the former system is counterbalanced by the fact that under STV all parliamentarians come from an electorate, albeit a multi-member one. To some extent, this criticism of MMP is founded upon a caricature of the system, rather than on an understanding of how it works in reality. In Germany, the list parliamentarians are selected from regional rather than national lists. Although this causes some loss of proportionality, it has the consequence that the parliamentarians identify with a specific geographic area, and provide service to voters in the region, in the same way as parliamentarians elected in individual electorates do.

Furthermore, it is important to recognise that MMP can operate without having a 50:50 split between electorate and list MPs. The crucial issue here is what is the minimum percentage of list seats that a system must have in order to achieve a sufficient degree of representivity or, to express the question differently, what percentage of electorate members can an MMP system tolerate without pushing its disproportionality index above that obtained under the significantly less proportional STV system? Empirical research on this question, by Taagepera and Shugart, indicates that in an electoral system where the electorate seats are filled in single member electorates, a minimum of 25% of the seats in the legislature should be filled from lists if overall proportionality is to be achieved.[37] However, this assumes an MMP system operating on the basis of nationwide lists, and so a slightly higher minimum percentage would be required to ensure proportionality if list seats were elected on a regional basis. For this reason, one should provide a margin of safety and assume that, in order to ensure a proportional outcome, 33% of the seats should be elected from lists.

Assuming, then, that the House of Representatives was elected under an MMP system with a 66:33 split between electorate and list seats, and with flexible lists, what impact would that have on the size of Parliament? Currently, the average number of voters in a federal electorate is approximately 84,400 voters. Moving to MMP with a 66:33 seat allocation would require either that the number of MPs was increased to 225 in order to maintain the same population per seat for the 150 electorate seats (with an additional 75 seats being elected from lists) or, if the total number of seats remained at the current 150, with 100 being chosen from electorates and 50 from lists, that the population of each electorate be increased to 113,000 voters. Such an increase would not put Australia markedly out of step with other democracies, where the ratio between voters and representatives is, in any event, very varied, from approximately 16,000 voters per member of the Dail in Ireland, to approximately 471,000 voters per member of the House of Representatives in the USA. In the case of Australia, however, it is geography rather than population which would, in all likelihood, be determinative of the question of whether to accommodate MMP by increasing the number of seats in the House, or of maintaining the number of seats and increasing the number of voters per seat. Following

37 Taagepera and Shugart, 1989, 131.

the latter course would result in already enormous electorates, such as those of Kalgoorlie in Western Australia (2,295,000 sq km), and Grey in South Australia (897,000 sq km), becoming even larger. Furthermore, given that the principles of proportional representation would require the abandonment of minimum representation of States in the House, it would seem unwise to move to MMP with only 100 electorate seats, as this would see Tasmania's electorate seat entitlement slip to two. MMP should, therefore, be implemented by increasing the number of members of the House to 225, with 150 being elected from existing electorates and 75 from lists. On current population distribution figures, the 150 electorate seats would be allocated among the States and Territories as follows:

New South Wales	51
Victoria	37
Queensland	28
Western Australia	15
South Australia	12
Tasmania	4
Australian Capital Territory	2
Northern Territory	1

So far as the list seats are concerned, the German model of having separate regional lists rather than of having one large national list (as in New Zealand) would cause list MPs to be identified with specific geographic areas, in the same way as are members of the Senate. States and Territories are obvious candidates as list seat regions. If the 75 list seats were allocated to States and Territories, the distribution would be as follows:

New South Wales	25
Victoria	19
Queensland	14
Western Australia	7
South Australia	6
Tasmania	2
ACT	1
NT	1

The total number of seats (both electorate and list) for each State and Territory would then be as follows:

New South Wales	76
Victoria	56
Queensland	42
Western Australia	22
South Australia	18
Tasmania	6
Australian Capital Territory	3
Northern Territory	2

Some provision would have to be made to cover the eventuality that a State or Territory's population fell below the quota required for a list seat. The only solutions would be either to set a minimum requirement of one list seat for each State and Territory, or for the voters in a State or Territory not entitled to separate representation to be included on another State's voters roll for list seat purposes. The first solution would introduce an element of disproportionality into the system, which is unacceptable given that the whole purpose of list seats is to correct disproportionality arising out of the electorate results. Inclusion of the unrepresented State or Territory voters on another State's roll would still result in those voters' opinions having an equal impact on the composition of the legislature as those of all other voters in Australia. The choice as to which State's voters roll the unrepresented voters should be added to should be determined by discovering which State's allocation would come closest to a whole number of seat entitlements after adding those voters.

Two points remain to be addressed: as stated above, the 5% threshold for entitlement to list seats is not a necessary feature of MMP. In Germany, it was adopted as a reaction to the multiplicity of small parties which obtained representation during the Weimar Republic. However, it is clearly inconsistent with the principle of proportional representation to have a threshold. I would, therefore, recommend that no threshold be imposed for representation if MMP was adopted in Australia. In any event, the fact that under the system proposed there would be only 75 list seats would mean that there was a practical threshold of 1.5%, which would filter out some of the 'micro parties'.

Finally, and very importantly, there should be no move to change the current method of election of the electorate MPs from the alternative vote system contained in the Commonwealth Electoral Act 1918 (Cth) to any other (such as FPP). Maintaining AV in individual electorates would counter one of the alleged weaknesses of proportional representation systems, namely, that because they usually require that coalition governments be formed (an objection which is addressed at length in the next section), they leave voters in the dark as to who the government will be until a coalition is negotiated, usually after the election. Given that the AV system requires parties to enter into co-operative agreements relating to exchange of preferences during an election, such agreements will provide an obvious pointer to voters before the election is held as to which parties are likely to enter into coalition with each other.[38]

8.4 COALITION GOVERNMENT

The usual outcome of any system of proportional representation is that no single party is able to form government on its own, and so coalition is the expected outcome when a government is formed after an election conducted under a proportional representation system. To some, this is a major drawback of proportional representation systems. They argue that coalition governments are inherently unstable, that they give excessive power to small parties, which those parties use to hold larger parties to ransom negotiations over the formation of a coalition, and that voters have no way of telling until after an election

38 United Kingdom Government, 1998, 127.

who their government will be, because that depends upon post-election negotiations between the parties.

Before addressing the propensity of proportional representation systems to produce coalition governments, it is apposite to note that systems using single member electorates do not inevitably produce single-party government. Indeed, a telling statistic produced by the Independent Commission on the Voting System, which reported to the United Kingdom government in 1998, was that in the 150 years prior to 1997, Britain had coalition governments for 43 years, and minority governments (in other words, governments which lacked a majority but which survived in office because of the support of other parties without being in coalition with them) for a further 34 years. In the case of Australia, coalition governments have held power for 49 of the 101 years the Commonwealth has been in existence. Of that period, 35 years are accounted for by the three long periods of Liberal/Country Party or Liberal/National Party coalitions from 1949–72, 1975–83 and 1996 to the present. It cannot, therefore, be said that coalition is either alien to the federal political scene or productive of governmental instability.

Turning now to proportional systems, the experience of the MMP system in Germany certainly has not been one of party proliferation or instability. As a study by Bogdanor concluded, fewer parties were represented in the Bundestag that in the House of Commons (the same also holding true for the Dail in Ireland elected by STV),[39] and Germany had only six chancellors during the period 1949–98, as compared with 11 Prime Ministers in the case of the United Kingdom.[40] Furthermore, although it is always possible that a coalition will break apart, leading to the government losing its majority in Parliament and thus calling an election, there is an obvious political disincentive to break-up because the voters may penalise the party(ies) which caused the break-up by denying them support at the resulting elections. Most importantly, however, it must be recognised that although coalition is the usual outcome of proportional systems, this is true only because voters wish it so. In the case of MMP, for example, voters could quite easily avoid coalitions if they gave their second (party list) vote to either of the major parties. However, the experience in Germany certainly has been that many voters deliberately cast their vote in favour of a different party from the one they voted for in their electorate, either because that is where their true sentiment lies (there, of course, usually being no point in voting one's heart in a single member electorate), or in order to ensure that neither major party can govern on its own.[41]

What is the effect of proportional representation on policy-making? The evidence adduced by Lijphart suggests that, whereas single-party government undoubtedly promotes quick decision-making, it does not necessarily promote wise decision-making.[42] The greater time for deliberation required for the type of consensual decision-making required when there is a coalition tends to produce policies which are better considered, and which reflect a wider range of interests. In so far as macro-economic policy is concerned, coalition governments tend to follow steady, centrist policies rather than to evince the swings from right to left that can occur in a two-party system, and the

39 Bogdanor, 1984, 149.

40 United Kingdom Government, 1998, para 60.

41 Farrell, 1997, 99.

42 Lijphart, 1999, 55 and 62–63.

empirical evidence shows that countries with proportional representation tend to have superior economic performance.[43] In general, proportional representation tends to reward moderation and centrism in politics, precisely because the balance of power between right and left is frequently held by a moderate centrist party. This has certainly been the case in Germany, where the centrist Free Democratic Party participated in coalitions for much of the post-Second World War period.[44] Of course, proportional representation can work to the advantage of small extremist parties on the fringe of politics. This has been the case in Israel, which has pure proportional representation, and where minor extremist parties have exerted undue influence over government policy, but has not been a characteristic of the MMP system in Germany. Similarly, the multi-member electorate system in Ireland has seen no more than four to five parties obtain representation in the Dail (the lower house of Parliament), while in the Senate in Australia, representation of the Liberal, National, Labor and Australian Democrats parties has only rarely been supplemented by representatives of minor parties or independents. Here, too, the position of the Australian Democrats illustrates the centripetal effect of proportional representation – as the centrist party, their vote is frequently crucial in securing the passage of legislation. This makes it appropriate to foreshadow the issue of parliamentary reform, and, in particular, the role of the Senate, discussed in Chapter 9: if, as is often stated, one of the advantages of current constitutional arrangements is that the Senate provides a forum for minor parties which cannot obtain representation in the House of Representatives,[45] the rationale for having a Senate with its current powers is weakened if the same effect can be achieved through reform of the electoral system for the House of Representatives. In fact, having proportional representation in the House of Representatives would give third parties a far more significant role than they serve at the moment. Currently, their role is primarily negative, that of blocking legislation in the Senate. If there was a system of proportional representation for the House, third parties would perform a far more positive role, because they would undoubtedly participate in government. Furthermore, because under proportional representation the government will, by definition, always have the support of more than 50% of the voters, the argument that under the current system the government in the House of Representatives does not necessarily have a mandate to implement its legislative programme, and ought, therefore, to be restrained by the Senate,[46] would also lose its force.

The most frequently stated objection to proportional representation is that voters do not know prior to, or even during, an election what alternative governments they are choosing between, because there is no way of predicting what combination of parties may form a post-election coalition. The current system, it is argued, at least has the advantage that voters have a clear choice between the Liberal/National coalition and Labor, and these blocs can commit to implementing a particular programme, which will not have to be compromised in post-election coalition negotiations. But is this true? First, given the balance of power held by the Australian Democrats in the Senate (something which voters produce as a conscious decision), no government can implement its programme

43 *Ibid*, 63–66.

44 Farrell, 1997, 96–97

45 Sharman, 1999(a), 158; and Evans, 2001, 10.

46 *Ibid*, Sharman, 154.

without compromise, so having minor parties hold the balance of power in the House of Representatives would not be revolutionary. Secondly, parties operating in a proportional representation environment experience a degree of pressure to declare to voters their intentions in relation to which parties they would or would not consider negotiating with, and what aspects of their policies they would not compromise on, before voters go to the polls. Parties which leave voters in uncertainty as to what their post-election intentions are, are likely to lose electoral support, precisely because they are being opaque on the issue. Of course, there is no way of enforcing pre-election pledges against a party after an election (short of punishing it at the next election), but, then, the same is true with regard to parties operating under non-proportional voting systems. Thirdly, and most significantly, opacity with regard to coalition intentions would be almost impossible to maintain in the context of Australian federal elections, given that electorate seats are elected by the Alternative Vote system, which requires parties to do preference deals at electorate level in order to achieve success. Which other party any given party did deals with at electorate level would obviously be indicative of their intentions with regard to coalition, even in the absence of any explicit statement on the matter. There is, therefore, every likelihood that Australian voters participating in an MMP election would know long before polling day which parties were likely to go into coalition, and could, therefore, make an informed choice, not only in relation to who they wish to have as their local representatives, but also which party or group of parties they wished to put into government.

Finally, in relation to the formation of governments under proportional representation, it must be emphasised that the key advantage conferred by proportional systems (apart from the fact that very voter's ballot is of equal value) is that the government will *always* be formed by parties which have the support of more than 50% of the voters. This can be contrasted with non-proportional systems, where the governing party almost always has fewer than 50% of the first preference votes, and frequently even has *fewer first preference votes than the party which loses the election*, as, indeed, has happened in Australia.

8.5 CONCLUSION

I started this chapter by noting that participation in elections is the most basic, and for most people the only, way in which the individual participates in the process of government. It would, therefore, seem to be axiomatic in a democracy that the vote of every person should, as far as possible, have the same effect as the vote of every other person, and that the legislature should, as far as possible, reflect the opinions of voters taken as a national whole. That is all that proportional representation seeks to achieve. What this chapter has sought to do is to identify the voting system which best serves those goals while retaining the equally important function of ensuring that voters have an identifiable representative in Parliament whose tenure they control.

PARLIAMENTARY REFORM

9.1 THE SENATE AND PARLIAMENTARY GOVERNMENT

The composition and role of the Senate are contentious issues in Australian constitutional law. The reason why the Senate forms such an inviting target for proponents of constitutional reform is because it manifests two serious flaws: one involving functional incompatibility with responsible government, and the other involving representational unfairness.

The first flaw is that the Senate's power to block supply is incompatible with the system of responsible government.[1] At the heart of this doctrine lies the obligation – imposed by convention rather than law – that a government which no longer enjoys the confidence of Parliament must resign. In the United Kingdom, 'not having the confidence of Parliament' is indicated where a government loses a formal vote of no confidence, when it fails to get through Parliament a piece of legislation which it (the government) has stated will be a test of confidence, or when Parliament blocks supply. The last of these is an indication of lack of confidence because a government which is unable to obtain authorisation for taxation or expenditure from Parliament cannot lawfully raise revenue or spend money, as was established in *R v Hampden* (*Ship Money* case).[2] This aspect of the doctrine of legislative confidence has a clear rationale, because a government which persists in office will ultimately be drawn into illegality. The same reasoning applies in Australia, where s 83 of the Constitution prohibits the expenditure of money in the absence of appropriations legislation. It, therefore, cannot be denied that failure to obtain supply is, under the conventions of responsible government we inherited from the United Kingdom, an event triggering the obligation of the government to resign.

In the case of a bicameral legislature, however, the system of responsible government encounters the difficult question of whether 'retaining the confidence of Parliament' means retaining the confidence of both houses, or just one. In England, the Commons and Lords came into conflict on several occasions during the 19th century over key reform measures, which the government in the House of Commons had been elected to implement, and which the Lords threatened to block.[3] Matters came to a head in 1909, when the Lords rejected the annual budget presented by Lloyd George. Whatever may have been the position under conventions governing relations between the two houses, there was no doubt that, as a matter of law, the assent of both houses was required for all legislation, and that the Lords thus had the power to block the budget. In the face of a threat by Lloyd George to advise King George V to create sufficient peers to give the government a majority in the Lords, the latter acceded to the Parliament Act 1911, which

1 Faulkner, 1999, 125–27.

2 (1637) 3 St Tr 826.

3 Hood Phillips and Jackson, 1978, 133–34.

provided that rejection of a Money Bill by the Lords could be overridden by the Commons after one month, and that the Lords could delay all other legislation[4] for only two years. That Act was amended by the Parliament Act 1949, which reduced the power of the Lords to block non-Money Bills to one year. The Parliament Acts of 1911 and 1949 thus remove the possibility of a government in the Commons failing to obtain supply because of the obduracy of the Lords, and so the only circumstance in which failure to obtain supply will trigger the obligation to resign is if the Commons itself refuses supply.

It is, perhaps, an unfortunate accident of history that the passage of the Commonwealth of Australia Act 1900 pre-dated the clash between Commons and Lords in 1909. If the chronology had been different, Australia's Constitution might well have included an appropriate restriction on the power of the Senate, either generally or, at least, in relation to financial legislation. But then again, it may be that a different sequence of events would have made no difference. The strength of feeling on the part of smaller States, and in particular Tasmania, South Australia and Western Australia, on the question of what power the Senate should have, suggests that the Constitution would have been drafted no differently even if Australian politicians had had the benefit of observing the clash between Commons and Lords.[5] The Convention debates reveal that the delegates were fully conscious of the implications for responsible government of giving the power of veto to the Senate.[6] Thus, at the 1891 Convention, Deakin said that to combine a government that was responsible to the House with a Senate having the power of veto would be 'to create on the one side an irresistible force and on the other an immovable object',[7] while, at the 1897 Convention, O'Connor said that 'it is utterly impossible to carry on responsible government with responsibility to two Houses'.[8] However, the giving of equal power to the Senate, including the power to block (but not to initiate or amend) financial legislation (the so-called 'Compromise of 1891'), was clearly a *sine qua non* of the smaller States joining the federation.[9] The only concession they were prepared to make was to have the deadlock-breaking provision of s 57 included in the Constitution. But, as the events of 1975 (addressed in Chapter 10) demonstrate, that provision is manifestly inadequate as a mechanism for resolving disputes within the time-frame that may be required for a government to obtain finance: s 57 contemplates an initial passage by the House and rejection by the Senate, followed by another passage by the House after the elapse of three months and then a rejection by the Senate, followed (if the government wishes to go that far) by a dissolution of both chambers, a general election and then, if the Senate again refuses to enact the legislation, a joint sitting which may (or may not) lead to the legislation being passed. Thus, quite apart from the section's

4 Except for a few categories excluded from the scope of the Act, such as legislation to extend the life of Parliament.

5 For a discussion of the smaller States' insistence on this point, see La Nauze, 1972, 43, 53, 119, 126 and 139–48; and Galligan, 1980, 1–10.

6 See, eg, the speech by Sir JW Hackett of Western Australia, at the 1891 Convention, who stated 'if that is the [model of] responsible government which it is proposed to graft on our new federation, there will be one of two alternatives – either responsible government will kill federation, or federation, in the form in which we shall, I hope, be prepared to accept it, will kill responsible government'; National Australasian Convention Debates, 1891, 280.

7 *Ibid*, 383.

8 National Australasian Convention Debates, 1897, 499.

9 Galligan, 1995, 75.

manifest uselessness given the time it takes to comply with the procedure it mandates, s 57 does not guarantee the supremacy of the House in financial matters, even if all its provisions are used.

We are thus left with a Constitution in which a fundamental provision (the power of the Senate in respect of financial legislation), can lead to a situation in which a government which enjoys the confidence of the House of Representatives (in the sense that it has a majority there), can yet simultaneously be said *not* to have the confidence of Parliament as a whole, because it cannot obtain supply. In such a situation, the doctrine of responsible government undoubtedly requires that such a government resign, failing which its continued expenditure of money will lead it into illegality. Irrespective of what one thinks about the legislative power of the Senate generally, the functional integrity of the Constitution requires that its power to block financial legislation be removed, or, at the very least, be reduced to that of delaying such legislation for a limited period, for example, in Ireland, where the Senead can delay financial legislation for only 21 days.[10] The powers currently conferred upon the Senate by the Constitution illustrate the harm that can arise where constitution-making is driven by political compromise rather than by principle. The smaller States' insistence on equal representation and on equal power for each chamber created an institution whose running was incompatible with the doctrines of parliamentary government.

9.2 ELECTORAL DISPARITY AND THE SENATE AS A 'STATES' HOUSE'

Assuming one accepts that the concept of 'one person, one vote, one value' is a fundamental principle of democratic government, it is clear that the current regime governing elections to the Senate does not conform to this fundamental principle. As was stated in Chapter 8, under the current system, a Tasmanian voter has 13 times the influence over the composition of the Senate as does a voter in New South Wales. Since the Senate has equal power with the House of Representatives, it follows that a Tasmanian voter has 13 times the influence over the passage of legislation as does a voter from New South Wales. In principle, it is unfair that the arbitrary fact of the State in which a voter lives should determine the degree of influence that voter has over the legislative process. The argument is often put forward that because the Australian Senate has a 'representative democratic nature'[11] it should enjoy equal power with the House of Representatives, unlike the House of Lords and the Canadian Senate which, because they are hereditary or appointive, have only a delaying power. However, I would argue that because of the gross disparity in the voting power enjoyed by individual voters (arising from the equality of representation given to each State), the Australian Senate can, at best, be classified only as 'less unrepresentative' than the House of Lords or the Canadian Senate. Indeed, to use the term 'proportional representation',[12] which assumes equal voting strengths for every voter, in relation to the Senate, where proportional

10 Constitution of Ireland 1937, Art 21.2.

11 Thompson, 1999, 42.

12 See, eg, Uhr, 1999.

representation is built on a grossly unequal foundation, is surely misleading. In short, on grounds of principle it must be acknowledged that the equal status the Senate enjoys with the House of Representatives is incompatible with the inequality of representation of individual voters in that chamber.[13] As King succinctly puts it, that 'the principle of equality of citizens is eroded where the equality of regional representation is entrenched'.[14]

An analysis purely on the level of principle ignores the history of constitution-making in Australia, and, in particular, the insistence on the part of the small States that each should have equal representation in the Senate, which, as has already been noted, was the crucial compromise which would be required to secure their agreement to Federation. This argument, as advanced by the small States, derives from a characterisation of the federal compact as being one between the federating States rather than their individual citizens, and that, as equal partners in the compact, each State deserves equal representation in the second chamber, which would be a 'States' House' representing their interests.

Three arguments can be made against this line of reasoning: first, the fact that the equal representation provision was the product of a political compromise does not, of course, vest it with moral authority. In other words, the principle of *pacta sunt servanda* does not serve to trump counter-arguments that may be raised as to why the Senate should be reformed. That would be to reduce the process of constitution-making to the status of a contract for the purchase of a second-hand car. Principles such as individual rights and equality cannot, in a society committed to democracy and freedom, be subordinated to a rule which is arbitrary and inequitable, simply because the rule is the product of an agreement. Perhaps the most stark illustration of this is provided by the example of the United States, whose Constitution was tainted at its inception by an agreement that slavery would be permitted to continue, notwithstanding the Constitution's commitment to individual freedom, a compromise which was unravelled by the Civil War. It cannot be imagined that, had an agreement been built into the Australian Constitution that slavery would be permitted in certain States, we would now say that the principle that agreements must be adhered to justifies a breach of fundamental human rights. Why, then, should the fact that inequality of representation was the product of an agreement entered into in the 1890s stand in the way of parliamentary reform?

Secondly, the assumption underpinning the 'States' house' argument – that voters from different States have State-specific interests, that they vote in accordance with those interests, and that, therefore, the inhabitants of States with a small population need protecting from those who live in States with large populations[15] – does not accord with voter behaviour, as even supporters of the Senate's power concede.[16] Furthermore, the Senate certainly has not performed the role of a 'States' house'. In reality, Senators have long voted along party lines rather than in accordance with the States they represent.[17] To

13 For a defence of the Senate by one of its members, see Bartlett, 2001.

14 King, 1993, 100.

15 For an example of this argument, see Sharman, 1999(a), 168–69.

16 Sharman, 1999(b), 157.

17 Craven, 1992, 49 and 60.

suggest that voters in Tasmania and Western Australia vote with an eye to restraining the large populations in New South Wales and Victoria, flies in the face of political reality. Similarly, to state, as Evans does,[18] that the 114 out of 148 members of the House of Representatives from New South Wales, Victoria and Queensland represent the 'three eastern states', and, therefore, that equal representation in the Senate is required to balance the 'domination' of those States, is misleading: Those representatives represent the citizens who happen to live in those States, not the States themselves, and in view of the populations of those States, the numbers of Representatives from them is quite properly far greater than those from the States with smaller populations. Voters in Australian federal elections vote overwhelmingly on national issues, usually in accordance with their socio-economic interests, so the argument based on State-specific interests is devoid of substance. Whether specific interest groups should be granted representation in the Senate is an issue which I address later in this chapter. But it is clear that the current recognition of interests of States does not reflect anything meaningful in contemporary Australian politics.

Thirdly, it is fundamentally wrong to think that protection of the interests of States in a federation require that they have equal representation in a second chamber, or that the second chamber have an absolute power of veto over legislation enacted by the first chamber.[19] In India, which is both the most populous democracy and the most populous federation in the world, seats in the upper house (the Council of States) are allocated between States on the basis of population.[20] Conflicts between the upper and lower houses (the House of the People) are resolved by means of a joint sitting,[21] and are almost inevitably resolved in favour of the lower house, given that it has 550 members, as compared to the 250 members of the upper house. In respect of financial legislation the powers of the upper house are restricted to that of a 14 day delay.[22] Similarly, in Germany, in the upper house (the Bundesrat) the representation of each State is dependant on its population,[23] and the consent of the Bundesrat is required only in respect of legislative topics which lie within the concurrent power of the federal and state governments.[24] In fact, a federation could operate quite happily without a second chamber at all (as, indeed, is shown by the example of the Republic of the Comoros, which has a unicameral federal Constitution),[25] because the key determinant of whether political power is distributed fairly in a federation is not whether there is an upper chamber, but, rather, how the Constitution distributes legislative competence between the State Parliaments, on the one hand, and the federal Parliament on the other. If that division is fair (an issue which is explored in Chapter 5), it is irrelevant whether there is a second chamber. Indeed, assuming that the States enjoy a sufficient degree of legislative and financial autonomy, how can one justify a special layer of influence over the federal government, which is chosen by a different electorate (the nation as a whole), to discharge different

18 Evans, 2001, 11.

19 This argument is made in Evans, 2001, 1–3 and 6, 11; and in Thompson, 1999, 44.

20 Constitution of India 1949, Schedule IV.

21 *Ibid*, s 108.

22 *Ibid*, s 109.

23 Constitution of Germany 1949, Art 51.

24 *Ibid*, Arts 74(2), 77 and 78.

25 Constitution of the Republic of the Comoros 1996, Art 31.

responsibilities (that is, those which are national in character and, to that extent, have nothing to do with the States individually),[26] and in relation to which the States' inhabitants are already represented in the House of Representatives?

9.3 CONTEMPORARY ARGUMENTS IN SUPPORT OF THE SENATE

Contemporary arguments in support of the powers of the Senate have focused on the protection supposedly given by the Senate against the 'tyranny of the House of Representatives or, rather, of the executive that dominates the House of Representatives',[27] which would be unrestrained if not curbed by the Senate. According to this argument, it is the very fact that it is difficult for governments to control both houses that is the strength of the system, and that, far from seeing the Senate as an obstructionist institution, voters deliberately cast their votes for opposition and/or minor parties in order to deny governments control over both chambers.[28] This argument is so frequently advanced that it has assumed the status of dogma in Australian constitutional debate. However, close analysis shows that it is erroneous.

The argument rests upon the unstated assumption that whether citizens are protected from governmental tyranny depends only upon the manner in which laws are made, rather than on their content. Nothing in the Constitution, as it now stands, prevents either house from enacting laws which infringe fundamental rights (with the exception of the few express and implied rights, discussed in Chapter 2). As a matter of pure law, the fact that legislation needs to be passed by two chambers rather than one provides no insurance against the end product being invasive of fundamental rights. Although Senate rejection may *sometimes* lead to the consequence that rights are protected (where a government that is bent on denying fundamental rights is resisted by an obstructionist Senate), the protection will prove nugatory either where the Senate colludes with the government in enacting oppressive legislation, or where the Senate *itself* imposes restrictions on fundamental freedoms as the price for its assent to legislation which has been enacted by the House. These possibilities (and, in particular, the second of them) are never alluded to by proponents of the current constitutional dispensation, who seem to assume that the Senate wields its power only in ways that protect individual freedom. If, for example, the House of Representatives introduced a Bill which would extend the ambit of anti-discrimination laws so as to prohibit discrimination on grounds of sexual orientation, how likely is it that a social conservative,such as Senator Brian Harradine, would vote in favour of it, given his opposition to access by lesbians to IVF treatment? What chance would a law liberalising immigration law have of passing the Senate if a Senator representing the One Nation party held the balance of power?

In short, there is no reason to suppose that Senators are any more immune to cynical use of power in order to achieve personal or party objectives than are members of the House of Representatives. Proponents of the argument that the Senate is protector of freedom appear to believe that the way to make a legislative system more just is to make

26 On this point, see Galligan, 1995, 67–68.

27 Sawer, 1999, 2. See also Sharman, 1999(a), 162–63; and Evans, 2001, 12.

28 See, eg, Bartlett, 2001, 164.

it less efficient – in other words, that simply by putting an impediment in the path of the House of Representatives (a 'spanner in the works', if you will), individual liberty is somehow guaranteed. As the examples discussed in the preceding paragraph have shown, this is clearly not necessarily the case. Sometimes a Senate will block oppressive legislation, sometimes it will not, and sometimes it might enact oppressive Acts or amendments itself as the price of approving a law passed by the House of Representatives, and whichever of these happens depends on the vagaries of party politics in that upper house. There is great irony that a country notoriously suspicious of politicians believes that fundamental freedoms are sufficiently safeguarded by reposing guardianship of them in a chamber consisting of politicians, rather than in a court staffed by independent judges. The argument that the Senate protects the people from 'tyrannical' legislation passed by the House is an argument that surely rests on a belief that laws should be blocked if they do not conform with a set of values. If the evil sought to be avoided is tyrannical laws (as contrasted with those that are in accordance with fundamental freedoms), then the remedy to the problem raised by that argument must be one that enables an institution to test such laws on grounds of values. As this paragraph has shown, the Senate is not at all circumscribed in relation to the grounds upon which it vetoes laws proposed by the House of Representatives. Rather, Senators act in accordance with the motive that actuates all legislators – namely, the perceived political interests of their party. The only sure protection against oppressive legislation is a Bill of Rights, which sets limits as to the substance of what either house may enact, rather than addressing only the procedures by which legislation is enacted, and which replaces political controls based on expediency with legal controls based on principle.

A second argument advanced in favour of the current constitutional dispensation, is that the Senate provides voters with an opportunity to give representation to minor parties, whose voices would not otherwise be heard in Parliament, given the geographic basis upon which elections are conducted for the House of Representatives. Sometimes this argument is advanced as a counter to that which challenges the appropriateness of the equal power of the Senate, in light of the gross inequality from State to State in the value of votes for that chamber.[29] Surely electoral reform in the House of Representatives is the obvious and most direct solution to this problem? The fact that proportional representation is used for Senate elections is used by some to distract attention from the fact that the value of the individual voter's vote for such elections depends upon the arbitrary fact of where they happen to live. While it may, indeed, be true that vote-splitting in House and Senate elections is actuated by a desire to break two-party dominance, and to give representation to third and minor parties, a better way to allow that to happen is to implement proportional representation for elections to the House of Representatives, as was argued in Chapter 8. In that situation, voters could quite happily vote according to their true sentiments in elections for the House of Representatives, even if that meant voting for a party other than one of the two major ones, as all parties would be represented in proportion to their shares of the national vote. In such a circumstance, the Senate would no longer be the only forum in which minor parties could obtain representation. Indeed, as was noted in Chapter 8, the position of minor parties would be greatly enhanced by proportional representation for the House of Representatives,

29 This argument is made in Sharman, 1999(a), 158, by Thompson, 1999, 43–46; and by Lees, 2000, 29.

because instead of being confined to the largely negative spoiling role they play in the Senate, proportional representation in the House of Representatives would give them a real chance of being a party to a coalition government, and of having their initiatives included in the government's legislative programme.

A further point that should be made in respect of minor party representation is that current arrangements shield voters from the consequences of their actions: the most common criticism of proportional representation is that it leads to governmental instability and gives excessive power to minor parties. I hope that the discussion in Chapter 8 has illustrated that that argument is by no means as strong as has been thought. But to the extent that vote-splitting in favour of minor parties impedes the operation of government, such an impediment already exists because of the way voters cast their votes for the Senate. In other words, while critics of proportional representation argue that the current electoral system for the House of Representatives is superior to one based on proportional representation, because it allows voters to elect a strong government with a clear parliamentary majority, this is to ignore the fact that voters hedge their bets by simultaneously using the Senate to deprive that government of the ability to carry through the platform on which it was elected. This is inconsistent. The system would be far more honest if the effect of vote-splitting was evident in the House where the government was formed. In such a situation, the effect of vote-splitting on the ability of a government to carry through its legislative programme – principally the need for governments to negotiate with minor parties – would be felt at first hand, and voters would be required to accept responsibility for their actions in a more direct way. If they continued to split votes so as to deprive any single party of a majority, so be it, but at least the effect on the ability of governments to get their legislation through would be obvious, rather than being shielded by the fact that the blockage occurs in the Senate.

A third argument in favour of the Senate is the role it performs in relation to ensuring governmental accountability,[30] and the scrutiny of legislation (in particular of delegated legislation) through its committee system. This function is undeniably important, as it provides an opportunity for inquiry into, and overview of, government policy in a less pressured forum than is provided by the House of Representatives. However, the Senate's discharge of this watchdog function does not depend upon its retention of a power of absolute veto. The restriction of the Senate's powers to that of delaying legislation for a year (advocated below) would still leave that chamber with a weapon of sufficient potency to ensure that governments complied with Senate requests for information, in order to avoid disruption of their legislative programme. Furthermore, the power of the Senate to require that members of the executive produce documents and answer questions would be unaffected, because that power (recently affirmed in relation to the New South Wales Legislative Council in *Egan v Willis*[31] and *Egan v Chadwick*[32]) derives from the privileges of Parliament rather than from the power to block legislation. In short, the powers and composition of the Senate could be reformed without at all reducing the valuable benefits conferred by the operation of Senate Committees.

30 For a discussion of the Senate's role in subjecting the government to accountability, see Evans, 1999; and Thompson, 1999, 49–51.

31 (1998) 195 CLR 424.

32 (1999) 46 NSWLR 563.

9.4 REFORMING THE SENATE

It is clear that the question of how the Senate should be elected is inextricably linked with the function it is to perform. If the Senate were to retain equal legislative power with the House of Representatives (even with the power to block financial legislation excepted, which, as has already been argued, has to be removed in order to allow the system of responsible government to operate properly), then the principle of equal weight for each voter would require that the electoral system for the Senate should be changed so that each voter has equal power. But while electing the Senate under the same proportional system as I have argued for in respect of the House of Representatives would remove the problem of unrepresentivity, it would also, in all likelihood, lead to the composition of one chamber mirroring that of the other, which then begs the question as to why have the Senate at all? The composition of the chambers might differ if we retained the current system under which the Senate is elected for different terms than the House, with half the Senate retiring every three years. However, this, too, is arguably inconsistent with representative government, as it may well be asked why a Senate, half of whose members reflect the popular will as it was some years before the most recent election for the House, should have the power to thwart the will of the House and the government formed in it. It therefore seems that whichever course is adopted, be it a fair electoral system for a Senate elected at the same time as the House of Representatives, or a fair electoral system for a Senate elected for terms that do not coincide with the House, there is a problem – redundancy in the first circumstance, or interference with the will of the government in the second.

The alternative to the above is to diminish the power of the Senate, so that its non-conformity to the principle of one person, one vote, one value, would not matter. If we were to limit the power of the Senate, depriving it of an absolute veto over legislation enacted by the House of Representatives, the unrepresentative electoral system used to choose its members would be unobjectionable. I have already noted that in the United Kingdom, the power of the House of Lords was reduced to that of delaying Bills for one year. If the same was done in respect of the Senate, the current disproportionate representation given to the States would cause no offence to democratic principles, because, ultimately, the will of the proportionately elected House of Representatives would prevail. This brings us to the heart of the reform – changing the very nature of the Senate to convert it from being a so-called 'house of review'[33] (which is really a euphemism for 'house of veto'), and making it, instead, what might be called a 'house of re-consideration' or a 'house of reflection'. The Senate would still be a forum in which detailed consideration was given to legislation passed by the House of Representatives, requiring that House to reconsider measures which the Senate felt were ill-considered or enacted in haste. The House would, if faced by amendments suggested by the Senate, have either to amend its legislation or accept a year's delay. Furthermore, the Senate would continue to exercise its supervisory role in respect of the executive branch in precisely the same way as it does as present because, as was stated above, that function is unrelated to the legislative powers of the chamber and derives from the powers it enjoys under the law of parliamentary privilege. The Constitution would then incorporate the

33 Evans, 2001, 11.

best of both worlds – consideration of legislation by a Senate, but without the fundamental principles of representative democracy being breached. This system currently operates in the United Kingdom, and, on balance, it is thought to work well, even by critics of the hereditary basis upon which the House of Lords operates. The government in the House of Commons regularly has measures rejected by the Lords, and must then either amend the legislation in a way that makes it palatable to the upper house, or else accept the delay imposed by that house. Sometimes the delay is forced in relation to legislation which is of crucial importance to the government, as in the case of the Lords' rejection of the Labour government's Trade Union and Labour Relations Bill in 1974, and their rejection of the Conservative government's legislation for the dissolution of the Greater London Council in 1984.[34] At the end of the day, however, the will of the more representative House of Commons prevails.

Assuming that the Senate's power was curbed in the way suggested above, and that, therefore, its State-based system of representation was no longer objectionable, what changes, if any, should be made to the composition of that chamber? A survey of second chambers around the world reveals a wide range of possibilities:[35] Some countries have the same system as is currently used Australia, with representation being accorded to States or provinces, sometimes on the basis of equal representation for each region (for example, the United States[36]), sometimes on the basis of representation for each region relative to its population (India[37] and Germany[38]). These countries also display differences in the way in which the regional representatives are chosen: in some, the second chamber is elected by the voters (Australia[39] and the United States[40]), while in India its members are elected by the State legislatures on the basis of proportional representation,[41] and in Germany they are nominated by the State governments.[42] In some countries, such as Malaysia[43] the upper chamber is partly nominated and partly elected. There is no elective element to the process at all in Canada, where Senators, who nominally represent the Provinces, are nominated by the federal government,[44] nor, of course, in the United Kingdom, where the House of Lords is partly hereditary and partly appointed. In other countries, the second chamber does not represent geographic regions, but, rather, consists of members elected or appointed to represent specific social groups. In Ireland, for example, the upper house (the Senead) is composed partly by members nominated by the Prime Minister, and partly by members elected by various social

34 Tsabelis and Money, 1997, 4.

35 Each variation in the composition and powers of second chambers could be illustrated by countless examples, from which I have selected just a few. For more comprehensive surveys, see Laundy, 1989, 3–10 and 143–54.

36 United States Constitution 1787, Art 1, s 3.

37 Constitution of India 1949, Schedule IV.

38 Constitution of Germany 1949, Art 51.

39 Commonwealth Constitution 1901, s 7.

40 United States Constitution 1787, Amendment XVII.

41 Constitution of India 1949, Art 80.

42 Constitution of Germany 1949, Art 51.

43 Constitution of Malaysia 1963, Art 45.

44 Constitution Act 1867, s 24.

interests groups, including universities, the professions, farmers' organisations, industry and commerce and labour organisations.[45]

In my view, there would be nothing to be gained by abandoning direct election of the Senate and replacing it with election by State Parliaments. That model, which was used in the United States until the passage of the Seventeenth Amendment in 1913, was consciously rejected by the drafters of our Constitution in favour of direct election by the people.[46] Furthermore, it is doubtful whether the Irish model of sectional representation would be suitable for adoption in Australia. The upper house in Ireland represents powerful social groups, and the adoption of such a system in Australia would fly in the face of the role the Senate was historically meant to perform – namely, of giving a voice to constituencies thought to be lacking in influence, which, in the late 19th century, were assumed to be the less populous States. It would also make it far less likely that minor parties would gain representation, and a change to a Senate dominated by representatives of professional organisations and unions, for example, would see a return to the situation that existed prior to 1949, with the Senate being dominated by the Liberals and Labor. Indeed, the very concept of sectional or group representation is highly problematic: should representation be given to prominent social groups, such as the professions, universities, farmers, trades unions and commerce and industry? How would the representatives of such groups be elected – directly by their members, or indirectly by bodies representing them? Furthermore, would it not entrench privilege to give representation to such groups, and should representation not, instead, be given to disadvantaged groups precisely in order that their voices might be heard? If the latter were the case, how would 'disadvantage' be measured? The concept of disadvantage involves a relative test which may give results which change over time: today's disadvantaged group may not be disadvantaged after the elapse of a decade, and social changes may have reduced the power and status of some other group which is thus more deserving of representation. In any event, who would speak for the disadvantaged? The most impoverished sectors of society – the illiterate, the homeless and the transient – are the least likely to participate in political processes, even at the most basic level of casting a vote, so how would they be fairly represented? The question of group representation is clearly one which is fraught with difficulty. In light of the problems identified in this paragraph, I would argue that it would be unwise to embed group representation in the Constitution, and that, with the exception of representation for indigenous people (already touched upon in Chapter 6, and elaborated upon below), the current system of equal representation for each State should be retained. I would also argue that, notwithstanding the increase in the number of members of the House of Representatives necessitated by the change to the MMP system, there should be no reduction in the number of senators, as to do that would impair the Senate's ability to staff its Committees.

Finally, given that under MMP the House of Representatives would be enlarged to 225 members, the existing constitutionally-mandated ratio of 2:1 between the

45 The range of interest groups represented in the second chamber in Ireland (the Senead) is specified in the Constitution of Ireland 1937, Arts 18.4 and 18.7. Note that the Senead does not have an absolute power to veto legislation which has been passed by the Dail (the lower house): Under Art 21.2, the Senead can block money bills for only 21 days, while in the case of all other legislation, Art 23.1 enables the Dail to override the Senead after 180 days.

46 Thompson, 1999, 41–42; and Uhr, 1999, 23–24.

membership of the House of Representatives and the Senate would be broken. However, that nexus was, in any event, a product of a desire to limit the power the House of Representatives would have in a s 57 joint sitting,[47] a procedure which would be redundant under the system proposed in this chapter.

9.5 INDIGENOUS REPRESENTATION

The other reform in the composition of the Senate is one which has already been discussed in Chapter 6, namely, that of reserving Senate seats for indigenous Australians. There it was noted that, although it would be possible to provide for separate representation in the House of Representatives, the fact that indigenous Australians comprise 2.2% of Australia's population would mean that, even if all people who were entitled to do so chose to go on a separate indigenous voters' roll, there would be a maximum of five representatives in a House expanded to 225. In the event that less than one fifth of those entitled to be registered took that option, separate representation would not occur. In view of this, it would surely be preferable to provide for separate indigenous representation in the Senate. The current size of the Senate is 76, consisting of 12 Senators from each of the six States, plus two Senators each for the Northern Territory and the ACT. According to the 2001 census, 410,000 Australians identified themselves as indigenous. How should representation of indigenous people be determined? A balance has to be struck between ensuring that indigenous people are adequately represented, and that such representation is not disproportionate to the size of the indigenous population relative to that of Australia as a whole. Perhaps the best basis upon which to proceed is to acknowledge that the indigenous population of Australia has at least equal claim to recognition as a separate entity as do the people of any of the States, and that, therefore, there should be 12 Senate seats reserved to represent voters on the indigenous voters' roll. That would bring the total complement of the chamber to 88. Assuming that all who were entitled to enrol on the indigenous voters' roll for Senate elections took that option, that would result in 2.2% of the population being represented by 13.6% of the seats in the Senate; in other words, being over-represented by a factor of 6.2, a degree of disproportionality which should not be considered alarming in light of the fact that, at present, the 2.4% of the population of Australia who live in Tasmania are represented by 16% of the seats in the Senate, an over-representation by a factor of 6.6.

9.6 CONCLUSION

The inequality of the strength of individual votes, resulting from the equal allocation of Senate seats to each State irrespective of population, makes it incompatible with democratic theory for the Senate to have equal power with the House of Representatives. In addition, the Senate's power to block supply is incompatible with the system of responsible government. For this reason, the power of the Senate should be reduced to that of delaying ordinary legislation for one year and money Bills for one month. Such a

47 Evans, 2001, 18.

reduction in the Senate's power would make its State-based allocation of seats unobjectionable, and would preserve the scrutiny role its Committees perform in ensuring accountability of the executive. Finally, and in accordance with the discussion in Chapter 6, the Constitution should accord special representation to indigenous people in the Senate in recognition of their special status in Australia.

THE HEAD OF STATE

10.1 THE ROLE OF THE HEAD OF STATE

Of all constitutional issues facing Australia, the identity of our Head of State is the least important from the perspective of the practical operation of the Constitution, and the least pressing of the reform measures recommended in this book. Nevertheless, attention needs to be paid to the issue because, even if Australia did not change the identity of the Head of State, there is a need for reform in relation to the status of the rules governing the exercise of the powers attaching to that office. However, if we did replace the Queen with an Australian Head of State, it would also be necessary to amend the Constitution to provide for matters such as the mechanics of choosing and dismissing such a person. Before addressing possible areas of reform, it is as well to give a brief overview of the current position and how the monarch, Governor-General and cabinet interact.

10.2 THE POWERS OF THE HEAD OF STATE

Whatever one's opinion on the merits of the republic issue, one must, at least, be clear who is currently Australia's Head of State. The phrase 'Head of State' is a colloquial term not mentioned in the Constitution. But if by 'Head of State' we mean the ultimate source of executive power under the Constitution, then it is quite clear from the text of the Constitution that that person is the monarch of the United Kingdom. The preamble to the Commonwealth of Australia Constitution Act 1900 refers to the establishment of a 'Federal Commonwealth *under the Crown of the United Kingdom*' (emphasis added), and s 61 of the Constitution states that:

> The executive power of the Commonwealth is vested in the Queen and is exercisable by the Governor-General *as the Queen's representative*, and extends to the execution and maintenance of this Constitution, and of the laws of the Commonwealth. [Emphasis added.]

Of all aspects of the public debate on the 1999 referendum, the suggestion by some elements within the monarchist camp that the Governor-General is Head of State was regrettable, because such a statement is explicable only as a manifestation of either profound ignorance or outright dishonesty. That statement was only marginally worse than one made by a federal government minister, Bronwyn Bishop (concurred in by yet another minister, Tony Abbott), to the effect that Australians should not vote for a republic, because the Weimar Constitution in Germany was republican in nature, and Hitler was able to overthrow it![1]

1 David Marr, 'Hitler's spectre becomes pundits' latter day tyranny' (1999) *Sydney Morning Herald*, 16 October, 1.

Given that the monarch of the United Kingdom is our Head of State in the sense used above, the question, then, is how do she, her representative – the Governor-General (acting in terms of Letters Patent issued by the Queen), and the cabinet interact? Here the difference, indeed, the frequent inconsistency, between law and convention are important. According to the law as embodied in the Commonwealth Constitution, the powers of the Governor-General (acting as the Queen's representative) can be divided into two classes: the first is a set of powers[2] which the Constitution expressly states are to be exercised by the 'Governor-General in Council' – in other words, by the Governor-General acting on the advice of the government of the day. The second consists of a set of unqualified and apparently independently exercised powers, such as those which vest in the Governor-General the authority to summon, prorogue and dissolve Parliament (s 5), to order a double dissolution and convene a joint sitting in certain circumstances (s 57), to assent to legislation (s 59), and to serve as Commander-in-Chief of the armed forces (s 68), to name but a few. Perhaps the most important power, conferred by s 64, is that the Governor-General has the power to appoint Ministers of State to administer Commonwealth government departments, who hold office 'during the pleasure of' the Governor-General – in other words, subject to dismissal by him at will. This, essentially, puts into Australian law the legal position that applies in the United Kingdom, where, in theory, the Queen can dismiss the Prime Minister or members of the cabinet.

However, to focus on the strict legal position in respect of the second set of powers (those which appear to be exercised independently) would, of course, be to give a completely misleading impression of how the Constitution actually works. The late 17th and early 18th centuries witnessed a crucial shift in power from Crown to Parliament in the United Kingdom following the Glorious Revolution of 1688, and the deposition by Parliament of James II. The practical effect of this shift in power was the gradual development of the conventions of responsible government during the 18th century, the most important of which are that a Prime Minister and cabinet (rather than the monarch) would exercise day to day executive power, that in choosing the Prime Minister, the monarch would select someone who has the support of the House of Commons, and that the monarch would always give assent to legislation passed by the two Houses of Parliament. Note that these changes, although of fundamental practical importance, were not mirrored in the law, which continues to vest complete executive power in the monarch. This, then, reveals the nature of conventions: they are rules of conduct which all participants in the system obey, but which are not laws, and for which there is thus no remedy obtainable from the courts.[3] Although the monarch could, in theory, dismiss the

2 These include the power to call an election for the House of Representatives (s 32), creating government departments (s 64), appointing public servants (s 67) and appointing federal judges (s 67).

3 For an illustration of this, see *Madzimbamuto v Lardner-Burke* [1969] 1 AC 645. This case addressed *inter alia* a convention which had been established between the United Kingdom government and the Southern Rhodesian government to the effect that the United Kingdom would not legislate for Southern Rhodesia except at its request, even though, as a Crown Colony, Southern Rhodesia was subject to the legislative power of the United Kingdom and the Colonial Laws Validity Act 1865. After the Southern Rhodesian government unilaterally declared independence on 11 November 1965, the United Kingdom Parliament passed the Southern Rhodesia Act 1965, in which that Parliament declared its continuing sovereignty over Southern Rhodesia. In *Madzimbamuto* the Privy Council rejected the argument that the establishment of the convention (which had even been recognised in correspondence between the United Kingdom and the Southern Rhodesian Premier) was enforceable at law. For an affirmation of this principle by the Supreme Court of Canada, see *Re Amendment to the Constitution of Canada* (1982) 125 DLR (3rd) 1.

United Kingdom Prime Minister and cabinet, and govern the country him or herself, to do so would create a political crisis. Moreover, although such steps would, in themselves, be legal, illegality could arise when, for example, government departments ran out of money, and Parliament refused to enact taxation and appropriations legislation.

At federation, it was understood that all these conventions of responsible government which had developed in the United Kingdom (and which had, indeed, operated in the separate colonies of Australia for decades prior to federation), would operate in tandem with the Commonwealth Constitution. Thus, in the case of the apparently independent powers of the summoning and dissolution of Parliament, assenting to legislation, acting as Commander-in-Chief of the armed forces, *et cetera*, it has always been understood that by convention the Governor-General usually exercises them on the advice of the cabinet.

However, it is also recognised that there are circumstances in which the Governor-General can exercise some of his powers independently of advice, albeit subject to conventional rules. These are commonly referred to as the 'reserve powers', but this is somewhat misleading – there is no separate set of powers known as reserve powers – rather, there are *circumstances* in which the statutory powers of the Governor-General (found in ss 5 and 64 of the Constitution), can be exercised independently. The key issue, and one over which there is some controversy (as the following paragraphs will demonstrate), is precisely what the conventions of the Constitution are in relation to these powers. Exactly when can the Governor-General act without advice, and what rules circumscribe his actions when he does so?

First, it is convenient to identify the powers which, in certain circumstances, the Governor-General can act independently. Undoubtedly of greatest political importance are the instances in which the Governor-General engages in independent exercise of the s 64 power to appoint and dismiss members of the executive. The power of selecting the Prime Minister is obviously a matter upon which the Governor-General cannot take advice. However, the exercise of this power is subject to the convention that the Governor-General chooses as Prime Minister the leader of the party or coalition which is able to command a majority in the House of Representatives, and then acts on the advice of that Prime Minister in appointing the other Ministers. The s 64 power to dismiss has proved to be more controversial. Most authorities would agree that, according to convention, the Governor-General may dismiss a Prime Minister who no longer has the confidence of the House of Representatives and who refuses to resign, or who persists in illegal conduct.[4] Still subject to heated debate, however, is what the rule is where, as in 1975, a government has a majority in the House of Representatives but cannot get supply through the Senate. This issue is addressed separately in the next paragraph. The other section of the Constitution which confers powers on the Governor-General which can sometimes be exercised independently is the s 5 power to dissolve Parliament. Normally, this power will be exercised on advice, but authorities agree that convention permits the Governor-General to dissolve Parliament on his own initiative if, having dismissed a

4 For an overview of the reserve powers, see Republic Advisory Committee, 1993, Vol 2, 242–69; Joseph and Castan, 2001, 103; and Booker, Glass and Watt, 1998, 144–45.

Prime Minister,[5] no-one else is able to command a majority in the House. More controversial is the suggestion that the Governor-General may refuse a Prime Minister's request to dissolve Parliament if, shortly after an election has been held, a government loses its majority (for example, through defections), and that, in those circumstances, the Governor-General could call upon someone who was able to command a majority to form a government.[6] There is some precedent for this from the international Commonwealth,[7] but, in general, the principle that the voters should be the ultimate arbiters of whether a government should survive militates against a Governor-General ever refusing a dissolution. The only obvious exception to this rule is where a Prime Minister has lost an election and the new Parliament has not yet assembled.[8] It would obviously subvert the democratic process if the Prime Minister was allowed to call another election in order to avoid a vote of no confidence by the new Parliament.[9] Interestingly, in the case of Ireland, where the Constitution expressly confers power on the President to refuse a dissolution,[10] that power has never been exercised. The reason for this is explained by Duffy, as follows:[11]

> The ability to ask for and get a dissolution is one of the key powers at the disposal of a Prime Minister. It enables him/her to threaten to call an election at times suitable for them and unsuitable for opponents whether inside or outside their political party. For a Taoiseach [Prime Minister] to have his request for an election turned down would at the very least be seen as humiliating. It could also strengthen the hands of his or her opponents in any attempt to depose them from the party leadership.

I would submit that those arguments would be equally applicable in any parliamentary democracy, including that of Australia.

The events of 1975 illustrate how the uncertain nature of conventions can give rise to a political crisis. The origin of the 1975 dispute lies in the fact that, as was noted in Chapter 9, the conferral of power on the Senate to block legislation which is a matter of confidence for the government situated in the House of Representatives, is inconsistent with the doctrines of responsible government: on the one hand, the conventions of responsible government inherited from the United Kingdom require the resignation of a government which cannot get money bills through Parliament, because failure to get money bills through is an indication of lack of confidence, as well as something which is

5 The argument has also been advanced that the Governor-General may dissolve Parliament without dismissing a Prime Minister if that Prime Minister has lost confidence or persists in unlawful action – see McGarvie, 1999, 173–76. On this basis, McGarvie argues that in 1975 Kerr should have simply dissolved Parliament and should not have dismissed Whitlam, as the latter still had the confidence of the House of Representatives. However, that argument rests on the assumption that it is in accordance with convention for a Governor-General to dissolve Parliament without the advice of the Prime Minister. This is not in accordance with the generally understood content of the conventions. Presumably, however, one could argue that having dismissed Whitlam and accepted Fraser's advice to dissolve Parliament, Kerr could safely have received the Speaker of the House of Representatives and re-appointed Whitlam on the basis of the House's vote of confidence in Whitlam just prior to the announcement of the dissolution, thus allowing the dissolution to stand and Whitlam to fight the election as Prime-Minister.

6 McGarvie, 1999, 51–53 and 160.

7 See, eg, the Byng-King controversy in Canada in 1925, discussed in Joseph, 1993, 601.

8 *Ibid*, 603.

9 Republic Advisory Committee, 1993, Vol 2, 268.

10 Constitution of Ireland 1937, Art 15.1.2.

11 Duffy, 1993, 125–26.

ultimately causative of a breach of law, when the government spends money without the approval of Parliament. In the setting of the United Kingdom, bicameralism presents no problem because, following the Parliament Act of 1911, a government which is able to get money bills through the House to which it is responsible (the House of Commons) cannot find itself blocked by the House of Lords (to which it is not responsible). In Australia, however, the fact that s 53 of the Constitution permits the Senate to block supply means that the position can arise, as it did in the case of the Whitlam government in 1975, that the government has a majority in the House of Representatives (an indication of having confidence), but, nevertheless, cannot obtain supply (an indication of not having confidence). Whether Kerr acted in accordance with convention in dismissing Whitlam depends upon one's view of which of these indications Kerr should have heeded. An inability to secure supply ultimately results in an inability to govern lawfully and, assuming that the Senate would have persisted in not passing the budget, and Whitlam would have persisted in clinging on to office, Kerr had either to exercise the power to dismiss for lack of confidence, on the assumption that inability to obtain supply equalled lack of confidence (which is what he did), or wait until the government ran out of money and the courts pronounced its continued activities unlawful, whereupon, if Whitlam had still stayed in office, Kerr could have dismissed him in accordance with the convention that the Governor-General can dismiss a Prime Minister who persists in illegal conduct. Finally, irrespective of whether Kerr was correct in equating lack of supply with lack of confidence, his dismissal of Whitlam can, of course, be justified without recourse to convention simply by saying that, in strict law, s 64 of the Constitution gave him the power to dismiss. Some argue that, because the Governor-General would then have been acting under the authority of a statutory provision, such an exercise of power could have been reviewed by the courts.[12] However, the use of the words 'during the pleasure of the Governor-General', and the obviously political reasons for which the discretion would be exercised, make it highly unlikely that judicial review would have succeeded.

I have already argued for parliamentary reform which would eliminate the problem that gave rise to the Whitlam-Kerr crisis – namely, the curtailing of the powers of the Senate. But even if the particular problems caused by bicameralism were removed from the Constitution, the preceding paragraphs indicate that there is a need to remove the uncertainties that surround other aspects of the Governor-General's independent exercise of ss 5 and 64 powers. The vagueness surrounding the conventions governing these powers, coupled with the fact that they are not rules of law and are, therefore, not legally enforceable, injects an element of uncertainty into constitutional law in relation to matters which are fundamental to its operation. For this reason, and irrespective of whether Australia became a republic or not, it would be helpful to codify the conventions and to elevate them to the status of legally enforceable provisions contained in the Constitution. This is neither as revolutionary nor as difficult as is sometimes alleged by those constitutional lawyers who seem to relish the vagueness of the conventions. Some argue that it is impossible to codify the conventions, and that a codification could never cover all the exigencies that might arise.[13] This argument seems to be founded on the view that constitutional practice is somehow different from all other areas of human endeavour, and incapable of being subject to comprehensive rules. Perfection is, of course,

12 Sawer, 1977, 148.

13 McGarvie, 1999, 161–62.

unattainable in any area of law, but there is nothing qualitatively different about the constitutional branch that prevents the reduction of its rules to codified form. Furthermore, if conventions were as ethereal as is alleged, surely it would be impossible to make definitive statements about them at all? Yet the strength with which competing views of them are held, and the vigour with which the correctness of these views is asserted, indicates that those who argue these competing points of view believe that at least some things can be stated with a degree of certainty. In simple terms, if language is capable of stating what the conventions are, then surely those statements can be put into the form of legal rules? To the extent that dispute exists in relation to the conventions, surely they are no different from the many other issues that drafters of a new Constitution would need to debate and reach agreement upon? In any event, the evidence that conventions can be codified is provided by the fact that many countries, both Commonwealth and non-Commonwealth, have Heads of State whose functions are the same as those currently performed by the Governor-General in Australia, and whose powers are specified in rules of law contained in the Constitution.[14] Thus in countries such as the Bahamas,[15] Barbados,[16] Grenada[17] and Jamaica,[18] – all of which are Commonwealth countries which are still constitutional monarchies like Australia – the Constitution states that the Governor-General must appoint whoever is able to command a majority in the legislature as Prime Minister, that the Governor-General must dismiss a Prime Minister who no longer commands a majority in the legislature and who refuses to resign or call an election, and either permits or requires the Governor-General to dissolve the legislature if a Prime Minister who has lost the confidence of the legislature fails to resign. Then there are a number of Commonwealth countries – Dominica,[19] Malta[20] and Mauritius,[21] – which are republics with a President as Head of State, whose Constitutions embody exactly the same rules. Finally, one can point to Germany and Ireland, republics which are not members of the Commonwealth, but where similar rules apply: in Germany, the President appoints as Chancellor whoever is elected by a majority of the Bundestag.[22] Where a Chancellor has lost the confidence of the Bundestag and the Bundestag has elected a successor, the President must dismiss the Chancellor.[23] Where the Bundestag fails to elect a new Chancellor, the president may dissolve the Bundestag.[24] In Ireland, the President must appoint as Taoiseach (Prime Minister) whoever is selected by the Dail (the lower house of Parliament),[25] and a Taoiseach who has lost the confidence of the Dail must resign or ask the President to dissolve the Dail (whereupon the new Dail will either confirm the existing Taoiseach, or elect a new one).[26]

14 A convenient summary of the constitutional powers of Heads of State of both Commonwealth and non-Commonwealth countries is to be found in Republic Advisory Committee, 1993, Vol 2, 6–18.

15 Constitution of Bahamas 1973, Arts 66, 73, 74.

16 Constitution of Barbados 1966, Arts 61, 65, and 66.

17 Constitution of Grenada 1973, Arts 52 and 58.

18 Constitution of Jamaica 1962, Arts 64, 70 and 71.

19 Constitution of Dominica 1978, Arts 59, 60 and 63.

20 Constitution of Malta 1964, Arts 76, 79, 80 and 81.

21 Constitution of Mauritius 1968, Arts 57, 59 and 60.

22 Constitution of Germany 1949, Art 63.

23 *Ibid*, Art 68.

24 *Ibid*, Art 63.

25 Constitution of Ireland 1937, Art 13.1.1.

26 *Ibid*, Art 28.10.

Another argument raised against codification is that the enforcement of codified rules by the courts would be impractical, because a Head of State who was determined to breach the Constitution would not heed a court order.[27] That argument would, if taken to its logical conclusion, mean that we should abandon constitutional law in its entirety – it is, of course, true that, practically speaking, the judiciary can do nothing where the executive refuses to comply with court orders; however, the entire constitutional system in countries such as ours, where the doctrine of constitutionalism is respected, rests upon the assumption that court orders will be complied with. The argument that, because a particular aspect of constitutional law (in this instance, a set of rules governing the conduct of a President) would be vulnerable to unconstitutional action, they should not be included in the document, implies that it is pointless to have a Constitution at all.

Codification the powers of the head of state would become particularly important if Australians decided to replace the Queen and Governor-General with a directly elected Head of State. The prospect of a Head of State who believed that, because he or she was popularly elected, he or she had a mandate to exercise the discretion attaching to the office in a politically partisan way, creates the risk that such a person could work very significant constitutional mischief. It is surely true to say that the greater the degree of vagueness in the definition of the powers of an office, the greater the opportunity there is for the abuse of those powers. For this reason, we should be absolutely sure that the holder of that office would be restrained by *legally enforceable* rules of constitutional law, and be compelled to respect the limited role we expect the Head of State to perform in our system of government. Assuming that was done, the risk of the politicisation of the office of Head of State, if direct election was used as the method of choosing that person, would be neutralised. Here, the analogy with the situation in Ireland is pertinent: in Ireland, the President's very limited role is prescribed by the Constitution; there is, therefore, nothing that candidates can promise to do or not do if elected, and, as a consequence, election campaigns for the office are not conducted on a political basis. This issue will be explored further below.

Of course, it would be entirely possible in Australia for the Queen and Governor-General to be replaced by a President exercising his or her powers subject to the same conventions as currently govern the exercise by the Governor-General of his powers. Such a step has been taken by yet other Commonwealth countries.[28] It is simply that a

---

27 McGarvie, 1999, 111–13.

28 Thus when South Africa became a Republic in 1961, the Republic of South Africa Constitution Act 1961 was simply amended in such a way as to substitute references to the Governor-General with those to a State President. Section 7 of the amending Act listed the functions of the State President, which were precisely the same as has been exercised by the Governor-General (to appoint ministers, to convene Parliament and prorogue it, to dissolve Parliament, *et cetera*), and in s 7(4) had a confirmatory provision as follows:

> 7(4) The State President shall in addition as head of the State have such powers and functions as were immediately before the commencement of this Act possessed by the Queen by way of the prerogative.

It was implicit in the 1961 Constitution that in exercising his powers, the State President would be subject to the same conventions as had regulated the conduct of the Governor-General. But any doubt in this regard was eliminated by the inclusion in the Republic of South Africa Constitution Act 1983, which stated as follows:

> 88 The constitutional and parliamentary conventions which existed immediately before the commencement of this Act shall continue to exist except in so far as they are inconsistent with the provisions of this Act.

codification of the conventions would remove uncertainty in an important area of the Constitution.

The conventions could be codified by putting the following rules into the Constitution: after an election, the House of Representatives should assemble and the Head of State (let us assume he was called the President) should appoint as Prime Minister whoever was able to command a majority in the House. That person should then have the power to advise the President as to whom to appoint and dismiss as Ministers heading Commonwealth government departments. The Constitution should also provide that, other than where an election has been held, and the House of Representatives has not yet assembled, the President should dissolve Parliament upon a request by the Prime Minister. The Prime Minister should be able to resign at any time, whereupon the President should appoint as Prime Minister whoever was able to command a majority of the House of Representatives. The same would apply if the Prime Minister died or was incapacitated. If the House passed a motion of no-confidence in the Prime Minister, or failed to pass a bill for the imposition of taxation or the appropriation of money,[29] the Prime Minister would have either to resign (whereupon the President would be required to appoint as Prime Minister whoever did have the confidence of the House of Representatives), or request that the President dissolve Parliament and call an election. If a Prime Minister refused to adopt either of those courses, the President could dismiss the Prime Minister, and appoint as his or her replacement whoever could command a majority in the House (or could secure the passage of the money bill). If there was no such person, the President would be required to dissolve Parliament. The President would also be able to dismiss a Prime Minister if the latter persisted in illegal conduct, which should be defined as refusal to comply with an order of the High Court (other than where there was an appeal pending against the order to the High Court in its appellate jurisdiction). Since that circumstance evinces an unwillingness of the government to comply with the doctrine of constitutionalism, the only remedy would be the dissolution of Parliament by the President, so as to give the voters the opportunity to pass judgment on the government.

Finally, the Constitution would have to make some provision for the continuance of government in circumstances where the President had dismissed the Prime Minister. Two different situations need to be addressed: the first would be where the Prime Minister had been dismissed for not resigning following loss of confidence, or for failure to secure the support of Parliament for a money bill, but there was no-one else who was able to command majority support in the House. In such circumstances, the country would be without government pending the election of a new Parliament. In that situation, I would argue that, since the (former) Prime Minister would obviously be an unsuitable person to appoint as caretaker, the President should be required to appoint as acting Prime Minister the leader of the largest party in Parliament which had not formed part of the dismissed government. This is, of course, precisely what happened in 1975, when Kerr appointed Fraser as caretaker Prime Minister pending the election of a new House of Representatives. The other situation in which the Constitution would have to make

29 This would be necessary in order to prevent governments tacking other pieces of legislation on to taxation or appropriation legislation, and thereby placing Parliament in the position either of passing some non-tax measure it did not want, or of running the political risks associated with unseating the government. Such a provision does, of course, already exist in the Constitution in s 55.

provision for a caretaker would be where the Prime Minister had been dismissed for illegal conduct. In that circumstance, the Prime Minister might still have majority support in the House, but here, too, it would obviously be inappropriate for him, or even another member of his government, to be appointed as acting Prime Minister. Here, too, the best option would be for the Constitution to require that the President appoint the leader of the largest non-governing party as acting Prime Minister until the new House of Representatives convenes after a general election has been held. The prospect, in either of these circumstances, of having the leader of the opposition appointed as Prime Minister, even in a caretaker role, would act as a powerful disincentive on Prime Ministers not to act unconstitutionally.

10.3 DO WE NEED A HEAD OF STATE?

I began this chapter by noting that the identity of the Head of State was of relatively little importance from the perspective of the operation of the Constitution. I then argued that of real importance was the definition in the Constitution of the powers of the Head of State, be that of the Queen exercising powers through the Governor-General, or of an Australian Head of State. In this section, however, I address the questions of whether we should replace the Crown with an Australian Head of State and, if so, how the incumbent of that office should be chosen.

Provided that the system of parliamentary government was not disturbed, the issue of whether we should sever the link with the Crown is essentially one of politics and symbolism, rather than of law. As a constitutional lawyer, I find that I have no strong views on the question one way or the other. However, approaching the issue purely as one of symbol, I think that it would be preferable for Australia to sever the link with the Crown in order to emphasise its own national identity. As proponents of an Australian republic have pointed out, it is anomalous that a country such as ours, populated by people with a diverse range of ethnicities, should look to a distant land with whom increasingly fewer number of us can have any connection, to provide us with a Head of State. Having the monarch of the United Kingdom as our Head of State is confusing to other countries, and compromises our independent role on the world stage in appearance, even if not in fact. However, the most persuasive argument in favour of an Australian republic is that, by severing the link with the Crown, it would become possible for an Australian to aspire to the highest office in the land, an aspiration which every citizen of a free country should surely be able to entertain.

Before addressing the issue of how best to choose an Australian President (and here I acknowledge that some people would prefer that an Australian Head of State be called the Governor-General rather than the President), we should perhaps pause to ask whether we need a separate office of Head of State at all. If the Head of State is to act in accordance with convention and, as I have argued above, it would be a good idea to codify the conventions, could we not do away with the office and include in the Constitution a set of self-executing rules specifying what was to happen in given circumstances without the intervention of a human agent?

An example of a system which operates without an office equivalent to that of a Head of State is provided by the Australian Capital Territory (Self-Government) Act 1988 (Cth), which operates as the Constitution for the Territory. The provisions of the Act show how the rules of parliamentary government can be made to operate automatically: the Territory's Assembly elects one of its number as Chief Minister (thus giving effect to the convention that the head of government is the person who has the confidence of the legislature).[30] The Chief Minister then selects the other members of the executive.[31] The Chief Minister must resign if the Assembly passes a vote of no confidence in him or her.[32] The Assembly must then elect one of its number to be the new Chief Minister,[33] but if a deadlock occurs and the Assembly is unable to elect a Chief Minister the Governor-General may dissolve the Assembly and elections will be held[34] or, if he does not, the Commonwealth Minister for Territories may call an election.[35] The system in the Territory departs from the normal rules of responsible government in that the Chief Minister cannot dissolve the Assembly (there being fixed three-year terms between elections) except in the already mentioned circumstance when there is deadlock over the choice of a Chief Minister, and the only ground upon which the Chief Minister is compelled to resign is a formal motion of no-confidence[36] which does not include failure to obtain supply.[37] The ACT model is not one which I would recommend for the Commonwealth. It is useful to have a person who represents the nation in a non-political way, and who is available to discharge ceremonial duties on behalf of the nation. The ACT example is adduced simply to show that, at least in one Australian jurisdiction, the operation of executive government has been codified to a significant extent without adverse political consequences, and that this suggests that we have little to fear from a codification of the type I recommended in the previous section of this chapter.

10.4 SELECTING A HEAD OF STATE

Assuming that the office of Head of State was retained – in other words, that the Governor-General's powers continued to be applied by a human being (albeit acting in accordance with codified rules) – what rules should govern the selection and dismissal of such an Australian Head of State? It was undoubtedly in relation to the appointment and dismissal of the Head of State that most confusion was evident during the 1999 republic referendum.

As matters stand, the monarch appoints the Governor-General, by convention acting on the advice of the Prime Minister – in other words, in reality the office of Governor-General is in the gift of the Prime Minister. The effective control that the Prime Minister currently enjoys over the selection of Governors-General makes it particularly ironic that,

30 Australian Capital Territory (Self-Government) Act 1988, s 40(1).

31 *Ibid*, s 39(1).

32 *Ibid*, s 46(1)(c)(ii).

33 *Ibid*, s 40(3).

34 *Ibid*, s 16(1)(a).

35 *Ibid*, s 48(2).

36 *Ibid*, s 19.

37 Crispin Hull, 'The rules of self-rule' (2000) *Canberra Times*, 1 July, 2.

although a majority of Australians appear to want a republic, the 1999 referendum proposal, which would have required the participation of a wider range of people in the selection of the Governor-General than at present, was roundly criticised by proponents of the 'No' case as creating a 'politicians' republic'[38] in which '[o]nly politicians will be allowed to pick the President'.[39] The 1999 proposal contemplated that a Presidential Nominations Committee would prepare a list of nominees for the presidency, that the Prime Minister and leader of the opposition would agree on a single nominee,[40] and that the choice would then be approved by a two-thirds majority at a joint sitting of the House of Representatives and the Senate. Far from what the monarchists referred to as 'removing the checks and balances of the current system'[41] (of which there are none), the proposed method for appointment would have made it far more likely that a non-partisan nominee would have become President (given that the agreement of both Prime Minister and leader of the Opposition, plus a two-thirds majority of Parliament was required), than does the current system, which effectively invites the Prime Minister to appoint a political crony as Governor-General. In short, the proposed selection method for the President maximised the chances that a politically neutral person – which is precisely who one needs in the post, given the constitutional powers vested in it – would have become President. Ironically, the 1999 proposal would have made it virtually impossible that a 'politician', in the sense of a partisan figure, would have obtained the office.

By contrast, that the Head of State should be directly elected – undoubtedly attractive because of its appeal to democratic principle – raises the risk that the office could become politicised. A particular danger would arise if candidates were selected by political parties, because even though the office carries no discretionary powers, the identification of the incumbent with a political party would undermine the image of political neutrality which the role requires. Indeed, some opponents of the direct election model argue that direct election raises the risk that the office of Head of State would become an alternate focus of power to that of the Prime Minister, who is head of government, and that the incumbent might come to believe that, because they were directly elected, they had a mandate to exercise the powers of the office in accordance with their own political discretion, something which would be incompatible with the neutral role the Head of State is expected to discharge in a system of parliamentary democracy.[42] The solution to this problem, already alluded to in the discussion relating to the powers of the Head of State in 10.2, above, is to codify the conventions that govern the exercise of those powers. In that event, it would be clear to everyone what the powers of the office were and, more importantly, how they were to be exercised. Because the circumstances in which the powers of the office could be exercise would be prescribed by the Constitution, and would involve little or no discretion, candidates for the office would be unable to pledge to the electorate that they would either do or not do something. Election campaigns might

38 Australian Electoral Commission, 1999, 9.

39 *Ibid*, 13.

40 The Prime Minister and the leader of the opposition would not have been bound to confine themselves to the list of nominees prepared by the Committee and could have put a name not on the Committee's list before Parliament.

41 Australian Electoral Commission, 1999, 9.

42 McGarvie, 1999, 117–18, 137–40 and 201.

be bland, becoming little more than popularity contests, but they certainly would not be political in the party political sense of that term, because it would be impossible to conduct a political campaign for an office the powers of which were wholly dictated by the Constitution. A good example of such a system in operation is that of Ireland, which has a Westminster system of responsible government, coupled with the direct election of a President[43] whose limited powers are laid down in the Constitution,[44] and where, in the words of Duffy:[45]

> It is also arguable that Irish politicians have, perhaps subconsciously, been influenced in how they perceive the office of President by the neighbouring British monarchy. Just as it would be unthinkable for Queen Elizabeth II or any of her immediate successors to become identifiable in the public mind as a rival source of political authority to the British government, so Irish governments and politicians have also been careful to ensure that the office of President is not too identified in the public mind as a rival source of authority to the Taoiseach and his ministers.

The powers of the Irish President are much less than those of an Australian Governor-General: according to the Constitution, the President must appoint as Taoiseach (Prime Minister) whoever is elected to that office by the Dail[46] (the lower House of Parliament). The President cannot dismiss the Taoiseach, but the Constitution requires a Taoiseach who has lost the confidence of the Dail either to resign or to ask the President to dissolve the Dail.[47] If the Taoiseach does not have the confidence of the Dail after the elections, he must then resign.[48] It is thus clear that the Irish Constitution successfully codifies the conventions of responsible government. Furthermore, the fact that the President's powers are prescribed by the Constitution makes the experience of that country a valid analogy for what would be the situation in Australia if the powers of the Head of State were codified: for much of the time since Ireland's Constitution came into force, a single candidate was nominated for President on a bipartisan basis.[49] However, even the contested elections of 1990 (won by Mary Robinson, who stood against the candidate sponsored by the major parties), and that of 1997 (won by Mary McAleese), were not conducted on a party political basis by the candidates, but, rather, focussed on the candidates' personalities, their experience and the likely effect their election would have on the country's image.[50] It is, therefore, reasonable to deduce from the Irish example that if an Australian President was directly elected to an office with strictly circumscribed powers, he or she would be no more likely to act in a partisan manner than any Irish President has done.

43 Constitution of Ireland 1937, Art 12.2.1.

44 For a discussion of the constitutional provisions relating to the powers of the President, see Duffy, 1993, 120–28.

45 *Ibid*, 137.

46 Constitution of Ireland 1937, Art 13.1.1.

47 *Ibid*, Art 28.10.

48 *Ibid*.

49 Thus a single candidate was returned unopposed in all presidential elections held prior to 1990 – see Hogan and Whyte, 1994, 84.

50 Duffy, 1993, 146–47.

Public opinion polls indicate strong support for a directly elected Head of State.[51] Realistically speaking, then, a new Constitution should be designed on the assumption that this is the most likely outcome of the republic issue. That being the case, the necessity for codifying the powers of the office of Head of State is vital. As stated earlier in this chapter, it would be fundamentally incompatible with the system of parliamentary government for the Head of State to believe that, because they had been directly elected, they had a political role to play. The Constitution must make clear that the Head of State is subject to rules in the way he or she exercises the powers of the office, that there is no political discretion involved in the exercise of those powers, and that a breach of the rules contained in the Constitution can be remedied by the courts.

10.5 DISMISSING A HEAD OF STATE

As in the case of the selection of the Governor-General, the current position is that effective power to dismiss the Governor-General lies in the hands of the Prime Minister, who needs simply to advise the monarch to dismiss the Governor-General for that to occur. Prior to the 1999 referendum, the suggestion was made that a Prime Minister who was seeking the dismissal of the Governor-General in politically charged circumstances would not be able to obtain immediate action from the Queen, and that dismissal would take a week or two.[52] This argument is untenable. Faced with a request to dismiss a Governor-General, the monarch would be obliged by convention to comply without equivocation – there would not, as McGarvie suggests, be anything for her to 'inquire or consult' about,[53] nor is it conceivable, as former Governor-General Sir William McKell suggested,[54] that the Monarch would make herself unavailable to a Prime Minister who was attempting to contact her for that purpose. Such overtly political (mis)conduct by a monarch would simply not occur. Furthermore, there is precedent from Australia that the monarch would act immediately, in that, within a day of making the request, Whitlam secured the dismissal of Sir John Hannah (who held the office of stand-by Administrator)[55] following a political attack on the government by the latter.

In Chapter 1, I identified the Prime Minister's control over dismissal of the Governor-General as a flaw in the Constitution. This became evident during the constitutional crisis of 1975, because the two major protagonists each had the power to dismiss the other – Kerr could dismiss Whitlam, and Whitlam could contact the Queen and request her to dismiss Kerr, and this possibility of being dismissed was a factor in Kerr's mind in deciding how long to allow the impasse between the government and the Senate to persist.[56] Had Kerr not had the threat of dismissal hanging over him, he might well have allowed a few more days to pass before deciding to dismiss Whitlam. Certainly, had

51 In January 1995, a nationwide Herald-AGB McNair poll indicated that 88% of respondents preferred direct election as the means of selecting an Australian Head of State – see Milton Cockburn, 'Voter support strong, but only when they decide who leads' (1995) *Sydney Morning Herald*, 7 June, 4.

52 McGarvie, 1999, 62 and 165–70.

53 *Ibid*, 168–69.

54 John O'Hara, 'Un-demonising of Sir John Kerr' (1996) *Weekend Australian*, 6–7 April, 12.

55 The Administrator stands ready to act for the Governor-General if the latter is unavailable.

56 McGarvie, 1999, 166–67.

Whitlam got wind of Kerr's plan to dismiss him, the risk of Whitlam launching a pre-emptive strike would obviously have been very great. It clearly makes no sense for each of these figures to have the power to dismiss the other, reducing the resolution of a constitutional crisis to the issue of who reaches for their telephone first.

The solution proposed to this problem by the 1999 referendum proposal was not satisfactory. Under that proposal, and in stark contrast to the appointment procedure which required bipartisan support, the Prime Minister, acting on his own, would have had the power to dismiss the President. The Prime Minister would have been required to obtain the approval of the House of Representatives within 30 days. This was, presumably, designed to ensure that a Prime Minister who no longer had the confidence of the House, and was going to be dismissed by the Governor-General, could not avoid dismissal by getting in first. Inexplicably, however, failure of the House to approve the dismissal was explicitly stated not to result in the restoration to office of the former President, which made the protection of the President nugatory. Although the proposed model was good, in that a dismissed President would be replaced by the most senior State Governor, who would be Acting President until the appointment procedure had been completed – in other words, the Prime Minister would not have been able to replace the dismissed President with his own choice – the fact remained that the 1999 proposal would still have seen the President and Prime Minister with the power to dismiss each other.

An equally unsatisfactory method of dismissing a Head of State would be by a vote of the legislature. Dismissal by a majority vote of the legislature would offer the Head of State no greater protection than would dismissal by the Prime Minister, because, in either case, the will of the governing party would be determinative of the issue. Furthermore, setting a special majority of the legislature – say two-thirds – would create the reverse problem, in that the opposition would be able to block a dismissal for its own partisan reasons even if dismissal was justified.[57]

Irrespective of whether an Australian Head of State was selected on a bipartisan basis by Parliament, or was directly elected by the voters, the most politically neutral way to address the question of dismissal would be to have the Head of State serve a fixed term,[58] subject only to impeachment upon application to the High Court on grounds of misbehaviour or incapacity. If impeachment occurred, the most senior State Governor should become Acting President, pending the choice of a new President in accordance with the procedures contained in the Constitution. This arrangement would ensure that an Australian Head of State would not be placed in the invidious position of Sir William Kerr, of fearing dismissal unless he acted first to dismiss a Prime Minister who had refused to comply with a constitutional obligation to resign.

---

57 *Ibid*, 98–101.

58 This term should not coincide with that of the House of Representatives, a device which would provide additional insurance (along with codification of the powers of the office) against elections to the office becoming identified with party politics. The current five-year term of the Governor-General would meet this requirement.

10.6 MOVING TOWARDS AN AUSTRALIAN HEAD OF STATE

This book is about constitutional reform in general, and proposes an entirely new Constitution of which a change to an Australian Head of State would be but one part. In the next chapter, I discuss how to achieve constitutional reform, and evaluate the relative strengths and weaknesses of a piecemeal approach, on the one hand, and the enactment of a new Constitution as a single process on the other. However, it is apposite, in light of the history of the 1999 referendum, to close this chapter with some remarks on the question of how, if the Head of State issue was being addressed in isolation, that change should be effected.

In retrospect, it appears that the process used by the government in 1999 was designed to ensure that the referendum would fail. The first stage in the process was the summoning in November 1998 of a Constitutional Convention. This body was of questionable legitimacy, given that it was only partly elected. The Convention was charged with the responsibility of agreeing upon a model for an Australian Head of State, which would then be put into the form of a constitutional amendment to be voted on in a s 128 referendum. What model should be put to referendum thus became the subject of manoeuvrings between the major factions in the Convention, namely, republicans who favoured a direct election model, republicans who rejected direct election, and monarchists who did not want a republic at all. As noted earlier in this chapter, the Convention eventually recommended that the Governor-General be replaced by a President elected by a two-thirds majority of Parliament, from a list prepared by a Nominations Committee made up of community groups. An objectionable part of the model was the provision for dismissal of the President by the Prime Minister, which was obviously inconsistent with the parliamentary appointment process. However, looking back at the events of 1998–99, it is clear that by far the greatest flaw lay not in the model put before the voters, but rather in the process used to arrive at it. The fusing together of what were two separate questions – whether the people wished to sever links with the Crown and, if so, what model of Australian republic should be adopted – left voters feeling that they had been presented by a *fait accomplis*. Combining these separate issues into one put many republicans in the position of either having to choose a type of republic they did not want, or of retaining the monarchy, and, as we know, many chose the latter course.

Recently, however, the republican debate has been re-ignited by a proposed process that would be radically different from that used in 1998–99. At the Peoples Conference, held in 2001 at Corowa (where in 1893 the first meeting was held that ultimately led to the formation of federation), a joint proposal by Bill Peach, George Winterton, Walter Phillips and the author was accepted as the process that should be used to place the issue of an Australian republic before the voters. Under the Corowa Plan (also known, with intended irony, as the Royal Hotel Resolution, after the establishment where it was drafted), a multi-party Parliamentary Joint Committee would draft a plebiscite which would ask the voters three questions: whether they wanted a republic with an Australian Head of State, whether they would like such a person to be called President or Governor-General, and which of four models of Head of State they would prefer. The models proposed were appointment by the Prime Minister, election by a two-thirds vote of the House of Representatives, selection by an electoral college, or direct election by the voters with the powers of the office codified. Following the plebiscite, a Constitutional Convention would be elected to flesh out the details of the model chosen by the people (assuming, of course, that an affirmative vote had been achieved in response to the first plebiscite question, regarding severing links with the monarchy). Once the Convention had completed the final draft of the model, it would be put to the voters in a s 128 referendum. The advantage of the Corowa Plan is that it gives voters a choice, both in relation to severing the links with the monarchy and the preferred model of republic, and requires the Convention to follow the wishes of the people rather than, as in the case of the 1998 Convention, giving that body the power to prescribe a model to the people. Finally, the Corowa Plan ensures that should the plebiscite result in the direct election model being chosen, the Convention would be required to codify the powers of the office of Head of State. The Convention could, if it wished, codify the powers of the Head of State if any of the other three models was chosen in the plebiscite, but codification would be mandatory in the case where the direct election model was chosen. This would avoid the danger alluded to earlier in this chapter of an elected Head of State seeking to supplant the Prime Minister in a manner inconsistent with our system of parliamentary government. The Corowa Plan thus makes it entirely possible to have an elected Head of State exercising codified powers which are exactly the same as those which are currently exercised by the Governor-General. Of course, whether the Corowa Plan (or any more general programme of constitutional reform) comes to fruition depends upon the extent to which it is possible to muster the political will in Parliament to initiate the plebiscite and referendum process. What is needed to achieve constitutional reform is discussed in the next chapter.

CHAPTER 11

ACHIEVING CONSTITUTIONAL REFORM

11.1 THE PROSPECTS OF CONSTITUTIONAL REFORM

At the beginning of this book, I said that anyone proposing constitutional reform in Australia is either over-optimistic or expects a lifespan beyond the expected norm. I hope that I have succeeded both in showing why constitutional reform is necessary, and in dispelling some of the misconceptions which abound, both in relation to the current constitutional order, and in relation to the consequences of changing it. Furthermore, some of those who took the opportunity to evaluate the Constitution during the centenary of federation year, came to the conclusion that the time was ripe for thorough-going constitutional reform.[1] Nevertheless, the problem remains as to how to effect constitutional reform, given the prevailing climate in which the attitude of voters towards reform can, at best, be described as being characterised by inertia, but among most of whom there is outright opposition born of profound suspicion about change.

A significant impediment to constitutional reform is the suspicion with which proposals to amend the Constitution are viewed. In the words of Colin Hughes:[2]

> To the extent that Canberra is perceived as a remote, hostile and selfish force in Australian politics, any proposal to tamper with the federal constitution is perceived as a potential Trojan horse for the aggrandizement of alien influences.

There is some excuse for this attitude on the part of voters: the only constitutional reforms thus far suggested by the Howard government have been the extension of terms for members of the House of Representatives from three years to four (with the extension of Senators' terms from six years to eight), and the resolution of deadlocks between the House and the Senate by a joint sitting without a double-dissolution election.[3] The first of these has, not surprisingly, been seen as a change which would primarily benefit politicians, while the second does not go far enough in addressing the issues of principle arising from the Constitution's conferral of a blocking power on the unrepresentative Senate.

However, I would suggest that there are more fundamental forces at work in creating impediments to constitutional change than a simple animus against the federal government.[4] It would not be stating anything novel to note that Australians are inherently suspicious of politicians. Because proposals for constitutional change usually

---

1 See Irving, 2001, 194. For earlier works containing proposals for a general review of the Constitution, see Solomon, 1998; and McMillan, Evans and Storey, 1983.

2 Hughes, 1994, 164.

3 Christina Jackman, 'Four-year terms wins Libs' vote' (2002) *Sunday Times*, 14 April, 29; Ross Peake, 'Libs seek to cut Senate powers' (2002) *Canberra Times*, 16 April, 8.

4 Galligan, 1995, 128–32 identifies partisanship, voter ignorance and apathy and a belief that amendments to the federal Constitution will automatically be inimical to the interests of the States.

emanate from the mouths of politicians, they are immediately tainted because of their source, irrespective of their substance. This means that most proposals for constitutional change are foredoomed to failure. At the core of this anti-politician attitude lies the absence of any conception in Australian society of the ordinary person as a *zoön politikon* – the Aristotelian citizen who bears political rights and responsibilities in equal measure with all other citizens, be they office holders or not. Of course, this view of the citizen was a product of the particular circumstances of Ancient Greek democracy, in which every citizen was a member of the legislature, and many were office holders as well. Nevertheless, I would argue that the obligation attaching to citizens to be involved, or at the very least, informed and interested, applies in modern representative democracies in the same way as in the direct democracies of the ancient world. The 'them' and 'us' attitude citizens have towards politicians is the product of a belief that politics is the realm of the professional politician, not the ordinary person. But the consequence of this stance of non-involvement is that people have only themselves to blame if the system has produced politicians they do not trust. The remedy for that circumstance is to become involved, and to change the system, rather than to withdraw and adopt an attitude which is negative and cynical. In short, it can be said that, as in other countries, Australians get the governments they deserve. So far as constitutional change is concerned, it is surely inconsistent for voters to say 'We have no interest being involved, leave politics to the politicians', and also to say 'We don't want constitutional reform because it is being promoted by politicians who, as a class, we do not trust'. Australians need to accept the obligations that go along with the rights enjoyed in a democracy and, if dissatisfied with those they have elected, to elect someone else or to stand as candidates themselves. Ultimately, the strength of a democracy depends upon the ordinary citizen's commitment to, and involvement in, its workings. Disengagement and, still worse, uniformed criticism from a position of disengagement, is wholly unsatisfactory.

Apart from active hostility to reform bred of cynicism about politicians, the other factor which stands as a barrier to constitutional reform is inertia. As I stated at the beginning of this book, the 'She'll be right' or 'If it ain't broke don't fix it' mentality is a recipe for mediocrity. As I have argued, we should strive for the best rather than what is merely adequate, and that surely applies in the field of constitutional law as in any other area of social activity. One of the challenges of those wishing to promote constitutional reform should, therefore, be to cultivate in the public a desire to have a Constitution which is the best that can be devised, through a process of public debate, not merely one which has creaked along for a hundred years. Here the experience of South Africa is instructive:[5] Part of the constitution-making process between 1993 and 1996 involved the solicitation of submissions from the general public. Their response was enthusiastic. In addition to formal submissions by organisations, submissions were made by individuals by means of petitions, letters, email and telephone calls to the Constitutional Assembly talk line. Petitions on various matters were signed by 1.9 million people, while 13,000 individual missives were sent. The Constitutional Assembly published a free magazine, *Constitutional Talk*, which was distributed to the public and which contained a draft of the Constitution on which comment was invited. In addition, there was a series of television and radio talk shows on constitutional issues, and face-to-face workshops were held in

5 Gloppen, 1997, 257–58.

remote areas where many of the people were literate or semi-literate. The result, according to public surveys, was that people felt that they had been consulted in the constitution-making process and that the Constitution was, to some extent at least, 'their' Constitution, which, in turn, impacted positively on the legitimacy of the Constitution.[6] The adoption of a similar process would clearly be beneficial once we embarked upon the journey of drafting a new Constitution for Australia.

11.2 CIVICS EDUCATION

It may be thought that the prospects of constitutional reform in Australia are slight, given current public attitudes. But despite this, I have every confidence that, furnished with adequate information, Australian voters have the ability adequately to assess what is being put before them. The key, then, is how to enhance the awareness and understanding Australians have of constitutional affairs. That, in turn, depends upon the development of a comprehensive programme of civics education. Surveys reveal how undeveloped public knowledge of our Constitution is. A survey taken in 1992 indicated that 33% of those surveyed were not even aware that a federal constitution existed, and that this proportion increased to 45% among those aged between 18 and 24.[7] Given the understandable propensity of voters to vote 'no' to a proposal they do not understand, the low success rate of constitutional amendment referenda comes as no surprise. Thus, it is clear that the success of any large-scale constitutional reform initiative will largely depend upon how well informed the public is.

What is the status of civics education in Australia at present? Given that education is a matter that falls within the legislative competence of the States and Territories, responsibility for civics education lies in the first instance, with them. However, the Commonwealth has also been active in the area, and has prepared a civics education programme called *Discovering Democracy*, which is aimed both primary and secondary schools, and which covers such issues as the nature of governmental power, the history of democracy from ancient times, the branches of government, judicial independence, the function of constitutions and civic involvement.[8] The programme has been developed as a resource available for use by education departments in the States and Territories. All States and Territories include civics-related subject matter as part of the syllabus in such subjects as Legal Studies or Studies of Society and the Environment (ACT), Society and the Environment (Queensland, Victoria, Tasmania, South Australia and Western Australia) or Human Society and its Environment (New South Wales), but the extent to which the civics programme is incorporated in these subjects varies from jurisdiction to jurisdiction, and even from school to school.[9] There is clearly a need for a comprehensive approach to this issue, and the ability of the Commonwealth to fund projects in the States by means of specific purpose payments (SPPs) provides an opportunity for the

6 *Ibid*, 264–67.

7 Denis Muller, 'Most want Constitution changed once they work out what it is' (1992) *Sydney Morning Herald*, 3 July, 6. See also Galligan, 1995, 129 and Hughes, 1994, 163.

8 The entire *Discovering Democracy* programme (including teaching materials) is available via the internet at www.curriculum.edu.au/democracy/.

9 See Margaret Cook, 'Breathing new life into civics' (2002) *The Age*, 27 March, 4.

Commonwealth to be proactive in this regard, by granting supplementary funds to the States, on condition that they are used to include at least a core element of the *Discovering Democracy* programme in school curricula.

Primary and secondary education aside, there is also a need for an education programme directed towards the general public. Both government and non-government organisations have a role to play here: even if our constitutional arrangements were the most perfect in the world, it would still be a public good for governments to foster knowledge of, and debate on, constitutional matters through broadly-targeted public education campaigns. The role of non-governmental organisations is particularly important. To take one example, during the 10 years of its existence, the Constitutional Centenary Foundation performed a positive role in surveying public opinion on constitutional matters, conducting public education programmes, hosting community debates, convening youth parliaments and publishing pamphlets on contemporary constitutional issues. Unfortunately, that organisation's charter required that it be wound up at the end of 2000, but there is clearly a need for successor organisations to carry on its work. A useful model from overseas is that provided by the United States – the Centre for Civic Education – which promotes understanding of the federal Constitution by constructing curricula for the teaching of civics education, and through its publication of student texts explaining the functioning of the Constitution.[10] An even more ambitious project is that being overseen by the National Constitution Centre,[11] which is constructing a museum and library opposite Independence Hall, in Philadelphia, which will function both as a monument to the Constitution and as the headquarters of an organisation which will engage in broad public education programmes.

11.3 HOW TO EFFECT CONSTITUTIONAL REFORM

An important tactical question that would need to be addressed is whether a programme of constitutional reform should proceed piecemeal, with voters being presented with different amendments on separate occasions, each effecting a distinct change to the Constitution, or whether voters should be asked to approve an entirely new Constitution on a single occasion.

For some, the lesson to be learned from the 1988 referendum, in which four amendments were presented simultaneously and all were defeated, is that the piecemeal approach stands a greater chance of success.[12] However, I would argue that the failure of the 1988 referendum had more to do with the haste with which it was presented to the voters, and its lack of bipartisan support, than with the fact that more than one change was proposed.[13] Furthermore, although the piecemeal approach offers the prospect of achieving at least some of the constitutional reform objectives our country needs, it has the disadvantage that proposed changes would have to be drafted in such a way as to be workable both within the existing Constitution and within the Constitution as finally

10 See, eg, Centre for Civic Education, 1998, which outlines a curriculum for teaching civics at high schools.

11 The Centre's website is at www.constitutioncenter.org/.

12 Hughes, 1994, 165.

13 McMillan, 1991, 63 and 69–71.

envisaged. This approach would, therefore, be far more complex from a technical point of view.

The opposite approach would involve the drafting of a completely new Constitution for approval in a single referendum. There is no doubt that this would be a gamble, and that failure might prejudice the cause of constitutional reform for years to come. However, this 'big bang' approach does, at least, have the advantage that a new Constitution is likely to have something for everyone, and that even if individual voters do not favour particular provisions, they may find that, looked at in its entirety, the new Constitution is worthy of adoption. Some voters may be persuaded to take the courageous decision to vote for change because it is the principled thing to do, even if they feel it to be against the interests of their specific societal group. However, in the case of those who take a more pragmatic view, I would argue that, provided that a new Constitution is presented as a cohesive whole, interest groups will find that, even if some part of the proposal is inimical to their particular interests, other parts are beneficial, and that, seen as a whole, the document is, on balance, worth supporting. If there is any lesson to be learned from the first century of federation, it is that piecemeal constitutional reform has a low rate of success. Surely it is time to give the comprehensive approach its chance.

Finally, the very holding of a referendum presupposes a Commonwealth government that has taken the political decision to commit itself to constitutional reform. Lobbying of the government by those who are interested in reform would assist in creating this political will. Perhaps the first step should be to request that the Commonwealth government establish a Constitutional Commission, similar to that which produced the 1988 report, to conduct public hearings and prepare a draft new Constitution. Ultimately, however, what is required is a political leader of sufficient courage to initiate the process. Only time will tell whether such a person exists in Australia.

11.4 A NEW CONSTITUTION FOR AUSTRALIA

This book ends with an Appendix containing a draft new Constitution for Australia, which embodies the recommendations made in the preceding chapters. This draft has been written on the assumption that the Commonwealth Constitution of 1901 would be replaced in its entirety. It should be remembered that the current Constitution is contained within s 9 of the Commonwealth of Australia Constitution Act 1900 (UK). Is there any way that the preamble to that Act and the other eight sections (the so-called 'covering clauses'), which are replete with references to Australia's status as a monarchy, could be expunged from Australian law? Some authorities have questioned whether s 128 of the Constitution could be used to repeal those sections, given that s 128 confers the power to amend only the Constitution – that is, only s 9 of the Act, rather than the whole Act. However, the generally accepted view is that the entirety of the United Kingdom Act could be repealed, by either of two methods:[14] the first is based on the argument that s 128 does confer the power to alter the entirety of the Act because, given Britain's disavowal of legislative authority over Australia by virtue of s 1 of the Australia Act 1986 (UK and Cth), if s 128 could not be used to do what the United Kingdom Parliament

14 See Winterton, 1995(b), 120–22.

cannot now do, then no-one would be able to do those things, which would mean that the covering clauses would be unamendable. The second view is that the covering clauses could be repealed by the Commonwealth Parliament using the avenue provided by s 15(1) of the Australia Act 1986 (UK and Cth), which permits the Commonwealth Parliament to amend that (United Kingdom) Act at the request of all the States. Obtaining the request of all the States would effectively put the Commonwealth Parliament into the shoes of the United Kingdom Parliament, and would, therefore, confer the power upon it to insert into the Australia Act 1986 (UK and Australia) a provision repealing the preamble and first eight sections of the Commonwealth of Australia Act 1900 (UK).[15]

Whatever the likelihood of constitutional reform in Australia, it is hoped that a draft document such as the one I offer for consideration will, at least, stimulate debate about constitutional matters, and lead to some positive change, even though falling short of the ideal. However, the struggle for constitutional reform will be half lost before it has begun if we start from a position of compromise. The years ahead will no doubt see compromise forced upon the proponents of constitutional reform. At least let the process begin with the statement of an ideal.

15 Apart from the two methods mentioned in the text above, it has also been suggested that the covering clauses could be repealed by using s 51(xxxviii) of the Constitution, which empowers the Commonwealth Parliament, with the consent of the States, to exercise such powers as were exercisable by the United Kingdom Parliament in 1900. However, the weakness of this argument is that all the s 51 powers are stated to be 'subject to' the Constitution, and could, therefore, not be used to amend the Constitution in a manner which was contrary to s 128.

THE CONSTITUTION OF THE COMMONWEALTH OF AUSTRALIA ACT 2002

PREAMBLE

We, the people of Australia, recognising the inherent dignity of every human being and their entitlement to fundamental rights; the original habitation of this country by its indigenous peoples, their original ownership its lands and seas, and their continued enjoyment of indigenous title rights subject to law; the contribution made to this country by immigrants from many lands; the multicultural nature of this country, and the commitment of this country to freedom, democracy and equality, do enact this Constitution.

CHAPTER 1 – THE CONSTITUTION

1 The Constitution

This Constitution is the supreme source of law in Australia.

2 Sources of law

Common law, indigenous customary law and statute law are recognised sources of law in Australia.

3 Invalidity of law

Any law, whether common law, indigenous customary law or statute law, is invalid to the extent that it is inconsistent with this Constitution.

4 Remedies

Anyone listed in this section has the right to approach a competent court, alleging that this Constitution has been infringed or is about to be infringed, and the court may grant such relief as it sees fit. The persons who may approach a court are:

(a) anyone acting in their own interest;

(b) anyone acting on behalf of another person who cannot act in their own name;

(c) anyone acting as a member of, or in the interest of, a group or class of persons;

(d) anyone acting in the public interest; and

(e) an association acting in the interest of its members.

CHAPTER 2 – THE AUSTRALIAN BILL OF RIGHTS

5 Recognition of rights

The rights listed in this Chapter are recognised as belonging to all persons in Australia. Nothing in this Chapter shall be construed as denying any rights not mentioned therein.

6 Application of this Chapter

This Chapter applies to all law, and binds the legislature, the executive, and the judiciary of Commonwealth, State and Territory governments and to all persons, both public and private.

7 Limitation of rights

Rights protected in this Chapter may be subject to such limitations imposed by law as are reasonable in a free and democratic society.

8 Life

All persons have a right to life.

9 Liberty

(1) All persons have a right to personal liberty.

(2) Any person who has been deprived of liberty must immediately be informed in a language they understand or through an interpreter:

- (i) of the reason for the deprivation of their liberty;
- (ii) of their right to contact a legal advisor without delay; and
- (iii) of their right to silence and of the consequences of waiving that right.

(3) Any person who has been deprived of their liberty must be charged with an offence or released within 24 hours.

(4) Any person who has been charged with an offence must be brought before a court of competent jurisdiction within 24 hours in order to have the validity of the continued deprivation of their liberty determined.

(5) A person deprived of liberty has a right to bail.

(6) A person charged with an offence has a right to trial in an open and impartial court within a reasonable time.

(7) A person charged with an offence has the right to be presumed innocent until proven guilty and the right not to be compelled to give evidence in their trial.

(8) A person who has been tried and acquitted in relation to an offence may not be charged or tried in relation to that same offence again.

(9) A person who has been convicted of an offence may not be charged, tried or punished in relation to that offence again.

10 Slavery, forced labour, torture and cruel or inhuman treatment or punishment

No one may be subject to slavery, forced labour (including military or civil conscription), torture or cruel or inhuman treatment or punishment. The death penalty shall not be imposed in Australia.

11 Expression

Every person has the right to freedom of expression, which includes the right to:

- (i) impart and receive information;
- (ii) engage in scientific research and artistic activity;

(iii) impart and receive ideas and opinions;

(iv) to engage in peaceful public assembly or protest.

12 Voting and candidacy

Subject to the provisions of sections 39(1) and 81(1), every adult citizen has the right to an equal vote and, if enrolled as a voter, to stand for election to public office.

13 Association

Every person has the freedom to associate and to decline to associate with others.

14 Religion

No law shall be made for the establishment of any religion, or for the imposition of any religious observance, or for prohibiting the free exercise of any religion.

15 Culture

Every person has the right to preserve and to engage in their culture.

16 Indigenous self-government

Subject to this Constitution, indigenous communities have the right to negotiate with the Commonwealth in relation to the establishment of institutions through which such communities may exercise self-government.

17 Privacy

Every person has a right to privacy in relation to the collection, dissemination, verification and correction of personal information relating to them.

18 Personal autonomy

Every person has a right to autonomy in relation to intimate choices relating to bodily integrity and personal relationships.

19 Equality

Every person has the right to equality. No one may discriminate against another person on any of the following grounds:

(i) sex;

(ii) sexual orientation;

(iii) trans-gender status;

(iv) residence in a particular part of Australia;

(v) marital status;

(vi) pregnancy;

(vii) family responsibility status;

(viii) breastfeeding;

(ix) age;

(x) race;

(xi) impairment;

(xii) physical features;

(xiii) religion or ethical belief;

(xiv) political belief or activity;

(xv) trade union activity;

(xvi) lawful sexual activity;

(xvii) association with a person with any of the attributes mentioned in sub-sections (i)–(xv) of this section.

20 Movement

Every person has the right to freedom of movement.

21 Commercial activity

Every person has the right to engage in commercial activity.

22 Food, shelter, medical care and primary education

Every person has, subject to the resources available to government, a right to basic food, shelter, medical care and primary education.

23 Judicial review

Every person has a right to judicial review of administrative action.

24 Compensation

Every person has the right to just terms compensation for deprivation of property.

CHAPTER 3 – THE EXECUTIVE

25 Executive power

Subject to this Constitution, the executive power of the Commonwealth vests in the President of Australia, and consists of such powers vested in the executive by this Constitution, by Parliament and by the common law, including the powers that formerly inhered in the Crown in right of the Commonwealth of Australia.

26 The President

The President shall be directly elected by the people of Australia for a term of five years.

27 Impeachment of the President

The President may be impeached on application to the High Court on grounds of misbehaviour in office or incapacity.

28 Acting President

If the President retires, is impeached, or dies in office, the longest serving State Governor shall become Acting President pending the election of a new President.

29 The Cabinet

The President shall be advised by a Cabinet consisting of the Prime Minister and other Ministers who direct the departments of state of the Commonwealth.

30 Exercise of power by the President

(1) All references to the President in this Constitution are to be taken as references to the President acting on the advice of the Cabinet, unless the reference is to the President acting on the advice of some other person or body, or as directed by this Constitution.

(2) The powers of the President include the power to summon, prorogue and dissolve Parliament and to be Commander-in-Chief of the defence forces.

31 Appointment of the Prime Minister

Subject to section 32(5), when the Prime Minister resigns, dies or is dismissed, the President must appoint as Prime Minister the person who has the support of a majority of members of the House of Representatives.

32 Dismissal of the Prime Minister

(1) Subject to sub-section (2) of this section the President must dismiss the Prime Minister when:

(i) the Prime Minister no longer has the support of a majority of members of the House of Representatives; or

(ii) Parliament has rejected a proposed law for the appropriation of money or the imposition of taxation,

and, in either of the circumstances mentioned in (i) or (ii), the Prime Minister refuses either to resign or to advise the President to dissolve the House of Representatives.

(2) After a general election for the House of Representatives the President may not exercise the power contained in sub-section (1) of this section until the House of Representatives elected at that election has met.

(3) The President must dismiss the Prime Minister when the Prime Minister has refused to comply with an order made by the High Court other than in circumstances when an appeal is pending against the order to the High Court in its appellate jurisdiction.

(4) If the President dismisses the Prime Minister in accordance with sub-section (3) of this section, he must immediately dissolve the House of Representatives.

(5) If the President has dismissed the Prime Minister in accordance with sub-section (1) of this section and there is no other person who has majority support of the House of Representatives, or has dismissed the Prime Minister in accordance with sub-section (3) of this section, the President shall appoint as Acting Prime Minister the parliamentary leader of the political party which has the most numerous members in the House but which did not have any members who were Ministers immediately before the dismissal of the Prime Minister. The Acting Prime Minister shall hold office until the day upon which the House of Representatives meets after a dissolution contemplated by sub-section (4) of this section or by section 34(1)(ii).

33 Appointment and dismissal of members of the Cabinet

The President, acting on the advice of the Prime Minister, shall appoint and dismiss members of the Cabinet.

34 Dissolution of the House of Representatives

(1) Subject to sub-section (2) of this section, the President must dissolve the House of Representatives when and only when the following circumstances exist:

(i) the President is advised to dissolve Parliament by the Prime Minister; or

(ii) the Prime Minister has been dismissed in accordance with section 32(1) and there is no other person who has the support of a majority of the members of the House of Representatives; or

(iii) the Prime Minister has been dismissed in accordance with section 32(4).

(2) The President is prohibited from dissolving the House of Representatives on the request of the Prime Minister where a general election for the House of Representatives has been held and the House has not yet met after the return of the writs.

35 Liability of the Commonwealth

(1) Subject to the law, the Commonwealth is liable under both procedural and substantive law.

(2) The liability of the Commonwealth under sub-section (1) of this section attaches to the Commonwealth even in cases where a servant or officer of the Commonwealth is exercising an independent discretion in the course and scope of their duties.

(3) Subject to any law Parliament may make, the courts may provide such remedies as they see fit against the Commonwealth or against a State or Territory.

(4) Nothing contained in sub-section (3) of this section enables Parliament to deprive the courts of the power to provide any remedy under section 4 of this Constitution.

(5) Notwithstanding the provisions of section 52(1), where an award of damages has been made against the Commonwealth, the judgment shall be satisfied from the Consolidated Revenue Fund.

CHAPTER 4 – THE LEGISLATURE

36 Legislative power

The legislative power of the Commonwealth is vested in a Parliament, which consists of the President, the Senate and the House of Representatives.

37 Sessions of Parliament

(1) After a general election the President must summon Parliament to meet not later than 30 days after the day appointed for the return of the writs.

(2) The President must convene a session of Parliament at least once in each calendar year.

38 Composition of the House of Representatives

(1) The House of Representatives shall consist of 225 members, 150 of whom shall fill electorate seats directly elected by the voters from electorates, and 75 of whom fill list seats directly elected by the voters from lists of candidates.

(2) In any general election for the House of Representatives, each voter shall receive:

(i) a ballot paper on which they may indicate ordered preferences among candidates in their particular electorate; and

(ii) a ballot paper on which the voter may indicate a single vote for a registered political party or for an individual.

(3) There shall be 150 electorates delineated for the purpose of electing the members of the House of Representatives to fill electorate seats, provided that no electorate shall cross the boundaries of any State or Territory, and provided further that the number of voters in each electorate shall vary by no more than 10% from the mean.

(4) For the purpose of elections of the 75 members of the House of Representatives to fill list seats, the 75 list seats in the House of Representatives shall be allocated to the States and Territories in proportion to the population of each, provided that, if a State or Territory does not have sufficient population to meet the quota required for a list seat, that State or Territory's population shall be counted as part of the population of whichever other State or Territory's population would come closest to a whole number of list seats after adding the population of the first mentioned State or Territory.

(5) In any election for the House of Representatives, the list seats in a State or Territory shall, as closely as possible, be allocated to parties and independents proportionately to the total number of votes that party or independent obtained in the State or Territory on the ballot papers referred to in sub-section (2)(ii) of this section.

(6) A registered political party nominating candidates for election to list seats in any State or Territory shall, prior to nomination day, publish a list indicating the party's ordered preference as to the election of its candidates.

(7) In casting ballots mentioned in sub-section (2)(ii) of this section, voters shall have the opportunity to vote for a registered political party, any individual candidate appearing on a list mentioned in sub-section (6) of this section, or for an independent.

(8) Seats allocated to a party in accordance with sub-section (5) of this section shall be filled by candidates named on that party's list, first in order of the number of votes received by individual candidates on ballot papers mentioned in sub-section (2)(ii) of this section, and then in accordance with the party's preference as indicated in accordance with sub-section (6) of this section.

39 Composition of the Senate

(1) The Senate shall consist of 12 members directly elected by the voters in each State, 2 members directly elected by the voters in each Territory, and 12 members directly elected by voters registered on the Indigenous Voters' Roll.

(2) In elections for the Senate, the voters in each State and Territory and on the Indigenous Voters' Roll shall vote as single electorates, and voters shall be able to indicate their preferences among ordered lists of candidates prepared by registered political parties.

(3) Senators shall be chosen for a term of six years, and the method for choosing the Senators from each State, Territory and by voters on the Indigenous Voters' Roll shall be uniform.

(4) The President must cause writs to be issued for elections to the Senate in fulfilment of the requirements contained in sub-section (1) of this section.

(5) As soon as the Senate first meets under this Constitution the Senate shall divide the Senators chosen for each State and Territory and from voters on the Indigenous Voters' Roll into two classes, as nearly equal in number as practicable; and the seats of the Senators of the first class shall become vacant at the expiration of three years, and the places of those of the second class at the expiration of six years, from the beginning of their term of service; and afterwards the places of senators shall become vacant at the expiration of six years from the beginning of their term of service. The election to fill

vacant places must be held within one year before the places are to become vacant. For the purposes of this section the term of service of a senator shall be taken to begin on the first day of July following the day of his election, except in the cases of the first election, when it shall be taken to begin on the first day of July preceding the day of his election.

40 Vacancies

(1) In this section references to the President are references to the President acting on the advice of the Australian Electoral Commission.

(2) If any vacancy shall occur in a seat in the House of Representatives filled in accordance with section 38(5) or in any seat in the Senate, the President shall determine which of the unelected candidates whose name was included in the same party list as the member whose seat has been declared vacant stood highest in the order of preference indicated by the party.

(3) If that candidate is still alive, the President shall then inquire of that candidate whether that candidate is willing to be a member of Parliament, and, if that candidate so indicates his or her willingness, the President shall declare that person to be elected.

(4) If that person has died or does not signify his or her willingness to be a member of Parliament, the Chief Electoral Officer shall proceed to make that inquiry of the following candidate in order of preference on the party list, and so on, in descending order of preference, until one of the candidates signifies his or her willingness to be a member of Parliament, in which case the Chief Electoral Officer shall declare that person to be elected.

(5) If no candidate signifies his or her willingness to be a member of Parliament, or there is no candidate lower in the order of preference on the party list than the member of Parliament whose seat has been declared vacant, he vacancy shall not be filled until the next general election.

41 The House of Representatives

(1) Every House of Representatives shall continue for three years and no longer, but may sooner be dissolved by the President in accordance with this Constitution.

(2) The President must cause writs to be issued for general elections of the House of Representatives following a dissolution of the House of Representatives in any of the circumstances mentioned in section 34(1) of this Constitution.

(3) Writs shall be issued within 10 days of the expiry of a House of Representatives or from the proclamation of a dissolution thereof.

(4) Whenever a vacancy for a seat elected under section 38(3) of this Constitution occurs in the House of Representatives, the President must issue a writ for the election of a new member.

(5) The House of Representatives shall, before proceeding to the despatch of any other business, choose a member to be the Speaker of the House, and whenever the office of Speaker become vacant, the House shall choose another Speaker.

(6) The Speaker shall cease to hold office if he ceases to be a member of the House of Representatives.

(7) The Speaker may be removed from office by a vote of the House and may resign his office by written notice to the President.

(8) Before or during the absence of the Speaker, the House of Representatives may choose a member to be Acting Speaker until the return of the Speaker.

(9) A member may resign his seat in the House of Representatives by written notice to the President, whereupon his seat shall become vacant.

(10) The quorum for the conduct of any business of the House shall be one third of the whole number of its members.

(11) Questions arising in the House of Representatives shall be determined by a majority of votes other than that of the Speaker. The Speaker shall not vote unless the numbers on either side of a question are equal, whereupon the Speaker shall have a casting vote.

42 The Senate

(1) The Senate shall, before proceeding to the despatch of any other business, choose a member to be the President of the Senate, and whenever the office of President of the Senate become vacant, the Senate shall choose another President of the Senate.

(2) The President of the Senate shall cease to hold office if he ceases to be a member of the Senate.

(3) The President of the Senate may be removed from office by a vote of the Senate and may resign his office by written notice to the President.

(4) Before or during the absence of the President of the Senate, the Senate may choose a member to be Acting President of the Senate until the return of the President of the Senate.

(5) A member may resign his seat in the Senate by written notice to the President, whereupon his seat shall become vacant.

(6) The quorum for the conduct of any business of the Senate shall be one third of the whole number of its members.

(7) Questions arising in the Senate shall be determined by a majority of votes other than that of the President of the Senate. The President of the Senate shall not vote unless the numbers on either side of a question are equal, whereupon the President of the Senate shall have a casting vote.

43 Disqualifications

(1) Any person who:

(i) has been convicted of treason, or has been convicted and is serving a sentence of imprisonment for more than a year for any offence punishable under the law of the Commonwealth or of a State or Territory; or

(ii) is of unsound mind; or

(iii) holds judicial office under the Commonwealth, a State or a Territory; or

(iv) is a member of the public service of the Commonwealth, a State or a Territory; or

(v) is a member of the defence forces; or

(vi) is an officer or employee of a public authority; or

(vii) has any direct or indirect pecuniary interest in any agreement with the Commonwealth otherwise than as a member in common with the other members of an incorporated company consisting of more than 25 persons, provided that Parliament may make laws disqualifying persons who have other interests which might create the risk of conflict of interest with their duties as a member of Parliament or who have committed offences relating to corrupt practices or improper influence,

shall be incapable of sitting or being chosen as a member of the House of Representatives or the Senate.

(2) A person who falls within a disqualifying category listed in sub-section (1) of this section may be chosen as a member for the House of Representatives or the Senate, but shall be deemed to have ceased to hold the disqualifying position on the day immediately before the day they are elected to the House of Representatives or the Senate.

(3) If a Senator or member of the House of Representatives becomes subject to any of the disabilities mentioned in sub-section (1) of this section, the place of that Senator or member of the House of Representatives shall thereupon become vacant.

(4) A member of either House of Parliament shall be incapable of sitting as a member of the other House or of the legislature of any State or Territory.

(5) Any question respecting the qualification of a Senator or of a member of the House of Representatives, or respecting a vacancy in either House of Parliament, and any question of a disputed election to either House, shall be determined by the High Court in the exercise of its jurisdiction under section 62(iii) of this Constitution.

44 Oaths

Every Senator and every member of the House of Representatives shall before taking their seat make and subscribe before the President or some person authorised by him an oath or affirmation of allegiance in the form set forth in the Schedule to this Constitution.

45 Privileges

Parliament shall have the power to make laws relating to the powers, privileges and immunities of the House of Representatives and the Senate and of the members and the committees of each House, pending which such powers, privileges and immunities shall remain as they were immediately prior to the coming into force of this Constitution.

46 Rules and orders

Each House of Parliament may make rules and orders with respect to the mode in which its powers, privileges and immunities may be exercised and upheld; and the order and conduct of its business and proceedings.

47 Enactment of laws

(1) A proposed law shall be taken to have been passed by a House of Parliament when it has been assented to by a majority of members present and voting.

(2) Subject to sub-sections (3) and (4) of this section, when a proposed law has been passed by the House of Representatives and by the Senate in accordance with this Constitution, the President must assent to it forthwith, whereupon it becomes law.

(3) When a proposed law has been passed by the House of Representatives, and the Senate has rejected or failed to pass it or has passed it with amendments to which the House of

Representatives will not agree, then if the House of Representatives again passes the same law after no less than one calendar year has elapsed since it was first passed by the House of Representatives, it must be signed by the President and becomes law.

(4) When a proposed law appropriating moneys or imposing taxation has been passed by the House of Representatives and the Senate has rejected or failed to pass it or has passed it with amendments to which the House of Representatives will not agree, then if the House of Representatives again passes the same law after no less than 30 days has elapsed since it was first passed by the House of Representatives it must be signed by the President and becomes law.

48 Proposed laws appropriating money or imposing taxation

(1) A proposed law appropriating money shall deal only with such appropriation, and a proposed law imposing taxation shall deal only with the imposition of taxation.

(2) A proposed law shall not be taken as appropriating money or as imposing taxation by reason only of its containing provisions for the imposition or appropriation of fines or other pecuniary penalties, or for the demand or payment or appropriation of fees for licences or fees for services under the proposed law.

49 Legislative powers of Parliament

Subject to this Constitution, the Parliament of the Commonwealth has the power to make laws for the peace, order, and good government with respect to the matters listed in sections 50 and 51.

50 Exclusive legislative powers

The matters listed in this section lie within the exclusive legislative power of the Parliament of the Commonwealth:

(i) taxes on the income of any person or corporation, and taxes on goods and services including duties of customs and excise;

(ii) the borrowing of money on the credit of the Commonwealth;

(iii) the appropriation of money for such purposes as the Commonwealth Parliament sees fit;

(iv) the granting of assistance to any State or Territory on such conditions as Parliament deems fit;

(v) defence, including the raising of defence forces;

(vi) external affairs;

(vii) aliens, naturalisation, citizenship and migration;

(viii) currency;

(ix) the service and execution throughout the Commonwealth of legal process, and of the judgments of Commonwealth and State and Territory courts;

(x) the recognition throughout the Commonwealth of State and Territory laws, State and Territory public records and State and Territory judicial proceedings;

(xi) principles of choice of law;

(xii) the seat of government of the Commonwealth, and all places acquired by the Commonwealth for public purposes;

(xiii) the Commonwealth public service.

51 Other legislative powers

The following powers additional to those listed in section 50 fall within then legislative power of the Parliament of the Commonwealth:

(i) trade and commerce;

(ii) corporations;

(iii) banking, excluding the operation of banks by State governments;

(iv) insurance, other than the operation of insurance schemes by State governments;

(v) negotiable instruments;

(vi) bankruptcy and insolvency;

(vii) intellectual property;

(viii) bounties on the production or export of goods;

(ix) marriage and family relationships;

(x) social welfare benefits and services and also pensions;

(xi) indigenous people;

(xii) telecommunications;

(xiii) air and sea navigation, including Admiralty and maritime matters;

(xiv) admiralty and maritime matters;

(xv) census and statistics;

(xvi) astronomical and meteorological observations;

(xvii) scientific research;

(xviii) nuclear energy;

(xix) quarantine;

(xx) fisheries beyond three nautical miles of the shore-line;

(xxi) weights and measures;

(xxii) the deprivation of property from any State or person for public purposes;

(xxiii) the giving of effect to the provisions of the Constitution;

(xxiv) any matter referred to the Parliament of the Commonwealth by the Parliament or Parliaments of any State or States, but so that the law shall extend only to States by whose Parliaments the matter is referred, or which subsequently adopt the law;

(xxv) matters incidental to the execution of any power vested by this Constitution in the legislative, executive or judicial branch of the Commonwealth.

52 Appropriation of money

(1) All moneys received by the Commonwealth shall form one Consolidated Revenue Fund, to be appropriated in accordance with the Constitution.

(2) Subject to sections 35(5) and 60(1)(iii) of this Constitution, no money shall be drawn from the Consolidated Revenue Fund except by appropriation made by law.

CHAPTER 5 – VOTER-INITIATED REFERENDA

53 Assistance in drafting a proposed law

Upon presentation to the President of a petition for the holding of a referendum on a proposed law signed by no less than one percent of persons entitled to vote in elections for the House of Representatives, the Attorney-General shall provide such reasonable assistance as may be required for the drafting of the proposed law.

54 Referendum on a proposed law

(1) Upon presentation to the President of a petition for the holding of a referendum on a proposed law signed by no less than three percent of persons entitled to vote in elections for the House of Representatives, the President shall call a referendum to be held on the first Monday of the following July, provided that the referendum on a proposed law presented to the President after the first Monday of April shall be held on the first Monday of July of the following year.

(2) No law proposing the appointment of any identifiable person to a public office, or the dismissal of an identifiable person from a public office, shall be able to be put to referendum.

55 Passage of a proposed law

A proposed law, other than a law mentioned in section 83, which receives at referendum the assent of a simple majority of persons entitled to vote in elections for the House of Representatives will be deemed to have been passed by the House of Representatives and the Senate and must be assented to by the President.

56 Amendment of a law enacted by referendum

A law enacted in accordance with section 55 may be amended only by means of a referendum held in accordance with that section or by a two thirds majority of votes cast in the House of Representatives and in the Senate.

57 Constitutional amendments

A proposed law to amend or repeal a provision in this Constitution must be signed into law by the President only if it obtains at referendum the assent of such majorities of voters as are required by section 83.

58 Inconsistent proposed laws

Where proposed laws put to referendum on the same day are in any respect inconsistent with each other, and both laws receive the assent that is required by section 55 or section 83, the proposed law which receives the greatest number of votes throughout Australia must be assented to by the President.

CHAPTER 6 – THE JUDICIARY

59 The judicial power of the Commonwealth

The judicial power of the Commonwealth shall, in accordance with the doctrine of separation of powers, be vested in the High Court of Australia, the Federal Court of Australia, courts of the Territories and such other federal courts as Parliament creates, and in such other courts as it invests with federal jurisdiction. The High Court shall consist of a Chief Justice, and so many other justices, not less than seven, as Parliament prescribes.

60 Appointment of judges

(1) Justices of the High Court, the Federal Court, courts of the Territories and other courts created by Parliament:

(i) shall be appointed by the President;

(ii) shall not be removed except by the President acting in accordance with an address by both Houses of Parliament in the same session, requesting removal on the ground of proven misbehaviour, unfitness or incapacity;

(iii) shall receive such remuneration as is fixed by the Judicial Services Commission, provided that, notwithstanding anything contained in section 52(1), such remuneration shall form a permanent charge on the Consolidated Revenue Fund, shall not be diminished during the judges' continuation in office, and shall be equal in the case of all judges of the same court.

(2) In appointing judges the President shall, in respect of each vacancy on the High Court, the Federal Court of Australia, courts of the Territories and such other courts as Parliament creates, select an appointee from a list of at least two names submitted by the Commonwealth Judicial Commission.

61 The Commonwealth Judicial Commission

(1) The Commonwealth Judicial Commission shall consist of:

(i) a person appointed by the President;

(ii) the Chief Justice of the High Court;

(iii) a person appointed by the President on the advice of the Law Council of Australia;

(iv) a person appointed by the President who has been elected from among their number by the heads of departments of law of those Universities offering a law degree recognised by a State or Territory Supreme Court;

(v) a female member of the House of Representatives appointed by the President on the advice of the parliamentary leader of the political party which has the most numerous members in the House but which does not have any members who are Ministers;

(vi) a Senator appointed by the President who has been elected by the Senators elected by voters on the Indigenous Voters Roll from among their number.

(2) The Commonwealth Judicial Commission shall, in respect of any vacancy on the High Court, the Federal Court of Australia, courts of the Territories and such other courts as Parliament creates, submit to the President the names of at least two persons from whom he shall select an appointee in accordance with section 60(2).

(3) In determining who to nominate under sub-section (2) of this section, the Commonwealth Judicial Commission shall select from applicants who are, or have

been, judges of an Australian court or who are admitted as a legal practitioner, and whose abilities and breadth of background and experience indicate that they merit appointment.

(4) The Commonwealth Judicial Commission shall determine the salaries of judges serving in courts mentioned in section 59, provided that each year the Commonwealth Judicial Commission shall direct that that the salaries of judges shall increase by at least the percentage by which the consumer price index has increased in the previous 12 months, and provided further that the salaries of each judge of the same court shall be the same.

(5) Notwithstanding anything contained in section 52, judicial salaries shall be paid from the Consolidated Revenue Fund upon the direction of the Commonwealth Judicial Commission.

62 Original jurisdiction of the High Court

The High Court shall have original jurisdiction in all matters:

(i) between the Commonwealth and a State or Territory, or between one State or Territory and another State or Territory;

(ii) arising under the Constitution or involving its interpretation;

(iii) relating to the validity of elections and returns, the qualification of members of Parliament and parliamentary vacancies.

63 Appellate jurisdiction of the High Court

(1) The High Court of Australia shall have appellate jurisdiction in all matters decided by:

 (i) any justice or justices exercising the original jurisdiction of the High Court;

 (ii) by the Federal Court of Australia, any other courts that Parliament creates and the Supreme Court of any State or Territory.

(2) The jurisdiction mentioned in sub-section (1) of this section may be subject to such conditions and regulations as Parliament provides, except that Parliament and the legislatures of the States and Territories shall not enact any law prohibiting the High Court from hearing an appeal in respect of which that court has granted special leave to appeal on grounds that the case raises questions of significant importance.

64 Jurisdiction of the Federal Court

The Federal Court of Australia shall have original jurisdiction in all matters:

(i) in which review is sought of the actions of an officer of the Commonwealth;

(ii) arising under laws made by the Parliament of the Commonwealth in relation to which Parliament confers jurisdiction on the Federal Court of Australia.

65 Cross-vesting of jurisdiction

(1) Parliament may confer such of the jurisdiction referred to in sections 62, 63 or 64 as it pleases on the courts of the States and Territories.

(2) The High Court, the Federal Court of Australia and such other courts as Parliament creates may exercise such jurisdiction as is conferred on them by the legislatures of the States and Territories.

66 Removal of judges

(1) An allegation that there are grounds to remove a judge from office under section 60(1)(ii) shall be made to the Commonwealth Judicial Tribunal, which shall consist of three persons who are judges of Supreme Courts of the States or Territories appointed by the President for terms of five years.

(2) Where the Commonwealth Judicial Tribunal finds that it has been presented with evidence which supports a prima facie case of misbehaviour, unfitness or incapacity, it shall request the President to suspend the judge against whom allegations have been made pending the outcome of proceedings mentioned in sub-section (3) of this section, and the President shall suspend the judge.

(3) If a *prima facie* finding has been made under sub-section (2) of this section, the Commonwealth Judicial Tribunal shall conduct a conclusive hearing into the question of whether a case of misbehaviour, unfitness or incapacity has been proved, and shall advise Parliament accordingly.

(4) In conducting proceedings under sub-section (3) of this section the Commonwealth Judicial Commission shall be bound by the rules of evidence.

(5) No address mentioned in section 60(1)(ii) may be made by Parliament to the President unless the Commonwealth Judicial Tribunal has made a finding of proven misbehaviour, unfitness or incapacity.

67 Liability of judicial officers

A judicial officer exercising the judicial power of the Commonwealth shall not be liable in tort for any judicial act done within jurisdiction, nor for any judicial act done outside jurisdiction unless it is proven that such act outside jurisdiction has been performed with actual knowledge of want of jurisdiction.

68 Exercise of judicial functions by military tribunals

Nothing in this Chapter shall prevent the exercise of jurisdiction by military tribunals in relation to the conduct of persons while members of the defence forces of Australia.

CHAPTER 7 – FEDERALISM

69 State Constitutions

Subject to this Constitution, the Constitutions of the States shall continue in force in the same way as they did immediately prior to the coming into force of this Constitution.

70 New States

The Northern Territory and the Australian Capital Territory shall be entitled, through a simple majority vote of voters enrolled to vote in the respective Territory elections, to become States, provided that in any referendum on statehood, a majority of the voters in a Territory approve a statehood Constitution which is not incompatible with this Constitution.

71 Commonwealth and State laws

(1) No law of the Commonwealth shall terminate the existence of any State or substantially curtail or interfere with the ability of any State government to function.

(2) No law of any State shall terminate the existence of the Commonwealth or substantially curtail or interfere with the ability of the Commonwealth to function.

(3) State and Territory governments are presumed to be immune from laws enacted by Parliament in the absence of an express statement in the law to the contrary.

(4) Subject to this Constitution, laws enacted by the State and Territory legislatures are presumed to bind the Commonwealth, unless the law does not bind the government of the State or Territory concerned, or unless the State or Territory law expressly states that it is not intended to bind the Commonwealth.

72 Inconsistency

When a law of a State is inconsistent with a law of the Commonwealth, the latter shall prevail, and the former shall, to the extent of the inconsistency, be invalid.

73 Equality of treatment of States and Territories

The Commonwealth shall not, by any law or regulation of trade, commerce or revenue, give preference to one State or Territory or any part thereof over any other State or Territory or any part thereof, irrespective of how such a part may be defined.

74 Taxation of Commonwealth, State or Territory property

Notwithstanding any other provision of this Constitution, a State or Territory shall not impose any tax on property of any kind belonging to the Commonwealth, nor shall the Commonwealth impose any tax on property of any kind belonging to a State or Territory.

75 Full faith and credit

Full faith and credit shall be given throughout the Commonwealth to the laws, public records and judicial proceedings of every State and Territory.

76 Territories

Subject to any restrictions and obligations to which Parliament is subject by this Constitution, Parliament shall have the power to legislate for the peace, order and good government of the Territories mentioned in section 70 until such Territories become States, and shall at all times have such capacity to legislate for all other Australian Territories.

77 Seat of government

Canberra shall be the seat of government of the Commonwealth.

78 The Council of Australian Heads of Government

(1) The Council of Australian Heads of Government shall consist of the Prime minister, the Premiers of the States and the Chief Ministers of the Territories however they may be described.

(2) The Council of Australian Heads of government shall meet not less than once in every calendar year.

(3) In voting on decisions, each member of the Council of Australian Heads of Government shall have one vote.

79 Revenue-sharing

(1) All revenue raised by the Commonwealth from taxes on the income of any person or corporation, and taxes on goods and services including duties of customs and excise

shall be allocated between the Commonwealth and the States according to the following percentages: 68% to the Commonwealth, 27% to the governments of the States and Territories unconditionally and 5% to the governments of the States and Territories subject to such conditions as the Parliament of the Commonwealth sees fit.

(2) The percentages mentioned in sub-section (1) of this section may be varied by a two thirds vote of the members of the Council of Australian Heads of Government.

CHAPTER 8 – INDIGENOUS PEOPLE

80 Indigenous Voters' Roll

There shall be an Indigenous Voters Roll upon which any adult indigenous person who is a citizen of Australia may choose to be enrolled, provided that if a person chooses to be so enrolled, they shall not be enrolled as a voter for elections to the Senate in any State or Territory.

81 Indigenous Peoples' Council

(1) The Indigenous Peoples' Council shall be directly elected by voters registered on the indigenous voters roll.

(2) The Indigenous Peoples' Council shall advise the Commonwealth on all matters pertaining to indigenous people and shall exercise such other powers as may be conferred upon it by Parliament.

82 Indigenous customary law

Indigenous customary law shall be applied where appropriate by courts and by institutions established under section 16.

CHAPTER 9 – AMENDMENT

83 Amendment of the Constitution

(1) This Constitution may be amended only in accordance with the following procedures.

(2) A proposed law for the amendment of any provision contained in this Constitution, must be passed by both Houses of Parliament or must satisfy the requirements of section 54, and in either case must also receive the approval of two thirds of the votes cast in a national referendum.

(3) A proposed law for the amendment of any provision of this Constitution which, if passed, would affect the representation of the States in the Commonwealth Parliament, the legislative powers of the Parliament of the Commonwealth or of the States, the ratio of distribution of Commonwealth revenue between the Commonwealth and the States and Territories, or which in any other way would affect the balance of power between the Commonwealth and the States, must in addition to fulfilling the conditions contained in sub-section (1) of this section, receive the approval of a majority of voters in a majority of States.

(4) The method of varying the ratio of distribution of Commonwealth revenues mentioned in sub-section (2) of this section is additional to the method permitted by section 79 of this Constitution.

(5) A proposed law for the amendment of any provision of this Constitution which, if passed, would alter the boundaries of a State or States, form a new State from the union of two or more States, form a new State from part of an existing State or in any way affected the rights of any State or States, must in addition to fulfilling the conditions contained in sub-section (2) of this section, obtain the assent of a majority of voters in the separate State or States which would be affected.

CHAPTER 10 – INTERPRETATION

84 Meaning of words

Words in this Constitution bear the following meaning unless the contrary is indicated:

'amendment' includes repeal;

'independent' means a person registered for the purposes of being eligible for an allocation of list seats under s 38(5);

'indigenous' in relation to a person means an Aboriginal person or a Torres Strait Islander;

'party' means a political party registered for the purposes of being eligible for an allocation of list seats under s 38(5);

'seat' means a place in the House of Representatives or the Senate filled by a single member.

SCHEDULE

Oath

I AB do swear that I will be faithful and bear true allegiance to the Commonwealth of Australia.

Affirmation

I AB do solemnly and sincerely affirm that I will be faithful and bear true allegiance to the Commonwealth of Australia.

1153111200 1558100602

BIBLIOGRAPHY

Advisory Council for Inter-Government Relations, *Constitutional Recognition of Local Government*, 1980, Hobart: Advisory Council for Inter-Government Relations

Allswang, J, *The Initiative and Referendum in California, 1898–1998*, 2000, Stanford: Stanford UP

ALRC, *The Judicial Power of the Commonwealth – A Review of the Judiciary Act 1903 and Related Legislation*, 2001, Canberra: ALRC

ALRC, *Equality Before the Law: Women's Equality*, 1994, Canberra: AGPS

ALRC, *The Recognition of Aboriginal Customary Laws*, 1986, Canberra: AGPS

Amankwah, H, 'Post-*Mabo*: the prospect of the recognition of a regime of customary (indigenous) law in Australia' (1994) 18 University of Queensland L Rev 15

ATSIC (Aboriginal and Torres Strait Islander Commission), *Recognition, Rights & Reform: Report to Government on Native Title Social Justice Measures*, 1995, Canberra: ATSIC

Australian Bureau of Statistics, *Government Finance Statistics – Australia 1999 – 2000 (5512.0)*, 2000, Canberra: Australian Bureau of Statistics

Australian Electoral Commission *Yes/No – Referendum '99 – Your Official Referendum Pamphlet*, 1999, Canberra: Australian Electoral Commission

Barker, F, Boston, J, Levine, S, McLeay, E and Roberts, N, 'An initial assessment of the consequences of MMP in New Zealand', in Shugart, M and Wattenberg, M (eds), *Mixed-member Electoral Systems – The Best of Both Worlds?*, 2001, Oxford: OUP, 297

Barnett, S, 'Sir Harry Gibbs and a representative bench' (2000) 25 Alternative LJ 148

Bartlett, A, 'Washminster revisited – the role of the Upper House', in Sampford, C and Round, T (eds), *Beyond the Republic – Meeting the Global Challenges to Constitutionalism*, 2001, Leichhardt: Federation Press, 164

Bartlett, A, 'A squeeze on the balance of power: using senate "reform" to dilute democracy', in Sawer, M and Miskin, S (eds), *Representation and Institutional Change: 50 Years of Proportional Representation in the Senate (Papers on Parliament No 34)*, 1999, Canberra: Department of the Senate, 111

Barwick, G, 'The external affairs power of the Commonwealth and the protection of world heritage' (1995) 25 University of Western Australia L Rev 233

Barwick, G, 'The state of the Australian judicature' (1977) 51 ALJ 480

Beaudoin, G and Mendes, E (eds), *The Canadian Charter of Rights and Freedoms*, 3rd edn, 1996, Scarborough: Carswell

Bennett, T, *A Sourcebook of African Customary Law for Southern Africa*, 1991, Cape Town: Butterworths

Bennett, T, *The Application of Customary Law in Southern Africa*, 1985, Cape Town: Juta & Co

Bishop, R and Glynn, T, *Culture Counts: Changing Power Relations in Education*, 1999, Palmerston North: Dunmore

Bix, B, 'Assault, sado-masochism and consent' (1993) 109 LQR 540

Blackshield, A, 'The appointment and removal of federal judges', in Opeskin, B and Wheeler, F (eds), *The Australian Federal Judicial System*, 2000, Carlton South: Melbourne UP, 400

Blackshield, T and Williams, G, *Australian Constitutional Law & Theory*, 3rd edn, 2002, Annandale: Federation Press

Blackstone, W, *Commentaries on the Laws of England*, 1979, Chicago: University of Chicago Press

Blay, S, 'The international covenant on civil and political rights and the recognition of customary law practices of indigenous tribes: the case of Australian Aborigines' (1986) 19 Comparative and International LJ of Southern Africa 199

Bloustein, E, 'Privacy as an aspect of human dignity: an answer to Dean Prosser' (1964) 39 New York UL Rev 962

Bogdanor, V, 'Western Europe', in Butler, D and Ranney, A (eds), *Referendums around the World – The Growing Use of Direct Democracy*, 1994, Washington DC: AEI, 24

Bogdanor, V, *What is Proportional Representation?*, 1984, Oxford: Martin Robertson

Bogdanor, V and Butler, D (eds), *Democracy and Elections*, 1983, Cambridge: CUP

Booker, K, Glass, A and Watt, R, *Federal Constitutional Law – An Introduction*, 2nd edn, 1998, Chatswood: Butterworths

Bowler, S and Donovan, T, *Demanding Choices – Opinion, Voting and Direct Democracy*, 1998, Ann Arbor: University of Michigan Press

Brennan, F, *Legislating Liberty? A Bill of Rights for Australia*, 1998, St Lucia: Queensland UP

Brennan, F, *One Land, One Nation*, 1995, St Lucia: Queensland UP

Brennan, F, *Sharing the Country*, 1994, Ringwood: Penguin

Brennan, G, *100 Years On: Strengths and Strains in the Constitution*, Fourth Geoffrey Sawer Lecture, Canberra, 18 July 2001

Bronner, E, *Battle for Justice: How the Bork Nomination Shook America*, 1989, New York: WW Norton

Browne, K, 'Title VII as censorship: hostile environment harassment and the First Amendment' (1991) 52 Ohio State LJ 481

Budge, I, *The New Challenge of Direct Democracy*, 1996, Cambridge: Polity

Burgess, M, 'Federalism and federation: a reappraisal', in Burgess, M and Gagnon, A (eds), *Comparative Federalism and Federations*, 1993, Hemel Hempstead: Harvester Wheatsheaf, 3

Butler, D and Ranney, A (eds), *Referendums Around the World – The Growing Use of Direct Democracy*, 1994, Washington DC: AEI

Campbell, E and Lee, H, *The Australian Judiciary*, 2001, Cambridge: CUP

Catt, H, Harris, P and Roberts, N, *Voter's Choice: Electoral Change in New Zealand?*, 1992, Palmerston North: Dunmore

Centre for Civic Education, *We the People ... The Citizen and the Constitution*, 6th edn, 1998, Calabasas: Centre for Civic Education

Chapman, R and Wood, M, *Australian Local Government – The Federal Dimension*, 1984, Sydney: Allen & Unwin

Chesterman, M, 'Criminal trials in Australia: from penal colonies to federal democracy', in Vidmar, N, *World Jury Systems*, 2000, Oxford: OUP, 125

Christie, G, Meeks, J, Prior, E and Sanders, J, *The Law of Torts*, 3rd edn, 1997, St Paul: West Publishing

Commonwealth Grants Commission, *Report on General Revenue Grant Relativities – 2000 Update*, 2000, Canberra: Commonwealth Grants Commission

Constitutional Centenary Foundation, *Report: A Decade of Experience*, 2000, Melbourne: Constitutional Centenary Foundation

Constitutional Commission, *Final Report of the Constitutional Commission*, 1998, Canberra: AGPS

Cooke, R, 'Fundamentals' [1988] New Zealand LJ 158

Coombs, H, *Aboriginal Autonomy – Issues and Strategies*, 1994, Cambridge: CUP

Council for Aboriginal Reconciliation, *Going Forward: Social Justice for the First Australians*, 1995, Canberra: AGPS

Craven, G (ed), *Australian Federation – Towards the Second Century*, 1992, Melbourne: Melbourne UP

Crommelin, M, 'The federal model', in Craven, G (ed), *Australian Federation – Towards the Second Century*, 1992, Melbourne: Melbourne UP, 33

Cronin, T, *Direct Democracy*, 1989, Cambridge, Mass: Harvard UP

Daes, E, 'Some considerations on the right of indigenous peoples to self-determination' (1993) 3 Transnational Law and Contemporary Problems 1

Davidson, S, *Human Rights*, 1993, Bristol: OUP

de Q Walker, G, *Ten Advantages of a Federal Constitution and How to Make the Most of Them*, 2001, St Leonard's: Centre for Independent Studies

de Q Walker, G, *Initiative and Referendum: The People's Law*, 1987, St Leonard's: Centre for Independent Studies

de Tocqueville, A, *Democracy in America*, Mayer, J (ed), 1969, New York: Harper & Rowe

Debelle, B, 'Aboriginal customary law: progress report', in Nettheim, G (ed), *Human Rights for Aboriginal People in the '80s*, 1983, Sydney: Legal Books

Department of the Treasury, *Budget Overview 2001*, 2001, Canberra: Department of the Treasury

Dicey, A, *Introduction to the Study of The Law of the Constitution*, 10th edn, 1959, London: Macmillan

Dobbs, D, Keeton, R and Owen, D, *Prosser and Keeton – The Law of Torts*, 5th edn, 1984, St Paul: West Publishing

Dority, B, 'Feminist moralism, "pornography" and "censorship"', in Baird, R and Rosenbaum, S (eds), *Pornography – Private Right or Public Menace?*, 1991, Buffalo: Prometheus, 113

Duffy, D, 'Ireland', in Republic Advisory Committee, *An Australian Republic – The Options*, 1993, Canberra: AGPS, Vol 2, 125

Dworkin, A and MacKinnon, C, *Pornography and Civil Rights: A New Day for Women's Equality*, 1988, Minneapolis: Organisation Against Pornography

Elazar, D, *Covenant and Constitutionalism*, 1998, New Bruswick: Transaction Publishers

Elazar, D, *The American Constitutional Tradition*, 1988, Lincoln: University of Nebraska Press

Elazar, D, 'Constitution-making: the pre-eminently political act', in Banting, K and Simeon, R (eds), *Redesigning the State: The Politics of Constitutional Change in Industrial Nations*, 1985, Toronto: University of Toronto Press, 244

Elazar, D, *American Federalism – A View from the States*, 3rd edn, 1984, New York: Harper & Row

Ely, R, *Unto God and Caesar – Religious Issues in the Emerging Commonwealth 1891–1906*, 1976, Melbourne: Melbourne UP

Emmerson, T, 'Towards a general theory of the First Amendment' (1963) 72 Yale LJ 877

Evans, H (ed), *Odger's Australian Senate Practice*, 10th edn, 2001, Canberra: Department of the Senate

Evans, H, *The Senate and Parliamentary Accountability (Discussion paper No 65, Australian National University, Graduate Program in Public Policy)*, 1999, Canberra: Australian National University

Evans, S, 'When is an acquisition of property not an acquisition of property? The search for a principles approach to s 51(xxxi)' (2000) 11 Public L Rev 183

Farrell, D, *Electoral Systems: A Comparative Introduction*, 2001, London: Palgrave

Farrell, D, *Comparing Electoral Systems*, 1997, London: Prentice Hall

Faulkner, J, 'A Labor perspective on senate reform', in Sawer, M and Miskin, S (eds), *Representation and Institutional Change: 50 Years of Proportional Representation in the Senate (Papers on Parliament No 34)*, 1999, Canberra: Department of the Senate, 119

Federal-State Relations Committee, *Federalism and the Role of the States: Comparisons and Recommendations*, 1999, Melbourne: Government Printer

Federal-State Relations Committee, Parliament of Victoria, *Australian Federalism: The Role of the States*, 1998, Melbourne: Government Printer

Feinberg, J, *Harm to Self*, 1986, New York: OUP

Fleming, D, *Legal Aid in Criminal Law Proceedings*, privately published monograph, 1994, Canberra

Galligan, B, *A Federal Republic – Australia's System of Constitutional Government*, 1995, Cambridge: CUP

Galligan, B, 'The Founders' design and intentions regarding responsible government', in Weller, P and Jaensch, D (eds), *Responsible Government in Australia*, 1980, Richmond: Drummond, 1

Galligan, B and Walsh, C, 'Australian Federalism – yes or no?', in Craven, G (ed), *Australian Federation – Towards the Second Century*, 1992, Melbourne: Melbourne UP, 193

Giles, M, '*R v Brown*: consensual harm in the public interest' (1994) 57 MLR 101

Gloppen, S, *South Africa: The Battle Over the Constitution*, 1997, Aldershot: Dartmouth

Goldsworthy, J, 'The constitutional protection of rights in Australia', in Craven, G (ed), *Australian Federation – Towards the Second Century*, 1992, Melbourne: Melbourne UP, 151

Grotius, H, *The Law of War and Peace*, Kelsey, F (trans), 1925, New York: Bobbs-Merrill

Grotius, H, *Introduction to the Jurisprudence of Holland*, Maasdorp, A (trans), 3rd edn, 1899, Cape Town: Juta & Co

Hall, R, *Abolish the States: A $30 billion Answer to our Tax Problems*, 1998, Sydney: Pan Macmillan

Hamilton, A, 'The Federalist No 78', in Schechter, S (ed), *Roots of the Republic – American Founding Documents Interpreted*, 1990, Madison: Madison House, 373

Hanks, P, *Constitutional Law in Australia*, 2nd edn, 1996, North Ryde: Butterworths

Hannum, H, *Autonomy, Sovereignty and Self-Determination: The Accommodation of Conflicting Rights*, 1990, Philadelphia: University of Pennsylvania Press

Hansen, M, *The Athenian Democracy in the Age of Demosthenes*, 1991, Oxford: Blackwell

Harding, A, Warren, N, Beer, G, Phillips, B and Osei, K, 'The distributional impact of selected Commonwealth outlays and taxes', unpublished paper presented at the Review of Commonwealth – State Funding Conference, Canberra, 14 March 2002

Harris, B, 'Race vilification laws: a comparative perspective' (1999) 6 Canberra L Rev 257

Harris, B, 'Appointments to the bench – the role of a Judicial Services Commission' (1993) 15 Adelaide L Rev 191

Hasen, R, 'Symposium: law, economics & norms: voting without law?' (1996) 144 University of Pennsylvania L Rev 2135

Haskell, J, *Direct Democracy or Representative Government? Dispelling the Populist Myth*, 2001, Boulder: Westview

Hicks, J and White, G, 'Nunavut: Inuit self-determination through a land claim and public government?', in Dahl, J, Hicks, J and Jull, P (eds), *Nunavut: Inuit Regain Control of Their Lands and Their Lives*, 2000, Copenhagen: International Work Group for Indigenous Affairs, 30

Hiebert, J, *Limiting Rights: The Dilemma of Judicial Review*, 1996, Montreal: McGill-Queen's UP

Higgins, R, *Problems and Processes: International Law and How We Use It*, 1994, Oxford: Clarendon

Hill, L, 'A great leveller: compulsory voting', in Sawer, M (ed), *Elections: Full, Free and Fair*, 2001, Annandale: Federation Press, 129

Hirst, J, *The Sentimental Nation: The Making of the Australian Commonwealth*, 2000, Melbourne: OUP

Hogan, G and Whyte, G, *The Irish Constitution*, 3rd edn, 1994, Sydney: Butterworths

Hogg, P, *Constitutional Law of Canada*, 3rd edn, 1992, Scarborough: Carswell

Hogg, P and Monahan, P, *Liability of the Crown*, 2nd edn, 2000, Scarborough: Carswell

Hood Phillips, O and Jackson, P, *O Hood Phillips' Constitutional and Administrative Law*, 6th edn, 1978, London: Sweet & Maxwell

Horowitz, D, *Ethnic Groups in Conflict*, 1985, Berkeley: University of California Press

House of Representatives Standing Committee on Aboriginal and Torres Strait Islander Affairs, *Torres Strait Islanders: A New Deal*, 1997, Canberra: AGPS

Hughes, C, 'Australia and New Zealand', in Butler, D and Ranney, A (eds), *Referendums around the World – The Growing Use of Direct Democracy*, 1994, Washington DC: AEI, 154

Indigenous Customary Law Forum, *Report of the Indigenous Customary Law Forum, Canberra, 18 October 1995*, 1996, Canberra: AGPS

Irving, H, 'Australia's constitutional identity: a conundrum for the 21st century', in Irving, H (ed), *Unity and Diversity – A National Conversation*, 2001, Sydney: ABC Books, 194

Irving, H (ed), *The Centenary Companion to Australian Federation*, 1999, Cambridge: CUP

Irving, H, *To Constitute a Nation: A Cultural History of Australia's Constitution*, 1997, Cambridge: CUP

Johnston, P and Hardcastle, R, 'State courts: the limits of *Kable*' (1998) 20 Sydney L Rev 216

Joseph, P, *Constitutional and Administrative Law in New Zealand*, 1993, North Ride: Lawbook Co

Joseph, S and Castan, M, *Federal Constitutional Law – A Contemporary View*, 2001, Sydney: Lawbook Co

Jull, P and Kajlich, H, 'First peoples, late admissions – recognising indigenous rights', in Sampford, C and Round, T (eds), *Beyond the Republic – Meeting the Global Challenges to Constitutionalism*, 2001, Leichhardt: Federation Press, 257

Justinian, *Institutes*, Thomas, J (trans), 1975, Amsterdam: North Holland

Kaminski, J and Bernstein, R, 'The Bill of Rights', in Schechter, S (ed), *Roots of the Republic: American Founding Documents Interpreted*, 1990, Madison: Madison House, 423

Kant, I, *Foundations of the Metaphysics of Morals*, Beck, L (trans), 1969, New York: Bobbs-Merrill

Kant, I, *The Metaphysical Elements of Justice*, Ladd, J (trans), 1965, New York: Bobbs-Merrill

Kasase, M, 'Personalised proportional representation: the "model" of the West German electoral system', in Lijphart, A and Grofman, B (eds), *Choosing an Electoral System*, 1984, New York: Praeger, 155

Kelsen, H, *General Theory of Law and State*, Wedberg, A (trans), 1945, New York: Russel and Russel

Kerr, J, *A Presumption of Wisdom – An Exposé of the Jury System of Injustice*, 1987, North Ryde: Angus and Robinson

King, P, 'Federation and representation', in Burgess, M and Gagnon, A (eds), *Comparative Federalism and Federations*, 1993, Hemel Hempstead: Harvester Wheatsheaf, 94

Kobach, K, 'Switzerland', in Butler, D and Ranney, A (eds), *Referendums Around the World – The Growing Use of Direct Democracy*, 1994, Washington DC: AEI, 98

La Nauze, J, *The Making of the Australian Constitution*, 1972, Melbourne: Melbourne UP

Lane, P, *A Manual of Australian Constitutional Law*, 6th edn, 1995, North Ryde: Lawbook Co

Laundy, P, *Parliaments in the Modern World*, 1989, Aldershot: Dartmouth

Lavarch, M, *Discussion Paper: Judicial Appointments – Procedure and Criteria*, 1993, Canberra: AGPS

Lawrence, C, 'If he hollers let him go: regulating racist speech on campus' (1990) Duke LJ 431

Leader, S, *Freedom of Association. A Study in Labour Law and Political Theory*, 1992, New Haven: Yale UP

Leaver, A, *Investigating Crime*, 1997, North Ryde: LBC Information Services

Lees, M, 'Parliamentary reform: the baby and the bathwater', in Costar, B (ed), *Deadlock or Democracy? The Future of the Senate*, 2000, Sydney: University of New South Wales Press, 29

Lerner, N, *Group Rights and Discrimination in International Law*, 1991, Dordrecht: Martinus Nijhoff

Lijphart, A, 'Australian democracy: modifying majoritarianism?', in Sawer, M and Miskin, S (eds), *Representation and Institutional Change: 50 Years of Proportional Representation in the Senate (Papers on Parliament No 34)*, 1999, Canberra: Department of the Senate, 55

Lijphart, A, *Electoral Systems and Party Systems*, 1994, Oxford: OUP

Lutz, D (ed), *Colonial Origins of the American Constitution*, 1998, Indianapolis: Liberty Fund

Lutz, D, 'The United States Constitution', in Schechter, S (ed), *Roots of the Republic: American Founding Documents Interpreted*, 1990, Madison: Madison House, 266

Lutz, D, *The Origins of American Constitutionalism*, 1988, Baton Rouge: Louisiana State UP

Macpherson, C, 'Natural rights in Hobbes and Locke', in Raphael, D (ed), *Political Theory and the Rights of Man*, 1967, London: Macmillan, 1

Maddock, K, 'Aboriginal customary law', in Hanks, P and Keon-Cohen, B (eds), *Aborigines and the Law*, 1984, Sydney: Allen & Unwin, 212

Magleby, D, 'Direct legislation in the American States' in Butler, D and Ranney, A (eds), *Referendums Around the World – The Growing Use of Direct Democracy*, 1994, Washington DC: AEI, 218

Magleby, D, *Direct Legislation – Voting on Ballot Propositions in the United States*, 1984, Baltimore: Johns Hopkins University

Marsh, M, 'The voters decide? Preferential voting in European list systems' (1985) 13 European Journal of Political Research 365

Mason, A, 'The appointment and removal of judges', in Cunningham, H (ed), *Fragile Bastion – Judicial Independence in the Nineties and Beyond*, 1997, Sydney: Judicial Commission of New South Wales

Mathews, A, *Freedom, State Security and the Rule of Law: Dilemmas of the Apartheid Society*, 1986, Kenwyn: Juta & Co

Mathews, R, *Revenue Sharing in Federal Systems*, 1980, Canberra: Centre for Research on Federal Financial Relations, ANU

McDowell, M and Webb, D, *The New Zealand Legal System: Structures, Processes and Legal Theory*, 1995, Wellington: Butterworths

McGarvie, R, *Democracy – Choosing Australia's Republic*, 1999, Carlton South: Melbourne UP

McKee, P, 'The Republic of Ireland', in Bogdanor, V and Butler, D (eds), *Democracy and Elections*, 1983, Cambridge: CUP, 167

McLaughlin, R, 'Some problems and issues in the recognition of indigenous customary law' (1996) 86 Aboriginal Law Bulletin 4

McMillan, J, 'Constitutional reform in Australia', in *One People, One Destiny (Papers on Parliament No 13)*, 1991, Canberra: Department of the Senate

McMillan, J, Evans, G and Storey, H, *Australia's Constitution: A Time for Change?*, 1983, Sydney: Law Foundation of New South Wales

Meagher, D, 'Appointment of judges' (1993) 2 Journal of Judicial Administration 190

Mill, JS, *On Liberty*, Grey, J and Smith, G (eds), 1991, London: Routledge

Montesquieu, C, *L'Esprit des Lois/The Spirit of the Law*, Nugent, T (trans), 1949, New York: Hafner

Mulholland, L, *Kant's System of Rights*, 1990, New York: Columbia UP

National Australasian Convention Debates, *Official Report of the National Australasian Convention Debates*, 1986, Sydney: Legal Books

New Zealand Parliament, *Report of the MMP Review Committee*, 2001, Wellington: New Zealand Parliament

Newland, R, *Comparative Electoral Systems*, 1982, London: Electoral Reform Society

O'Donoghue, L, 'One nation: promise or paradox?', speech at the National Press Club, Canberra, 20 May 1992

Office of Indigenous Affairs, Department of the Prime Minister and Cabinet, *Aboriginal Customary Law – Report on Commonwealth Implementation of the Recommendations of the Australian Law Reform Commission*, 1994, Canberra: AGPS

Olivier, N, *Indigenous Law*, 1995, Durban: Butterworths

Orr, G, 'Agency shops in Australia? Compulsory bargaining fees, union (in)security and the rights of free-riders' (2001) 14 Australian Journal of Labour Law 1

Palmer, G and Palmer, M, *Bridled Power – New Zealand Government Under MMP*, 1997, Auckland: OUP

Parker, S, 'The independence of the judiciary', in Opeskin, B and Wheeler, F (eds), *The Australian Federal Judicial System*, 2000, Carlton South: Melbourne UP

Parliament of Victoria, *Report of the Australian Federalism Conference*, 1994, Melbourne: Government Printer

Paust, J, 'Human dignity as a constitutional right: a jurisprudentially based inquiry into criteria and content' (1984) 27 Howard LJ 145

Pearson, N, 'Reconciliation: to be or not to be: nationhood, self-determination or self-government?' (1993) 61 Aboriginal Law Bulletin 14

Piotrowicz, R and Kaye, S, *Human Rights in International and Australian Law*, 2000, Chatswood: Butterworths

Quick, J and Garran, R, *The Annotated Constitution of the Australian Commonwealth*, 1976, Sydney: Legal Books

Rava, W, 'State constitutional protections for the poor' (1998) 71 Temple L Rev 543

Rawls, J, *Political Liberalism*, 1993, New York: Columbia UP

Rawls, J, 'Kantian constructivism in moral theory' (1980) 77 Journal of Philosophy 515

Rawls, J, *A Theory of Justice*, 1971, Cambridge, Mass: Harvard UP

Republic Advisory Committee, *An Australian Republic – The Options*, 1993, Canberra: AGPS

Review of Commonwealth – State Funding, *Background Paper*, 2002, Melbourne: Review of Commonwealth – State Funding

Rich, W, 'Constitutional law in the United States and Australia: finding common ground' (1995) 35 Washburn LJ 1

Rishworth, P, 'Affirming the fundamental values of the nation: how the Bill of Rights Act and the Human Rights Act affect New Zealand law', in Huscroft, G and Rishworth, P (eds), *Rights and Freedoms*, 1995, Wellington: Brookers

Roberts, D, 'Self-determination and the struggle for Aboriginal equality', in Bourke, C, Bourke, E and Edwards, E (eds), *Aboriginal Australia – An Introductory Reader in Aboriginal Studies*, 1994, St Lucia: University of Queensland Press, 212

Rossum, R and Tarr, G, *American Constitutional Law – Volume I: The Structure of Government*, 5th edn, 1999, Boston: Bedford/St Martin's

Rotenstreich, N, *Man and his Dignity*, 1983, Jerusalem: Magnes

Rotunno, N, 'Student note: State constitutional social welfare provisions and the right to housing' (1996) 1 Hofstra Law & Policy Symposium 111

Royal Commission on Aboriginal People, *Partners in Confederation*, 1993, Ottawa: Royal Commission on Aboriginal People

Sanders, A (ed), *The Internal Conflict of Laws in South Africa*, 1990, Durban: Butterworths

Sawer, M, 'Overview: institutional design and the role of the Senate', in Sawer, M and Miskin, S (eds), *Representation and Institutional Change: 50 Years of Proportional Representation in the Senate (Papers on Parliament No 34)*, 1999, Canberra: Department of the Senate, 1

Sawer, G, *Federation Under Stress*, 1977, Melbourne: Melbourne UP

Sawer, M and Miskin, S (eds), *Representation and Institutional Change: 50 Years of Proportional Representation in the Senate (Papers on Parliament No 34)*, 1999, Canberra: Department of the Senate

Scarrow, S, 'Germany: the mixed-member system as a political compromise', in Shugart, M and Wattenberg, M (eds), *Mixed-Member Electoral Systems – The Best of Both Worlds?*, 2001, Oxford: OUP, 55

Schachter, O, *International Law in Theory and Practice*, 1991, Dordrecht: Martinus Nijhoff

Schachter, O, 'Human dignity as a normative concept' (1983) AJIL 848

Schechter, S (ed), *Roots of the Republic – American Founding Documents Interpreted*, 1990, Madison: Madison House

Schmidt, D, *Citizen Lawmakers –The Ballot Initiative Revolution*, 1989, Philadelphia: Temple UP

Seddon, N, *Government Contracts – Federal, State and Local*, 2nd edn, 1999, Leichhardt: Federation Press

Senate Standing Committee on Constitutional and Legal Affairs, *Two Hundred Years Later*, 1983, Canberra: AGPS

Sharman, C, 'The Senate and good government', in *The Senate and Good Government and Other Lectures in the Senate Occasional Lecture Series (Papers on Parliament No 33)*, 1999(a), Canberra: Department of the Senate, 153

Sharman, C, 'The representation of small parties and independents', in Sawer, M and Miskin, S (eds), *Representation and Institutional Change: 50 Years of Proportional Representation in the Senate (Papers on Parliament No 34)*, 1999(b), Canberra: Department of the Senate, 149

Shestack, J, 'The philosophical foundations of human rights', in Symonides, J (ed), *Human Rights: Concepts and Standards*, 2000, Aldershot: Dartmouth, 31

Shugart, M and Wattenberg, M (eds), *Mixed-Member Electoral Systems – The Best of Both Worlds?*, 2001, Oxford: OUP

Smolla, R, *Free Speech in an Open Society*, 1993, New York: Vantage

Solomon, D, *Coming of Age: Charter for a New Australia*, 1998, St Lucia: Queensland UP

Standing Committee on Law and Justice, *A New South Wales Bill of Rights*, 2001, Sydney: New South Wales Parliament

Stark, B, 'Economic rights in the United States and international human rights law: toward an entirely new strategy' (1992) 44 Hastings LJ 79

Steiner, H and Alson, P, *International Human Rights in Context*, 2nd edn, 2000, Oxford: OUP

Sterritt, N, 'Defining indigenous governance', paper delivered at the Indigenous Governance Conference, Canberra, 3–5 April 2002

Strossen, N, 'A feminist critique of "the" Feminist Critique of Pornography' (1993) 79 Virginia L Rev 1099

Taagepera, R and Shugart, M, *Seats and Votes – The Effects and Determinants of Electoral Systems*, 1989, New Haven: Yale UP

Tasmanian Department of Justice and Industrial Relations, *Discussion Paper – Judicial Appointments in Tasmania*, 1999, Hobart: Department of Justice Tasmania

Thompson, E, 'The Senate and representative democracy', in Sawer, M and Miskin, S (eds), *Representation and Institutional Change: 50 Years of Proportional Representation in the Senate (Papers on Parliament No 34)*, 1999, Canberra: Department of the Senate, 41

Thompson, B, *Sadomasochism*, 1994, London: Cassell

Treson, F, 'International human rights and cultural relativism' (1985) 25 Virginia Journal of International Law 117

Tribe, L, *American Constitutional Law*, 2nd edn, 1988, Mineloa: Foundation Press

Tronc, K, Crawford, C and Smith, D, *Search and Seizure in Australia and New Zealand*, 1996, North Ryde: LBC Information Services

Tsabelis, G and Money, J, *Bicameralism*, 1997, Cambridge: CUP

Uhr, J, 'Why we chose proportional representation', in Sawer, M and Miskin, S (eds), *Representation and Institutional Change: 50 Years of Proportional Representation in the Senate (Papers on Parliament No 34)*, 1999, Canberra: Department of the Senate, 13

United Kingdom Government, *Report of the Independent Commission on the Voting System (the Jenkins Report)*, 1998, London: HMSO

United Kingdom Law Commission, *Consent and Offences Against the Person (Consultation Paper No 134)*, 1994, London: HMSO

van der Vyver, J, 'Human rights aspects of the dual system applying to Blacks in South Africa' (1982) 15 Comparative and International Law Journal of Southern Africa 306

van Wyk, D (ed), *Rights and Constitutionalism: The New South African Legal Order*, 1994, Kenwyn: Juta & Co

Vile, J, *A Companion to the United States Constitution and its Amendments*, 2001, Westport: Praeger

Vowles, J (ed), *Voters' Victory? New Zealand's First Election Under Proportional Representation*, 1998, Auckland: Auckland UP

Wade, H, *Administrative Law*, 6th edn, 1988, Oxford: Clarendon

Warren, S and Brandeis, L, 'The right to privacy' (1890) 4 Harvard L Rev 193

Weisbrot, D, 'Introduction to Report of the National Pro Bono Task Force and recommended action plan', in Arup, C and Laster, K (eds), *For the Public Good: Pro Bono and the Legal Profession in Australia*, 2001, Annandale: Federation Press, 214

Williams, G, *A Bill of Rights for Australia*, 2000: Sydney: University of New South Wales Press

Williams, G, *Human Rights under the Australian Constitution*, 1999, Melbourne: OUP

Winterton, G, *Judicial Remuneration in Australia*, 1995(a), Carlton South: Australian Institute of Judicial Administration Inc

Winterton, G, 'The States and the Republic: a constitutional accord?' (1995(b)) 6 Public L Rev 107

Winterton, G, 'Extra-constitutional notions in Australian constitutional law' (1986) 16 Federal L Rev 223

Zdenkowski, G, 'Customary punishment and pragmatism: some unresolved dilemmas' (1994) 68 Aboriginal Law Bulletin 26

Zimmerman, J, *The Referendum – The People Decide Public Policy*, 2001, Westport: Praeger

INDEX

For Product Safety Concerns and Information please contact our EU representative GPSR@taylorandfrancis.com Taylor & Francis Verlag GmbH, Kaufingerstraße 24, 80331 München, Germany